ENGLISH RECUSANT LITERATURE
1558–1640

Selected and Edited by
D. M. ROGERS

Volume 145

MATTHEW WILSON
Mercy and Truth
1634

MATTHEW WILSON

Mercy and Truth

1634

The Scolar Press

1973

ISBN 0 85417 960 7

Published and Printed in Great Britain by
The Scolar Press Limited, 20 Main Street,
Menston, Yorkshire, England

1756346

Reproduced (original size) from a copy in the library of Ampleforth Abbey, by permission of the Abbot and Community.

References: Allison and Rogers 897; STC 25778.

MERCY & TRVTH.

OR

CHARITY

MAINTAYNED

by Catholiques.

By way of Reply vpon an Anſwere lately framed by **D. POTTER** to a Treatiſe which had former-ly proued, That CHARITY was MISTAKEN by Proteſtants: With the want whereof Catholi-ques are vniuſtly charged for affirming, That Pro-teſtancy vnrepented deſtroyes SALVATION.

Deuided into tvvo Parts.

Mercy and Truth haue met togeather. *Pſalm. 84. v. 11.*

Better are the wounds of him that loueth, then the fraudulent kiſſes of him that hateth. Prou. cap. 27. v. 6.

We loue you Brethren, and deſire the ſame things for you, which we doe for our ſelues. S. *Aug. Ep. 166.*

Permiſſu Superiorum, M. DC. XXXIIII.

TO THE
MOST HIGH

Mighty, *Iuſt*, and *Clement* Prince,

CHARLES

King of *Great-Brittaine*, *France*,
and *Ireland* , *&c.*

Heſe Titles (moſt gracious Soueraigne) partly flovving from your Royall Authority , and partly appropriated to your Sacred Perſon, haue by their happy coniunction emboldened me to lay at your Princely Feet,

A 2   vvith

vvith moſt humble reſpects, and profound ſubmiſſion, this R E P L Y of mine to a Booke, lately vvritten in obedience, as the Author therof affirmes, to your Maieſties particular Commaund.

For, though your Regal Authority may ſeeme to be an Obiect of only Dread and Avve; yet doth it not ſo much auert, as inuite men to a confident approach, vvhen it appeares ſo ſvvetly tempered, and adorned vvith ſuch rare Perſonall Qualities as your Maieſties are; *Iuſtice* to all; *Clemency* to euery one of your meaneſt Subiects; *VViſdome* to diſcerne vvith quicknes & depth, and to determine vvith great maturity of Iudgment, betvvene right and vvrong; A Princely diſdaine, and iuſt indignation againſt

the

the leaſt diſſimulation, vvhich may
be repugnant to the ſecret teſtimony of Conſcience; An heroicall Affection, and euen as it vvere a naturall kind of ſympathy vvith all
Sincerity, and Truth.

So that, vvhen your Maieſty
thought fit to impoſe a Commandement of vvriting vpon one ; I
could not but conceiue it to be alſo
your gracious Pleaſure and Will,
that in Vertue of the ſame Royal
Commaund, others vvho are of
contrary Iudgment, vvere ſuffered
at leaſt, if not obliged, to anſvvere
for themſelues; but yet vvith all due
reſpect, and Chriſtian moderation:
Which, I haue as carefully endeauoured to obſerue, as if I had vvritten by the expreſſe Commaund, &
ſpoken in the Hearing, and acted

the part of *Truth*, in the prefence of
fo *Great*, fo *Modeft*, and fo *Iudici-*
ous a Monarch, as your Maiefty is.

I vvas therfore fupported by con-
templation of thefe your rare En-
dovvments of Mind : vvhich, as
they are the *Happines* of all your
Subiects; fo vvere they no leffe a
Hope to me , that your Maiefty
vvould not difdaine to caft an eie of
Grace vpon this R E P L Y, not according to the face of prefent times,
but vvith regard to the Plea's of
Truth, appearing in times more
ancient, and in places more diffu-
fed, by the allegation of one, vvho
doth fo cordially profeffe himfelfe
your Maiefties moft humble fubiect, as that from the depth of a fin-
cere hart, and vvith all the povvers
of his foule, he vvishes that God be

no

no longer mercifull , and good to him , and all your other Catholiques Subiects , then they, and he shall both in defire, and deed , approue themfelues vpon all occafions, fincerely Loyall to the moft Excellent Perfon, and thrice hopefull Iffue of your Sacred Maiefty.

This our Catholique Religion teaches vs to profeffe and performe : and heervvith I lay this poore Worke, and proftrate the Author thereof, at the Throne of your Royall Feet.

Your Maiefties moft humble and moft loyall Subiect.

I. H.

Aduertisement of the Printer.

THis *REPLY*, *Good Rea-*
der, vvas indeed long since fi-
nished by the Author: but by reason
of some impediment, it could not be
commodiously transported, so soone as
he vvished, and desired it should.

TO THE

READER·

I v e me leaue (good Reader)
to informe thee, by way of
Preface, of three points. The
firſt concernes *D. Potters Anſ-*
were to Charity Miſtaken. The
ſecond relates to this *Reply* of
mine. And the third containes
ſome *Premonitions*, or *Preſcriptions* in caſe *D. Pot-*
ter, or any in his behalfe thinke ſit to reioyne.

2.   For the firſt point concerning *D. Potters* A generall
Anſwere, I ſay in generall, reſeruing particu- conſidera-
lars to their prioper placeſ, that in his whole tion of D.
Booke he hath not ſo much as once truly and Potters
really fallen vpon the point in̄ queſtion, which Anſwere.
was, Whether both Catholiques and Prote-
ſtants can be ſaued in their ſeuerall profeſſions.
And therefore *Charity Miſtaken* iudiciouſly preſ-

B

ſing

fing thofe particulars, wherein the difficultie
doth precifely confift, proues in generall, that
there is but one true Church; that all Chriftiās
are obliged to hearken to her; that fhe muft be
euer vifible, and infallible; that to feparate ones
felfe from her Communion is Schifme, and to
diffent from her doctrine is Herefie, though
it be in points neuer fo few, or neuer fo fmall
in their own nature; and therefore that the diftinction of points fundamentall, and not fundamentall is wholy vaine, as it is applied by
Proteftants. Thefe (I fay) and fome other generall grounds *Charity Miſtaken* handles, and
out of them doth cleerely euince, that any leaft
difference in faith cannot ftand with faluation
on both fides: and therefore fince it is apparent,
that Catholiques and Proteftants difagree in
very many points of Faith, they both cannot
hope to be faued without repentance: and confequently, as we hold, that Proteftancy vnrepented *deſtroies Saluation*; fo muft they alfo belieue that we cānot be faued, if they iudge their
own Religion to be true, and ours to be falfe.
And whofoeuer difguizeth this truth, is an enemy to foules, which he deceiues with vngrounded falfe hopes of faluation, indifferent Faiths,
and Religions. And this, *Charity Miſtaken* performed exactly, according to that which appeares to haue been his defigne, which was not
to defcend to particuler difputes, as *D.Potter* affectedly does, namely, Whether or no the Ro-

man

mã Church be the only true Church of Chriſt ;
and much leſſe whether Generall Councels be
infallible; whether the Pope may erre in his Decrees common to the whole Church ; whether
he be aboue a Generall Councell ; whether all
points of fayth be contained in Scripture; whether Fayth be reſolued into the authority of the
Church, as into his laſt *formall Obiect*, and *Motiue* ; and leaſt of all did he diſcourſe of Images,
Communion vnder both kinds, publique Seruice in an vnknowne Tongue, Seauen Sacraments, Sacrifice of the Maſſe, Indulgences, and
Index Expurgatorius : all which and diuers o-
ther articles *D. Potter* (as I ſaid) drawes by violence into his Booke : & he might as well haue
brought in Pope *Ioane*, or Antichriſt, or the
Iewes who are permitted to liue in Rome ,
which are common Themes for men that want
better matter, as *D. Potter* was forced to fetch
in the aforſayd Controuerſies, that ſo he might
dazle the eyes, & diſtract the mynd of the Reader, and hinder him from perceiuing that in his
whole Anſwere he vttered nothing to the purpoſe, & point in queſtion : which if he had followed cloſely, I dare well ſay , he might haue
diſpatched his whole Booke in two or three
ſheetes of paper. But the truth is , he was loath
to affirme plainely, that generally both Catholiques and Proteſtants may be ſaued : and yet
ſeeing it to be moſt euident that Proteſtants
cannot pretend to haue any true Church be-

fore

fore *Luther* except the Roman, and such as a-
greed with her, and consequently that they
cannot hope for saluation, if they deny it to vs;
he thought best to auoid this difficulty by con-
fusion of language, & to fill vp his Booke with
points which make nothing to the purpose.
Wherein he is lesse excusable, because he must
graunt, that those very particulers to which he
digresseth, are not fundamentall errors, though
it should be granted that they be errors, which
indeed are Catholique verities. For since they be
not fundamentall, nor destructiue of saluation,
what imports it whether we hold them or no,
for as much as concernes our possibility to be
saued?

3.   In one thing only he will perhaps seeme
to haue touched the point in question, to wit, in
his distinction of points fundamentall, and not
fundamentall: because some may thinke, that
a difference in points which are not fundamentall breakes not the Vnity of Faith, and hinders
not the hope of saluation in persons so disagreeing. And yet in this very distinction, he neuer
speakes to the purpose indeed, but only sayes,
that there are some points so fundamentall, as
that all are obliged to know and *belieue* them
explicitely, but neuer tells vs, whether there be
any other points of faith, which a man may deny or *disbelieue*, though they be sufficiently presented to his vnderstanding, as truths reuealed,
or testified by almighty God; wch was the only
thing

thing in queſtiō. For if it be dānable, as certainly it is, to deny, or disbelieue any one truth wit-
neſſed by almighty God, thogh the thing be not
in it ſelf of any great conſequence, or moment ;
& ſince of two diſagreeing in matters of faith,
one muſt neceſſarily deny ſome ſuch truth ; it
cleerly followes that amongſt men of different
Faiths, or Religions, one omely can be ſaued,
though their difference conſiſt of diuers, or but
euen one point, which is not in his owne nature fundamentall, as I declare at large in diuers places of my *firſt Part*. So that it is cleere,
D. Potter euen in this his laſt refuge and diſtinction, neuer comes to the point in queſtion:
to ſay nothing that he himſelfe doth quite ouerthrow it, and plainly contradict his whole deſigne, as I ſhew in the third Chapter of my *firſt*
Part.

4. And as for *D. Potters* manner of handling thoſe very points, which are vtterly beſide
the purpoſe, it conſiſts, only in bringing vulgar
meane obiections, which haue been anſwered
a thouſand tymes, yea, and ſome of them are
cleerely anſwered euen in *Charity Miſtaken* ; but
he takes no knowledge at all of any ſuch anſwers, and much leſſe doth he apply himſelfe to
confute them. He alledgeth alſo Authors with
ſo great corruption and fraude, as I would not
haue belieued, if I had not found it by cleere,
and frequent experience. In his ſecond *Edition*,
he hath indeed left out one or two groſſe cor-

rupti-

ruptions , amongſt many others no leſſe notoꝛ
rious, hauing as it ſeemes been warned by ſome
friends , that they could not ſtand with his credit : but euen in this his ſecond *Edition* he re-
tracts them not at all , nor declares that he was
miſtaken in the *Firſt*, and ſo his Reader of the
firſt *Edition* ſhall euer be deceiued by him,thogh
withall he reade the *Second* . For preuenting
of which inconuenience, I haue thought it neceſſary to take notice of them , and to diſcouer
them in my *Reply*.

5.   And for concluſion of this point I will
only ſay , that *D. Potter* might well haue ſpared
his paines if he had ingenuouſly acknowledged,
where the whole ſubſtance . yea and ſometime
the very words & phraſes of his booke may be
found in farre briefer manner , namely , in a
Sermon of *D. Vſhers* preached before our late ſoueraigne Lord *King Iames* the 20. of Iune. 1624.
at *Wanſted*, containing *A Declaration of the Vniuerſality of the Church of Chriſt , and the Vnity of
Fayth , profeſſed therein* , which Sermon hauing
been roundly and wittily confuted by a Catholike Diuine , vnder the name of *Paulus Ve-
ridicus*, within the compaſſe of about 4. ſheetes
of Paper , *D. Potters Anſwere to Charity Miſtaken* was in effect confuted before it appeared .
And this may ſuffice for a generall Cenſure of
his Anſwere to *Charity Miſtaken*.

6.   For the ſecond , touching my *Reply* : if
you wonder at the Bulke thereof , compared
eyther

eyther with *Charity Mistaken,* or *D. Potters An-* Concer-
fwer, I defire you to confider well of what now ning my
I am about to fay, and then I hope you will fee, Reply.
that I was caft vpon a meere neceffity of not
being fo fhort, as otherwife might peraduenture be defired. *Charity Mistaken* is fhort I grant,
and yet very full, and large for as much as concerned his defigne, which you fee was not to
treate of particuler Controuerfies in Religion,
no not fo much as to debate, whether or no the
Roman Church be the onely true Church of
Chrift, which indeed would haue required a
larger Volume, as I haue vnderftood there was
one then coming forth, if it had not been preuented by the Treatife of *Charity Mistaken* ,
which feemed to make the other intéded worke
a little leffe feafonable at that tyme. But *Charity Mistaken* proues onely in Generall out of
fome Vniuerfall Principles, well backed and
made good by choyce and folide authorities,
that of two difagreeing in points of Fayth, one
onely without repentance can be faued; which
ayme exacted no great bulke. And as for *D.
Potters Anfwere,* euen that alfo is not fo fhort as
it may feeme. For if his marginall notes printed in a fmall letter were transfered into the
Text, the Booke would appeare to be of fome
bulke: though indeed it might haue been very
fhort, if he had kept himfelf to the point treated
by *Charity Miflaken,* as fhall be declared anon.
But contrarily, becaufe the queftion debated
betwixt

betwixt *Charity Mistaken* & *D. Potter*, is a point of
the higheft confequence that can be imagined,
& in regard that there is not a more pernicious
Herefy, or rather indeed ground of Atheifme,
then a perfuafion that men of different Religions may be faued, if otherwife forfooth they
lead a kind of ciuill and morall life : I concea-
ued, that my chiefe endeauour was not to be
employed in anfwering *D. Potter*, but that it was
neceffary to handle the Queftion it felfe fomewhat at large, and not only to proue in generall, that both Proteftants and Catholikes cannot be faued ; but to fhew alfo, that Saluation
cannot be hoped for out of the Catholique Roman Church ; and yet withall, not to omit to
anfwere all the particules of *D. Potters* Booke
which may any way import. To this end I
thought it fit, to deuide my *Reply* into *two Parts*:
in the former whereof, the maine queftion is
handled by a continued difcourfe without ftep-
ping afide to confute the particulers of *D. Potters Anfwere*, though yet fo as that euen in this
firft *Part*, I omit not to anfwere fuch paffages of his, as I find directly in my way, and
naturally belong to the points wherof I treat :
& in the fecond *Part* I anfwere *D. Potters* Treatife, *Section* by *Section*, as they lie in order I heer
therefore intreate the Reader, that if hartily
he defire fatisfaction in this fo important queftion, he do not content himfelfe with that
which I fay to *Doctour Potter* in my fecond
Part,

Part, but that he take the *First* before him, eyther all, or at leaſt ſo much as may ſerue moſt
to his purpoſe of being ſatisfied in thoſe doubts
which preſſe him moſt. For which purpoſe I
haue cauſed a Table of the Chapters of the firſt
Part, together with their Titles & Arguments,
to be prefixed before my Reply.

7. This was then a chiefe reaſon why I
could not be very ſhort. But yet there wanted
not alſo diuers other cauſes of the ſame effect.
For there are ſo ſeuerall kinds of Proteſtants,
through the difference of Tenets which they
hold, as that if a man conuince but one kind
of them, the reſt will conceiue themſelues to be
as truly vnſatisfyed and euen vnſpoken to, as
if nothing had been ſaid therein at all. As for
example, ſome hold a neceſſity of a perpetuall
viſible Church, and ſome hold no ſuch neceſſity. Some of them hold it neceſſary to be able to
proue it diſtinct from ours; & others, that their
buſineſſe is diſpatched when they haue proued
ours to haue beene alwayes viſible : for then
they will conceiue that theirs hath been ſo: and
the like may be truly ſaid of very many other
particulers. Beſides, it is *D. Potters* faſhion,
(wherein as he is very far from being the firſt,
ſo I pray God he proue the laſt of that humour)
to touch in a word many triuiall old obiectiõs,
which if they be not all anſwered, it will, and
muſt ſerue the turne, to make the more ignorant
ſort of men belieue, and brag, as if ſome maine

vnanſ-

vnanfwerable matter had been fubtily & purpofely omitted; and euery body knowes that
fome obiection may be very plaufibly made in
few words the cleere and folid anfwere whereof will require more leaues of paper then one.
And in particuler *D. Potter* doth couch his corruption of Authors within the compaffe of fo
few lines, and with fo great confufeones and
fraude, that it requires much time, paines, and
paper to open them fo diftinctly, as that they
may appeare to euery mans eye. It was alfo neceffary to fhew, what *D. Potter* omits in *Charity
Miftaken*, and the importance of what is omitted, and fometimes to fet downe the very words
themfelues that are omitted, all which could
not but add to the quantity of my *Reply*. And as
for the *quality* thereof, I defire thee (good Reader) to belieue, that whereas nothing is more
neceffary the Bookes for anfwering of Bookes:
yet I was fo ill furnifhed in this kind, that I was
forced to omit the examination of diuers Authors cited by *D. Potter*, meerely vpon neceffity;
though I did very well perceaue by moft apparant circumftances, that I muft probably haue
been fure inough to find them plainely mifal-
leadged, and much wronged: and for the few
which are examined, there hath not wanted
fome difficulties to do it. For the times are not
for all men alike; and *D. Potter* hath much aduantage therein. But Truth is Truth, and will
euer be able to iuftify it felfe in the midft of all

diffi.

difficulties which may occurre. As for me, when I alledge Proteſtant Writers as well do-meſticall, as forraine, I willingly and thanke-fully acknowledge my ſelfe obliged for diuers of them to the Author of the Booke entituled, *The Proteſtants Apology for the Roman Church,* who calls himſelfe *Iohn Brerely,* whoſe care, exactnes, and fidelity is ſo extraordinary great, as that he doth not only cite the Bookes, but the Editions alſo, with the place and time of their printing, yea and often the very page, and line where the words are to be had. And if you hap-pen not to find what he cites, yet ſuſpend your iudgment, till you haue read the corrections placed at the end of his booke; though it be alſo true, that after all diligence and faithfulnes on his behalfe, it was not in his power to amend all the faults of the print: in which prints we haue difficulty inough for many euident rea-ſons, which muſt needs occur to any prudent man.

8.   And for aſmuch as concernes the man-ner of my *Reply,* I haue procured to do it with-out all bitternes, or gall of inuectiue words, both for as much as may import either Prote-ſtants in generall, or *D. Potters* perſon in parti-culer; vnles, for example, he will call it bitter-neſſe for me to terme a groſſe impertinency, a *ſleight,* or a *corruption,* by thoſe very names, without which I do not know how to expreſſe the things: and yet wherein I can truly affirme

that I haue ſtudied how to deliuer them in the
moſt moderate way, to the end I might giue as
little offence as poſſibly I could, without be-
traying the Cauſe. And if any vnfit phraſe may
peraduenture haue eſcaped my pen (as I hope
none hath)it was beſide, and againſt my intention;though I muſt needs profeſſe,that *D.Potter*
giues ſo many and ſo iuſt occaſions of being
round with him , as that perhaps ſome will
iudge me to haue been rather remiſſe , then
moderate. But ſince in the very Title of my
Reply I profeſſe to *maintaine Charity* , I conceiue
that the exceſſe will be more excuſable a-
mongſt all kinds of men , if it fall to be in
mildnes , then if it had appeared in too much
zeale.And if *D.Potter* haue a mind to charge me
with ignorance or any thing of that nature , I
can , a nd will eaſe him of that labour , by acknowledging in my ſelfe as many & more perſonall defects , then he can heape vpon me .
Truth only and ſincerity I ſo much valew and
profeſſe, as that he ſhall neuer be able to proue
the contrary in any one leaſt paſſage or particle againſt me .

Rules to be obſerued if *D.Potter* intend a Reioynders .

9. In the third & laſt place, I haue thought
fit to expreſſe my ſelfe thus If *D. Potter,* or any
other reſolue to anſwere my *Reply*; I deſire that
he will obſerue ſome things which may tend to
his owne reputation , the ſauing of my vnneceſſary paines, and eſpecially to the greater aduantage of truth. I wiſh then that he would be

care

carefull to confider , wherein the point of euery difficulty confifts , and not impertinently to
fhoote at Rouers , and affectedly miftake one
thing for another . As for example , to what
purpofe (for as much as cocernes the queftion
betweene *D. Potter* and *Charity Miftaken*) doth
he fo often and ferioufly labour to proue , that
fayth is not refolued into the Authority of the
Church , as into the formall *Obiect* and *Motiue*
thereof ? Or that all points of Fayth are contained in Scripture ? Or that the Church cannot make new Articles of fayth ? Or that the
Church of *Rome*, as it fignifies that particuler
Church or dioceffe, is not all one with the vniuerfall Church ? Or that the Pope as a priuate
Doctour may erre ? With many other fuch
points as will eafily appeare in their proper places. It wil alfo be neceffary for him not to put
certaine Doctrines vpon vs , from which he
knowes we difclaime as much as himfelfe.

10. I muft in like manner intreate him not to
recite my reafons & difcourfes by halfes , but to
fet thé down faythfully & entirely, for as much
as in very deed concernes the whole fubftance
of the thing in queftió ; becaufe the want fom-
time of one word, may chance to make voyd, or
leffen the force of the whole argumét. And I am
the more folicitous about giuing this particuler
caueat, becaufe I find how ill he hath complied
with the promife which he made in his Preface
to the Reader , not to omit *without anfwere any*

one

*one thing of moment in all the difcourfe of Charity
Miftaken*. Neither will this courfe be a caufe
that his *Reioynder* grow too large, but it will be
occafion of breuity to him , and free me alfo
from the paines of fetting downe all the words
which he omits , and himfelf of demonftrating
that what he omitted was not materiall . Nay
I will affure him, that if he keep himfelfe to the
point of euery difficulty , and not weary the
Reader , and ouercharge his margent, with vnneceffary quotations of Authors in Greeke and
Latin, and fometime alfo in Italian and French,
togeather with prouerbs , fentences of Poets ,
and fuch grammaticall ftuffe , nor affect to cite
a multitude of our Catholique Schoole deuines
to no purpofe at all; his Booke will not exceed
a competent fize, nor wil any man in reafon
be offended with that length which is regula-
ted by neceffity. Agayne before he come to fet
downe his anfwere, or propofe his Arguments,
let him confider very wel what may be replied,
and whether his owne obiections may not be
retorted againft himfelfe , as the Reader will
perceiue to haue hapned often to his difaduantage in my *Reply* againft him But efpecially I
expect , and Truth it felfe exacts at his hand ,
that he fpeake cleerly and diftinctly , and not
feeke to walke in darknes , fo to delude and deceiue his Reader , now faying, and then denying, and alwayes fpeaking with fuch ambiguity, as that his greateft care may feeme to confift

in

in a certaine art to find a ſhift, as his occaſions might chance, eyther now, or heereafter to require, and as he might fall out to be vrged by diuerſity of feuerall arguments. And to the end it may appeare, that I deale plainely, as I would haue him alſo do, I deſire that he declare himſelfe concerning theſe points.

11.   Firſt, whether our Sauiour Chriſt haue not alwayes had, and be not euer to haue a viſible true Church on earth: & whether the contrary doctrine be not a damnable Hereſy.

12.   Secondly, what viſible Church there was before *Luther*, diſagreeing from the *Roman* Church, and agreeing with the pretended Church of Proteſtants.

13.   Thirdly, Since he will be forced to grant that there cā be aſſigned no viſible true Church of Chriſt, diſtinct from the Church of Rome, and ſuch Churches as agreed with her when *Luther* firſt appeared, whether it do not follow, that ſhe hath not erred fundamentally; becauſe euery ſuch errour deſtroies the nature and being of the Church, and ſo our Sauiour Chriſt ſhould haue had no viſible Church on earth.

14.   Fourthly, if the *Roman* Church did not fall into any fundamentall errour, let him tell vs how it can be *damnable* to liue in her Communion, or to maintaine errours, which are knowne & confeſſed, not to be fundamentall, or *damnable*.

15.   Fiftly, if her Errours were not damnable,

ble, nor did exclude faluation, how can they be excufed from *Schifme*, who forfooke her Communion vpon pretence of errours, which were not damnable?

16.   Sixtly, if *D. Potter* haue a mind to fay, that her Errours are damnable, or fundamentall, let him do vs fo much charity, as to tell vs in particuler what thofe fundamentall errours be. But he muft ftill remember (and my felfe muft be excufed, for repeating it) that if he fay the Roman Church erred fundamentally, he will not be able to fhew, that Chrift our Lord had any vifible Church on earth, when *Luther* appeared: & let him tel vs how Proteftants had, or can haue any Church which was vniuerfall, and extended herfelfe to all ages, if once he grant, that the Roman Church ceafed to be the true Church of Chrift; and confequently how they can hope for Saluation, if they deny it to vs.

17.   Seauenthly, whether any one Errour maintayned againft any one Truth though neuer fo fmall in it felfe, yet fufficiently propounded as teftified or reuealed by almighty God, do not deftroy the Nature and Vnity of Faith, or at leaft is not a grieuous offence excluding Saluation.

18.   Eightly, if this be fo, how can *Lutherans*, *Caluinifts*, *Zuinglians*, and all the reft of difagreeing Proteftãts, hope for faluation, fince it is manifeft that fome of them muft needs erre

againft

againſt ſome ſuch truth as is teſtified by almighty God, either fundamentall, or at leaſt not
fundamentall.

19. Ninthly, we conſtantly vrge, and require to haue a particuler Catalogue of ſuch
points as he calls fundamentall. A catalogue,
I ſay, in *particuler*, and not only ſome *generall* definition, or deſcription, wherein Proteſtants
may perhaps agree, though we ſee that they
differ when they come to aſſigne what points
in particuler be fundamentall; and yet vpon
ſuch a particuler Catalogue much depends: as
for example in particuler, whether or no a mã
do not erre in ſome point fundamentall or neceſſary to ſaluation; and whether or no *Lutherans*, *Caluiniſts*, and the reſt do diſagree in fundamentals, which if they do, the ſame Heauen
cannot receiue them all.

20. Tenthly, and laſtly I deſire that in anſ-
wering to theſe points, he would let vs know
diſtinctly, what is the doctrine of the Proteſtant
Engliſh Church concerning them, and what
he vtters only as his owne priuate opinion.

21. Theſe are the queſtions which for the
preſent I find it fit and neceſſary for me to aske
of *D. Potter*, or any other who will defend his
cauſe, or impugne ours. And it willbe in vaine
to ſpeake vainely, and to tell me, that a Foole
may aske more queſtions in an houre, then a
wiſeman can anſwere in a yeare; with ſuch idle
Prouerbs as that. For I aske but ſuch queſtions

as for which he giues occafion in his **Booke,**
and where he declares not himfelfe but after fo
ambiguous and confufed a manner, as that
Truth it felfe can fcarce tell how to conuince
him fo, but that with ignorant and ill-iudging
men he will feeme to haue fomewhat left to fay
for himfelfe, though Papifts (as he calls them)
and Puritans fhould preffe him contrary wayes
at the fame tyme : and thefe queftions concerne things alfo of high importance, as where-
vpon the knowledge of Gods Church, & true
Religion, and confequently Saluation of the
foule depends. And now becaufe he fhall not
taxe me with being like thofe men in the Gofpell whom our bleffed Lord and Sauiour charged with laying heauy burdens vpon other
mens fhoulders, who yet would not touch them
with their finger : I oblige my felfe to anfwere
vpon any demaund of his, both to all thefe
Queftions, if he find that I haue not done it already, and to any other concerning matter of
faith that he fhall aske. And I will tell him very
plainly, what is Catholique doctrine, and what
is not, that is, what is defined or what is not defined, and refts but in difcuffion among Deuines.

22. And it will be heere expected, that he
performe thefe things, as a man who profeffeth learning fhould doe, not flying from queftions which concerne things as they are confidered in their owne nature, to accidentall, or
rare

rare circumſtances of ignorance, incapacity, want of meanes to be inſtructed, erroneous cōſcience, and the like, which being very various and different, cannot be well comprehended vnder any generall Rule. But in deliuering generall doctrines we muſt conſider things as they be *ex natura rei,* or *per ſe loquendo* (as Deuines ſpeake) that is, according to their natures, if all circumſtances concurre proportionable thereunto. As for example ſome may for a time haue inuincible ignorance, euen of ſome fundamentall article of fayth, through want of capacity, inſtruction, or the like, and ſo not offend eyther in ſuch ignorance or errour; and yet we muſt abſolutely ſay, that errour in any one fundamentall point is damnable, becauſe ſo it is, if we conſider things in themſelues, abſtracting from accidentall circumſtances in particuler perſons : as contrarily if ſome man iudge ſome act of vertue, or ſome indifferent action to be a ſinne, in him it is a ſinne indeed, by reaſon of his erroneous conſcience; and yet we ought not to ſay abſolutely, that vertuous, or indifferent actions are ſinnes : and in all ſciences we muſt diſtinguiſh the generall Rules from their particuler Exceptions. And therefore when, for example, he anſwers to our demand, whether he hold that Catholiques may be ſaued, or whether their pretended errours be fundamentall and damnable, he is not to change the ſtate of the queſtion, and haue re

courſe

courſe to Ignorance, and the like, but to anſwere concerning the errours being conſidered what they are apt to be in themſelues, and as they are neyther increaſed nor diminiſhed, by accidentall circumſtances.

23. And the like I ſay of all the other points, to which I once againe deſire an anſwere without any of theſe, or the like ambiguous termes, *in ſome ſort, in ſome ſenſe, in ſome degree*, which may be explicated afterward as ſtrictly or largely as may beſt ſerue his turne; but let him tell vs roundly and particulerly, in what ſort, in what ſenſe, in what degree he vnderſtands thoſe, & the like obſcure mincing phraſes. If he proceed ſolidly after this manner, and not by way of meere words, more like a Preacher to a vulgar Auditour, then like a learned man with a pen in his hand, thy patience ſhall be the leſſe abuſed, and truth will alſo receiue more right. And ſince we haue already layed the grounds of the queſtion, much may be ſayd heereafter in few words, if (as I ſayd) he keep cloſe to the reall point of euery difficulty without wandring into impertinent diſputes, multiplying vulgar and threed-bare obiections and arguments, or labouring to proue what no mā denies, or making a vaine oſtentation by citing a number of Schoolemen, which euery Puny brought vp in Schooles is able to doe; and if he cite his Authours with ſuch ſincerity, as no time need be ſpent in opening his corruptions;

and

and finally if he fet himfelfe a worke with this confideration, that we are to giue a moſt ſtrict accompt to a moſt iuſt, and vnpartiall Iudge, of euery period, line, and word that paſſeth vnder our pen. For if at the later day we ſhall be arraigned for euery idle word which is ſpoken, ſo much more will that be done for euery idle word which is written, as the deliberation wherwith it paſſeth makes a man guilty of more malice, and as the importance of the matter which is treated of in bookes concerning true fayth and religion, without which no Soule can be faued, makes a mans Errours more materiall, then they would be, if queſtion were but of toyes.

D 3　　　　　　　　**A**

A TABLE OF THE
Chapters , and Contents of
this enfuing Firſt Part
of Reply .

CHAP. I.

THE true ſtate of the *Queſtion:*
VVith a Summary of the Reaſons, for vvhich , amongſt men
of different Religions , one ſide only
can be ſaued.

CHAP. II.

VVhat is that meanes vvherby the
reuealed truths of God are conueyed to
our Underſtanding, and vvhich muſt
determine Controuerſies in Fayth and
Religion.

CHAP.

CHAP. III.

That the diftinction of points fun-damentall, and not fundamentall, is neither pertinent, nor true in our pre-fent Controuerfy. And that the Ca-tholique vifible Church cannot erre in eyther kind of the fayd points.

CHAP. IIII.

To fay, that the Creed containes all points necefsarily to be belieued, is neyther pertinent to the Queftion in hand, nor in it felfe true.

CHAP. V.

That Luther, Caluin, their affo-ciates, and all vvho began, or conti-nue the feparation from the externall Communion of the Roman Church, are guilty of the proper, and formall finne of Schifme.

CHAP.

CHAP. VI.

That Luther, and the rest of Prote-
stants haue added Heresy to Schisme.

CHAP. VII.

In regard of the Precept of Charity
towwards ones selfe , Protestants are
in state of Sinne, as long as they re-
maine separated from the Roman
Church.

THE

THE FIRST PART.

The State of the Question; with a
Summary of the reasons for which
amongst men of different Religi-
ons, one side onely can be saued.

CHAP. I.

NEVER is Malice more indiſ-
creet, then when it chargeth
others with imputation of
that, to which it ſelfe becoms
more liable, euen by that very
act of accuſing others. For,
though guiltines be the effect
of ſome errour, yet vſually it begets a kind of
Moderation, ſo far forth, as not to let men caſt
ſuch aſperſions vpon others, as muſt apparant-
ly reflect vpon themſelues. Thus cannot the

Poet

Quis tulerit
Gracchum
&c.

Poet endure, that *Gracchus*, who was a factious
and vnquiet man, fhould be inueighing againft
Sedition: and the Roman Oratour rebukes Philofophers, who, to wax glorious, fuperfcribed
their Names vpon thofe very Bookes which
they entitled, *Of the contempt of glory*. What then
fhall we fay of D. *Potter*, who in the *Title*, and
Text of his whole Booke doth fo tragically
charge *Want of Charity on all fuch Romanifts, as
dare affirme, that Proteftancy deftroyeth Saluation*;
while he himfelfe is in act of pronouncing the
like heauy doome againft Roman Catholiques?
For, not fatisfied with much vnciuil language,

(a) *Pag.* 11. in affirming the Roman Church *many* (a) *wayes
to haue played the Harlot, and in that regard defer-
ued a bill of diuorce from Chrift, and deteftation of
Chriftians*; in ftiling her, that *proud* (b) *and curft*

(b) *Ibid.* *Dame of Rome, which takes vpon her to reuell in the
Houfe of God*; in talking of an *Idoll* (c) to be wor-

(c) *Pag.* 4. fhiped at Rome; he comes at length to thun-
Edit. 1. der out this fearefull fentence againft her: *For*

(d) *Pag.* 20 *that* (d) *Maffe of Errors* (faith he) *in iudgment
and practife, which is proper to her, and wherein she
differs from vs, we iudge a reconciliation impofsible,
and to vs* (*who are conuicted in confcience of her corruptions*) *damnable*. And in another place he

(e) *Pag.* 81. faith: *For vs who* (e) *are conuinced in confcience,
that she ers in many things, a necefsity lyes vpon vs,
euen vnder paine of damnation, to forfake her in thofe
Errors* By the acerbity of which Cenfure, he
doth not only make himfelfe guilty of that,
whic

which he iudgeth to be a haynous offence in
others, but freeth vs alſo from all colour of
crime by this his vnaduiſed recrimination.For,
if Roman Catholikes be likewiſe *conuicted in
conſcience* of the Errours of Proteſtants ; they
may,and muſt, in conformity to the *Doctours*
owne rule,iudge a reconciliation with them to
be alſo *damnable.* And thus, all the *Want of Charity* ſo deeply charged on vs,diſſolues it ſelfe into this poore wonder, *Roman Catholiques belieue
in their conſcience, that the Religion which they profeſſe is true, and the contrary falſe.*

2.   Neuertheleſſe, we earneſtly deſire, and
take care, that our doctrine may not be defa-
med by miſinterpretation. Far be it from vs, by
way of inſultation, to apply it againſt Proteſtants, otherwiſe then as they are comprehended vnder the generality of thoſe who are diuided from the only one true Church of Chriſt
our Lord,within the Communion whereof he
hath confined ſaluation. Neither do we vnderſtand,why our moſt deere Countrymen ſhould
be offended, if the Vniuerſality be particula-
rized vnder the *Name* of *Proteſtants*, firſt giuen
(g) to certaine *Lutherans*, who *proteſting* that
they would ſtand out againſt the Imperiall decrees, in defence of the Confeſſion exhibited
at *Auſburge*, were termed *Proteſtants*, in re-
guard of ſuch their *proteſting* : which *Confeſſio
Auguſtana* diſclayming from, and being diſ-
claymed by *Caluiniſts,* and *Zuinglians*, our na-

(g) *Sleidan.
l. 6. fol.*84.

ming or exemplifying a generall doctrine vnder
the particuler name of Proteftantifme, ought
not in any particuler manner to be odious in
England.

3.   Moreouer, our meaning is not, as misin-
formed perfons may conceiue, that we giue
Proteftants ouer to reprobation; that we offer
no prayers in hope of their faluation; that we
hold their cafe defperate. God forbid ! We
hope, we pray for their Conuerfion; and fometimes we find happy effects of our charitable
defires. Neither is our Cenfure immediatly directed to particuler perfons. The Tribunall of
particuler Iudgment is Gods alone. When any
man efteemed a Proteftant, leaueth to liue in
this world, we do not inftantly with precipitation auouch, that he is lodged in Hell. For we
are not alwayes acquainted with what fufficiency or meanes he was furnifhed for inftruction; we do not penetrate his capacity to vnderftand his Catechift; we haue no reuelation
what light might haue cleered his errours, or
Contrition retracted his finnes, in the laft moment before his death. In fuch particuler cafes,
we wifh more apparent fignes of faluation, but
do not giue any dogmaticall fentence of perdition. How grieuous finnes, *Difobedience*, *Schifme*, and *Herefy* are, is well knowne. But to difcerne how far the naturall malignity of thofe
great offences might be checked by Ignoráce,
or by fome fuch leffening circumftance, is the
office,

office, rather of *Prudence*, then of *Faith*.

4. Thus we allow Proteſtants as much
Charity, as *D.Potter* ſpares vs, for whom, in the
words aboue mentioned, and elſe where, he *(h)*
makes *Ignorāce* the beſt hope of ſaluation. Much
leſſe comfort, can we expect from the fierce doctrine of thoſe chiefe Proteſtants, who teach
that for many ages before *Luther*, Chriſt had
no viſible Church vpon earth. Not theſe men
alone or ſuch as they, but euen the 39. Articles,
to which the Engliſh Proteſtant Clergy ſub-
ſcribes, cenſure our beliefe ſo deeply, that Ignorance can ſcarce, or rather not at all, excuſe vs
from damnation. Our doctrine of *Tranſubſtan-*
tiation, is affirmed to be *repugnant* to the plaine
words of *(i)* Scripture ; our *Maſſes* to be blaſ-
phemous *(k)* *Fables*, with much more to be ſeen
in the *Articles* themſelues. In a certaine Confeſſion of the Chriſtian faith, at the end of their
bookes of Pſalmes collected into Meeter, and
printed *Cum priuilegio Regis Regali*, they call vs
Idolaters, and *limmes of Antichriſt*; and hauing
ſet downe a Catalogue of our doctrines, they
conclude, that for thē we ſhall after the General
Reſurrection be *damned to vnquenchable fire.*

5. But yet leſt any man ſhould flatter himſelfe with our charitable Mitigations, and therby waxe careles in ſearch of the true Church,
we deſire him to reade the *Concluſion* of the *Se-*
cond Part, where this matter is more explayned.

6. And, becauſe we cannot determine,

E 3   what

(h)*See Pag.*
39.

(i) *Art. 28.*
(k) *Art. 31.*

what *Iudgmēt* may be efteemed *rash*, or *prudent*, except by weighing the reafons vpon which it is grounded, we will heere, vnder one afpect, prefent a Summary of thofe Principles, from which we infer, that Proteftancy in it felfe vn-repented deftroyes Saluation: intending after-ward to proue the truth of euery one of the grounds, till, by a concatenation of fequels, we fall vpon the *Conclufion*, for which we are char-ged with *Want of Charity*.

7. Now, this is our gradation of reafons. Almighty God, hauing ordained Mankind to a fupernaturall *End* of eternall felicity; hath in his holy Prouidence fetled competent and con-uenient *Meanes*, whereby that end may be at-tained. The vniuerfall grand Origen of all fuch meanes, is the Incarnation and Death of our Bleffed Sauiour, whereby he merited internall grace for vs; and founded an *externall* vifible Church, prouided and ftored with all thofe helps which might be neceffary for Saluation. From hence it followeth, that in this Church amongft other aduantages, there muft be fome effectuall meanes to beget, and conferue fayth, to maintaine Vnity, to difcouer and condemne Herefies, to appeafe and reduce Schifmes, and to determine all Controuerfies in Religion. For without fuch meanes, the Church fhould not be furnifhed with helps fufficient to faluation, nor God affoard fufficient meanes to attayne that End, to which himfelfe ordained Man-

kind

kind. This meanes to decide Controuerfies in fayth and Religion (whether it fhould be the holy Scripture, or whatfoeuer elfe) muft be indued with an Vniuerfall Infallibility, in whatfoeuer it propoundeth for a diuine truth, that is, as reuealed, fpoken, or teftifyed by Almighty God, whether the matter of its nature, be great or fmall. For if it were fubiect to errour in any one thing, we could not in any other yield it infallible affent; becaufe we might with good reafon doubt, whether it chanced not to erre in that particuler.

8.   Thus farre all muft agree to what we haue faid, vnlefle they haue a mind to reduce *Faith* to *Opinion.* And euen out of thefe grounds alone, without further proceeding, it vndenyably followes, that of two men diffenting in matters of faith, great or fmall, few or many, the one cannot be faued without repentance, vnles Ignorance accidentally may in fome particuler perfon, plead excufe. For in that cafe of cótrary beliefe, one muft of neceffity be held to oppofe Gods word, or Reuelation fufficiently reprefented to his vnderftāding by an infallible Propounder; which oppofitió to the Teftimony of God is vndoutedly a damnable fin, whether otherwife, the thing fo teftifyed, be in it felfe great or fmall. And thus we haue already made good, what was promifed in the argument of this Chapter, that *amongft men of different Religions,* one is only capable of being faued.

9. Neuertheles, to the end that men may know in particular what is the sayd infallible meanes vpon which we are to rely in all things concerning Fayth , and accordingly may be able to iudge in what safety or danger , more or lesse they liue ; and becaufe *D. Potter* defcendeth to diuers particulers about Scriptures and the Church &c. we will go forward, & proue, that although Scripture be in it felfe moft facred, infallible, & diuine ; yet it alone cannot be *to vs a Rule*, or Iudge, fit and able to end all doubts and debates emergent in matters of Religion ; but that there muft be fome externall, vifible, publique, liuing Iudge, to whome all forts of perfons both learned & vnlearned, may without danger of errour , haue recourfe ; and in whofe Iudgment they may reft , for the interpreting and propounding of Gods Word or Reuelation . And this liuing Iudge, we will moft euidently proue to be no other , but that Holy, Catholique , Apoftolique, and Vifible Church, which our Sauiour purchafed with the effufion of his moft precious bloud.

10. If once therefore it be granted, that the Church is that means, which God hath left for deciding all Cōtrouerfies in faith, it manifeftly will follow, that fhe muft be infallible in all her determinations, whether the matters of thefelues be great or fmall ; becaufe as we fayd aboue, it muft be agreed on all fides, that if that meanes which God hath left to determine Contro-

uerfies were not infallible in all things propofed by it as truths reuealed by Almighty God, it
could not fettle in our minds a firme, and infallible beliefe of any one.

11. From this Vniuerfail Infallibility of
God's Church it followeth, that whofoeuer
wittingly denieth any one point propofed by
her, as reuealed by God, is iniurious to his diuine Maiefty, as if he could either deceiue, or be
deceiued in what he teftifieth. The auerring
whereof, were not only a *fundamentall* error,
but would ouerthrow the very foundation of
all fundamentall points, and therefore without repentance could not poffibly ftand with
faluation

12 Out of thefe grounds, we will fhew,
that although the diftinction of points *funda-*
mentall, and not *funaamentall,* be good and vfe-
full, as it is deliuered and applied by Catholique
Deuines, to teach what principall Articles of
faith, Chriftians are obliged *explicitely* to belieue: yet that it is impertinent to the prefent
purpofe of excufing any man from grieuous
finne, who knowingly *disbelieues*, that is, belieues the contrary of that which Gods Church
propofeth as diuine Truth. For it is one thing
not to know explicitly fome thing teftifyed by
God, & another pofitiuely to oppofe what we
know he hath reftified. The former may often
be excufed from finne, but neuer the latter,
which only is the cafe in Queftion.

F   13. In

13. In the fame manner fhall be demon-ftrated, that to alleadge the *Creed*, as contay-ning all Articles of faith neceffary to be expli-citely belieued, is not pertinent to free from finne the voluntary deniall of any other point knowen to be defined by Gods Church. And this were fufficient to ouerthrow all that *D. Potter* alleadgeth, concerning the *Creed:* though yet by way of Supererogation, we will proue, that there are diuers importāt matters of Faith which are not mentioned at all in the Creed.

14. From the aforefaid maine principle, that God hath alwayes had, and alwaies will haue on earth, a Church *Vifible*, within whofe Communion Saluation muft be hoped, and *in-fallible*, whofe definitions we ought to belieue; we will proue, that *Luther*, *Caluin*, and all o-ther, who continue the diuifion in Commu-nion, or Faith, from that Vifible Church, which at, and before *Luthers* appearance, was fpread ouer the world, cannot be excufed from *Schif-me*, and *Herefy*, although they oppofed her faith but in *one only* point; wheras it is manifeft, they diffent from her, in *many* and weighty matters, concerning as well *beliefe*, as *practife*.

15. To thefe reafons drawne from the ver-tue of *Faith*, we will add one other taken from *Charitas propria*, the Vertue of *Charity*, as it obli-geth vs, not to expofe our foule to hazard of perdition, when we can put our felues in a way much more fecure, as we will proue, that of the

Roman

Roman Catholiques to be.

16. We are then to proue thefe points.
Firft, that the infallible meanes to determine
controuerfies in matters of faith, is the vifible
Church of Chrift. Secondly, that the diftinction of points *fundamentall*, and *not fundamentall*, maketh nothing to our prefent Queftion.
Thirdly, that to fay the *Creed* containes all fundamentall points of faith, is neither *pertinent*,
nor *true*. Fourthly, that both *Luther*, & all they
who after him, perfift in diuifion, from the *Communion*, and *Faith* of the Roman Church, cannot be excufed from *Schifme* Fifthly, nor from
Herefy. Sixtly and laftly, that in regard of the
precept of *Charity* towards ones felfe, Proteftants be in ftate of finne, as long as they remaine diuided from the *Roman* Church. And
thefe fix points, fhall be feuerall Arguments for
fo many enfuing Chapters.

17. Only I will heere obferue, that it feemeth very ftrange, that Proteftants fhould charge vs fo deeply with *Want of Charity*, for only
teaching that both they, and we cannot be faued, feeing themfelues muft affirme the like of
whofoeuer oppofeth any leaft point deliuered
in Scripture, which they hold to be the fole Rule
of Faith Out of which ground they muft be
enforced to let all our former Inferences paffe
for good. For, is it not a grieuous finne, to deny
any one truth contained in holy Writ? Is there
in fuch deniall, any diftinction betwixt points

fun-

fundamentall, and not fundamentall, sufficient
to excufe from herefy? Is it not impertinent, to
alleadge the Creed contayning all fundamentall points of faith, as if belieuing it alone, we
were at liberty to deny all other points of Scripture? In a word: According to Proteftants;
Oppofe not Scripture, there is no Errour a-
gainft faith. Oppofe it in any leaft point, the error (if Scripture be fufficiently propofed, which
propofition is alfo required before a man can
be obliged to belieue euen fundametall points)
muft be damnable. What is this, but to fay with
vs, *Of perfons contrary in whatfoeuer point of beliefe,*
one party only can be faued? And *D. Potter* muft
not take it ill, if Catholiques belieue they may
be faued in that Religion for which they fuffer.
And if by occafion of this doctrine, men will
ftill be charging vs with *Want of Charity*, and
be refolued to *take* fcandall where none is *giuen*;
we muft comfort our felues with that graue,
and true faying of *S. Gregory*: *If fcandall (*1*) be*
taken from declaring a truth, it is better to permit
fcandall, then forfake the truth. But the folid
grounds of our Affertion, and the fincerity of
intention in vttering what we thinke, yield vs
confidence, that all will hold for moft reafonable the faying of Pope *Gelafius* to *Anaftafius* the
Emperour: *Farre be it from the Roman Emperour*
that he should hold it for a wrong to haue truth de-
clared to him. Let vs therefore begin with that
point which is the fuft that can be controuerted

ted betwixt Proteſtāts & vs, for as much as concernes the preſent Queſtion, & is contained in
the Argument of the next enſuing Chapter.

CHAP. II.

*VVhat is that meanes, vvherby the
reuealed Truthes of God are conueyed to our Vnderſtanding, and
vvhich muſt determine Controuerſies in Faith and Religion.*

F our eſtimation, reſpect, and
reuerence to holy Scripture
euen Proteſtants themſelues do
in fact giue teſtimony, while
they poſſeſſe it from vs, & take
it vpon the integrity of our cuſtody No cauſe imaginable could auert our wil
frō giuing the functiō of ſupreme & ſole Iudge
to holy Writ, if both the thing were not impoſſible in it ſelfe, & if both reaſon & experiēce did
not conuince our vnderſtanding, that by this
aſſertion Contentions are increaſed, and not
ended. We acknowledge holy Scripture, to be a
moſt perfect Rule, for as much as a writing
can be a Rule: We only deny that it excludes either diuine Tradition though it be vnwritten,
or an externall Iudge to keep, to propoſe, to in-

terpret

terpret it in a true, Orthodoxe, and Catholique
fenſe . Euery ſingle Booke, euery Chapter, yea
euery period of holy Scripture is infallibly true,
& wants no due perfection. But muſt we therfore infer, that all other Bookes of Scripture, are
to be excluded, leaſt by addition of them, we
may ſeeme to derogate from the perfection of
the former? When the firſt Bookes of the old &
New Teſtament were written, they did not exclude vnwritten Traditions, nor the Authority
of the Church to decide Controuerſies; & who
hath then ſo altered their nature, & filled them
with ſuch iealouſies, as that now they cannot
agree for feare of mutuall diſparagemēt? What
greater wrong is it for the written Word, to be
compartner now with the vnwritten, then for
the vnwritten, which was once alone, to be afterward ioyned with the written ? Who euer
heard, that to commend the fi elity of a Kee-
per, were to diſauthorize the thing committed
to his cuſtody ? Or that, to extoll the integrity
and knowledge, and to auouch the neceſſity of
a Iudge in ſuits of law, were to deny perfection
in the law? Are there not in Common wealths
beſides the lawes written & vnwritten cuſtomes, Iudges appointed to declare both the one,
the other. as ſeuerall occaſions may require ?

    2.   That the Scripture alone cannot be
Iudge in Controuerſies of faith , we gather very cleerlv. From the quality of a writing in generall : From the nature of holy Writ in particuler

culer, which muſt be believed as true, and infallible: From the Editions, & Tranſlations of it:
From the difficulty to vnderſtand it without
hazird of Errour: From the inconueniences
that muſt follow vpon the aſcribing of ſole Iudicature to it: & finally from the Confeſſions
of our Aduerſaries. And on the other ſide, all
theſe difficulties ceaſing, and all other qualities
requiſite to a Iudge concurring in the viſible
Church of Chriſt our Lord, we muſt conclude,
that ſhe it is, to whom in doubts concerning
Faith and religion, all Chriſtians ought to haue
recourſe.

3. The name, notion, nature, and proper-
ties of a Iudge cannot in common reaſon a-
gree to any meere writing, which, be it otherwiſe in its kind, neuer ſo highly qualified with
ſanctity and infallibility; yet it muſt euer be, as
all writings are, deafe, dumb, and inanimate. By
a Iudge, all wiſe men vnderſtand a Perſon endued with life, and reaſon, able to heare, to examine, to declare his mind to the diſagreeing
parties, in ſuch ſort as that ech one may know
whether the ſentence be in fauour of his cauſe,
or againſt his pretence; and he muſt be applia-
ble, and able to do all this, as the diuerſity of
Controuerſies, perſons, occaſions, and circumſtances may require. There is a great & plaine
diſtinction betwixt a *Iudge* and a *Rule.* For as in
a kingdome, the Iudge hath his Rule to follow
which are the receiued Lawes and cuſtomes;

fo are not they fit or able to declare, or be Iudges to themfelues, but that office muft belong to a liuing Iudge. The holy Scripture may be, and is a Rule,but cannot be a Iudge, becaufe it being alwayes the fame, cannot declare it felfe any one time, or vpon any one occafion more particularly then vpon any other; and let it be read ouer an hundred times, it wilbe ftill the fame,and no more fit alone to terminate controuerfies in faith, then the Law would be to end fuites, if it were giuen ouer to the phanfy, & gloffe of euery fingle man.

4.   This difference betwixt a Iudge and a Rule, *D.Potter* perceiued,when more then once, hauing ftiled the Scripture a *Iudge*, by way of correcting that terme, he adds *or rather a Rule*, becaufe he knew that an inanimate writing could not be a *Iudge*. Frō hence alfo it was,that though Proteftants in their beginning,affirmed Scripture alone to be the Iudge of Controuerfies; yet vpon a more aduifed reflection, they changed the phrafe, and fayd, that not Scripture, but the Holy Ghoft fpeaking in Scripture, is Iudge in Controuerfies. A difference without a difparity. The Holy Ghoft fpeaking only in Scripture is no more intelligible to vs, then the Scripture in which he fpeakes; as a mā fpeaking only Latin, can be no better vnderftood, then the tongue wherein he fpeaketh. And therefore to fay, a Iudge is neceffary for deciding controuerfies, about the meaning of
Scrip-

Scripture, is as much as to fay, he is neceſſary
to decide what the Holy Ghoſt ſpeakes in Scripture. And it were a conceyt, equally foolifh
and pernicious, if one ſhould ſeeke to take away
all Iudges in the kingdome, vpon this nicity,
that albeit Lawes cânot be Iudges, yet the Law-
maker ſpeaking in the Law, may performe that
Office ; as if the Law-maker ſpeaking in the
Law, were with more perſpicuity vnderſtood,
then the Law wherby he ſpeaketh.

5. But though ſome writing were granted
to haue a priuiledge, to declare it ſelfe vpon
ſuppoſition that it were maintayned in being,
and preferued entire from corruptions : yet it is
manifeſt that no writing can conſerue it ſelfe,
nor can complayne, or denounce the falſifier
of it; and therefore it ſtands in need of ſome
watchfull and not erring eye, to guard it, by
meanes of whoſe aſſured vigilancy, we may vndoubtedly receiue it ſincere and pure.

6. And ſuppoſe it could defend it ſelfe from
corruption, how could it aſſure vs that it ſelfe
were Canonicall, and of infaillible Verity ? By
ſaying ſo ? Of this very *affirmation*, there will
remaine the ſame Queſtion ſtill ; how it can
proue it ſelfe to be infallibly true ? Neyther can
there euer be an end of the like multiplyed demands, till we reſt in the externall Authority
of ſome perſon or perſons bearing witnes to the
world, that ſuch, or ſuch a booke is Scripture :
and yet vpon this point according to Proteſtāts

all other Controuersies in fayth depend.

7.   That Scripture cannot aſſure vs, that it ſelfe is Canonicall Scripture, is acknowledged by ſome Proteſtants in expreſſe *words*, and by all of them in deeds. *M. Hooker,* whome *D. Pot-* (a) *ter* ranketh (a) among men of great *learning and iudgement,* ſayth : *Of thinges* (b) *neceſſary, the very chiefeſt is to know what bookes we are to eſteeme holy ; which point is confeſſed impoſsible for the Scripture it ſelfe to teach.* And this he proueth by the ſame argument, which we lately vſed, ſaying thus : *It is not* (c) *the word of God which doth, or poſsibly can, aſſure vs, that we doe well to thinke it his word. For if any one Booke of Scripture did giue teſtimony of all, yet ſtill that Scripture which giueth teſtimony to the reſt, would require another Scripture to giue credit vnto it. Neyther could we come to any pauſe whereon to reſt, vnles beſids Scripture, there were ſomething which might aſſure vs &c.* And this he acknowledgeth to be the (d) Church. By the way. If, *of things neceſſary the very chiefeſt cannot poſsibly be taught by Scripture,* as this *man of ſo great learning and iudgment affirmeth,* and demonſtratiuely proueth ; how can the Proteſtant Clergy of England ſubſcribe to their ſixth Article? Wherein it is ſayd of the Scripture : *Whatſoeuer is not read therein, nor may be proued thereby, is not to be required of any man, that it ſhould be belieued as an Article of the fayth, or be thought requiſite or neceſſary to ſaluation :* and concerning their beliefe and profeſſion of this Article

(a) *Pag. 131.*
(b) *In his firſt booke of Eccleſ. Policy Sect. 14. pag. 68.*

(c) *Ibid. lib. 2. Sect. 4. p. 102.*

(d) *l. 3. Sect. 8. p. 17. 1. 146. & alibi*

Article, they are particulerly examined when
they be ordayned Priefts and Bifhops . With
Hooker, his defendant *Couell* doth punctually a-
gree. *Whitaker* likewife confeffeth , that the
queftion about Canonicall Scriptures, is defined to vs , not by *testimony of the priuate spirit* ,
which (fayth he) *being priuate and secret* , *is (* e)
vnfit to teach and refell others ; but (as he acknowledgeth) *by the (* f) *Ecclesiasticall Tradition* : *An*
argument (fayth he *) whereby may be argued, and*
conuinced what bookes be Canonicall , and what be
not . *Luther* fayth : *This (* g) *indeed the Church*
hath, that she can discerne the word of God , from the
word of men : as *Augustine confesseth , that he be-*
lieued the Ghospell, being moued by the authority of
the Church, which did preach this to be the Gospell.
Fulke teacheth, that *the Church (* h) *hath iudgment*
to discerne true writings from counterfaite , and the
word of God from the writing of men, and that this
iudgment she hath not of herselfe , but of the Holy
Ghost. And to the end that you may not be ignorant, from what Church you muft receiue
Scriptures , heare your firft Patriarch *Luther*
fpeaking againft thē, who (as he faith) brought
in *Anabaptisme*, that fo they might defpight the
Pope. *Verily* (faith he *) these (* i) *men build vpon a*
weake foundation. For by this meanes they ought to
deny the whole Scripture, and the Office of Preaching.
For , all these we haue from the Pope : otherwise we
must goe make a new Scripture.

8.   But now in deedes, they all make good,

(e) Aduerfus
Stapl. l. 2.
cap. 6. pag.
270 & pag.
357.
(f) Aduerfus
Stapl. l. 2 c.
4. pag 300.
(g) lib. de
capt. Babyl:
tom. 2. Wit-
temb. fol. 18,
(h) In his
answere to a
countefaite
Catholique
pag. 5.

(i) Epist. côt:
Anabap. ad
duos Paro-
chos. tom. 2:
Germ. Wit-
temb.

44 *Part.1. Charity maintayned*

that without the Churches authority, no cer-
tain can be had what Scripture is Canonicall, while they cannot agree in affigning the
Canon of holy Scripture. Of the Epiftle of *S.*

(k) *Prefat.* *Iames, Luther* hath thefe words : *The* (k) *Epiftle*
in epift. Iac. *of Iames is contentions, fwelling, dry, ftrawy, and vn-*
inedit. Ie- *worthy of an Apoftolicall Spirit.* Which cenfure of
nenfi. *Luther, Illyricus* acknowledgeth and maintai-
neth. *Kemnitius* teacheth, that *the fecond Epiftle*
(l) *In Enchi-* (l) *of Peter, the fecond and third of Iohn, the Epiftle*
rid. pag. 63. *to the Hebrewes, the Epiftle of Iames, the Epiftle of*
Iude, and the Apocalyps of Iohn are Apocryphall, as
not hauing fufficient Teftimony (m) *of their autho-*
(m) *In exa-* *rity,* and therefore that *nothing in controuerfy can*
min. Conc.
Trid.part.1. *be proued out of thefe* (n) *Bookes.* The fame is
pag. 55. taught by diuers other Lutherans : and if fome
(n) *Ibid.* other amongft them, be of a contrary opinion
fince *Luthers* time, I wonder what new infallible ground they can alleadge, why they leaue
their Maifter, and fo many of his prime Schollers ? I know no better ground, then becaufe
they may with as much freedome abandon
him, as he was bould to alter that Canon of
Scripture, which he found receiued in Gods
Church.

9. What Bookes of Scripture the Proteftants of England hold for Canonicall, is not
eafy to affirme. In their *fixt Article* they fay : *In*
the name of the Holy Scripture, we do vnderftand
thofe Canonicall Bookes of the Old and New Tefta-
ment, of whofe authority was neuer any doubt in the
Church.

Church. What meane they by thefe words? That by the Churches confent they are affured what Scriptures be Canonicall? This were to make the Church Iudge, and not Scriptures alone. Do they only vnderftand the agreement of the Church to be a probable inducement? Probability is no fufficient ground for an infallible affent of fayth. By this rule *(of whofe authority was N E V E R any doubt in the Church)* the whole booke of *Efther* muft quit the Canon, becaufe fome in the Church haue excluded it from the Canon, as *(o)Melito Afianus,* (p)*Athanafius,* and (q *)Gregory Nazianzen.* And *Luther* (if Proteftants will be content that he be *in the Church)* faith : *The Iewes* (r *)place the booke of Efther in the Canon, which yet, if I might be Iudge, doth rather deferue to be put out of the Canon.* And of *Ecclefiaftes* he faith : *This* (s *)booke is not full; there are in it many abrupt things : he wants boots and fpurs, that is, he hath no perfect fentence, he rides vpon a long reed like me when I was in the Monaftery.* And much more is to be read in him : who *(t)* fayth further, that the faid booke was not written by *Salomon,* but by *Syrach* in the tyme of the Machabees, and that it is like to *the Talmud (* the Iewes bible *) out of many bookes heaped into one worke, perhaps out of the Library of king Ptolomeus.* And further he fayth, that *(u)* he doth not belieue all to haue been donne as there is fet downe. And he teacheth the (w) booke of *Iob* to be *as it were an argument for a fable (* or Comedy)

G 3

(o) *Apud Eufeb.l. 4. hift.cap.26.*
(p)*in Synop.*
(q)*In carm. de genuinis Scripturis.*
(r)*lib.de feruo arbitrio contra Eraf. tom.2. Witt. fol.471.*
(s)*In latinis Sermonibus conuiuiali-bus Francof. in 8. impr. Anno 1571.*
(t)*In Germanicis colloq. Lutheri ab Aurifabroe-ditis Franco-furti tit. de libris veteris & noui Teft. fol.379.*
(u)*Ibid. tit. de Patriar-chis & Pro-phet. fol. 282.*
(w)*Tit. de lib. Vet. & Noui Teft.*

dy) *to set before vs an example of Patience.* And he
(*x*)*Fol.*380. (x) deliuers this generall cenſure of the Prophets Bookes: *The Sermons of no Prophet, were
written whole, and perfect, but their diſciples, and
Auditors ſnatched, now one ſentence, and then another, and ſo put them all into one booke, and by this
meanes the Bible was conſerued.* If this were ſo, the
Bookes of the Prophets, being not written by
themſelues, but promiſcuouſly, and caſually, by
their Diſciples, will ſoone be called in queſtion.
Are not theſe errours of *Luther*, fundamentall?
and yet if Proteſtants deny the infallibility of
the Church, vpon what certaine ground can
they diſproue theſe *Lutherian*, and *Luciferian*
blaſphemies? ô godly Reformer of the Roman
Church! But to returne to our Engliſh Canon
of Scripture. In the New Teſtament by the a-
boue mentioned rule (*of whoſe authority was neuer any doubt in the Church*) diuers Bookes of the
New Teſtament muſt be diſcanonized, to wit,
all thoſe of which ſome Ancients haue doubted, and thoſe which diuers *Lutherans* haue of
late denied. It is worth the obſeruation how the
before mentioned *ſixt Article*, doth ſpecify by
name all the Bookes of the *Old Teſtament* which
they hold for Canonicall; but thoſe of the *New*,
without naming any one, they ſhuffle ouer
with this generality: *All the Bookes of the New
Teſtament, as they are commonly receiued, we do receiue, and account them Canonicall.* The myſtery
is eaſily to be vnfolded. If they had deſcended

to

to particulers , they muſt haue contradicted
ſome of their chiefeſt Brethren. *As they are com-*
monly receiued &c . I aske : By whom ? By the
Church of *Rome?* Then, by the ſame reaſon they
muſt receiue diuers Bookes of the Old Teſtament , which they reiect. By *Lutherans?* Then
with *Lutherans* they may deny ſome Bookes of
the New Teſtament. If it be the greater , or
leſſe number of voyces , that muſt cry vp, or
downe, the Canon of Scripture, our *Roman*
Canon will preuaile: and among Proteſtants
the *Certainty* of their *Fayth* muſt be reduced to
an *Vncertaine* Controuerſy of *Fact,* whether the
number of thoſe who reiect , or of thoſe others
who receiue ſuch and ſuch Scriptures , be greater. Their faith muſt alter according to yeares,
and dayes. When *Luther* firſt appeared, he, and
his Diſciples were the greater number of that
new Church ; and ſo this claime (*Of being com-*
monly receiued) ſtood for them , till *Zuinglius*
& *Caluin* grew to ſome equall, or greater number then that of the *Lutherans* , and then this
rule of (*Commonly receaued*) will canonize their
Canon againſt the *Lutherans.* I would gladly
know, why in the former part of their Article,
they ſay both of the *Old* and *New Teſtament: In*
the name of the Holy Scripture , we do vnderſtand
thoſe Canonicall Bookes of the Old and New Teſta-
ment, of whoſe authority was neuer any doubt in the
Church: and in the latter part, (ſpeaking againe
of the *New Teſtament* , they giue a far different
rule,

rule, saying : *All the Bookes of the New Testament, as they are commonly receiued, we do receiue, and account them Canonicall*. This I say is a rule much different from the former (*Of whose authority was NEVER any doubt in the Church.*) For some Bookes might be said to be *Commonly receiued*, although they were *sometime* doubted of by *some*. If to be *Commonly receiued*, passe for a good rule to know the Canon of the *New Testament* ; why not of the *Old*? Aboue all we desire to know, vpon what infallible ground, in some Bookes they agree with vs against *Luther*, and diuers principall *Lutherans*, and in others iump with *Luther* against vs ? But seeing they disagree among themselues, it is euident that they haue no certaine rule to know the Canon of Scripture, in assigning whei of some of them must of necessity erre, because of contradictory propositions both cannot be true

10.   Moreouer the letters, syllables, words, phrase, or matter contained in holy Scripture haue no necessary, or naturall connexion with diuine *Reuelation* or *Inspiration* and therefore by seeing, reading, or vnderstanding them, we cannot inferre that they proceed from God or be confirmed by diuine authority , as because *Creatures* inuolue a necessary relation , connexion, and dependance on their *Creator*, Philosophers may by the light of naturall reason , demonstrate the existence of one prime cause of all things. In Holy Writ there are innumerable
truths

truths not furpaffing the fpheare of humane
wit,which are, or may be deliuered by Pagan
Writers, in the felfe fame words and phrafe as
they are in Scripture. And as for fome truths
peculiar to Chriftians, (for Example , the
myftery of the Bleffed Trinity &c.) the only
fetting them downe in *Writing* is not inough to
be affured that fuch a *Writing* is the vndoubted
word of God : otherwife fome fayings of *Plato,*
Trifmegiflus, Sybills, Ouid &c. muft be efteemed
Canonicall Scripture, becaufe they fall vpon
fome truths proper to Chriftian Religion. The
internall *light,* and *infpiration* which directed &
moued the Authors of Canonicall Scriptures,is
a hidden *Quality* infufed into their vnderftanding and will,and hath no fuch particuler fen-
fible influence into the externall *Writing* , that
in it we can difcouer,or *from it* demonftrate any
fuch fecret *light,* and *infpiration* ; and therefore
to be affured that fuch a *Writing* is diuine, we
cannot know from it felfe alone, but by fome
other extrinfecall authority.

11. And heere we appeale to any man of
Iudgement , whether it be not a vaine brag of
fome Proteftants to tell vs , that they wot full
well what is Scripture , by the light of Scripture it felfe, or(as *D.Potter* word's it) *by* (y)*that*
glorious beame of diuine light which shines therein ; (y) *Pag.141.*
euen as our eye diftinguifheth light from dark-
nes , without any other help then light it felfe ;
and as our eare knowes a voyce, by the voyce

H it

it felfe alone. But this vanity is refuted, by what we fayd euen now ; that the externall Scripture hath no apparent or neceffary connexion with diuine *infpiration* , or *reuelation* . Will *D* . *Potter* hold all his Brethren for blind men , for not fe-ing *that glorious beame of diuine light which shines* in Scripture , about which they cannot agree ? Corporall light may be difcerned by it felfe a-lone , as being euident , proportionate, & con-natural to our faculty of feeing. That Scripture is diuine , and infpired by God, is a truth excee-ding the naturall capacity and compaffe of mãs vnderftanding, to vs obfcure , and to be belie-ued by diuine fayth, which according to the *A-*

(z) Heb. v.1 *poftle* is ; *argumentum (z) non apparentium* ; *an ar-gument* , or conuiction, *of things not euident:* and therefore no wonder if Scripture doe not ma-nifeft it felfe by it felfe alone , but muft require fome other meanes for app'ying it to our vn-derftanding . Neuertheles their owne fimilitu-des and inftances , make againft themfelues . For fuppofe a man had neuer read , or heard of Sunne, Moone , Fire, Candle &c and fhould be brought to behold a light , yet in fuch fort as that the Agent , or Caufe Efficient from which it proceeded , were kept hidden from him ; could fuch an one, by only beholding the light , certainly know , whether it were proou-duced by the Sunne , or Moone &c ? Or if one heare a voyce , and had neuer known the 'pea-ker , could he know from whome in particuler

that

that voyce proceeded? They who looke vpon
Scripture, may well fee, that fome one wrote
it, but that it was written by diuine infpiration,
how shall they know? Nay, they cannot fo
much as know who wrote it, vnles they firft
know the writer, and what hand he writes : as
likewife I cānot know whofe voice it is which
I heare, vnles I firft both know the perfon who
fpeakes, & with what voice he vfeth to fpeake ;
and yet euen all this fuppofed, I may perhaps
be deceyued. For there may be voyces fo like,
and Hand fo counterfaited, that men may be
deceyued by them, as birds were by the grapes
of that skillfull Painter. Now fince Proteftants
affirme knowledge concerning God as our *fupernaturall* end, muft be taken from Scripture,
they cannot in Scripture alone difcerne that it
is his voyce, or writing, becaufe they cannot
know from whome a writing, or voyce proceeds, vnles firft they know the perfon who
fpeaketh, or writeth. Nay I fay more: By Scripture alone, they cannot fo much as know,
that any perfon doth in it, or by it, fpeake any
thing at all: becaufe one may write without in-
tent to fignify, or affirme any thing, but only
to fet downe, or as it were paint, fuch chara-
ĉters, fyllables, and words, as men are wont
to fet copies, not caring what the fignification
of the words imports: or as one tranfcribes a
writinge which himfelfe vnderftands not; or
when one writes what another dictates, and

in other such cases, wherein it is cleere, that
the writer speakes, or signifies nothing in such
his writing; & therefore by *it* we cannot heare,
or vnderstand *his* voyce. With what certainty
then can any man affirme, that by Scripture it
self they can see, that the writers did inted to signify any thing at all; that they were Apostles,
or other Canonical Authours; that they wrote
their owne sense, and not what was dictated by
some other man; and finally, & especially, that
they wrote by the infallible direction of the
Holy Ghost?

12.   But let vs be liberall, and for the present suppose (not grant) that Scripture is, like
to corporall light, by it selfe alone able to determine, & moue our vnderstanding to assent;
yet the similitude proues against theselues. For
light is not visible, except to such as haue eyes,
which are not made by the light, but must be
presupposed as produced by some other cause.
And therefore, to hold the similitude, Scripture can be cleere only to those who are endewed with the eye of fayth; or, as *D. Potter* a-
(a) *Pag.*141. boue cited fayth, to all that *haue* (a) *eyes to dif-*
cerne the shining beames thereof; that is, to the *be-*
lieuer, as immediatly after he speaketh. Fayth
then must not originally proceed from Scripture, but is to be presupposed, before we can see
the light thereof; and consequently there must
be some other meanes precedent to Scripture, to
beget Fayth, which can be no other then the
Church

Church .

13. Others affirme, that they know Canonicall Scriptures to be such , by the *Title* of the
Bookes. But how shall we know such *Inscripti-*
ons, or *Titles* to be infallibly true ? From this
their Answere our argument is strengthned, because diuers Apocryphall writings haue appeared , vnder the *Titles*, and Names of sacred Authours, as the Ghospell of *Thomas* mentioned by
S (b) *Augustine* : the Ghospell of *Peter*, which
the *Nazarei* did vse, as (c) *Theodoret* witnesseth,
with which *Seraphion* a Catholique Bishop, was
for sometyme deceiued , as may be read in (d)
Eusebius, who also speaketh of the *Apocalyps* of
(e) *Peter.* The like may be sayd of the Ghospells
of *Barnabas*, *Bartholomew* , and other such writings specifyed by Pope (f) *Gelasius*. Protestants
reiect likewise some part of *Esther* and *Daniel*,
which beare the same *Titles* with the rest of
those Bookes , as also both wee, and they hould
for Apochryphall the third and fourth Bookes
which go vnder the name of *Esdras* , and yet
both of vs receiue his first and second booke .
Wherefore Titles are not sufficient assurances
what bookes be Canonicall: which (h) *D. Co-*
uell acknowledgeth in these words : *It is not the*
word of God , which doth , or possibly can assure vs ,
that we doe well to thinke it is the word of God : the
first outward motion leading men so to esteeme of the
Scripture , is the Authority of Gods Church , which
teacheth vs to receiue Marks Ghospell, who was not

(b) *Cont. A-*
dimantum c.
17.
(c) *l.2.hare-*
tic fab .
(d) *lib.6.cap.*
10.
(e *lib.6.cap.*
11.
(f) *Dist. Can.*
Sancta Ro-
mana.

(h) *In his de-*
defence art.4.
Pag.31 .

an Apoſtle, and to refuſe the Ghoſpell of Thomas who was an Apoſtle: and to retaine Lukes Ghoſpell who ſaw not Chriſt, and to reiect the Ghoſpell of Nicodemus who ſaw him.

14. Another Anſwere, or rather Obiection they are wont to bring: That the Scripture being a *principle needs no proofe among Chriſtians.* So
(i) *Pag.*234 D. (i) *Potter.* But this it either a plaine begging of the queſtion, or manifeſtly vntrue, and is directly againſt their owne doctrine, and practiſe. If they meane, that Scripture is one of thoſe principles, which being the firſt, and the moſt knowne in all Sciences, cannot be demonſtrated by other Principles, they ſuppoſe that which is in queſtion, whether there be not ſome principle (for example, the Church) wherby we may come to the knowledge of Scripture. If they intend, that Scripture is a Principle, but not the firſt, and moſt knowne in Chriſtianity, then Scripture may be proued. For principles, that are not the firſt, nor knowne of themſelues, may, & ought to be proued, before we can yield aſſent, either to them, or to other verities depending on then. It is repugnant to their owne doctrine, and practiſe, in as much as they are wont to affirme, that one part of Scripture may be knowne to be Canonicall, and may be interpreted by another. And ſince euery ſcripture is a principle ſufficient, vpon which to ground diuine faith, they muſt grant, that one Principle may, and ſometime muſt be proued

by

by another. Yea this their Anfwere, vpon due ponderation, falls out to proue, what we af-firme. For fince all Principles cannot be pro-ued, we muft (that our labour may not be end-les) come at length to reft in fome principle, which may not require any other proofe. Such is *Tradition*, which inuolues an euidence of fact, and from hand to hand, and age to age, brin-ging vs vp to the *times*, and *perfons* of the Apo-ftles, and our Sauiour himfelfe cometh to be confirmed by all thofe miracles, and other ar-guments, whereby they conuinced their do-ctrine to be true. Wherefore the ancient Fa-thers auouch that we muft receiue the facred Canon vpon the credit of Gods Church. S. (k *Athanafius* faith, that only foure Gofpels are to be receiued, becaufe the *Canons of the Holy, and Catholique Church haue fo determined.* The third Councell of (l) *Carthage* hauing fet downe the Bookes of holy Scripture, giues the reafon, be-caufe, *We haue receiued from our Fathers that thefe are to be read in the Church.* S. *Auguftine* (m) fpea-king of the *Acts* of the *Apoftles*, faith: *To which booke I muft giue credit, if I giue credit to the Gofpel, becaufe the Catholique Church doth a lik recomend to me both thefe Bookes.* And in the fame place he hath alfo thefe words: *I would not belieue the Gofpell, vnles the authority of the Catholique church did moue me.* A faying fo plaine, that *Zuinglius,* is forced to cry out: *Heere I* (n) *implore your e-quity to fpeake freely, whether this faying of Au-*
guftine

(k) *In Sy-nopfi.*

(l) *Can.* 47.

(m) *Cont. ep. Fundam. c.* 5,

(n) *Tom.* 1. *fol.* 135.

guſtine ſeeme not ouerbould, or els vnaduiſedly to
haue fallen from him.

15. But ſuppoſe they were aſſured what
Bookes were Canonicall, this will little auaile
them, vnles they be likewiſe certaine in what
language they remaine vncorrupted, or what
Tranſlations be true. *Caluin* (o) acknowledgeth
corruption in the Hebrew Text; which if it be
taken without points, is ſo ambiguous, that
ſcarcely any one Chapter, yea period, can be
ſecurely vnderſtood without the help of ſome
Tranſlation. If with points: Theſe were after
S. Hierom's time, inuented by the perfidious
Iewes, who either by ignorance might miſtake,
or vpon malice force the Text, to fauour their
impieties. And that the Hebrew Text ſtill retaines much ambiguity, is apparent by the diſagreeing *Tranſlations* of *Nouelliſts* ; which alſo
proues the Greeke, for the New Teſtament, not
to be void of doubtfulnes, as *Caluin* (p) confeſſeth it to be corrupted. And although both the
Hebrew and Greeke were pure, what doth this
help, if only Scripture be the rule of faith, and
ſo very few be able to examine the Text in theſe
languages. All then muſt be reduced to the certainty of *Tranſlations* into other tongues, wherin no priuate man hauing any promiſe, or aſſu-
rance of infallibility, Proteſtants who rely v-
pon Scripture alone, will find no certaine
ground for their faith; as accordingly *Whitaker*
(q) affirmeth : *Thoſe who vnderſtand not the He-*
brew

(o) *Inſtit. c.*
6. §. 11.

(p) *Inſtit. ca.*
7. §. 12.

(q) *lib. de*
ſancta Scri-
ptura p. 52;.

brew and Greeke do erre often,and vnauoydably.

16. Now concerning the Tranſlations of
Proteſtants , it will be ſufficient to ſet downe
what the laborious , exact, and iudicious Author of the *Proteſtants Apology &c.* dedicated to
our late King *Iames* of famous memory , hath
to this (r) purpoſe. To omit (ſaith he) particulers,whoſe recitall would be infinite,& to touch
this point but generally only , the Tranſlation
of the New Teſtament by *Luther* is condemned
by *Andreas, Oſiander, Keckermannus* , and *Zuin-*
glius, who ſayth hereof to *Luther. Thou doſt cor-*
rupt the word of God , thou art ſeene to be a manifeſt
and common corrupter of the holy Scriptures : how
much are we aſhamed of thee who haue hitherto eſtee-
med thee beyond all meaſure,and now proue thee to be
ſuch a man? And in like maner doth *Luther* reiect
the Tranſlation of the *Zuinglians* terming them
in matter of diuinity,fooles, Aſſes, Antichriſts,
deceauers, and of Aſſe-like vnderſtanding. In
ſo much that when *Proſcheuerus* the Zwinglian
Printer of *Zurich* ſent him a Bible tranſlated by
the diuines there, *Luther* would not receyue the
ſame, but ſending it backe reiected it , as the
Proteſtant Writers *Hoſpinians,* and *Lauatherus*
witneſſe. The tranſlation ſet forth by *Oecolam-*
padius, and the Deuines of *Baſil,* is reproued by
Beza, who affirmeth that the *Baſil Tranſlation is*
in many places wicked,and altogeather differing from
the mynd af the Holy Ghoſt. The tranſlation of *Ca-*
ſtalio is condemned by *Beza ,* as being *ſacrilegi-*

(r)Tract. 1.
Sect.10.
ſubd.4.ioy-
ned with
tract. 2.
cap. 2.Sect.
10.ſubd.2.

ous

ous, wicked, and Ethnicall. As concerning *Caluins* tranſlation, that learned Proteſtant Writer *Carolus Molinæus* ſaith thereof: *Caluin in his Harmony maketh the Text of the Goſpell to leape vp and downe : he vſeth violence to the letter of the Goſpell; and beſides this addeth to the Text.* As touching *Beza's* tranſlation (to omit the diſlike had therof by *Seluecerus* the German Proteſtant of the Vniuerſity of *Iena)* the foreſaid *Molinæus* ſaith of him, *de facto mutat textum; he actually changeth the text*; and giueth further ſundry inſtances of his corruptions: as alſo *Caſtalio that learned Caluiniſt, and moſt learned in the tongues*, reprehendeth *Beza* in a whole booke of this matter, and ſaith; that to note all his errours in tranſlation, *would require a great volume.* And *M. Parkes* ſaith: *As for the Geneua Bibles, it is to be wiſhed that either they may be purged from thoſe manifold errors, which are both in the text, and in the margent , or els vtterly prohibited.* All which confirmeth your Maieſties graue and learned Cenſure, in your *thinking the Geneua tranſlation to be worſt of all* ; and that in the *Marginall notes annexed to the Geneua tranſlation, ſome are very partiall, vntrue, ſeditious, &c.* Laſtly concerning the Engliſh Tranſlations , the Puritanes ſay : *Our tranſlation of the Pſalmes comprized in our Booke of Common Prayer, doth in addition , ſubtraction, and alteration , differ from the Truth of the H brew in two hundred places at the leaſt.* In ſo much as they do therefore profeſſe to reſt doubtfull , *whether a man with a*

ſafe

safe conscience may subscribe thereto. And *M. Caer-lile* saith of the Englifh Tranflators, that they haue *depraued the senfe, obscured the truth, and deceiued the ignorant; that in many places they do detort the Scriptures from the right fenfe.* And that, *they shew themfelues to loue darknes more then light, falshood more then truth.* And the Minifters of Lincolne Dioceffe giue their publike teftimony, terming the Englifh Tranflation : *A Tranflation that taketh away from the Text; that addeth to the Text; and that, fometime to the changing, or obscuring of the meaning of the Holy Ghoft.* Not without caufe therefore did your Maiefty affirme, that you *could neuer yet fee a Bible well tranflated into Englifh.* Thus far the *Author* of the *Proteftants Apology &c.* And I cannot forbeare to mention in particuler that famous corruption of *Luther,* who in the Text where it is faid (*Rom. 3. v. 28.*) *We accompt a man to be inftified by faith, without the works of the Law,* in fauour of Iuftification by faith *alone,* tranflateth (*Iuftified by faith ALONE.*) As likewife the falfification of *Zuinglius* is no leffe notorious, who in the Gofpels of *S. Mathew, Mark,* and *Luke,* and in *S. Paul,* in place of, *This is my Body; This is my bloud;* tranflates, *This fignifies my Body; This fignifies my bloud.* And heere let Proteftants confider duely of thefe points. Saluation cannot be hoped for without true faith: Faith according to them relies vpon Scripture alone: Scripture muft be deliuered to moft of them by the Tranflations:

Tranflations depend on the skill and honefty of
men, in whom nothing is more certaine then a
moft certaine poffibility to erre, and no greater euidence of Truth, then that it is euident
fome of them imbrace falfhood, by reafon of
their contrary tranflations. What then remaineth, but that truth, faith, faluation, & all, muft
in them rely vpon a fallible, and vncertaine
ground? How many poore foules are lamenta-
bly feduced, while from preaching Minifters,
they admire a multitude of Texts of diuine
Scripture, but are indeed the falfe tranflations,
and corruptions of erring men? Let them therfore, if they will be affured of true Scriptures,
fly to the alwayes vifible Catholique Church,
againft which the gates of hell can neuer fo far
preuaile, as that fhe fhall be permitted to deceiue the Chriftian world with falfe Scriptures. And *Luther* himfelfe, by vnfortunate experience, was at length forced to confeffe thus

(s) *lib. cont.* much, faying: *If the* (s) *world laſt longer, it will be*
Zwingl. de *againe neceffary to receiue the Decrees of Councels, &*
verit. corp. *to haue recourfe to them, by reafon of diuers interpre-*
Chrifti in *tations of Scripture which now raigne.* On the con-
Euchar. trary fi e, the Tranflation approued by the Roman Church, is commended euen by our Ad-
(t) *In his an-* uerfaries: and *D.Couell* in particuler fayth, *that*
fwere vnto *it was vfed in the Church, one thoufand* (t) *three*
M. John *hundred yeares agoe*, and doubteth not *to prefer*
Burges pag. (u) *that Tranflation before others.* In fo much, that
94. whereas the Englifh tranflations be many, and
(u) *Ibid.* _____
                                                   among

among themfelues difagreeing, he concludeth, that of all thofe *the approued tranflation authori-zed by the Church of England, is that which com-meth neareſt to the vulgar, and is commonly called the Bishops Bible.* So that the truth of that tran-flation which we vfe, muſt be the rule to iudge of the goodneſſe of their Bibles : and therefore they are obliged to maintaine our Tranflation if it were but for their owne fake.

17.   But doth indeed the fource of their ma-nifjld vncertainties ftop heer? No! The chiefeſt di ficulty remaines, concerning the true mea-ning of Scripture: for attayning whereof , if Proteſtants had any certainty , they could not difagree fo hugely as they do. Hence, M.Hooker faith: *We are* (w) *right fure of this ,that Nature, Scripture, and Experience haue all taught the world to feeke for the ending of contentions, by fubmitting it felfe vnto fome iudiciall, and definitiue fentence, whereunto neither part that contendeth may, vnder any pretence,refufe to ſtand.* D.*Fields* words are re-markable to this purpofe : *Seeing* (faith he) *the controuerfies* (x) *of Religion in our times are growne in number fo many, and in nature fo intricate , that few haue time and leafure, fewer ſtrength of vnder-ſtanding to examine them; what remaineth for men defirous of fatisfaction in things of fuch confequence, but diligently to fearch out which among all the focie-tyes in the world,is that bleſſed Company of ho'y Ones, that houſhould of Faith, that Spoufe of Chriſt , and Church of the liuing God , which is the Pillar and*

(w) *In his Preface to his Bookes of Ecclefiaſti-call Policy. Sect.6. 26.*

(x) *Jn his Treatife of the Church In his Epiſtle dedicatory to the* L.*Arch-bishop.*

ground

ground of Truth, that so they may imbrace her com-
munion, follow her directions , and rest in her iudg-
ment .

18.   And now that the true Interpretation
of Scripture , ought to be receiued from the
Church, it is alfo proued by what we haue already demonftrated, that ihe it is, who muft declare what Bookes be true Scripture; wherein if
ihe be affifted by the Holy Ghoft , why fhould
we not belieue her , to be infallibly directed
concerning the true meaning of them? Let Proteftants therfore eyther bring fome proofe out
of Scripture, that the Church is guided by the
Holy Ghoft in difcerning true Scripture , and
not in deliuering the true fenfe thereof; Or els
giue vs leaue to apply againft them , the argument, which *S. Auguftine* oppofed to the *Ma-*
(x)*Cont. ep.* *nicheans,* in thefe words : *I would not (y) belieue*
Fund.cap.5. *the Gofpel,vnles the authority of the Church did moue*
me.Them therfore whom I obeyed faying, Belieue the
Gofpell , why should I not obey faying to me , Do not
belieue Manichæus (Luther, Caluin, &c.) *Choofe*
what thou pleafeft.If thou shalt fay , Belieue the Ca-
tholiques ; They warne me not to giue any credit to
you.If therefore I belieue them, I cannot belieue thee.
If thou fay, Do not belieue the Catholiques, thou fhalt
not do well inforcing me to the faith of Manichæus,
becaufe by the preaching of Catholiques I belieued the
Gofpell it felfe. If thou fay,you did well to belieue them
(Catholiques) commending the Gofpell,but you did
not well to belieue them,difcommending Manichæus;
D.*ft*

Dost thou thinke me so very foolish, that without any reason at all, I should beleeue what thou wilts, & not beleeue what thou wilts not? And do not Protestāts perfectly resemble these men, to whom *S. Augustine* spake, when they will haue men to beleeue the *Roman* Church deliuering Scripture, but not to beleeue her condemning *Luther,* and the rest? Against whom, when they first opposed themselues to the Roman Church, *S. Augustine* may seeme to haue spoken no lesse prophetically, then doctrinally, when he said: *Why should I not most (z) diligently inquire what Christ commanded of them before all others, by whose authority I was moued to beleeue, that Christ commanded any good thing? Canst thou better declare to me what he said, whom I would not haue thought to haue been, or to be, if the beliefe thereof had been recommended by thee to me? This therefore I beleeued by fame, strengthned with celebrity, consent, Antiquity. But euery one may see that you, so few, so turbulent, so new, can produce nothing deseruing authority. What madnes is this? Beleeue them (* Catholiques *) that we ought to beleeue Christ; but learne of vs what Christ said. Why. I beseech thee? Surely if they (* Catholiques *) were not at all, and could not teach me any thing, I would more easily perswade my selfe, that I were not to beleeue Christ, then that I should learne any thing concerning him from any other then them by whom I beleeued him* If therefore we receiue the knowledge of Christ, and Scriptures from the Church, from her also must we take his doctrine,

(z) *lib. de vtil. cre. cap.* 14.

&ctrine, and the interpretation thereof.

19.   But befides all this, the Scriptures cannot be Iudge of Controuerfies, who ought to be
fuch, as that to him not only the learned, or Ve-
terans, but alfo the vnlearned, and Nouices,
may haue recourfe; for thefe being capable of
faluation, and endued with faith of the fame
nature with that of the learned, there muft be
fome vniuerfall Iudge, which the ignorant may
vnderftand, and to whom the greateft Clerks
muft fubmit. Such is the Church : and the Scripture is not fuch .

20.   Now, the inconueniences which follow by referring all Controuerfies to Scripture
alone, are very cleare. For by this principle, all
is finally in very deed and truth reduced to the
internall priuate Spirit, becaufe there is really no
middle way betwixt a *publique externall*, and a
priuate internall voyce; & whofoeuer refufeth
the one, muft of neceffity adhere to the other.

21.   This Tenet alfo of Proteftants, by taking the office of Iudicature from the Church,
comes to conferre it vpon euery particuler mã,
who being driuen from fubmiffion to the
Church, cannot be blamed if he truft himfelfe
as farre as any other, his confcience dictating,
that wittingly he meanes not to cozen himfelf,
as others malicioufly may do. Which inference
is fo manifeft, that it hath extorted from diuers
Proteftants the open Confeffion of fo vaft an
abfurdity . Heare *Luther* : *The Gouernours (a) of*
                                        Churches

(a) *Tom. 2.*
Wittemberg.
fol. 375.

Churches and Pastours of Christs sheep haue indeed
power to teach, but the sheep ought to giue Iudgment
whether they propound the voyce of Christ, or of Ali- (b) *In lib. de*
ens . Lubbertus fayth: *As we haue (* b *) demonstra-* *principijs*
ted that all publique Iudges may be deceiued in inter- *Christian.*
preting ; fo we affirme, that they may erre in iudging. *dogm. lib.* 6.
All faythfull men are priuate Iudges , and th y alfo *cap. 13.*
haue power to Iudge of doctrines and interpretations.
Whitaker, euen of the vnlearned , fayth : *They*
(c *) ought to haue recourfe vnto the more learned, but* (c) *De Sacra*
in the meane tyme we must be carefull not to attribute *Scriptura*
to them ouer-much , but fo, that still we retaine our *pag.* 529.
owne freedome. Bilfon alfo affirmeth ; that , *The*
people (d *) must be difcerners, and Iudges of that* (d) *In his*
which is taught. This fame pernicious doctrine is *true differen-*
deliuered by *Brentius, Zanchius, Cartwright* , and *ce part. 2.*
others exactly cited by (e) *Brereley* ; & nothing (e) *Tract.2 .*
is more common in euery Proteftants mouth, *cap.1.Sect.*
then that he admits of Fathers, Councells, 1.
Church &c. as far as they agree with Scripture; which vpon the matter is himfelfe. Thus
Herefy euer fals vpon extremes *:* It pretends to
haue Scripture alone for Iudge of Controuerfies , and in the meane time fets vp as many
Iudges, as there are men, and women in the
Chriftian world. What good Statefmen would
they be, who fhould idëate , or fancy fuch a
Common wealth, as thefe men haue framed to
themfelues a Church? They verify what *S. Au-*
gustine obiecteth againft certaine Heretiques. (f) *lib.* 32.
You fee (f *) that you goe about to ouerthrow all cu-* *cont.Fauft,*
                    K   *thority*

thority of Scripture, and that euery mans mind may be to himselfe a Rule, what he is to allow, or disallow in euery Scripture.

22. Moreouer what côfusion to the Church, what danger to the Common wealth, this deniall of the authority of the Church, may bring, I leaue to the consideration of any Iudicious, indifferent man. I will only set downe some words of *D. Potter*, who speaking of the Proposition of reuealed Truths, sufficient to proue him that gaine-faith them to be an Heretique, fayth thus: *This Proposition* (g) *of reuealed truths, is not by the infallible determination of Pope, or Church;* (Pope, and Church being excluded, let vs heare what more secure rule he will prescribe) *but by whatsoeuer meanes a man may be conuinced in conscience of diuine reuelation. If a Preacher do cleare any point of fayth to his Hearers; if a priuate Christian do make it appeare to his Neighbour, that any conclusion, or point of faith is deliuered by diuine reuelation of Gods word; if a man himselfe (without any Teacher) by reading the Scriptures, or hearing them read, be conuinced of the truth of any such conclusion: this is a sufficient proposition to proue him that gainfaith any such proofe, to be an Heretique, and obstinate opposer of the faith.* Behold what goodly safe Propounders of fayth arise in place of Gods vniuersall visible Church, which must yield to a single Preacher, a Neighbour, a man himselfe if he can read, or at least haue eares to heare Scripture read. Verily I do not see, but

(g) *pag.*247

that

that euery well-gouerned Ciuill Common-
wealth, ought to concur towards the exterminating of this doctrine, whereby the Interpretation of Scripture is taken from the Church,
and conferred vpon euery man, who, whatſoeuer is pretended to the contrary, may be a paſ-
ſionate ſeditions creature.

23. Moreouer, there was no Scripture, or
written word for about two thouſand yeares
from *Adam* to *Moyſes*, whom all acknowledge
to haue been the firſt Author of Canonicall
Scripture: And againe for about two thouſand
yeares more, from *Moyſes* to Chriſt our Lord,
holy Scripture was only among the people of
Iſrael; and yet there were Gentils endewed in
thoſe dayes with diuine Faith, as appeareth in
Iob, and his friends. Wherefore during ſo many
ages, the Church alone was the deciſder of
Controuerſies, and Inſtructor of the faithfull.
Neither did the Word written by *Moſes*, depriue that Church of her former Infallibility,
or other qualities requiſite for a Iudge: yea *D.*
Potter acknowledgeth, that beſides the *Law*,
there was a liuing *Iudge* in the Iewiſh Church,
endewed with an *abſolutly infallible direction in*
caſes of moment; as all points belonging to diuine Faith are. Now, the Church of Chriſt our
Lord, was before the Scriptures of the New
Teſtament, which were not written inſtantly,
nor all at one time, but ſucceſſiuely vpon ſeuerall occaſions; and ſome after the deceaſe of

moſt of the Apoſtles : & after they were written, they were not preſently knowne to all
Churches: and of ſome there was doubt in the
Church for ſome Ages after our Sauiour. Shall
we then ſay, that according as the Church by
little and little receiued holy Scripture, ſhe was
by the like degrees deueſted of her poſſeſſed Infallibility, and power to decide Controuerſies
in Religion? That ſome Churches had one Iudge of Controuerſies, and others another? That
with moneths, or yeares, as new Canonicall
Scripture grew to be publiſhed, the Church altered her whole Rule of faith, or Iudge of Controuerſies? After the Apoſtles time, and after
the writing of Scriptures, Hereſies would be
ſure to riſe, requiring in Gods Church for their
diſcouery and condemnation, *Infallibility*, either to write new Canonicall Scripture as was
done in the Apoſtles time by occaſion of emergent hereſies; or *infallibility* to interpret Scriptures, already written, or, without Scripture,
by diuine vnwritten Traditions, and aſſiſtance
of the holy Ghoſt to determine all Controuer-
(h) *De teſt.* ſies, as *Tertullian* ſaith: *The ſoule is* (h) *before the*
anim. cap. 5. *letter; and ſpeach b fore Bookes; and ſenſe before Stile.*
Certainly ſuch *addition* of Scripture, with de-
rogation, or *ſubtraction* from the former power
and infallibility of the Church, would haue
brought to the world *diuiſion* in matters of
faith, and the Church had rather loſt, then gained by holy Scripture (which ought to be far
from

from our tongues and thoughts,) it being manifeſt, that for deciſion of Controuerſies, infallibility ſetled in a liuing Iudge, is incomparably
more vſefull and fit, then if it were conceiued,
as inherent in ſome inanimate writing. Is there
ſuch repugnance betwixt Infallibility in the
Church, and Exiſtence of Scripture, that the
production of the one, muſt be the *destruction* of
the other? Muſt the Church wax dry, by giuing to her Children the milke of ſacred Writ?
No, No. Her Infallibility was, and is deriued
from an inexhauſted fountaine. If *Proteſtants*
will haue the *Scripture* alone for their Iudge, let
them firſt produce ſome *Scripture* affirming, that
by the *entring* thereof, Infallibility *went out* of
the Church. *D. Potter* may remember what himſelfe teacheth; That the Church is ſtil endewed
with infallibility in points fundamentall, and
conſequently, that infallibility in the Church
doth well agree with the truth, the ſanctity, yea
with the ſufficiency of Scripture, for all matters neceſſary to Saluation. I would therfore
gladly know, out of what Text he imagineth
that the Church by the comming of Scripture,
was d priued of infallibility in ſome points, &
not in others? He affirmeth that the Iewiſh Synagogue retained infallibility in her ſelfe, notwithſtanding the writing of the *Old* Teſtament; and will he ſo vnworthily and vniuſtly
depriue the Church of Chriſt of infallibility
by reaſon of the *New* Teſtament? Eſpecially

K 3   if

of we confider , that in the Old Teftament ,
Lawes, Ceremonies, Rites, Punifhments, Iudgments, Sacraments , Sacrifices &c. were more
particulerly , and minutely deliuered to the
Iewes, then in the New Teftament is done ; our
Sauiour leauing the determination, or declaration of particulers to his Spoufe the Church,
which therefore ftands in need of Infallibility
more then the Iewifh Synagogue. *D. Potter*, (i)
againft this argument drawne from the power
and infallibility of the Synagogue, obiects; that
we might as well infer, that *Chriftians muft haue
one foueraigne Prince ouer all, becaufe the Iewes had
one chiefe Iudge.* But the difparity is very cleare.
The Synagogue was a type, and figure of the
Church of Chrift, not fo their ciuill gouernmēt
of Chriftian Common-wealths, or kingdomes.
The Church fucceeded to the Synagogue, but
not Chriftian Princes to Iewifh Magiftrates:
And the Church is compared to a howfe, or (k)
family; to an (l) Army, to a (m) body ; to a (n)
kingdome &c. all which require one Maifter,
one Generall, one head , one Magiftrate, one
fpirituall King; as our bleffed Sauiour with *fiet
Vnum ouile*, (o) ioyned *Vnus Paftor: One fheepe-
fold, one Paftour:* But all diftinct kingdomes, or
Common-wealths, are not one Army, Family,
&c. And finally, it is neceffary to faluation, that
all haue recourfe to one Church; but for temporall weale, there is no need that all fubmit ,
or depend vpon one temporall Prince, kingdome,

(i) *Pag.*24.

(k) *Heb. 13.*
(l) *Cant.* 2.
(m) *1. Cor.*
10. *Ephef.*4.
(n)*Matt.*12

(o) *Ioan.* 5.
10.

dome , or Common-wealth: and therefore our
Saviour hath left to his whole Church , as being *One*, one Law,one Scripture , the same Sacraments &c. Whereas kingdomes haue their
seuerall Lawes, different gouernments, diuersi-
ty of Powers, Magistracy &c. And so this obiection returneth vpon *D. Potter*. For as in the *One*
Community of the Iewes,there was one Power
and Iudge, to end debates, and resolue difficulties: so in the Church of Christ, which is *One*,
there must be some *one* Authority to decide all
Controuersies in Religion.

24. This discourse is excellently proued by
ancient *S. Irenæus* (p) in these words : *What if* (p)*lib.3.c.4*
the Apostles had not left Scriptures , ought we not
to haue followed the order of Tradition which they
deliuered to those to whom they committed the Chur-
ches ? to which order many Nations yield assent,who
belieue in Christ, hauing saluation written in their
harts by the spirit of God,without letters or Inke, and
diligently keeping ancient Tradition. It is easy to re-
ceiue the truth from God's Church, seing the Apo-
stles haue most fully deposited in her, as in a rich
Storehowse,all things belonging to truth. For what?
if there should arise any contention of some small que-
stion, ought we not to haue recourse to the most an-
cient Churches,and from them to receiue what is cer-
taine and cleare concerning the present question?

25 Besides all this, the doctrine of Protestants is destructiue of it selfe. For either they
haue certaine,and infallible meanes not to erre
in

in interpreting Scripture; or they haue not. If not; then the Scripture (to them) cannot be a sufficient groũd for infallible faith, nor a meete Iudge of Controuersies. If they haue certaine infallible meanes, and so cannot erre in their interpretations of Scriptures; then they are able with infallibility to heare, examine, and determine all controuersies of faith, and so they may be, and are *Iudges* of Controuersies, although they vse the Scripture as a *Rule*. And thus, against their owne doctrine, they constitute an other Iudge of Controuersies, besides Scripture alone.

26. Lastly, I aske *D. Potter*, whether this Assertion, (*Scripture alone is Iudge of all Controuersies in faith*,) be a fundamentall point of faith, or no? He must be well aduised, before he say, that it is a fundamentall point. For he will haue against him, as many Protestants as teach that by Scripture alone, it isimpossible to know what Bookes be Scripture, which yet to Protestants is the most necessary and chiefe point of

(q) *In his de-fence of M. Hokers bookes art. 4. p. 31.*

all other. *D.Couell* expressely saith : *Doubtles* (q) *it is a tolerable opinion in the Church of Rome, if they goe no further, as some of them do not* (he should haue said as none of them doe) *to affirme, that the Scriptures are holy and diuine in themselues, but so esteemed by vs, for the authority of the Church*. He will likewise oppose himselfe to those his Brethren, who grant that Controuersies cannot be ended, without some externail liuing authority,

ty, as we noted before. Befides, how can it be in
vs a fundamentall errour to fay, the Scripture
alone is not Iudge of Controuerfies, feing (notwithftanding this our beliefe) we vfe for interpreting of Scripture, all the meanes which they
prefcribe, as Prayer, Conferring of places, Confulting the Originals &c. and to thefe add the
Inftruction, and Authority of God's Church,
which euen by his Confeffion *cannot* erre damnably, and *may* affoard vs more *help*, then can
be expected from the induftry, learning, or wit
of any priuate perfon.;& finally *D. Potter* grants,
that the Church of Rome doth not maintaine
any fundamentall error againft faith; and confequently, he cannot affirme that our doctrine
in this prefent Controuerfy is damnable. If he
anfwere, that their Tenet, about the *Scriptures*
being *the only Iudge of Controuerfies,* is not a fundamentall point of faith : then, as he teacheth
that the vniuerfall Church may erre in points
not fundamentall ; fo I hope he will not deny,
but particuler Churches, and priuate men, are
much more obnoxious to error in fuch points;
and in particuler in this, that *Scripture alone is*
Iudge of Controuerfies : And fo, the very principle
vpon which their whole faith is grounded, remaines to them yncertaine ; and on the other
fide, for the felfe fame reafon, they are not certaine, but that the Church is Iudge of Controuerfies, which if fhe be, then their cafe is lamentable, who in *generall* deny her this authority, &

in *particular* Controuerſies oppoſe her definitions. Beſides among publique Concluſions defended in *Oxford* the yeare 1633. to the queſtions, *Whether the Church haue authority to determine Controuerſies in faith* ; And, *To interpret holy Scripture?* The anſwere to both is *Affirmatiue.*

27. Since then , the Viſible Church of Chriſt our Lord is that infallible *Meanes Whereby the reuealed Truths of Almighty God are conueyed to our Vnderſtanding*; it followeth that to oppoſe her definitions is to reſiſt God himſeife ; which bleſſed *S. Auguſtine* plainely affirmeth, when ſpeaking of the Controuerſy about *Rebaptization* of ſuch as were baptized by Heretiques, he ſaith. *This* (r) *is neither openly, nor euidently read, neither by you nor by me ; yet if there Were any Wiſe man of whom our Sauiour had giuen teſtimony, and that he should be conſulted in this queſtion, we ſhould make no doubt to performe What he should ſay , leaſt we might ſceme to gainſay not him ſo much as Chriſt, by whoſe teſtimony he Was recommended. NoW Chriſt beareth witnes to his Church.* And a little after: *Whoſoeuer refuſeth to folloW the practiſe of the Church, doth reſiſt our Sauiour himſelfe , Who by his teſtimony recommends the Church.* I conclude therfore with this argument . Whoſoeuer reſiſteth that meanes which infallibly propoſeth to vs God's Word or Reuelation , commits a ſinne, which, vnrepented, excluds ſaluation. But whoſoeuer reſiſteth Chriſts viſible Church, doth reſiſt that meanes, which infallibly propoſeth
                                                                    God's

(r) *De vnit. Eccleſ.c.* 22.

God's word or reuelation to vs: Therfore whofoeuer refilteth Chrifts vifible Church, commits a finne, which, vnrepented, excluds faluation. Now, what vifible Church was extant,
when *Luther* began his pretended Reformation, whether it were the Roman, or Proteftant
Church; & whether he, and other Proteftants
do not oppofe that vifible Church, which was
fpread ouer the world, before, and in *Luthers*
time, is eafy to be determined, and importeth
euery one moft ferioufly to ponder, as a thing
wheron eternall faluation dependeth. And becaufe our Aduerfaries do heere moft infift vpon
the diftinction of points fundamentall, and not
fundamentall, and in particular teach, that the
Church may erre in points not fundamentall, it
will be neceffary to examine the truth, and
weight of this euafion, which fhall be done in
the next Chapter.

CHAP. III.

That the distinction of points funda-
mentall and not fundamentall, is
neither pertinent, nor true in our
present Controuersy. And that the
Catholique Visible Church can-
not erre, in either kind of the said
points.

THIS distinction is abused by
Protestants to many purposes
of theirs, and therfore if it be
either vntrue or impertinent
(as they vnderstand, & apply
it) the whole edifice built ther-
on, must be ruinous and false. For if you obiect their bitter and continued discords in matters of faith, without any meanes of agreement;
they instantly tell you (as *Charity Mistaken*
plainely shewes) that they differ only in points
not fundamentall. If you conuince them euen
by their owne Confessions, that the ancient
Fathers taught diuers points held by the *Roman*
Church against Protestants; they reply, that
those

thofe Fathers may neuertheles be faued, becaufe thofe errors were not fundamentall. If you will them to remember, that Chrift muft alwayes haue a vifible Church on earth, with admini-ftration of Sacraments, and fucceffion of Pa-ftors, and that when *Luther* appeared there was no Church diftinct from the Roman, whofe *Communion* and *Doctrine, Luther* then forfooke, and for that caufe muft be guilty of *Schifme* and *Herefy*; they haue an Anfwere (fuch as it is) that the Catholique Church cannot perifh, yet may erre in points not fundamentall, and ther-fore *Luther* and other Proteftants were obliged to forfake her for fuch errors, vnder paine of *Damnation*; as if (forfooth) it were *Damnable,* to hold an error not *Fundamentall*, nor *Damna-ble.* If you wonder how they can teach, that both Catholiques, and Proteftants may be fa-ued in their feuerall profeffions ; they falue this contradiction, by faying, that we both a-gree in all fundamentall points of faith, which is inough for faluation. And yet, which is pro-digioufly ftrange, they could neuer be induced to giue a Catalogue what points in particular be fundamentall, but only by fome generall def-cription or by referring vs to the *Apoftles Creed,* without determining, what points therein be fundamentall, or not fundamentall for the matter; and in what fenfe, they be , or be not fuch : and yet concerning the meaning of di-uers points contained, or reduced to the *Creed,*

they

they differ both from vs and amóg themfelues. And indeed, it being impoßible for them to exhibite any fuchCatalogue, the faid diftinction of points, although it were pertinent, and true, cannot ferue them to any purpofe, but ftill they muft remaine vncertaine, whether or not they difagree from one another; from the ancient Fathers; and from the Catholique Church, in points fundamentall: which is to fay, they haue no certainty, whether they enioy the fubftance of Chriftian Faith, without which they cannot hope to be faued. But of this more heerafter.

2.　And to the end, that what fhall be fayd concerning this diftinction, may be better vnderftood, we are to obferue; that there be two precepts, which concerne the vertue of fayth, or our obligation to *belieue* diuine truths. The one is by Deuines called *Affirmatiue*, wherby we are obliged to haue a pofitiue, explicite beliefe of fome chiefe Articles of Chriftian faith. The other is termed *Negatiue*, which ftrictly binds vs not to disbelieue, that is, not to belieue the cótrary of any one point fufficiently reprefented to our vnderftáding, as reuealed, or fpoken by Almighty God. The fayd *Affirmatiue Precept* (according to the nature of fuch commands) inioynes fome act to be performed, but not at all *tymes*, nor doth it equally bind all forts of *perfons*, in refpect of all *Obiects* to be belieued. For *obiects*; we grant that fome are more neceffary

fary to be explicitely, and feuerall belieued then
other: eyther becaule they are in themfelues
more great, and weighty ; or els in regard they
inftruct vs in fome neceflary Chriftian duty towards God , our felues, or our Neyghbour. For
perfons; no doubt but fome are obliged to know
diftinctly more then others , by reafon of their
office, vocation, capacity or the like. For *tymes* ;
we are not obliged to be ftill in act of exerci-
fing acts of fayth , but according as feuerall occafions permit , or require. The fecond kind of
precept called *Negatiue* , doth (according to
the nature of all fuch commands) oblige *vniuerfally* , all *perfons*, in refpect of all *obiects* ; & at
all *tymes* ; *femper & pro femper* , as Deuines fpeake. This generall doctrine will be more cleere
by examples. I am not obliged to be alwayes
helping my Neighbour , becaufe the *Affirmatiue* precept of *Charity* , bindeth onely in fome
particuler cafes : But I am alwayes bound by a
Negatiue precept , neuer to doe him any hurt, or
wrong. I am not alwayes bound to vtter what
I know to be true : yet I am obliged , neuer to
fpeake any one leaft vntruth, agaynft my knowledge. And (to come to our prefent purpofe)
there is no *Affirmatiue* precept , commanding
vs to be at *al times* actually belieuing any *one*, or
all Articles of faith: But we are obliged, *neuer* to
exercife any act againft any one truth, knowne
to be reuealed. All forts of *perfons* are not bound
explicitely, and diftinctly to know all things teftified

ftified by God either in Scripture, or otherwife:
but euery one is obliged, not to belieue the contrary of any one point, knowne to be teftified
by God. For that were in fact to affirme, that
God could be deceiued, or would deceiue; which
were to ouerthrow the whole certainty of our
faith, wherin the thing moft principall, is not
the point which we belieue, which Deuines cal
the *Materiall Obiect*, but the chiefeft is the *Mo-*
tiue for which we belieue, to wit, Almighty
God's infallible reuelation, or authority, which
they terme the *Formall obiect* of our faith. In two
fenfes therefore, and with a double relation,
points of fayth may be called fundamentall,
and neceffary to faluation. The one is taken
with reference to the *Affirmatiue* Precept,
when the points are of fuch quality that there
is obligation to know and belieue them explicitely and feuerally. In this fenfe we grant that
there is difference betwixt points of faith,
(a) *Pag.* 209 which *D. Potter* (a) to no purpofe laboureth
to proue againft his Aduerfary, who in expreffe
(b) *Charity* words doth grant and explicate (b) it. But the
Miftaken *c.* *Doctor* thought good to diffemble the matter, &
8. *pag.* 75. not fay one pertinent word in defenfe of his
diftinction, as it was impugned by *Charity* *Mi-*
ftaken, and as it is wont to be applied by Proteftants. The other fenfe, according to which,
points of faith may be called *Fundamentall*, and
neceffary to faluation, with reference to the
Negatiue precept of faith, is fuch, that we cannot

not without grieuous finne, and forfeiture of faluation, disbelieue any one point, fufficiently propounded, as reuealed by Almighty God. And in this fenfe we auouch, that there is no diftinction in points of faith, as if to reiect fome muft be damnable, and to reiect others, equally propofed as God's word, might ftand with faluation. Yea the obligation of the *Negatiue* precept is far more ftrict, then is that of the *Affirmatiue*, which God freely impofed, & may freely releafe. But it is impoffible, that he can difpenfe, or giue leaue to disbelieue, or deny what he affirmeth: and in this fenfe, finne & damnation are more infeparable from *error* in points *not fundamentall*, then from *ignorance* in Articles *fundamentall*. All this I fhew by an Example, which I wifh to be particularly noted for the prefent, and for diuers other occafions hereafter. The *Creed* of the *Apoftles* containes diuers fundamentall points of faith, as the Deity, Trinity of Perfons, Incarnation, Paffion, and Refurrection of our Sauiour Chrift &c. It containes alfo fome points, for their matter, and nature in themfelues not fundamentall, as vnder what Iudge our Sauiour fuffered, that he was buried, the circumftance of the time of his Refurrection the third day &c. But yet neuerthelefle, whofoeuer once knowes, that thefe points are contained in the Apoftles *Creed*, the deniall of them is damnable, and is in that fenfe a *fundamentall* error: & this is the precife point

M   of

of the prefent queftion.

3. And all that hitherto hath been faid, is fo manifeftly true, that no Proteftant or Chriftian, if he do but vnderftand the termes, and ftate of the Queftion, can poffibly deny it: In fo much as I am amazed, that men who otherwife are endued with excellent wits, fhould fo enflaue themfelues to their Predeceffors in Proteftantifme, as ftil to harp on this diftinction, & neuer regard how impertinently, and vntruly it was applyed by them at firft, to make all Proteftants feeme to be of one fayth, becaufe forfooth they agree in fundamentall points. For the difference among Proteftants, confifts not in that fome belieue fome points, of which others are ignorant, or not bound expreffely to know (as the diftinction ought to be applyed;) but that fome of them disbelieue, and directly, wittingly, and willingly oppofe what others do belieue to be teftifyed by the word of God, wherein there is no difference betweene points fundamentall, and not fundamentall ; Becaufe till points fundamentall be fufficiently propofed as reuealed by God, it is not agaynft faith to reiect them, or rather without fufficient propofition it is not poffible prudently to belieue them ; and the like is of points not fundamentall, which affoone as they come to be fufficiently propounded as diuine Truths, they can no more be denyed, then points fundamentall propounded after the fame manner. Neither wil

it

it auayle them to their other end, that for pre-
feruation of the Church in being, it is fufficient
that fhe do not erre in poins fundamentall. For
if in the meane time fhe maintaine any one Errour againft Gods reuelation, be the thing in it
felfe neuer fo fmall, her Errour is damnable,
and deftructiue of faluation.

4. But *D. Potter* forgetting to what purpofe Proteftants make vfe of their diftinction,
doth finally ouerthrow it, & yields to as much
as we can defire. For, fpeaking of that *meafure*
(c) and quantity of faith without which none can be (c) *pag.* 211;
faued, he fayth : *It is inough to beliue fome things*
by a vertuall faith, or by a generall, and as it were, a
negatiue faith, whereby they are not denied or contra-
dicted. Now our queftion is in cafe that diuine
truths, although not fundamentall, be denied
and contradicted ; and therefore, euen according to him, all fuch deniall excludes faluation.
After, he fpeakes more plainely. *It is true (* faith
he *) whatfoeuer (d) is reuealed in Scripture, or prc-* (d) *pag.* 212;
pounded by the Church out of Scripture, is in fome
fenfe fundamentall, in regard of the diuine authority
of God, and his word, by which it is recommended :
that is, fuch as may not be denied, or contradicted
without Infidelity : fuch as euery Chriftian is bound
with humility, and reuerence to beliue, whenfoeuer
the knowledge thereof is offered to him. And further:
Where (e) the reuealed will or word of God is fuffi- (c) *pag.* 250.
ciently propounded; there he that oppofeth, is conuin-
ced of error, and he who is thus conuinced is an Here-
M 2   *tique,*

tique, and Herefie is a worke of the flefh which excludeth from heauen. (*Gal.* 5. 20. 21.) *And hence it foloweth, that it is F V N D A M E N T A L L to a Chriſtians F A I T H, and neceſſary for his ſaluation, that he belieue all reuealed Truths of God, whereof he may be conuinced that they are from God.* Can any thing be ſpoken more crearely or directly for vs, that it is a *Fundamentall* error to deny any one point, though neuer ſo ſmall, if once it be ſufficiently propounded, as a diuine truth, and that there is , in this ſenſe, no diſtinction betwixt points fundamentall, and not fundamentall? And if any ſhould chance to imagine, that it is againſt the foundation of faith, not to belieue points *Fundamentall*, although they be not ſufficiently propounded, *D.* Potter doth not admit of this (f) difference betwixt points fundamentall, and not fundamentall. For he teacheth, that *ſufficient propoſition of reuealed truth is required before a man can be conuinced,* and for want of ſufficient conuiction he excuſeth the Diſciples from hereſy, although they belieued not our Sauiours Reſurrection , (g) which is a very fundamentall point of faith. Thus then I argue out of *D. Potters* owne confeſſon : No error is damnable vnles the contrary truth be ſufficiently propounded as reuealed by God: Euery error is damnable, if the contrary truth be ſufficiently propounded as reuealed by God : Therfore all errors are alike for the generall effect of damnation, if the difference

(f) *Pag.*246.

(g) *pag.*246.

                                                                        ariſe

arife not from the manner of being propounded. And what now is become of their diftinction?

5.   I will therfore conclude with this Argument. According to all Philofophy and Diuinity, the *Vnity,* and diftinction of euery thing
followeth the Nature & Effence thereof, and
therfore if the *Nature* and *being* of fayth, be not
taken from the matter which a man belieues,
but from the motiue for which he belieues,
(which is God's word or Reuelation) we muft
likewife affirme that the *Vnity,* and *Diuerfity* of
faith, muft be meafured by God's reuelation
(which is alike for all obiects) and not by the
fmalnes, or greatnes of the matter which we
belieue. Now, that the nature of faith is not
taken from the greatnes, or fmallnes of the
things belieued, is manifeft; becaufe otherwife
one who belieues only fundamentall points,
and another who together with them, doth alfo belieue points not fundamentall, fhould haue
faith of different natures, yea there fhould be as
many differences of faith, as there are different
points which men belieue, according to differét capacities, or inftruction &c all which confequences are abfurd, & therfore we muft fay,
that *Vnity in Fayth* doth not depend vpó points
fundamentall, or not fundamentall, but vpon
God's reuelation equally or vnequally propofed: and Proteftants pretending an *Vnity* only
by reafon of their agreement in fundamentall

points,

points, do indeed induce as great a multiplicity of faith as there is multitude of different obiects which are belieued by them, & since they disagree in things *Equally reuealed* by Almighty God, it is euident that they forsake the very *Formall motiue* of faith, which is Gods reuelation and consequently loose all *Faith*, and *Vnity* therin.

6. The first part of the Title of this Chapter (*That the distinction of points fundamentall & not fundamentall in the sense of Protestants, is both impertinent and vntrue*) being demonstrated; let vs now come to the second : *That the Church is infallible in all her definitions, whether they concerne points fundamentall, or not fundamentall.* And this I proue by these reasons.

7. It hath beene shewed in the precedent Chapter, that the Church is Iudge of Controuersies in Religion; which she could not be, if she could erre in any one point, as *Doctor Potter* would not deny, if he were once persuaded that she is Iudge. Because if she could erre in some points, we could not rely vpon her *Authority* and Iudgment in any one thing.

8. This same is proued by the reason we alledged before, that seeing the Church was infallible in all her definitions ere Scripture was written (vnles we will take away all certainty of fayth for that tyme) we cannot with any shew of reason affirme, that she hath been depriued thereof by the adioined comfort, & help

of

of sacred Writ .

9. Moreouer to say , that the Catholique Church may propose any false doctrine , maketh her lyable to *damnable* sinne and errour; & yet *D. Potter* teacheth that the Church cannot erre *damnably*. For if in that kind of Oath,which Deuines call *Assertorium*, wherin God is called to witnes, euery falshood is a deadly sinne in any priuate person whatsoeuer , although the thing be of it selfe neither materiall, nor preiudiciall to any ; because the quantity,or greatnes of that sinne is not measured so much by the thing which is affirmed , as by the manner, & authority whereby it is auouched, and by the iniury that is offered to Almighty God in applying his testimony to a falshood : in which respect it is the vnanimous consent of all Deuines, that in such kind of Oaths, no *leuitas materiæ*, that is, *smallnes of matter* , can excuse from a mortall sacriledge, agaynst the *morall* vertue of Religiō which respects worship due to God : If, I say , euery least falshood be deadly sinne in the foresayd kind of Oath; much more pernicious a sinne must it be in the *publique person* of the Catholique Church to propound vntrue Articles of fayth , thereby fastning Gods *prime Verity* to falshood,and inducing and obliging the world to doe the same. Besids, according to the doctrine of all Deuines, it is not only iniurious to Gods Eternall Verity , to disbelieue things by him reuealed,but also to propose as

reuea-

reuealed truths , thinges not reuealed : as in
commonwealths it is a haynous offence to coyne eyther by counterfeyting the mettall or the
ſtamp , or to apply the Kings ſeale to a writing
counterfeyt , although the contents were ſuppoſed to be true . And whereas , to ſhew the
deteſtable ſinne of ſuch pernicious fictions , the
Church doth moſt exemplarly puniſh all broa-
chers of faygned reuelations, viſions, miracles,
(h) *Sub Le-* prophecies &c. as in particuler appeareth in the
*on.*10. *Seſſ.* Councell of *(h) Lateran* , excommunicating
11. ſuch perſons; if the Church her ſelfe could propoſe falſe reuelations, ſhe herſelfe ſhould haue
beene the firſt , and chiefeſt deſeruer to haue
been cenſured , and as it were excommunicated
by herſelfe. For (as the holy Ghoſt ſayth in
(i) *Cap.* 13. *(1) Iob)* doth God need your lye, that for him you may
v. 7. *ſpeake deceypts ?* And that of the *Apocalyps* is
moſt truly verifyed in fictitious reuelations : *If
any (k)ſhall add to theſe things , God will add vnto
him the plagues which are written in this Booke :* &
(k) *Cap.vlt.* *D. Potter* ſayth, *To add (l) to it* (ſpeaking of
v. 18. the Creed *)is high preſumption, almoſt as great as
(l, *pag.* 222. *to detract frō it.* And therfore to ſay the Church
may add falſe Reuelations, is to accuſe her of
high preſumption , and of pernicious errour
excluding ſaluation.

10.   Perhaps ſome will heere reply that although the Church may erre , yet it is not im-
puted to her for ſinne , by reaſon ſhe doth not
erre vpon malice , or wittingly, but by ignorance,

rance, or miſtake.

11.　But it is eaſily demonſtrated that this excuſe cānot ſerue. For if the Church be aſſiſted only for points fundamentall, ſhe cannot but know, that ſhe may erre in points not fundamentall, at leaſt ſhe cannot be certaine that ſhe cānot erre, & therfore cannot be excuſed from headlong & pernicious temerity, in propoſing points not fundamētall, to be belieued by Chriſtians, as matters of faith, wherin ſhe can haue no certainty, yea which alwayes imply a falſhood. For although the thing might chance to be true, and perhaps alſo reuealed; yet for the *matter* ſhe, for her part, doth alwaies expoſe herſelfe to danger of falſhood & error; and in fact doth alwayes erre in the *manner* in which ſhe doth propound any matter not fundamentall; becauſe ſhe propoſeth it as a point of faith *certainly* true, which yet is alwayes vncertaine, if ſhe in ſuch things may be deceiued.

12.　Beſides, if the Church may erre in points not fundamentall, ſhe may erre in propoſing ſome Scripture for Canonicall, which is not ſuch: or els erre in keeping and conſeruing from corruptions ſuch Scriptures as are already belieued to be Canonicall For I will ſuppoſe, that in ſuch Apocryphall Scripture as ſhe deliuers, there is no fundamentall error againſt faith, or that there is no falſhood at all but only want of diuine teſtification: in which caſe *D. Potter* muſt either grant, that it is a fundamenmentall error, to apply diuine reuelation to any point not reuealed, or els muſt yield, that the Church may erre in her *Propoſition*, or *Cuſtody* of the Canon of Scripture: And ſo we cannot be ſure whether ſhe haue not been deceiued already, in Bookes recommended by her, and accepted by Chriſtians. And thus we ſhall haue no certainty of Scripture, if the Church want certainty in all her definitions. And it is worthy to be obſerued, that ſome Bookes of Scripture which were not alwayes knowne to be Canonicall, haue been afterward receiued for ſuch; but neuer any one Booke, or ſyllable defined by the Church to be Canonicall, was afterward queſtioned, or reiected for Apocryphall. A ſigne, that God's Church is infallibly aſſiſted by the holy Ghoſt, neuer to propoſe as diuine truth, any thing not reuealed by God: & that, *Omiſſion* to define points not ſufficiently diſcuſſed is laudable, but *Commiſſion* in propounding things not reuealed, inexcuſable; into which precipitation our Sauiour Chriſt neuer hath, nor neuer will permit his Church to fall.

13.   Nay, to limit the generall promiſes of our Sauiour Chriſt made to his Church to points only fundamétall, namely, that *the gates* (m) *of hell ſhall not preuaile againſt her*: and that, *the holy Ghoſt* (n) *ſhall lead her into all truth &c.* is to deſtroy all Faith. For we may by that doctrine, and manner of interpreting the Scripture, limit the Infallibility of the Apoſtles words,

(m) *Matt.*
16 18.
(n) *Ioan.16.*
13.

words, & preaching, only to points fundamentall: and whatſoeuer general Texts of Scripture
ſhall be alleadged for their Infallibility, they
may, by *D. Potters* example be explicated, & reſtrained to points fundamentall. By the ſame
reaſon it may be further affirmed, that the Apoſtles, and other Writers of Canonicall Scripture, were endued with infallibility, only in
ſetting downe points fundamentall. For if it be
vrged, that *all Scripture is diuinely inſpired;* that it
is the word of God &c. *D. Potter* hath affoarded
you a ready anſwere to ſay, that *Scripture is inſ-*
pired &c. only in thoſe parts, or parcels, wherin
it deliuereth fundamentall points. In this manner *D. Fotherby* ſayth: *The Apoſtle (o) twice in*
one Chapter profeſſed, that this he ſpeaketh, & not
the Lord ; He is very well content that where he lacks
the warrant of the expreſſe word of God, that part of
his writings ſhould be eſteemed as the word of man. D.
Potter alſo ſpeakes very dangerouſly towards
this purpoſe, *Sect.* 5. where he endeauoureth to
proue, that the infallibility of the Church is limited to points fundamētall, becauſe *as Nature,*
ſo God is neither defectiue in (p) *neceſſaries, nor la-*
uiſh in ſuperfluities. Which reaſon doth likewiſe
proue that the infallibility of Scripture, and of
the Apoſtles muſt be reſtrained to points neceſſary to ſaluation, that ſo God be not accuſed, *as*
defectiue in neceſſaries, or lauiſh in ſuperfluities. In
the ſame place he hath a diſcourſe much tending to this purpoſe, where ſpeaking of theſe

(o) *In his*
Sermōs ſerm.
2. *pag.* 50.

(p) *pag.* 150.

words: *The Spirit shall leade you into all truth, and*
shall abide with (q) *you for euer* , he sayth : *Though
that promise was* (r) *directly, and primarily made to
the Apostles* (*who had the Spirits guidance in a more
high and absolute manner, then any since them*) *yet it
is made to them for the behoofe of the Church, and
is verified in the Church Vniuersall. But all truth is
not simply all, but all of some kind. To be led into all
truths, is to know, and belieue them. And who is so
simple as to be ignorant, that there are many millions
of truths* (*in Nature, History, Diuinity*) *whereof the
Church is simply ignorant. How many truths lye vnreuealed in the infinite treasury of God's wisdome,
wherewith the Church is not acquainted &c. so then,
the truth it selfe enforceth vs to vnderstand by* (*all
truths*) *not simply all, not all which God can possibly
reueale, but all pertayning to the substance of faith,
all truth absolutely necessary to saluation.* Marke
what he sayth. That promise (*The spirit shall
lead you into all truth,*) *was made directly to the A-
postles, & is verified in the vniuersall Church* , but by
all truth is not vnderstood simply ail, but all apper-
tayning to the *substance of faith,* and absolutely *necessary to saluation.* Doth it not hence follow,
that the promise made to the Apostles of being
led into all truth, is to be vnderstood only of all
truth absolutly necessary to saluation ? & consequently their preaching, and writing, were
not infalliblein points not fundamentall ? or if
the Apostles were infallible in all things which
they proposed as diuine truth , the like must be
                                                    affirmed

affirmed of the Church , becaufe *D. Potter* teacheth , the fayd promife *to be verifyed in the
Churh.* And as he limits the aforefayd wordes
to points fundamentall; fo may he reftrayne
what other text foeuer that can be brought for
the vniuerfail infallibility of the Apoftles or
Scriptures. So he may ; and fo he muft, leaft o-
therwife he receiue this anfwere of his owne
from himfelfe , *How many truths lye vnreuealed in
the infinite treafury of Gods wifdome, wherewith the
Church is not acquainted?* And therefore to verify fuch generall fayings , they muft be vnderftood of truths abfolutely neceffary to Saluation. Are not thefe fearefull cōfequences? And
yet *D. Potter* will neuer be able to auoyd them ,
till he come to acknowledge the Infallibility of
the Church in al points by her propofed as diuine truths; & thus it is vniuerfally true that fhe is
lead into al truth,in regard that our Sauiour neuer permits her to define, or teach any fallhood.

14.   All, that with any colour may be replied to this argument is ; That if once we call a-
ny one Booke , or parcell of Scripture in queftion; although for the matter it containe no
fundamentall errour , yet it is of great importance and fundamentall, by reafon of the con-
fequéce; becaufe if once we doubt of one Booke receiued for Canonicall , the whole Canon
is made doubtfull and vncertayne , and therefore the Infallibility of Scripture muft be vniuerfall, and not confined within compaffe of

points

points fundamentall.

15.   I anſwere : For the thing it ſelfe it is
very true, that if I doubt of any one parcell of
Scripture receaued for ſuch, I may doubt of all:
And thence by the ſame parity I inferre , that if
we did doubt of the Churches Infallibility in
ſome points , we could not belieue her in any
one, and conſequently not in propounding *Canonicall* Bookes, or any other points fundamentall, or not fundamentall ; which thing being
moſt abſurd, and withall moſt impious, we muſt
take away the ground thereof, & belieue that
ſhe cannot erre in any point great or ſmall: and
ſo this reply doth much more ſtrengthen what
we intended to proue. Yet I add , that Proteſtants cannot make vſe of this reply , with any
good coherence to this their diſtinction, and
ſome other doctrines which they defend. For if
D. Potter can tell what points in particuler be
fundamentall (as in his *7. Sect.* he pretendeth)
then he may be ſure, that whenſoeuer he meets
with ſuch points in Scripture, in them it is infallibly *true,* although it might erre in others: &
not only *true,* but *cleere* , becauſe Proteſtants
teach , that in matters neceſſary to Saluation ,
the Scripture is ſo cleere , that all ſuch neceſſary
Truths are eyther manifeſtly contayned therein, or may be cleerely deduced from it . Which
doctrines being put togeather , to wit : That
Scriptures cannot erre in points fundamentall;
that they cleerely containe all ſuch points ; and
that

that they can tell what points in particuler be such, I meane fundamentall; it is manifeft, that it is fufficiēt for Saluation, that Scripture be infallible only in points fundamentall . For fuppofing thefe doctrines of theirs to be true, they may be fure to find in Scripture all points neceffary to faluation, although it were fallible in other points of leffe moment . Neyther will they be able to auoyde this impiety againft holy Scripture, till they renounce their other doctrines : and in particuler, till they belieue that Chrifts promifes to his Church, are not limited to points fundamentall.

16 . Befides, from the fallibility of Chrifts Catholique Church in fome points, it followeth, that no true Proteftant learned, or vnlearned , doth or can with affurance belieue the vniuerfall Church in any one point of doctrine . Not in points of leffer momēt, which they call *not fundamentall*; becaufe they belieue that in fuch points fhe may erre. Not in *fundamentalls*; becaufe they muft know what points be fundamentall, before they go to learne of her, leaft otherwife they be rather deluded, then inftructed ; in regard that her certaine, and infallible direction extēnds only to points fundamentall. Now, if before they addreffe themfelues to the Church they muft know what points are fundamentall , they learne not of her, but will be be as fit to teach, as to be taught by her : How then are all Chriftians fo often , fo ferioufly,

vpon so dreadfull menaces, by Fathers, Scriptures, and our blessed Sauiour himselfe, coun-
selled and commaunded to seeke, to heare, to
obey the Church? *S. Augustine* was of a very
different mind from Protestants: *If (sayth he)*
the (s) *Church through the whole world practise any*
of these things, to dispute whether that ought to be
so done, is a most insolent madnes. And in another
place he sayth. *That which* (t) *the whole Church*
holds, and is not ordained by Councels, but hath alwaies
beene kept, is most rightly beleeued to be deliuered by
Apostolicall authority. The same holy Father teacheth, that the custome of baptizing children
cannot be proued by Scripture alone, and yet
that it is to be beleeued, as deriued from the
Apostles. *The custome of our Mother the* (u)
Church (saith he) in baptizing infants is in no wise
to be contemned, nor to be accounted superfluous, nor
is it at all to be beleeued, vnles it were an Apostoli-
call Tradition. And elsewhere. *Christ* (w) *is of*
profit to Children baptized; Is he therefore of profit
to persons not beleeuing? But God forbid, that I should
say Infants doe not beleeue. I haue already sayd, he be-
leeues in another, who sinned in another. It is sayd, he
beleeues, & it is of force, and he is reckoned among the
faythfull that are baptized. This the authority of our
Mother the Church hath; against this strength, against
this inuincible wal whosoeuer rusheth shalbe crushed in
pieces. To this argument the Protestants in the
Conference at *Ratisbon*, gaue this round answer:
Nos ab Augustino (x) *hac in parte liberè dissentimus.*

In

(s) *Epist.*
118.

(t) *lib. 4.*
de Bapt. c.
24.

(u) *lib. 10.*
de Genesi ad
liter. cap.
23.
(w) *Serm.*
14. *de verbis*
Apost. c. 18.

(x) *See Pro-*
tocoll. Mo.
nac. edit. 2.
pag. 367.

In this we plainely disagree from Augustine. Now if this doctrine of baptizing Infants be not fundamentall in *D.Potters* sense, then according to *S.Augustine,* the infallibility of the Church extends to points not fundamentall. But if on the other side it be a fundamentall point; then according to the same holy *Doctour,* we must rely on the authority of the Church, for some fundamentall point, not contained in Scripture, but deliuered by Tradition. The like argument I frame out of the same Father about the not rebaptizing of those who were baptized by Heretiques, whereof he excellently to our present purpose speaketh in this manner. *We follow* (y) *indeed in this matter euen the most certaine authority of Canonicall Scriptures.* But how? Consider his words : *Although verily there be brought no example for this point out of the Canonicall Scriptures, yet euen in this point the truth of the same Scriptures is held by vs, while we do that, which the authority of Scriptures doth recommend, that so, becauſe the holy Scripture cannot deceiue vs, whoſoeuer is afraid to be deceiued by the obſcurity of this queſtion, muſt haue recourſe to the ſame Church concerning it, which without any ambiguity the holy Scripture doth demonſtrate to vs.* Amõg many other points in the aforesaid words, we are to obſerue, that according to this holy Father, when we proue some points not particulerly contained in Scripture, by the authority of the Church, euen in that caſe we ought not to be ſaid to belieue ſuch

(y) *lib. 1. cont . Creſ-con. cap.32, & 33.*

O   points

points without Scripture, becaufe Scripture it felfe recommends the Church; and therfore relying on her we rely on Scripture, without danger of being deceiued by the obfcurity of any queftion defined by the Church. And elfe where he fayth: *Seing this is* (z) *written in no Scripture, we muſt belieue the teſtimony of the Church, which Chriſt declareth to fpeake the truth.* But it feemes D. *Potter* is of opinion that this doctrine about not rebaptizing fuch as were baptized by Heretiques, is no neceffary point of faith, nor the contrary an herefy: wherin he cotradicteth *S. Auguſtine,* from whom we haue now heard, that what the Church teacheth, is truly faid to be taught by Scripture ; and confequently to deny this particuler point, deliuered by the Church, is to oppofe Scripture it felfe. Yet if he will needs hold, that this point is not fundamentall, we muft conclude out of S. *Auguſtine,* (as we did concerning the baptizing of Children) that the infallibility of the Church reacheth to points not fundamentall. The fame Father in another place, concerning this very queftion of the validity of Baptifme conferred by Heretiques, fayth: *The* (a) *Apoſtles indeed haue prefcribed nothing of this, but this Cuſtome ought to be belieued to be originally taken from their tradition, as there are many things that the vniuerfall Church obfcrueth which are therfore with good reafon belieued to haue be-ne commanded by the Apoſtles, although they be not written.* No lefle cleere is S. *Chryfoſtome*

(z) *De vnit. Ecclef. c.19.*

(a) *De Bapt. cont. Donat. lib.5.cap.23.*

sistome for the infallibility of the Traditions of
the Church. For treating these words (2. *Thess.*2.
Stand, and hold the Traditions which you haue lear-
ned whether by speach or by our Epistle) faith: *Hence*
it is (b) manifest that they deliuered not all things by
letter, but many things also without writing, & these
also are worthy of beliefe. Let vs therfore account the
tradition of the Church to be worthy of beliefe. It is a
Tradition : Seeke no more. Which words are so
plaine against Protestants, that *Whitaker* is as
plaine with S. *Chrysostome*, saying: *I answere (c)*
that this is an inconsiderate speach, and vnworthy so
great a Father. But let vs conclude with S. *Augu-*
stine, that the Church cannot approue any error against fayth, or good manners. *The Church*
(sayth he) being (d) placed betwixt much chaffe &
cockle, doth tollerate many things ; but yet she doth
not approue, nor dissemble, nor do those things which
are against fayth, or good life.

    17.   And as I haue proued that Protestants,
according to their grounds, cannot yield infallible assent to the Church in any one point : so
by the same reason I proue, that they cannot
rely vpon Scripture it selfe in any one point of
fayth. Not in points of lesser moment (or not
fundamentall,) because in such points the Catholique Church, (according to *D. Potter*) and
much more any Protestant may erre, & thinke
it is contained in Scripture, when it is not. Not
in points fundamentall, because they must first
know what points be fundamentall, before

               O 2   they

(b)Hom. 4.

(c)*De Sacra*
Script. pag.
678.

(d] *Ep.* 119.

they can be aſſured, that they cannot erre in vnderſtanding the Scripture, and conſequently independantly of Scripture, they muſt fore-know all fundamentall points of fayth: and therfore they do not indeed rely vpon Scripture, either for fundamentall, or not fundamentall points.

18. Beſides, I mainely vrge *D. Potter*, and other Proteſtants, that they tell vs of certaine points which they call fundamentall, and we cannot wreſt from them a liſt in particuler of ſuch points, without which no man can tell whether or no he erre in points fundamentall, and be capable of ſaluation. And which is moſt lamentable, inſteed of giuing vs ſuch a Catalogue, they fall to wrangle among themſelues about the making of it.

19. *Caluin* holds the (e) Popes Primacy, Inuocation of Saints, Freewill, and ſuch like, to be fundamentall errors ouerthrowing the Goſpell. Others are not of his mind, as *Melancthon* who ſayth, in (f) the opinion of himſelfe, and other his Brethren, *That the Monarchy of the Biſhop of Rome is of vſe, or profit to this end, that Conſent of Doctrine may be retained. An agreement therfore may eaſily be eſtabliſhed in this Article of the Popes Primacy, if other Articles could be agreed vpon. If the Popes Primacy be a meanes, that conſent of Doctrine may be retained,* firſt ſubmit to it, and other articles wilbe *eaſily agreed vpon. Luther* alſo ſayth of the Popes Primacy,

(e) *Inſtit. l. 4. cap. 2.*

(f) *Cent. Ep. Theolog. ep. 74.*

.nacy, it may be *borne* (g) *withal.* And why then,
O *Luther*, did you not beare with it? And how
can you, and your followers be excufed from
damnable Schifme, who chofe rather to deuide Gods Church, then to beare with that,
which you confeffe may be *borne withall?* But
let vs go forward. That the doctrine of freewill, Prayer for the dead, worfhipping of I-
mages, Worfhip and Inuocation of Saints,
Reall prefence, Tranfubftanciation, Receauing vnder one kind, Satisfaction, and Merit of workes, and the Maffe, be not fundamentall Errours, is taught (*refpectiuè*) by diuers Proteftants, carefully alledged in the *Pro-
t. ft..nts* (h) *Apology &c.* as namely by *Perkins*,
Cartwright, *Frith*, *Fulke*, *Henry Spark*, *Goade*, *Lu-*
ther, *Reynolds*, *Whitaker*, *Tindall*, *Francis Iohn-*
fon, with others. Contrary to thefe, is the *Con-*
feffion of the Chriftian fayth, fo called by Proteftats, which I mentioned (1) heeretofore, wherin we are damned vnto *vnquencheable fire*, for
the doctrine of Maffe, Prayer to Saints, and for
the dead, Freewill, Prefence at Idol-feruice,
Mans merit, with fuch like. Iuftificatiõ by faith
alone is by fome Proteftants affirmed to be the
foule of the (k) *Church*: *The only principall origen*
of (l) *Saluation*: *of all other points of* (m) *doctrine*
the chiefeft and weightieft. Which yet, as we haue
feen, is cõtrary to other Proteftants, who teach
that merit of good workes is not a fundamentall Errour; yea, diuers Proteftants defend me-

(g) *In Affer-*
tionibus art.
36.

(h) *Tract 2.*
cap. 2. Sect.
14. *after F.*

(i) *Cap.1.n.*
4.
(k) *Chark:*
in the Tower
difputation
the 4. dayes
conference.
(l) *Fox Act.*
Monn. pag.
402.
(m) *The Con-*
feffion of Bo-
hemia in the
Harmony of
Confeffions
pag. 253.

rit

rit of good works, as may be seene in (n) *Brere-ley*. One would thinke that the Kings Supremacy, for which some blessed men lost their liues was once among Protestants held for a Capitall point; but now *D. Andrewes* late of *Winchester* in his booke agaynst *Bellarmine* tells vs, that it is sufficient to reckon it among *true doctrines*. And *Watton* denies that *Protestants* (o) *Hold the Kings Supremacy to be an essentiall point of fayth*. O freedome of the new Ghospell? Hold with Catholiques, the Pope; or with Protestants, the King; or with Puritanes, neyther Pope, nor King, to be Head of the Church, all is one, you may be saued. Some, as *Castalio*, (p) and the whole Sect of the Academicall Protestants, hold, that doctrines about the Supper, Baptisme, the state and office of Christ, how he is one with his Father, the Trinity, Predestination, and diuers other such questions are not necessary to Saluatio. And (that you may obserue how vngrounded, and partiall their Assertions be) *Perkins* teacheth, that the Reall presence of our Sauiours Body in the Sacramet as it is belieued by Catholiques, is a fundamentall errour; and yet affirmeth the Consubstantiation of Lutherans not to be such, notwithstading that diuers chiefe *Lutherans*, to their Consubstantiation ioyne the prodigious Heresy of Vbiquitation. *D. Vshher* in his Sermon of the *Vnity of the Catholique fayth*, grants Saluation to the *Æthiopians*, who yet with Christian Baptisme ioyne Circu-cision

(n) Tract. 3. Sect. 7. vnder m. n. 15.

(o) In his answere to a Popish pamphlet. p. 68.

(p) Vid. Gul. Reginald. Calu. Turcism. lib. 2. cap. 6.

cifion *D. Potter*(q) cites the doctrine of fome
whome he termeth men of great learning and
iudgement: that, *all who profeſſe to loue and honour*
I ᴇ s v s - C h r i s t *are in the viſible Chriſtian
Church, and by Catholiques to be reputed Brethren.*
One of theſe men of great learning and iudgment, is *Thomas Morton* by *D. Potter* cited in his
Margent, whoſe loue & honour to *Ieſus-Chriſt,*
you may perceyue, by his ſaying, that the *Churches of Arians* (who denyed our Sauiour Chriſt
to be God) *are to be accounted the Church of God,
becauſe they doe hold the foundation of the Ghoſpell ,
which is Fayth in Ieſus-Chriſt the Sonne of God, and
Sauiour of the world.* And, which is more , it ſeemeth by theſe charitable men, that for being a
member of the Church it is not neceſſary to belieue one only God. For *D. Potter* (r) among
the arguments to proue *Hookers, & Mortons* opinion, brings this : *The people of the ten Tribes after
their defection, notwithſtanding their groſſe corruptions, and Idolatry,* remained ſtill a true Church.
We may alſo , as it ſeemeth by theſe mens rea-
ſoning , deny the Reſurrection, and yet be mē-
bers of the true Church. For a learned man
(ſayth *D. Potter* (s) in behalfe of *Hookers* , and
Mortons opinion) was anciently made a Biſhop
of the Catholique Church , though he did pro-
feſſedly doubt of the laſt Reſurrectiō of our bodies. Deere Sauiour! What tymes doe we behold ? If one may be a member of the true
Church, and yet deny the Trinity of Perſons ,

the

(q) *Pag.* 113,
114.

Morton in
his Treatiſe
of the King
dome of
Iſrael. pag:
94.
(r) *pag.* 121.

(s) *pag.* 122.

the Godhead of our Sauiour , the necessity of Baptisme, if we may vse Circumcision , and with the worship of God ioyne Idolatry, wherin doe we differ from Turks, and Iewes ? or rather are we not worse, then eyther of them ? If they who deny our Sauiours diuinity might be accounted the Church of God , how will they deny that fauour to those ancient Heretiques , who denyed our Sauiours true humanity? and so the totall denyall of Christ will not exclude one from being a member of the true Church .

(t) *Commēt.* S. *Hilary* (t) maketh it of equall necessity for
in Matt. c. Saluation, that we belieue our Sauiour to be
16. true God , and true Man , saying : *This manner of Confession we are to hold , that we remember him to be the Sonne of God , and the Sonne of Man , because the one without the other , can giue no hope of Saluation.* And yet D. *Potter* sayth of the aforesayd doctrine of *Hooker* and *Morton* : *The* (u)
(u) *pag.* 123. *Reader may be pleased to approue , or reiect it , as he*
(w) *pag.* 253. *shall find cause.* And in another place(w)he sheweth so much good liking of this doctrine, that he explicateth and proueth the Churches perpetuall Visibility by it. And in the second Edition of his booke , he is carefull to declare, and illustrate it more at large , then he had done before: howsoeuer, this sufficiently sheweth, that they haue no certainty , what points be fundamentall. As for the *Arians* in particuler , the Authour whome D. *Potter* cites for a *moderate Catholike,* but is indeed a plaine *Heretique* , or

ra-

rather Atheift, *Lucian*-like iefting at all Religion, placeth *Arianifme* among fundamentall errors : But *(x)* contrarily an Englifh Proteftant Deuine masked vnder the name of *Irenæus Philalethes,* in a little Booke in Latin entituled, *Differtatio de pace & concordia Ecclefiæ,* endeauoureth to proue, that euen the deniall of the bleffed Trinity may ftand with faluation. Diuers Proteftants haue taught,that the Roman Church, erreth in fundamentall points: But *D. Potter,* and others teach the contrary, which could not happen if they could agree what be fundamentall points. You brand the *Donatifts* with the note of an Error, *in the matter (y) and nature of it properly hereticall;* becaufe they taught that the Church remained only with them,in the part of *Donatus :* And yet many Proteftants are fo far from holding that Doctrine to be a fundamentall error,that themfelues goe further, and fay; that for diuers ages before *Luther* there was no true vifible Church at all. It is then too too apparent,that you haue no agreement in fpecifying, what be fundamentall points; neither haue you any meanes to determine what they be ; for if you haue any fuch meanes, why do you not agree? You tell vs, the *Creed* containes all points fundamentall, which although it were true,yet you fee it ferues not to bring you to a particuler knowledge, and agreement in fuch points. And no wonder. For (befides what I haue faid already

(x) A moderate examination &c. c. 1. paulo poft initium.

(y) pag.126

in the beginning of this Chapter, & am to deliuer more at large in the next) after so much labour and paper spent to proue that the *Creed* cō-
taynes all fundamentall points , you conclude:
It remaines (a) very probable , that the Creed is the
perfect Summary of those fundamentall truths, wher-
of consists the Vnity of fayth , and of the Catholique
Church . Very *probable?* Then , according to all
good Logick , the contrary may *remaine very*
probable , and so all remaine as full of yncertain-
ty , as before. The whole *Rule* , say you , & the
sole *Iudge* of your faith, must be Scripture. Scripture doth indeed deliuer diuine Truths , but
seldome doth qualify them, or declare whether
they be, or be not, absolutly necessary to saluation. You fall (b) heauy vpon *Charity Mistaken,*
because he demands a particuler Catalogue of
fundamental points , which yet you are obliged in conscience to doe , if you be able. For
without such a Catalogue , no man can be assured whether or no, he haue fayth sufficient to
Saluation. And therefore take it not in ill part,
if we agayne and agayne demand such a Catalogue. And that you may see we proceed faire-
ly , I will performe , on our behalfe , what we
request of you, & do heer deliuer a Catalogue ,
wherein are comprized all points by vs taught
to be necessary to Saluation , in these wordes :
We are obliged, vnder payne of damnation, to belieue
whatsoeuer the Catholique visible Church of Christ
proposeth, as reueaaled by Almighty God. If any be
of

(a) *pag.241.*

(b) *pag.215.*

of another mind, all Catholiques denounce
him to be no Catholique. But inough of this.
And I go forward with the Infallibility of the
Church in all points.

20. For, euen out of your owne doctrine
that the Church cannot erre in points necessary to saluation, any wise man will infer, that it
behooues all, who haue care of their soules, not
to forsake her in any one point. 1. Because they
are assured, that although her doctrine proued
not to be true in some point, yet euen according
to *D.Potter*, the error cannot be fundamentall,
nor destructiue of fayth, and saluation : neither
can they be accused of any least imprudence in
erring (if it were possible) with the vniuersall
Church. Secondly, since she is, vnder paine of
eternall damnation, to be belieued, and obeyed
in some things, wherin confessedly she is endewed with infallibility; I cannot in wisdome
suspect her credit in matters of lesse moment.
For who would trust another in matters of
highest consequence, and be afraid to rely on
him in things of lesse moment? Thirdly, since
(as I said) we are vndoubtedly obliged not to
forsake her in the chiefest, or fundamentall
points, and that there is no Rule to know precisely what, and how many those fundamentall
points be; I cannot without hazard of my soule,
leaue her in any one point, lest perhaps that
point or points wherin I forsake her, proue indeed to be fundamentall, and necessary to sal-

uation.

uation. Fourthly, that visible Church which cannot erre in points fundamentall, doth without distinction, propound all her Definitions concerning matters of faith to be belieued vnder Anathema's or Curses, esteeming all those who resist, to be deseruedly cast out of her Communion, and holding it as a point necessary to saluation, that we belieue she cannot erre: wherin if she speake true, then to deny any one point in *particuler*, which she defineth, or to affirme in *generall*, that she may erre, puts a man into state of damnation. Wheras to belieue her in such points as are not necessary to saluation, can not endanger saluation; as likewise to remaine in her Communion, can bring no great harme, becaufe she cannot maintaine any damnable error, or practife: but to be deuided frō her, (she being Chrifts Catholique Church) is most certainely damnable. Fifthly, the true Church, being in lawfull, and certaine possession of Superiority and Power, to command & require Obedience, from all Chriftians in some things; I cannot without grieuous sinne withdraw my obedience in any one, vnles I euidently know, that the thing commanded comes not within the compasse of those things to which her Power extendeth. And who can better informe me, how far God's Church can proceed, then God's Church herselfe? Or to what Doctor can the Children, and Schollers, with greater reason, and more security, fly for direction,

then

then to the *Mother*, and appointed *Teacher* of
all Chriſtians ? In following her , I ſhall ſooner
be excuſed , then in cleauing to any particuler
Seĉt, or Perſon, teaching, or applying Scriptures
againſt her doĉtrine , or interpretation. Sixtly,
the fearefull examples of innumerable perſons
who forſaking the Church vpon pretence of
her errours , haue failed, euen in fundamentall
points , and ſuffered ſhipwracke of their Saluation ought to deter all Chriſtians, from oppo-
ſing her in any one doĉtrine, or praĉtiſe : as (to
omit other, both ancient and moderne hereſies)
we ſee that diuers chiefe Proteſtants , pretending to reforme the corruptions of the Church,
are come to affirme , that for many Ages , ſhe
erred to death, and wholy periſhed ; which *D.*
Potter, cannot deny to be a fundamentall Errour againſt that Article of our Creed , *I belieue*
the Catholike Church , as he affirmeth it of the
Donatiſts, becauſe they confined the vniuerſall
Church , within *Africa* , or ſome other ſmall
traĉt of ſoile. Leaſt therefore I may fall into
ſome fundamentall errour, it is moſt ſafe for me
to belieue al the Decrees of that Church, which
cánot erre fundamentally: eſpecially if we add ;
That according to the Doĉtrine of Catholique
Deuines , one errour in fayth , whether it be
for the matter if ſelfe, great or ſmall , deſtroyes
fayth, as is ſhewed in *Charity Miſtaken*; and có-
ſequently to accuſe the Church of any one Errour, is to affirme, that ſhe loſt all fayth , and
erred

erred damnably : which very faying is damnable, becaufe at leaues Chrift no vifible Church on earth.

21. To all thefe arguments I add this demóftration: *D. Potter* teacheth, that *there neyther was* (c) *nor can be any iuft caufe to depart frō the Church of Chrift, no more then from Chrift himfelfe.* But if the Church of Chrift can erre in fome points of fayth, men not only may, but muft forfake her in thofe, (vnles *D. Potter* will haue them to belieue one thing, and profeffe another :) and if fuch errours, and corruptions fhould fall out to be about the Churches Liturgy, publique Seruice, adminiftration of Sacraments, & the like; they who perceiue fuch errours, muft of neceffity leaue her externall Cōmunion. And therefore if once we grant the Church may erre, it followeth that men may, and ought to forfake her (which is againft *D. Potters* owne wordes,) or elfe they are inexcufable who left the Communion of the *Roman* Church, vnder pretence of Errors, which they grant, not to be fundamentall. And if *D. Potter* thinke good to anfwere this argument, he muft remember his owne doctrine to be, that euen the *Catholique* Church may erre in points not fundamentall.

22. An other argument for the vniuerfall infallibility of the Church, I take out of *D. Potters* owne words. If (fayth he) we (d) did not diffent in fome opinions from the prefent Roman Church, we could not agree with the Church truly Catho-

(c) *pag. 75.*

(d) *pag. 97.*

Catholique. These words cannot be true, vnlesse he presuppose that the *Church truly Catholique*, cannot erre in points not fundamentall. For if she may erre in such points, the *Roman* Church which he affirmeth to erre only in points *not fundamentall*, may agree with the *Church truly Catholique*, if she likewise may erre in points *not fundamentall*. Therfore either he must acknowledge a plaine contradiction in his owne words, or else must grant, that the *Church truly Catholique* cannot erre in points *not fundamentall*, which is what we intended to proue.

23. If *Words* cannot perswade you, that in all Controuersies you must rely vpon the infallibility of the Church; at least yield your assent to *Deeds*. Hitherto I haue produced Arguments drawne, as it were, *ex naturâ rei*, from the Wisdome, and Goodnes of God, who cannot faile to haue left some infallible meanes to determine Controuersies, which, as we haue proued, can be no other, except a Visible Church, infallible in all her Definitions. But because both Catholiques and Protestants, receiue holy Scripture, we may thence also proue the infallibility of the Church in all matters which concerne Faith and Religion. Our Sauiour speaketh cleerely: *The gates of Hell* (e) *shall not preuaile against her.* And, *I will aske my* (f) *Father, and he will giue you another Paraclete, that he may abide with you for euer, the Spirit of truth.* And, *But when he, the Spirit of* (g) *truth cometh, he shall*

(e) *Matt. 16.*
(f) *Ioan. 14.*

(g) *Ioan. 16.*

teach

teach you all truth. The Apoſtle ſayth, that the
Church is, *the Pillar, and ground* (h) *of Truth.*
And, *He gaue, ſome Apoſtles, and ſome Prophets,
and otherſome Euangeliſts, and otherſome Paſtors
and Doctors, to the conſummation of the Saints, vnto the worke of the Miniſtery, vnto the edifying of the
body of Chriſt: vntill we meete all into the vnity of
faith, and knowledge of the Sonne of God, into a perfect man, into the meaſure of the age of the fulnes of
Chriſt: that now we be not Children wauering, and
carried about with euery wind of doctrine in the wickednes of men, in craftines, to the circumuention*
(i) *of Errour.* All which wordes ſeeme cleerely
inough to proue, that the Church is vniuerſally infallible, without which, Vnity of faith
could not be conſerued agaynſt *euery wind of
Doctrine*: And yet *Doctor Potter* (k) limits theſe
promiſes & priuiledges to *fundamentall* points,
in which he grants the Church cannot erre.
I vrge the wordes of Scripture, which are v-
niuerſall, and doe not mention any ſuch re-
ſtraint. I alleadge that moſt reaſonable, and
receaued Rule, that Scripture is to be vnderſtood literally, as it ſoundeth, vnleſſe ſome
manifeſt abſurdity force vs to the contrary.
But all will not ſerue, to accord our different
interpretations. In the meane tyme diuers of
Doctor Potters Brethren ſteppe in, and reiect his
limitation, as ouer large, and ſomwhat taſting
of Papiſtry: And therfore they reſtraine the
mentioned Texts, either to the Infallibility
which

(h) 1. *Tim.*
cap. 3.

(I) *Epheſ. 4.*

(k) *pag. 151.
153.*

which the Apoftles, and other facred Writers
had in penning of Scripture: or elfe to the *inui-*
fible Church of the *Elect*; and to them, not abfolutely, but with a double reftriction, that they
fhall not fall *damnably*, & *finally*; and other men
haue as much right as thefe, to interpofe their
opinion & interpretation. Behold we are three
at debate about the felfe fame words of Scripture: We confer diuers places and Text: We
confult the Originals: We examine Tranflations: We endeauour to pray hartily: We profeffe to fpeake fincerely; To feeke nothing but
truth and faluation of our owne foules, & that
of our Neighbours; and finally we vfe all thofe
meanes, which by Proteftants themfelues are
prefcribed for finding out the true meaning of
Scripture: Neuertheles we neither do, or haue
any poffible meanes to agree, as long as we are
left to our felues; and when we fhould chance
to be agreed, the doubt would ftill remaine
whether the thing it felfe be a *fundamentall*
point or no: And yet it were great impiety to
imagine that God, the Louer of foules, hath left
no certaine infallible meanes, to decide both
this, and all other differences arifing about the
interpretation of Scripture, or vpon any other
occafion. Our remedy therfore in thefe contentions muft be, to confult, and heare God's
Vifible Church, with fubmiffiue acknowledg-
ment of her Power, and Infallibility in whatfoeuer fhe propofeth as a reuealed truth: accor-

Q   ding

ding to that diuine aduice of *S. Augustine* in
thele words. *If at length* (1) *thou seeme to be suffi-*
ciently tossed, and hast a desire to put an end to thy
paines, follow the way of the Catholique Discipline,
which from Christ himselfe by the Apostles hath come
downe euen to vs, and from vs shall descend to all
posterity. And though I conceiue that the distinction of points *fundamentall*, and *not funda-*
mentall hath now beene sufficiently confuted ;
yet that no shadow of difficulty may remaine,
I will particulerly refell a common saying of
Protestants, that it is sufficient for saluation, to
belieue the Apostles Creed, which they hold to
be a Summary of all fundamentall points of
Fayth.

(1) *De vtil.*
cred. cap. 8.

CHAP.

CHAP. IIII.

To say, that the Creed containes all points necessarily to be believed, is neyther pertinent *to the Question in hand, nor in it selfe* true.

 SAY, neyther *pertinent*, nor *true*. Not *pertinent* : Becaufe our Queſtion is not, what points are neceſſary to be explicitely belieued; but what points may be lawfully *diſbelieued*, or reiected after ſufficient Propoſitiō that they are diuine Truths. You ſay, the Creed cōtaynes all points neceſſary to be belieued. Be it ſo. But doth it likewiſe containe all points not to be diſbelieued? Certainly it doth nor. For how many truths are there in holy Scripture not contayned in the Creed, which we are not obliged diſtinctly, and particulerly to know & belieue, but are bound vnder paine of damnation not to reiect, as ſoone as we come to know that they are found in holy Scripture? And we hauing already ſhewed, that whatſoeuer is pro-

poſed

poſed by Gods Church as a point of fayth, is infallibly a truth reuealed by God; it followeth that whoſoeuer denyeth any ſuch point, oppoſeth Gods ſacred teſtimony, whether that point be contayned in the Creed, or no. In vaine then was your care imploied to proue that al points of fayth neceſſary to be *explicitely* belieued, are contained in the Creed. Neyther was that the Catalogue which *Charity Miſtaken* demanded. His demand was (and it was moſt reaſonable) that you would once giue vs a liſt of all fundamentals, the denyall whereof deſtroyes Saluation; whereas the denyall of other points not fundamentall, may ſtand with ſaluation, although both theſe kinds of points be equally propoſed as reuealed by God. For if they be not equally propoſed, the difference will ariſe from diuerſity of the *Propoſall*, and not of the *Matter* fundamentull, or not fundamentall · This Catalogue only, can ſhew how farre Proteſtants may diſagree without breach of Vnity in fayth; and vpon this many other matters depend, according to the ground of Proteſtants. But you will neuer aduenture to publiſh ſuch a Catalogue. I ſay more: You cannot aſſigne any one point ſo *great*, or fundamentall, that the denyall thereof will make a man an Heretique, if it be not ſufficiently propounded, as a diuine Truth: Nor can you aſſigne any one point ſo *ſmall*, that it can without hereſy be reiected, if once it be ſufficiently repreſented as reuea-

reuealed by God.

2.   Nay, this your inftance in the Creed, is
not only impertinent but directly agaynft you.
For, all points in the Creed are not of their
own nature fundamentall, as I fhewed (a) before: And yet it is damnable to deny any one
point contayned in the Creed. So that it is
cleere, that to make an errour damnable, it is
not neceffary that the matter be of it felfe fundamentall.

3.   Moreouer you cannot ground any certainty vpon the Creed it felfe, vnleffe firft you
prefuppofe that the authority of the Church is
vniuerfally infallible, and confequently that it
is damnable to oppofe her declarations, whether they concerne matters great, or fmall, co-
tayned, or not contained in the Creed. This
is cleere. Becaufe we muft receaue the Creed it
felfe vpon the credit of the Church, without
which we could not know that there was any
fuch thing as that which we call the *Apoftles
Creed:* and yet the arguments whereby you endeauour to proue, that the Creed contaynes all
fundamentall points, are grounded vpon fuppofition, that the *Creed* was made *eyther by the
Apoftles themfelues, or by the* (b) *Church of their
tymes from them:* which thing we could not certainly know, if the fucceeding and ftill continued Church, may erre in her Traditions:
neyther can we be affured, whether all fundamentall Articles which you fay were out of

Q 3   the

(a) *Chap.* 3.
n. 3.

(b) *pag.* 216

the Scriptures, *summed, and contracted into the Apostles Creed* , were faythfully summed and contracted , and not one pretermitted , altered , or miftaken , vnleffe we vndoubtedly know that the Apoftles compofed the Creed ; and *that* they intended to contract all fundamentall points of faith into it ; or at leaft *that the Church of their tymes (* for it feemeth you doubt whether indeed it were compofed by the Apoftles themfelues) did vnderftand the Apoftles aright ; & *that the Church of their tymes ,* did intend that the Creed fhould containe all fundamentall points . For if the Church may erre in points not fundamentall , may fhe not alfo erre in the particulers which I haue fpecifyed ? Can you fhew it to be a fundamentall point of fayth , that the Apoftles intended to copiize all points of fayth neceffary to Saluation in the Creed ? Your felfe fay no more then that it is *very (* d *)* (d) *pag.* 241. *probable* ; which is farre from reaching to a fundamentall point of fayth . Your probability is grounded vpon *the Iudgment of Antiquity , and euen of the Roman Doctours ,* as you fay in the fame place. But if the Catholique Church may erre, what certainty can you expect from Antiquity , or Doctours ? Scripture is *your* totall Rule of fayth . Cite therefore fome Text of Scripture, to proue that the Apoftles , or *the Church of their tymes* compofed the Creed , and compofed it with a purpofe that it fhonld contayne all fundamentall points of fayth . Which

being

being impoffible to be done, you muft for the Creed it felfe rely vpon the infallibility of the Church.

4. Moreouer, the Creed confifteth not fo much in the words, as in their fenfe and meaning. All fuch as pretend to the name of Chriftians, recite the Creed, & yet many haue erred fundamentally, as well againft the Articles of the Creed, as other points of faith. It is then very friuolous to fay, the Creed containes all fundamentall points, without fpecifying, both in what fenfe the Articles of the Creed be *true*, and alfo in what *true* fenfe, they be *fundamental*. For, both thefe taskes, you are to performe, who teach that all truth is not fundamentall: & you do but delude the ignorant, when you fay, that the Creed, *taken in a Catholique* (e) *fenfe*, comprehendeth all points fundamentall; becaufe (e) *pag.* 216. with you, all *Catholique fenfe* is not fundamentall: for fo it were neceffary to faluation that all Chriftians fhould know the whole Scripture, wherin euery leaft point hath a *Catholique fenfe*. Or if by Catholique fenfe, you vnderftand that fenfe which is fo vniuerfally to be knowne, and belieued by all, that whofoeuer failes therein cannot be faued, you trifle and fay no more then this: *All points of the Creed in a fenfe necefary to faluation, are necefary to faluation.* Or: *All points fundamentall, are fundamentall.* After this manner it were an eafy thing to make many true Prognoftications, by faying it will certainely

raine

raine, when it raineth. You fay the Creed (f) was opened and explaned, *in fome parts* in the Creeds of *Nice* &c . but how fhall we vnderftand the other *parts*, not explained in thofe Creeds?

5. For what Article in the Creed is more fundamentall, or may feeme more cleere, then that, wherin we belieue IESVS CHRIST to be the Mediatour, Redeemer, and Sauiour of mankind, and the founder, and foundation of a *Catholique Church* expreffed in the Creed? And yet about this Article, how many different doctrines are there, not only of old Heretiques, as *Arius, Neſtorius, Eutiches &c.* but alfo of Proteftants, partly againft Catholiques, and partly againft one another? For the faid maine Article of Chrift's being the *only* Sauiour of the world &c. according to different fenfes of difagreeing Sects, doth inuolue thefe, and many other fuch queftions; That Faith in IESVS CHRIST doth iuftify alone; That Sacraments haue no efficiency in Iuftification; That Baptifme doth not auaile Infants for faluation; vnleffe they haue an Act of faith; That there is no Sacerdotall Abfolution from finnes; That good works proceeding from God's grace are not meritorious; That there can be no Satisfaction for the temporall punifhment due to finne after the guilt, or offence is pardoned; No, Purgatory; No Prayers for the dead; No Sacrifice of the Maffe; No Inuocation; No Mediation, or interceffion

of

of Saints; No inherent Iuſtice : No ſupreme Paſtor, yea no Biſhop by diuine Ordinance; No Reall preſence, no Tranſubſtantiation, with diuers others. And why? Becauſe (forſooth) theſe Doctrines derogate from the Titles of Mediator, Redeemer, Aduocate, Foundation &c. Yea and are againſt the truth of our Sauiours humane nature, if we belieue diuers Proteſtants, writing againſt Tranſubſtantiation. Let then any iudicious man conſider, whether *Doctour Potter*, or others doe really ſatisfy, when they ſend men to the Creed for a perfect Catalogue, to diſtinguiſh points fundamentall, from thoſe which they ſay are not fundamentall. If he will ſpeake indeed to ſome purpoſe, let him ſay : This Article is vnderſtood in this ſenſe : and in this ſenſe it is fundamentall. That other is to be vnderſtood in ſuch a meaning; yet according to that meaning, it is not ſo fundamentall, but that men may diſagree, and deny it without damnation. But it were no policy for any Proteſtant to deale ſo plainely.

6.   But to what end ſhould we vſe many arguments ? Euen your ſelfe are forced to limit your owne Doctrine, and come to ſay, that the *Creed* is a perfect Catalogue of fundamentall points, *taken as it was further opened and explained in ſome parts (by occaſion of emergent Hereſies) in the other Catholique Creeds of Nice, Conſtantinople,* (g) *Epheſus, Chalcedon, and Athanaſius.* But this

R   ex-

explication, or reſtriction ouerthroweth your
Aſſertion. For as the Apoſtles Creed was not to
vs a ſufficient Catalogue, till it was explained
by the firſt Councell, nor then till it was declared by another &c. ſo now alſo, as new Hereſies may ariſe, it will need particular explanation againſt ſuch emergent errors; and ſo it is
not yet, nor euer will be of it ſelfe alone, a particular Catalogue, ſufficient to diſtinguiſh betwixt fundamentall, and not fundamentall
points.

7. I come to the ſecond part: *That the Creed*
doth not containe all maine and principall points of
faith. And to the end we may not ſtriue about
things either granted by vs both, or nothing
concerning the point in queſtion, I muſt pre-
miſe theſe obſeruations.

8. Firſt : That it cannot be denied, but that
the Creed is moſt full and complete, to that
purpoſe for which the holy Apoſtles, inſpir'd
by God, meant that it ſhould ſerue, and in that
māner as they did intend it, which was, not to
comprehend all particular points of faith, but
ſuch generall heads as were moſt befitting, and
requiſite for preaching the faith of Chriſt to
Iewes, and Gentiles, and might be briefly, and
compendiouſly ſet downe, and eaſily learned,
and remembred. And therfore, in reſpect of
Gentiles, the Creed doth mētion God, as Creator of all things; and for both Iewes and Gentiles, the Trinity, the Meſſias, and Sauiour, his
birth,

Birth, life, death, resurrection, and glory, from
whom they were to hope remission of sinnes, &
life euerlasting, and by whose sacred Name they
were to be distinguished from all other professions, by being called Christians. According to
which purpose *S. Thomas of Aquine* (h) doth distinguish all the Articles of the Creed into
these generall heads : That some belong to the
Maiesty of the *Godhead* ; others to the Mistery
of our Sauiour Christs *Humane nature* : Which
two generall obiects of faith, the holy Ghost
doth expresse, and conioyne *Ioan.* 17. *Hæc est vita
æterna &c. This is life euerlasting, that they know
thee true GOD, and whom thou hast sent I E S V S
C H R I S T.* But it was not their meaning to
giue vs as it were a course of Diuinity, or a Ca-
techisme, or a particular Expression of all
points of Faith, leauing those things to be performed, as occasion should require, by their
owne word or writing, for their time, and afterwards by their Successours in the Catholique Church. Our question then is not, whether
the Creed be perfect, as far as the end for which
it was composed, did require ; For we belieue &
are ready to giue our liues for this: but only we
deny, that the Apostles did intend to comprize
therin all particular points of beliefe, necessary
to saluation, as euen by *D. Potters* owne (i) confession, it doth not comprehend *agenda,* or
things belonging to practise, as *Sacraments,
Commandements,* the Acts of *Hope,* and dutyes

(h) *2. 2. q,
1. art.* 8.

(i) *pag.* 235,
215.

R 2　　　　　of

of Charity, which we are obliged not only to practise, but alſo to *belieue* by diuine infallible fayth. Will he therefore inferre that the Creed is not perfect, becauſe it contaynes not all thoſe neceſſary, and fundamentall Obiects of fayth? He will anſwere. No : becauſe the Apoſtles intended only to expreſſe *credenda*, thinges to be belieued, not practiſed. Let him therefore giue vs leaue to ſay, that the Creed is perfect, becauſe it wanteth none of thoſe Obiects of beliefe which were intended to be ſet downe, as we explicated before.

9. The ſecond obſeruation is, that to ſatisfy our queſtion what points in particuler be fundamentall, it will not be ſufficient to alledg the Creed, vnleſſe it containe all ſuch points eyther expreſſely & immediatly; or els in ſuch manner, that by euident, and neceſſary conſequence they may be deduced from Articles both cleerely, and particulerly contayned therin. For if the deduction be *doubtfull*, we ſhal not be *ſure*, that ſuch Concluſions be fundamental: or if the Articles themſelues which are ſayd to be fundamentall, be not diſtinctly, and particuerly expreſſed, they will not ſerue vs to know, and diſtinguiſh all points fundamental, from thoſe which they call, not fundamentall. We doe not deny, but that all points of fayth, both fundamentall, and not fundamentall, may be ſaid to be contained in the Creed in ſome ſenſe; as for example, implicitely, generally

sally, or in some such inuolued manner. For
when we explicitely belieue the *Catholique
Church*, we do implicitely belieue whatsoeuer
she proposeth as belonging to faith. Or else by
way of *reduction*, that is, when we are once in-
structed in the beliefe of particular points of
faith, not expressed, nor by necessary conseque-
ce deducible frō the Creed; we may afterward,
by some analogy, or proportion, and resem-
blance, reduce it to one, or moe of those Articles which are explicitely contayned in the
Symbole. Thus *S. Thomas* the Cherubim among
Deuines teacheth (l) that the miraculous existence of our Blessed Sauiours body in the *Eucharist*, as likewise all his other *miracles*, are
reduced to Gods *Omnipotency*, expressed in the
Creed. And *Doctor Potter* sayth : *The Eucharist*
(m) *being a seale of that holy Vnion which we haue
with Christ our head, by his Spirit and Fayth, and
with the Saints his members by Charity, is euidently
included in the Communion of Saints.* But this re-
ductiue way, is farre from being sufficient to
inferre out of the Articles of *Gods Omnipotency*,
or of the *Communion of Saints*, that our Sauiours
body is in the Eucharist, and much lesse whether it be only in figure, or els in reality ; by
Transubstantiation, or Consubstantiation &c.
and least of all, whether or no these points be
fundamentall. And you hyperbolize, in saying,
the Eucharist is *euidently included in the Communion of Saints*, as if there could not haue been, or

*(l) 2.2: q.i\
art. 8. ad 6.*

(m) pag. 237.

Was not a Communion of Saints, before the
Bleſſed Sacrament was inſtituted. Yet it is
true, that after we know, and belieue, there
is ſuch a Sacrament, we may referre it to ſome
of thoſe heads expreſſed in the Creed, and yet
ſo, as *S. Thomas* referrs it to one Article, and
D. Potter to another; and in reſpect of different
analogies or effects, it may be referred to ſeuerall Articles. The like I ſay of other points of
faith, which may in ſome ſort be reduced to the
Creed, but nothing to *D. Potters* purpoſe: But
contrarily it ſheweth, that your affirming ſuch
and ſuch points to be fundamentall or not fundamentall, is meerely arbitrary, to ſerue your
turne, as neceſſity, and your occaſions may require. Which was an old cuſtome amongſt Heretiques, as we read in *(n) S. Augustine. Pelagius*
and *Celestius, deſiring fraudulently to auoyde the
hatefull name of Hereſies, affirmed that the question
of Originall Sinne may be diſputed without danger of
fayth.* But this holy Father affirmes that it belongs to the foundation of fayth. *We may (faith*
he) *endure a diſputant who erres in other questions
not yet diligently examined, not yet diligently established by the whole authority of the Church, their
errour may be borne with: but it muſt not paſſe ſo far
as to attempt to ſhake the foundation of the Church.*
We ſee *S. Augustine* places the being of a point
fundamentall or not fundamentall, in that it
hath beene *examined*, and *established* by the
Church, although the point of which he ſpeaketh

(n) *De pec-*
cat. Orig.
cont. Pelag.
l.2. cap.22.

keth, namely Originall Sinne, be not contayned in the Creed.

10. Out of that which hath beene fayd, I inferre, that *Doctour Potters* paines in alledging Catholique Doctours, the ancient Fathers, and the Councell of Trent, to proue that the Creed containes all points of faith, was needlesse, since we grant it in manner aforesayd. But *Doctour Potter*, can not in his conscience belieue, that Catholique Deuines, or the Councell of Trent, and the holy Fathers did intend, that all points in particuler which we are obliged to belieue, are contayned explicitely in the Creed; he knowing well inough, that all Catholiques hold themselues obliged, to belieue all those points which the sayd Councell defines to be belieued vnder an Anathema, and that all Christians belieue the commandments, Sacraments &c. which are not expressed in the Creed.

11. Neither must this seeme strange. For who is ignorant, that Summaries, Epitom'es, & the like briefe Abstracts, are not intended to specify all particulars of that Science, or Subiect to which they belong. For as the Creed is said to containe all points of *Fayth*: so the Decalogue comprehends all Articles, (as I may terme them) which concerne *Charity*, and good life: and yet this cannot be so vnderstood, as if we were disobliged from performance of any duty, or the eschewing of any vice, vnlesse it be

ex-

expreffed in the ten Commandments. For, (to omit the precepts of receauing Sacraments, which belong to practife,or manners , and yet are not contained in the Decalogue) there are many finnes, euen againft the Law of nature, and light of reafon,which are not contained in the ten Commandments, except only by fimilitude, analogy, reduction or fome fuch way. For example, we find not expreffed in the Decalogue , either diuers finnes , as Gluttony, Drunkenneffe , Pride , Sloth , Couetoufnes in defiring either things fuperfluous , or with too much greedines ; or diuers of our chiefe obligations,as Obedience to Princes. and all Superiours, not only Ecclefiafticall but alfo Ciuill, whofe Lawes *Luther* , *Melancthon* , *Caluin* . and fome other Proteftants do dangeroufly affirme not to oblige in confcience , and yet thefe men thinke they know the ten Commandments: as likewife diuers Proteftants defend Vfury , to be lawfull;and the many Treatifes of *Ciuilians,Canonifts*, and *Cafuifts,* are witneffes , that diuers finnes againft the light of reafon , and Law of nature,are not diftinctly expreffed in the ten Commandements ; although when by other diligences they are found to be vnlawfull , they may be reduced to fome of the Commandments, and yet not fo euidently, and particularly , but that diuers doe it in diuers manners .

12.   My third Obferuation is: That our prefent

sent queſtion being, whether or no the Creed
containe ſo fully all fundamentall points of
faith, that whoſoeuer do not agree in all, and
euery one of thoſe fundamentall Articles, cannot haue the ſame ſubſtance of faith, nor hope
of Saluation; if I can produce one, or more
points, not contained in the Creed, in which if
two do not agree, both of them cannot expect
to be ſaued, I ſhall haue performed as much as I
intend; and *D.Potter* muſt ſeeke out ſome other
Catalogue for points fundamentall, then the
Creed. Neither is it materiall to the ſaid purpoſe, whether ſuch fundamentall points reſt
only in knowledge, and ſpeculation or beliefe,
or elſe be further referred to work and practiſe.
For the *Habit*, or Vertue of *Fayth*, which incli-
neth, and enableth vs to belieue both ſpeculatiue, and practicall verities, is of one and the
ſelfe ſame nature, and eſſence. For example, by
the ſame *Fayth*, wherby I ſpeculatiuely belieue
there is a God, I likewiſe belieue, that he is to be
adored, ſerued, and loued, which belong to practiſe. The reaſon is, becauſe the *Formall Obiect*, or
motiue, for which I yield aſſent to thoſe different ſorts of materiall obiects, is the ſame in
both, to wit, the reuelation, or word of God.
Where, by the way I note, that if the *Vnity*, or
Diſtinction, and nature of Fayth, were to be taken from the diuerſity of things reuealed, by
one Fayth I ſhould belieue ſpeculatiue verities,
and by another ſuch as tend to practiſe, which

I doubt whether *D. Potter* himſelfe will admit.

13. Hence it followeth, that whoſoeuer denieth any one maine practicall reuealed truth, is
no leſſe an Heretique, then if he ſhould deny a
point reſting in beliefe alone. So that when *D.
Potter*, (to auoid our argument, that all fundamentall points are not contained in the Creed,
becauſe in it there is no mention of the Sacra-
mēts, which yet are points of ſo maine importā-
ce, that Proteſtants make the due adminiſtratiō
of them to be neceſſary & eſſentiall to conſtitute
a Church) anſwereth, that the *Sacraments are to
be* (p) *reckoned, rather among the* Agenda *of the
Church, then the* Credenda; *they are rather diuine
rites & ceremonies, then Doctrines,* he either grants
what we affirme, or in effect ſayes; Of two
kinds of reuealed truths, which are neceſſary to
be belieued, the Creed containes one ſort only,
ergo, it containes all kind of reuealed truths neceſſary to be belieued. Our queſtion is not, *de no-
mine* but *re*; not what be called points of Fayth,
or of practiſe, but what points indeed be neceſſarily to be belieued, whether they be termed
Agenda, or *Credenda :* eſpecially the chiefeſt part
of Chriſtian perfection conſiſting more in
Action, then in barren Speculation; in good
workes, then bare beliefe; in doing, then
knowing. And there are no leſſe contentions
concerning practicall, then ſpeculatiue truths :
as Sacraments, obtayning remiſſion of ſinne,
Innocation of Saints, Prayers for dead, Adora-

(p) *pag.*235.

tion

tion of Chrift in the Sacrament, & many others
all which do fo much the more import, as on
them, befide right beliefe, doth alfo depend our
practife, and the ordering of our life. Though
D. Potter could therfore giue vs (as he will neuer be able to do) a minute, and exact Catalogue of all truths to be belieued ; that would not
make me able inough to know, whether or no
I haue faith fufficient for faluation ; till he alfo
did bring in a particular Lift, of all belieued
truths, which tend to practife, declaring which
of them be fundamentall, which not, that fo
euery man might know whether he be not in
fome *Damnable* Errour, for fome Article of
fayth, which further might giue influence into
Damnable works.

14. Thefe Obferuations being premifed, I
come to proue, that the Creed doth not containe all points of Fayth neceffary to be
knowne, & belieued. And, to omit that in generall it doth not tell vs, what points be fundamentall, or not fundamentall, which in the
way of Proteftants, is moft neceffary to be
knowne; in particular, there is no mention of
the greateft Euils, from which mans calamity
proceeded, I meane, the finne of the Angels, of
Adam, and of Originall finne in vs: nor of the
greateft good from which we expect all good,
to wit, the neceffity of *Grace* for all works tending to piety. Nay, there is no mention of Angels, good, or bad. The meaning of that moft

S 2

generall head *(Oportet accedentem &c. It behooues*
(q) Heb.11.
6.
(q) *him that comes to God, to belieue that he is, and is*
a remunerator,) is queſtioned, by the deniall of
Merit, which makes God, a Giuer, but not a Re-
warder. It is not expreſſed whether the Article
of *Remiſsion of ſinnes* be vnderſtood by fayth a-
lone, or elſe may admit the efficiency of Sacraments. There is no mention of Eccleſiaſticall,
Apoſtolicall, *Diuine Traditions*, one way or o-
ther; or of holy Scriptures in generall, and
much leſſe of euery booke in particuler; nor
of the Name Nature, Number, Effects, Matter,
Forme, Miniſter, Intention, Neceſſiry of Sacraments, and yet the due adminiſtration of Sacraments, is with Proteſtants an eſſentiall Note of
the Church There is nothing for Baptiſme of
Children, nor againſt Rebaptization. There is
no mention in fauour, or againſt the Sacrifice of
the Maſſe, of Power in the Church to inſtitute
Rites, Holy dayes &c. and to inflict Excommunication, or other Cenſures: of Prieſthood,
Biſhops, and the whole Eccleſiaſticall Hierarchy, which are very fundamentall points;
of *S. Peters* Primacy, which to *Caluin* ſeemeth a
fundamentall error; nor of the poſſibility, or
impoſſibility to keep Gods commandments; of
the proceſſion of the holy Ghoſt from the Father and the Sonne; of Purgatory, or Prayer for
the dead, in any ſenſe: And yet *D. Potter* doth
not deny, but that *Aerius* was eſteemed an He-
(r) pag. 35. retique, for denying (r) all ſort of Commemoration

ration for the dead. Nothing of the Churches
Vifibility or Inuifibility, Fallibility or Infallibility; nor of other points controuerted betwixt
Proteftants themfelues, and betweene Proteftants and Catholiques, which to *D. Potter* feeme
fo haynous corruptions, that they cannot without damnation ioyne with vs in profeffion
therof. There is no mention of the Ceffation
of the Old Law, which yet is a very maine
point of faith. And many other might be alfo
added.

15. But what need we labour to fpecify
particulars? There are as many importat points
of faith not expreffed in the Creed, as fince the
worlds beginning, now, & for all future times,
there haue been, are, and may be innumerable,
groffe, damnable, Herefies, whofe contrary
truths are not contained in the Creed. For,
euery fundamental Error muft haue a contrary
fundamentall truth; becaufe of two contradictory propofitions, in the fame degree, the one
is falfe, the other muft be true. As for example,
if it be a damnable error to *deny* the Bl. Trinity,
or the God-head of our Sauiour, the *beliefe* of
them muft be a truth neceffary to faluation; or
rather, if we will fpeake properly, the *Error* is
damnable, becaufe the oppofite *Truth* is neceffary; as death is frightfull, becaufe life is fweet;
and according to Philofophy, the Priuation is
meafured by the Forme to which it is repugnant. If therfore the Creed containe in particu-

ler

ler all fundamentall points of fayth, it minst explicitely, or by cleere consequence, coprehend all truths opposite to innumerable Herefies of all Ages past, present, and to come, which no man in his wits will affirme it to doe.

16.   And heer I cannot omit to fignify how you (s) applaude the faying of *D. Vfher. That in those Propofitions which without all controverfy are vniuerfally receiued in the whole Chriftian world, fo much Truth is contained, as being ioyned with holy Obedience may be fufficient to bring a man to euerlaft-ing faluation; Neither haue we caufe to doubt, but that as many as walke according to this Rule (neither ouerthrowing thatwhich they haue builded, by fuperin-ducing any damnable herefies therupon, nor otherwife vitiating their holy fayth with a lewd and wicked con-uerfation) peace fhall be vpon them, and vpon the Ifrael of God.* Now, *D. Potter* knowes, that the Miftery of the B. Trinity is not vniuerfally re-ceiued in the whole Chriftian world, as appea-res in very many Heretiques, in *Polony, Hunga-ry,* and *Tranfiluania,* and therfore according to this Rule of *D. Vfher,* approued by *D. Potter,* the deniall of the B. Trinity, fhall not exclude fal-uation.

17.   Let me note by the way, that you might eafily haue efpied a foule contradiction in the faid words of *D. Vfher,* by you recited, and fo much applauded. For he fuppofeth, that a man agrees with other Churches in beliefe, which ioyned with holy Obedience may bring him to

euer-

(s) *pag.* 255.

euerlasting saluation, and yet, that he may *superinduce damnable herefies.* For how can he *superinduce damnable herefies* , who is suppofed to belieue all *Truths* neceffary to faluation? Can there
be any damnable herefy, vnleffe it contradict
fome neceffary truth, which cannot happen in
one who is suppofed to belieue all necefsary
Truths? Befides if one belieuing all fundamentall Articles in the Creed, may *superinduce damnable herefies* ; it followeth that the fundamétall
truths contrary to thofe damnable herefies, are
not contained in the Creed .

18.   According to this Modell of *D. Potters*
foundation , confifting in the agreement of
fcarcely one point of fayth ; what a ftrange
Church would he make of men concurring in
fome one of few Articles of beliefe , who yet
for the reft fhould be holding conceyts plainly contradictory : fo patching vp a Religion of
mé who agree only in the Article, that Chrift is
our Sauiour, but for the reft, are like to the parts
of a Chimæra , hauing the head of a man , the
necke of a horfe , the fhoulders of an Oxe , the
foote of a Lion &c. I wrong them not heerein.
For in good Philofophy there is greater repu-
gnancy betweene affent and diffent , affirmation and negation , *eft eft , non non* (efpecially
when all thefe contrradictories pretend to relye vpon one and the felfe fame *Motiue*, the in-
infallible Truth of Almighty God) then betweene the integrall parts , as head , necke ,
&c.

&c.of a mā, horſe, lion, &c. And thus Proteſtāts
are farre more bold to diſagree euen in matters
of fayth, then Catholique Deuines in queſtions meerely Philoſophicall, or not determined
by the Church. And while thus they ſtand only vpon *fundamentall* Articles, they do by their
owne confeſſion deſtroy the Church, which
is the *houſe of God.* For the *foundation* alone of a
houſe, is not a houſe, nor can they in ſuch an
imaginary Church any more expect Saluation,
then the foundation alone of a houſe is fit to affoard a man habitation.

19.   Moreouer, it is moſt euident that Proteſtants by this Chaos rather then Church, doe
giue vnauoydable occaſion of deſperation to
poore ſoules. Let ſome one who is deſirous to
ſaue his ſoule repaire to *D. Potter,* who main-
taynes theſe grounds, to know vpon whome
he may rely, in a matter of ſo great conſequence; I ſuppoſe the Doctours anſwere will be: V-
pon the truly Catholique Church. She cannot
erre danably. What vnderſtand you by the Catholike Church? Cannot generall Councells,
which are the Church *repreſentatiue,* erre? Yes,
(t) *pag. 167.* *they may weakely, or (t) wilfully miſapply, or miſ-*
vnderſtand, or neglect Scripture, and ſo erre damna-
bly. To whome then ſhall I goe for my particuler inſtructiō? I cannot confer with the vnited
body of the whole Church about my particuler difficulties, as your ſelfe affirmes, that the
(u) *pag. 27.* Catholique Church *cannot be told* (u) *of priuate*
iniu-

iniuries. Muſt I then conſult with euery particular perſon of the Catholique Church ? So it
ſeemes, by what you write in theſe wordes :
The whole (w *) militant Church (that is all the mem-*
bers of it) cannot poſsibly erre, eyther in the whole　(w)*pag.*150
fayth, or any neceſſary Article of it. You ſay, *M.*　151.
Doſtour, I cannot for my inſtruction acquaint
the vniuerſall Church with my particuler ſcru-
ples : You ſay, the Prelates of Gods Church
meeting in a lawfull generall Councel may erre
damnably : It remaynes then, that for my neceſſary inſtruction, I muſt repaire to euery particuler member of the vniuerſall Church ſpread
ouer the face of the earth : & yet you teach that
the promiſes (x *) which our Lord hath made vnto his*　(x)*pag.*151.
Church for his aſsiſtance, are intended not to any par-
ticuler perſons or Churches, but only to the Church
Catholike, with which (as I ſayd) it is impoſſible for me to confer. Alas, O moſt vncomfor-
table Ghoſtly Father, you driue me to deſperation. How ſhall I confer with euery Chriſtian
ſoule, man and woman, by ſea and by land,
cloſe priſoner, or at liberty &c. ? Yet vpon ſup-
poſall of this *miraculous* Pilgrimage for *Fayth,*
before I haue the *fayth* of *Miracles,* how ſhall I
proceed at our meeting ? Or how ſhall I know
the man on whome I may ſecurely relye ? Procure (will you ſay) to know whether he belieue all fundamentall points of fayth. For if
he doe, his fayth, for point of beliefe, is ſufficient for ſaluation, though he erre in a hundred

things of ieffe moment. But how fhall I know
whether he hold all fundamentall points or no?
For til you tel me this, I cannot know whether
or no his beliefe be found in all fundamentall
points. Can you fay the Creed? Yes. And fo
can many damnable Heretikes. But why doe
you aske me this queftion? Becaufe the Creed
containes all fundamentall points of fayth. Are
you fure of that? not fure: I hould it very *proba-*
(y)*pag.* 241. *ble* (y). Shall I hazard my foule on *probabilities*,
or euen wagers? This yields a new caufe of def-
paire. But what? doth the Creed contayne all
points neceffary to be belieued, whether they
reft in the vnderftanding, or elfe do further extend to practife? No. It was copofed to deliuer
Credenda, not *Agenda* to vs; Fayth, not *Practife.*
How then fhall I know what points of beliefe,
which direct my practife, be neceffary to faluation? Still you chalke out new pathes for Def-
peration. Well, are all Articles of the Creed, for
their nature and matter, fundamentall? I cannot fay fo. How then, fhall I know which in
particuler be, and which be not fundamentall?
Read my Anfwere to a late Popifh Pamphlet
intituled *Charity Miftaken &c.* there you fhall
find, that fundamentall doctrines are fuch *Ca-*
(z)*pag.* 211. *tholique Verities, as principally, and effentially per-*
213. 214. *taine* (z) *to the Faith, fuch as properly conftitute a*
Church, and are neceffary (in ordinary courfe) to be
diftinctly belieued by euery Chriftian that will be fa-
ued. They are thofe grand, and capitall doctrines
which

*which make vp our Fayth in Christ; that is, that common fayth which is alike precious in all, being one & the same in the highest Apostle, & the meanest belieuer, which the Apostle else-where cals the first principles of the oracles of God, and the forme of sound words.*But how shall I apply these generall definitions, or descriptions, or (to say the truth) these only varied words, and phrases (for I vnderstand the word, *fundamentall,* as well as the words, *principall, essentiall, grand, and capitall doctrines &c.*) to the particular Articles of the Creed, in such sort, as that I may be able precisely, exactly, particularly to distinguish fundamentall Articles, from points of lesse moment? You labour to tell vs *what* fundamentall points be, but not *which* they be : and yet vnlesse you do this, your Doctrine serues onely, either to make men despaire, or els to haue recourse to those whom you call Papists, and who giue one certaine Rule, that all points defined by Christs visible Church belong to the foundation of Fayth, in such sense, as that to deny any one cannot stand with saluation. And seing your selfe acknowledges that these men do not erre in points fundamentall, I cannot but hold it most safe for me to ioyne with them, for the securing of my soule, and the auoyding of desperation, into which this your doctrine must cast all them who vnderstand, and belieue it. For the whole discourse, and inferences which heer I haue made, are either your owne direct Assertions,

T 2   tions,

tions, or euident confequences cleerly deduced from them.

20.   But now let vs anfwere fome few Obiections of *D. Potters*, againft that which we
haue faid before, to auoid our argument, That
the Scripture is not fo much as mentioned in
the Creed, he fayth : *The Creed is an abstract of*
(a)*pag.*234. *fuch* (a) *neceffary Doctrines as are deliuered in Scri-*
pture, or collected out of it; and therfore needs
not expreffe the authority of that which it fuppofes.

21.   This anfwere makes for vs. For by giuing a reafon why it was needles that Scripture
fhould be expreffed in the Creed, you grant as
much as we defire , namely that the Apoftles
iudged it *needles* to exprefse all necefsary points
of fayth in their Creed. Neither doth the Creed
fuppofe, or depend on Scripture, in fuch fort as
that we can by any probable confequence, infer
from the Articles of the Creed, that there is any
Canonicall Scripture at all; and much lefse that
fuch Bookes in particular be Canonicall : Yea
the Creed might haue been the fame although
holy Scripture had neuer been written; and,
which is more, the Creed euen in priority of
time, was before all the Scripture of the new
Teftament, except the Gofpell of *S. Mathew.*
And fo according to this reafon of his the Scripture fhould not mention Articles conteined
in the Creed. And I note in a word , how little
connexion *D. Potters* arguments haue , while he

tels

tels vs, that *the Creed* (b) *is an Abstract of such* (b) *pag. 234.*
necessary doctrines as are deliuered in Scripture, or
collected out of it, and therfore needs not expresse the
authority of that which it supposes; it doth not follow: The Articles of the Creed are deliuered in
Scripture: therfore the Creed supposeth Scripture. For two distinct writings may well deliuer the same truths, and yet one of them not
suppose the other, vnlesse *D. Potter* be of opinion
that two Doctours cannot, *at one time,* speake
the same truth.

22. And notwithstanding, that *D. Potter*
hath now told vs, it was *needles* that the Creed
should expresse Scripture, whose *Authority it*
supposes, he comes at length to say, that the *Ni-*
cene Fathers in their Creed confessing that the holy
Ghost spake by the Prophets, doth therby sufficiently
auow the diuine Authority of all Canonicall Scri-
pture. But I would aske him, whether the *Nicene*
Creed be not also an Abstract of Doctrines deliuered in Scripture, as he said of the Apostles
Creed, and thence did infer, that it was needles
to expresse Scripture, *whose authority it supposes?*
Besides, we do not only belieue in generall, that
Canonicall Scripture is of diuine authority,
but we are also bound vnder paine of damnation to belieue, that such and such particular
Bookes, not mentioned in the *Nicene* Creed,
are Canonicall. And lastly *D. Potter* in this Answere grants as much as we desire, which is
that all points of fayth are not contained in the

Apo-

Apoftles Creed, euen as it is *explained* by other
Creeds. For thefe words (*who fpake by the Pro-*
phets) are no wayes contained in the Apoftles
Creed, and therfore containe an *Addition*, not
an *Explanation* therof.

23.   But, *how can it be neceffary* (fayth *D. Pot-*
ter) *for any Chriftian, to haue more in his Creed then*
(c)*pag.* 221. *the* (c) *Apoftles had , and the Church of their ty-*
mes ? I anfwere ; You trifle, not diftinguifh be-
tweene the Apoftles beliefe, and that abridge-
ment of fome Articles of fayth , which we call
the Apoftles *Creed* ; and withall you begg the
queftion, by fuppofing that the Apoftles belieued no more , then is contaned in their Creed,
which euery vnlearned perfon knowes and belieues : and I hope you will not deny but the A-
poftles were endued with greater knowledge
then ordinary perfons .

24.   Your pretended proofe out of the Acts,
that the Apoftles *reuealed to the Church the whole*
(d) *Act.* 20. *Counfell of God, keeping* (d) *backe nothing* , with
27 ;   your gloffe (*needfull for our faluatiõ*) is no proofe
vnleffe you ftill beg the queftion, and doe fup-
pofe , that whatfoeuer the Apoftles reuealed
to the Church , is contayned in the Creed.
And I wonder you do not reflect that thofe
words were by *S. Paul* particularly directed to
Paftors, and Gouernours of the Church , as is
cleere by the other wordes ; *He called the An-*
cients of the Church. And afterward : *Take heed to*
your felues , and to the whole flocke wherin the holy
                                              Ghoft

Ghoſt hath placed you Biſhops, to rule the Church.
And your ſelfe ſay, *that more knowledge is* (e) *ne-* (e)*pag.*244
*ceſſary in Biſhops, and Prieſts, to whom is committed
the gouernment of the Church, and the care of ſoules,
then in vulgar Laickes.* Do you thinke that the
Apoſtles taught Chriſtians nothing but their
Creed ? Said they nothing of the Sacraments,
Cōmandments, Duties of Hope, Charity &c ?

25. Vpon the ſame affected ambiguity is
grounded your other obiection: *To ſay the whole
fayth of thoſe times* (f) *is not contained in the Apo-* (f)*pag.*222.
les Creed, is all one, as if a man should ſay, this is not 223.
the Apoſtles Creed, but a part of it . For the fayth of
the Apoſtles is not all one with that which we
commōly call their Creed. Did not, I pray you,
S. Mathew , and *S. Iohn* belieue their writings
to be Canonicall Scripture? and yet their wri-
tinges are not mentioned in the Creed. It is
therfore more then cleere, that the Fayth of the
Apoſtles is of a larger extent, then the Apoſtles
Creed.

26. To your demaund, why amongſt many
things of equall *neceſsity to be belieued, the Apoſtles ſhould* (g) *ſo diſtinctly ſet downe ſome, and be
altogether ſilent of others?* I anſwere: That you (g) *pag.*223.
muſt anſwere your owne demaund. For in the
Creed there be diuers points in their nature,
not fundamentall, or neceſſary to be explicitely and diſtinctly belieued, as aboue we ſhewed;
why are theſe points which are not fundamentall expreſſed, rather then other of the ſame
quali-

quality? Why our Sauiours defcent to Hell, &
Buriall expreffed, and not his Circumcifion, his
manifeftation to the three Kings, working of
Miracles &c? Why did they not expreffe Scriptures, Sacraments, and all fundamentall points
of Fayth tending to practife, as well as thofe
which reft in beliefe? Their intention was, particularly to deliuer fuch Articles as were fitteft
for thofe times, concerning the Deity, Trinity,
and Meffias (as heretofore I haue declared) leauing many things to be taught by the *Catholique
Church,* which in the Creed we all profeffe to
belieue. Neither doth it follow, as you infer,
*That as well, nay better, they might haue giuen no
Article, but that (of the Church) and fent vs to the
Church for all the reft. For in fetting downe others
befides that, and not all, they make vs belieue we haue
all, when* (h) *we haue not all.* For by this kind of
arguing, what may not be deduced? One might,
quite contrary to your inference, fay: Jf the
Apoftles Creed containe all points necefsary
to faluation, what need we any Church to
teach vs? and confequently what need of the
Article concerning the *Church?* What need we
the Creeds of *Nice, Conftantinople &c.* Superfluous are your Catechifms, wherin befide the
Articles of the Creed, you add diuers other particulars. Thefe would be poore confequences,
and fo is yours. But fhall I tell you newes? For
fo you are pleafed to efteeme it. We grant your
inference, thus far: That our Sauiour Chrift referred,

(h)*pag.*223.

ferred vs to his Church , by her to be taught, &
by her alone. For, fhe was before the Creed, and
Scriptures; And fhe to difcharge this impofed
office of inftructing vs , hath deliuered vs the
Creed, but not it alone , as if nothing els were
to be belieued. We haue befides it , holy Scripture; we haue vnwritten, diuine , Apoftolicall
Ecclefiafticall Traditions. It were a childifh argument : The Creed containes not all things
which are neceffary to be belieued: *Ergo*, it is not
profitable. Or; The Church alone is fufficient to
teach vs by fome conuenient meanes: *Ergo* , fhe
muft teach vs without all meanes , without
Creeds, without Councels , without Scripture
&c. If the Apoftles had exprefsed no Article,
but that of the Catholique Church , fhe muft
haue taught vs the other Articles in particular,
by Creeds, or other meanes, as in fact we haue
euen the Apoftles Creed from the Tradition of
the Church. If you will *belieue you haue all in the
Creed, when you haue not all*, it is not the Apoftles,
or the Church, that makes you fo belieue , but
it is your owne error , wherby you will needs
belieue, that the Creed muft containe *all* . For
neither the Apoftles , nor the Church , nor the
Creed it felfe tell you any fuch matter ; and
what necefsity is there, that one meanes of inftruction, muft inuolue whatfoeuer is contained
in all the reft ? We are not to recite the Creed
with anticipated perfwafion, that it muft containe what we imagine it ought , for better

maintayning fome opinions of our owne; but
we ought to fay, and belieue that it containes
what we find in it; of which one Article is to
belieue the *Catholique Church*,furely to be taught
by her, which prefuppofeth that we need other
inftruction befide the Creed : and in particuler
we may learne of her, what points be contained
in the Creed , what otherwife; and fo we fhall
not be deceiued, by belieuing we haue all in the
Creed, when we haue not all : and you may in
the fame manner fay : *As well,nay better,the Apoftles might haue giuen vs no Articles* at all , as haue
left out Articles tending to practife. For in fetting down one fort of articles, & not the other,
they make vs belieue we haue all, whē we haue not all.

27.   To our argument, that Baptifme is not
contayned in the Creed ; *D. Potter* , befides his
anfwere, that Sacraments belong rather to practife then fayth , (which I haue already confuted , and which indeed maketh agaynft himfelfe , and ferueth only to fhew that the Apoftles intended not to comprize all points in
the Creed which we are bound to belieue)
adds, that the *Creed of* (i) *Nice expreffed Bap-*
(i) *pag.* 237. *tifme by name ; confeffe one Baptifme for the remifsiō
of Sinne.* Which anfwere is directly againft him-
felfe,and manifeftly proues that Baptifme is an
Article of fayth , and yet is not contained in
the Apoftles Creed , neyther explicitely , nor
by any neceffary confequence from other Articles expreffed therein . If to make it an Article

cle of fayth be fufficient that it is contayned in
in the Nicene Councell; he will find that Proteftants maintayne many errours againft faith,
as being repugnant to definitions of Generall
Councels: as in particuler, that the very Coun- (k) *In his*
cell of *Nice* (which fayth *M. Whitgift*, (k) *is of defence pag:*
all wife and learned men reuerenced, efteemed & im- 330.
*braced, next vnto the Scriptures themfelues)*decreed
that, *to thofe who were chofen to the Miniftry vn-*
marryed, it was not lawfull to take any wife afterward,
is affirmed by Proteftants. And your grand Reformer *Luther (lib. de Concilijs part. prima)*fayth,
that he vnderftands not the Holy Ghoft in that
Councell. For in one Canon it fayth that thofe
who haue gelded themfelues are not fit to be
made Priefts; in another it forbids them to haue
wiues. *Hath (* fayth he*) the Holy Ghoft nothing to*
doe in Councells, but to binde, and loade his Mini-
sters which impofsblie, dangerous, and vnneceffary
lawes ? I forbeare to fhew that this very Article
I confeffe one Baptifme for the remifsion of finnes,
wilbe vnderftood by Proteftants in a farre different fenfe from Catholiques, yea Proteftants
among themfelues doe not agree, how Baptifme forgiues finnes, nor what grace it confers.
Only concerning the Vnity of Baptifme againft
rebaptization of fuch as were once baptized
(which I noted as a point not contained in the
Apoftles Creed) I cannot omit an excellent
place of *S. Auguftine*, where fpeaking of the
Donatifts he hath thefe words. *They are fo bold*

(m) *lib. de Hæref.in 6 9.*

as (m) *to rebaptize Catholiques, wherein they shew themselues to be the greater Heretiques, since it hath pleased the vniuersall Catholique Church not to make Baptisme void euen in the very Heretiques theselues.* In which few words this holy Father deliuereth agaynst the Donatists these points which doe also make against Protestants ; That to make an Heresy, or an Heretique, knowne for such, it is sufficient, to oppose the definition of Gods Church ; That a proposition may be Hereticall though it be not repugnant to any Texts of Scripture. For *S. Augustine* teacheth that the doctrine of rebaptization, is hereticall, and yet acknowledgeth it cannot be couinced for such out of Scripture. And that neyther the Heresy of rebaptization of those who were baptized by Heretiques, nor the contrary Catholique truth being expressed in the Apostles Creed, it followeth that it doth not containe all points of fayth necessary to saluation. And so we must conclude that to belieue the *Creed* is not sufficient for Vnity of fayth, and Spirit in the same Church, vnles there be also a totall agreement both in *beliefe* of other points of fayth, and in *externall profession,* and Communion also (wherof we are to speake in the next Chapter) according to the saying of *S. Augustine: You are* (n) *with vs in Baptisme,* and *in the Creed; but in the Spirit of Vnity, and bond of peace, and lastly in the Catholique Church you are not with vs.*

(n) *Aug.ep. 48.*

CHAP.

CHAP. V.

*That Luther, Caluin, their affociates,
and all vvho began, or continue
the feparation from the externall
Cōmunion of the Roman Church,
are guilty of the proper, and formall finne of Schifme.*

H E Searcher of all Hearts, is witneffe with how vnwilling mindes, we Catholiques are drawne to faften the denomination of Schifmatiques, or Heretiques, on them, for whofes foules, if they employed their beft bloud, they would iudge that it could not be better fpent. If we reioyce, that they are contriftated at fuch titles, our ioy rifeth not from their trrouble or griefe, but, as that of the Apoftles did, from the fountaine of Charity, *becaufe they are contriftated to repentance* ; that fo after vnpartiall examination, they finding themfelues to be what we fay, may by Gods holy grace,

be-

beginne to diſlike, what themſelues are. For our
part, we muſt remember that our obligation is,
to keep within the meane, betwixt vncharitable bitternes, & pernicious flatery; not yielding
to worldly reſpects, nor offending Chriſtian
Modeſty, but vttering the ſubſtance of truth in
ſo *Caritable* manner, that not ſo much we, as
Truth, and Charity may ſeeme to ſpeake, according to the wholeſome aduiſe of *S. Gregory
Nazianzen* in theſe diuine words : *We doe not af-*
(a)Orat.32. *fect peace with* (a)*preiudice of the true doctrine, that
ſo we may get a name of being gentle, and milde : &
yet we ſeeke to conſerue peace, fighting in a lawfull
manner, and contayning our ſelues within our compaſſe, and the rule of Spirit. And of theſe thinges
my iudgement is, and for my part I preſcribe the
ſame Law to all that deale with ſoules, and treate of
true doctrine, that neyther they exaſperate mens
minds by harſhnes, nor make tl̄e haughty or inſolent,
by ſubmiſſion ; but that in the cauſe of fayth they
behaue themſelues prudently, and aduiſedly, and doe
not in eyther of theſe things exceed the meane.* With
whome agreeth *S. Leo* ſaying : *It behoueth vs in*
(b)Epiſt. 8. *ſuch cauſes to be* (b)*moſt carefull, that without noiſe
of contentions, both Charity be conſerued, and Truth
maintayned.*

2. For better Methode, we will handle
theſe points in order. Firſt we will ſet downe
the nature, and eſſence, or as I may call it, the
Quality of *Schiſme.* In the ſecond place, the
greatnes & grieuouſnes, or (ſo to terme it) the

Quan-

Quantity thereof . For the Nature , or Quality will tell vs , who may without iniury be iudged Schifmatiques : and by the greatnes , or quantity, fuch as find themfelues guilty therof, will remaine acquainted with the true ftate of their foule, and whether they may conceiue any hope of faluation or no. And becaufe Schifme wil be found to be a diuifion from the Church, which could not happen , vnles there were alwayes a vifible Church; we wil, Thirdly proue, or rather take it as a point to be granted by all Chriftians, that in all ages there hath been fuch a Vifible Congregation of Faythfull People . Fourthly , we will demonftrate , that *Luther, Caluin* , and the reft, did feparate themfelues from the Communion of that alwayes vifible Church of Chrift, and therfore were guilty of *Schifme.* And fifthly we will make it euident, that the vifible true Church of Chrift , out of which *Luther* and his followers departed , was no other but the *Roman Church,* & confequently that both they, and all others who perfift in the fame diuifion, are Schifmatiques by reafon of their feparation from the Church of *Rome.*

3. For the firft point touching the *Nature,* or *Quality* of Schifme: as the naturall perfection of man confifts in his being the *image* of God his Creator, by the powers of his foule; fo his fupernaturall perfection is placed in *fimilitude* with God , as his laft End and Felicity ; and by hauing the faid fpirituall faculties , his *Vnder-Standing*

1. Point.

The nature of Schifme.

Standing and *Will* linked to him. His Vnderſtanding is vnited to God by *Fayth* ; his Will, by
Charity. The former relies vpon his infallible
Truth : The latter carrieth vs to his infinite
Goodnes. *Fayth* hath a deadly oppoſite, *Hereſy*.
Contrary to the Vnion, or Vnity of *Charity*, is
Separation and *Diuiſion*. Charity is twofold. As
it reſpects *God*, his Oppoſite Vice is *Hatred* a-
gainſt *God* : as it vniteth vs to our *Neighbour*, his
contrary is *Separation* or diuiſion of affections,
and will from our *Neighbour*. Our Neighbour
may be conſidered, either as one priuate perſon
hath a ſingle relation to another, or as all concur to make one Company or Congregation,
which we call the Church; and this is the moſt
principall reference and Vnion of one man
with another: becauſe the chiefeſt Vnity is that
of the *Whole*, to which the particular Vnity of
Parts is ſubordinate. This Vnity, or Oneneſſe
(if ſo I may call it) is effected by Charity vniting
all the members of the Church in one *Myſticall Body*; contrrary to which, is *Schiſme*, from
the Greeke word ſignifying *Sciſſure*, or *Diuiſion*.
Wherfore vpon the whole matter, we find that
Schiſme, as the Angelicall Doctor *S. Thomas* defines it, is ; *A voluntary ſeparation* (c) *from the
Vnity of that Charity, whereby all the members of the
Church are vnited*. From hence he deduceth, that
Schiſme is a ſpeciall and particular vice, diſtinct
from *Hereſy*, becauſe they are oppoſite to two
different Vertues: Hereſy, to Fayth: Schiſme, to
Cha-

(c) 2.2.q.39
art. in corp.
& ad 3.

Charity. To which purpofe he fitly alleadgeth
S. Hierome vpon thefe words, (*Tit.* 3.) *A man
that is an Heretique after the firft and fecond admo-
nition auoide,* faying : *I conceiue that there is this
difference betwixt Schifme and Herefy, that Herefy
inuolues fome peruerfe affertion: Schifme for Epifco-
pall diffention doth feparate men from the Church.*
The fame doctrine is deliuered by *S. Auguftine*
in thefe words: *Heretiques (d) and Schifmatiques
call their Congregations, Churches: but Heretiques
corrupt the Fayth by belieuing of God falfe things: but
Schifmatiques by wicked diuifions breake from fra-
ternall Charity, although they belieue what we belieue. Therefore the Heretique belongs not to the
Church, becaufe fhe loues God : nor the Schifmatique, becaufe she loues her Neighbour.* And in another place he fayth. *It is wont to be demaunded
(e) How Schifmatiques be diftinguifhed from Heretiques: and this difference is found, that not a diuers fayth, but the deuided Society of Communion
doth make Schifmatiques.* It is then euident that
Schifme is different from Herefy . Neuerthelefle (fayth *Saint Thomas* (f) as he who is depriued of faith muft needs want Charity; fo euery
Heretique is a Schifmatique, but not conuerfi-
uely, euery Schifmatique is an Heretique; thogh
becaufe want of Charity difpofes and makes
way to the deftruction of fayth (according to
thofe wordes of the Apoftle, *Which* (a good cō-
fcience) *fome cafting off, haue fuffered fhipwrack
in their fayth)* Schifme fpeedily degenerates to

(d) *lib.* 1. *de
fid. & Symb.
cap.* 10.

(e) *Queft.
Euangel. ex
Matt. q.* 11.

(f) *vbi fupra*

Herefy,

Herefy, as *S. Hierome* after the rehearfed words teacheth, faying: *Though Schifme in the beginning may in fome fort be vnderftood different from Herefy; yet there is no Schifme which doth not faigne fome herefy to it felfe, that fo it may feeme to haue departed from the Church vpon good reafon.* Neuertheles when Schifme proceeds originally from Herefy, Herefy as being in that cafe the predominant quality in thefe two peccant humours, giueth the denomination of an *Heretique*; as on the other fide we are wont, efpecially in the beginning, or for a while, to call *Schifmatiques,* thofe men who firft began with only *Schifme,* though in procefle of time they fell into fome *Herefy,* and by that meanes are indeed both Schifmatiques and Heretiques.

4.   The reafon why both Herefy and Schifme are repugnant to the being of a good *Catholique*, is: Becaufe the *Catholique,* or Vniuerfall Church fignifies *One* Congregation, or Company of Faithfull people, and therfore implies not only *Faith,* to make them *Faithfull* belieuers, but alfo *Communion,* or *Common Vnion,* to make them *One* in Charity, which excludes Separation, and *Diuifion*: and therfore in the Apoftles Creed, *Communion of Saints* is immediately ioyned to the *Catholique Church.*

5.   From this definition of Schifme may be inferred, that the guilt therof is contracted, not only by diuifion from the Vniuerfall Church; but alfo, by a Separation from a particular Church

Church or Dioceſſe which agrees with the V-
niuerſall. In this manner *Meletius* was a Schiſmatique,but not an Heretique , becauſe as we
read in *S.Epiphanus*, (h) he was *of the right Faith:*   (h)*Hæreſ.*
for his fayth was not altered at any time from the ho- 68.
ly Catholique Church &c. He made a Sect, but depar-
ted not from Fayth. Yet becauſe he made to himſelfe a particular Congregation againſt *S.Peter*
Archbiſhop of *Alexandria* his lawfull Superiour,and by that meanes brought in a diuiſion
in that particular Church , we was a Schiſmatique. And it is wel worth the noting , that the
Meletians building new Churches put this title
vpon them, *The Church of Martyrs*: and vpon the
ancient Churches of thoſe who ſucceeded *Pe-*
ter, was inſcribed , *The Catholique Church.* For ſo
it is. A new Sect muſt haue a new name which
though it be neuer ſo gay and ſpecious , as *the*
Church of Martyrs : the Reformed Church &c . yet
the Nouelty ſheweth that it is not the Catholique,nor a true Church. And that Schiſme may
be committed by diuiſion from a particular
Church,we read in *Optatus Mileuitanus (*i*)* theſe
remarkable words , (which do well declare (i) *Lib. 1.*
who be Schiſmatiques *)* brought by him to *cont. Par-*
proue that not *Cæcilianus* but *Parmenianus* was a *men.*
Schiſmatique: For *Cæcilianus went not out from*
Maiorinus thy Grand-Father (he meanes his next
predeceſſour but one, in the Biſhopricke, *) but*
Maiorinus from Cæcilianus : neither did Cæcilianus
depart from the Chaire of Peter,or of Cyprian (who
X 2   **was**

was but a particular Bishop,) *but Maiorinus, in whose Chaire thou sittest which had no beginning before Maiorinus himselfe. Seing it is manifestly knowne, that these things were so done, it euidently appeareth, that you are heires both of traditors (* that is, of those who deliuered vp the holy Bible to be burned) *and of Schismatiques.* And it seemeth that this kind of Schisme must principally be admitted by Protestants, who acknowledge no one visible Head of the whole Church, but hold that euery particular Diocesse, Church, or Countrey is gouerned by it selfe independantly of any one Person, or Generall Councell, to which all Christians haue obligation to submit their iudgments, and wills.

2. Point.

The grieuousnes of Schisme.

(1) *Supra art. 2. ad 3.*

6. As for the grieuousnes or quantity of Schisme (which was the second point proposed) S. *Thomas* teacheth, that amongst sinnes against our Neighbour, *Schisme* (1) is the most grieuous ; because it is against the spirituall good of the *multitude*, or *Community*. And therfore as in a *Kingdome* or *Common-wealth*, there is as great difference betweene the crime of rebellion or sedition, and debates among priuate men, as there is inequality betwixt one man, & a whole kingdome; so in the Church, *Schisme* is as much more grieuous then *Sedition* in a *Kingdome*, as the spirituall good of soules surpasseth the ciuill and politicall weale. And S. *Thomas* adds further, that they loose the spirituall *Power* of *Iurisdiction*; and if they goe about to absolue

from

from finnes, or to excommunicate, their actions
are inualid; which he proues out of the Canon
*Nouatianus. Caufa 7.quaeſt.1.*which fayth: *He that
keepeth neither the Vnity of fpirit, nor the peace of
agreement, and feparates himfelfe from the bond of
the Church, and the Colledge of Prieſts, can neither
haue the Power, nor dignity of a Biſhop.* The *Power*
alfo of *Order* (for example to confecrate the
Euchariſt, to ordaine Prieſts &c.) they cannot
lawfully exercife.

7. In the iudgment of the holy Fathers,
Schifme is a moſt grieuous offence. *S.Chryſoſtome*
(m) compares thefe Schifmaticall deuiders of
Chriſts *myſticall* body, to thofe who facrile- (m)Hom.11. in ep. ad E- phef.
gioufly pierced his *naturall* body, faying : *No-
thing doth fo much incenfe God, as that the Church
ſhould be deuided. Although we ſhould do innumerable good works, if we deuide the full Eccleſiaſticall
Congregation, we ſhall be puniſhed no leſſe then they
who tore his (*naturall*) *body. For that was done to
the gaine of the whole world, although not with that
intention: but this hath no profit at all, but there ari-
feth from it moſt great harme. Thefe things are
fpoken, not only to thofe who beare office, but alfo to
thofe who are gouerned by them.* Behold how neither a morall good life (which conceipt decei-
ueth many) nor authority of Magiſtrates, nor
any neceſſity of Obeying Superiours can excufe Schifme from being a moſt haynous of-
fence. *Optatus Mileuitanus* (o) calls Schifme, *In-* (o)lib.cont. Parmen.
gens flagitium: a huge crime. And fpeaking to the

Dona-

Donatists, fayth; that *Schifme is euill in the higheſt degree, euen you are not able to deny.* No leſſe patheticall is *S.* *Auguſtine* vpon this fubiect. He reckons Schifmatiques among Pagans, Heretiques, and Iewes, faying: *Religion is to be fought,* (p) *neither in the confuſion of Pagans, nor* (p) *in the filth of Heretiques, nor in the languiſhing of Schifmatiques, nor in the Age of the Iewes ; but among thoſe alone who are called Chriſtian Catholiques, or Orthodox, that is, louers of Vnity in the whole body, and followers of truth.* Nay he eſteems them worſe then Infidels and Idolaters, faying : *Thoſe whom the Donatiſts* (q) *heale from the wound of Infidelity and Idolatry, they hurt more grieuouſly with the wound of Schifme.* Let here thoſe men who are pleaſed vntruly to call vs Idolaters, reflect vpon themſelues, and confider, that this holy Father iudgeth Schifmatiques (as they are) to be worſe then Idolaters, which they abſurdly call vs: and this he proueth by the example of *Core, Dathan,* and *Abiron* and other rebellious Schifmatiques of the Old Teſtament, who were conuayed aliue downe into Hell, and puniſhed more openly then Idolaters. *No doubt* (fayth this holy Father) *but* (r) *that was committed moſt wickedly, which was puniſhed moſt feuerely.* In another place he yoaketh Schifme with Hereſy, faying vpon the Eight Beatitude : *Many* (s) *Heretiques, vnder the name of Chriſtians, deceiuing mens foules,* do fuffer many fuch things ; but therfore they are excluded from this reward, becauſe it is not only

ly

(p) *lib. de vera Relig. cap.* 6.

(q) *Cont. Donatiſt. l. 1. cap. 8.*

(r) *Ibid. lib. 2. cap. 6.*

(s) *De ſerm. Dom. in monte c.* 5.

ly faid, Happy are they who fuffer perfecution, „
but there is added, for Iuftice. But where there „
is not found fayth, there cannot be iuftice. Nei- „
ther can Schifmatiques promife to themfelues „
any part of this reward, becaufe likewife where „
there is no Charity, there cannot be iuftice. „
And in another place, yet more effectually he
faith: *Being out of (t) the Church, and diuided from*
the heape of Vnity, and the bond of Charity, thou
fhouldeft be punifhed with eternall death, though thou
fhouldeft be burned aliue for the name of Chrift. And
in another place, he hath thefe words: *If he heare*
not the Church let him be to (v) thee, as an Heathen
or Publican; which is more grieuous then if he were
fmitten with the fword, confumed with flames, or caft
to wild beafts. And elfe where: *Out of the Catho-*
lique Church (fayth he) one (w) may haue Fayth,
Sacraments, Orders, and in fumme, all things except
Saluation. With S. *Auguftine*, his Countreyman
and fecond felfe in fympathy of fpirit, S. *Ful-*
gentius agreeth, faying: *Belieue this (x) ftedfaftly*
without doubting, that euery Heretique, or Schifma-
tique, baptized in the name of the Father, the Sonne,
and the Holy Ghoft, if before the end of his life, he be
not reconciled to the Catholique Church, what Almes
foeuer he giue, yea though he should fhed his bloud for
the name of Chrift, he cannot obtaine Saluation.
Marke againe how no morall honefty of life,
no good deeds, no Martyrdome, can without
repentance auaile any Schifmatique for faluation. Let vs alfo add that *D. Potter* fayth : Schif-

(t) *Epift.204*

(u)*cont. ad-*
uerf. leg. &
prophet. lib.
2.cap.17.

(w) *de geft.*
cum Emerit.

(x)*de fide ad*
Pet.

me

(y)*Pag.* 42.

me is no leſſe (y) damnable, then Hereſy.

8.   But ô you Holy, Learned, Zealous Fathers, and Doƈtours of God's Church; out of theſe premiſes, of the grieuouſnes of Schiſme, & of the certaine damnation which it bringeth (if vnrepented) what concluſion draw you for the inſtruƈtion of Chriſtians? *S. Auguſtine* maketh this wholeſome inference. *There is (z) no iuſt neceſsity to diuide Vnity.* S. *Ireneus* concludeth : *They cannot* (a) *make any ſo important reformation, as the euill of the Schiſme is pernicious.* S. *Denis* of *Alexandria* ſayth : *Certainely* (b) *all things ſhould rather be indured, then to conſent to the diuiſion of the Church of God: thoſe Martyrs being no leſſe glorious, that expoſe themſelues to hinder the diſmembring of the Church, then thoſe that ſuffer rather then they will offer ſacrifice to Idols.* Would to God all thoſe who diuided thĕmſelues from that viſible Church of Chriſt, which was vpon earth when *Luther* appeared, would rightly conſider of theſe things! And thus much of the ſecond Point.

(z) *Cont.* *Parm.lib.*2. *cap.*62.
(a)*cont. he-reſ.lib.*4.*c.* 62.
(b) *Apud* *Euſeb. Hiſt.* *Eccleſ.lib.*6.

9.   We haue iuſt and neceſſary occaſion, eternally to bleſſe Almighty God, who hath vouchſafed to make vs members of the Catholique *Roman* Church, from which while men fall, they precipitate themſelues into ſo vaſt abſurdities, or rather ſacrilegious blaſphemies, as is implyed in the doƈtrine of the totall deficiency of the viſible Church, which yet is maintayned by diuers chiefe Proteſtants, as may at large

3. Point.

Perpetuall viſibility of the Church

large be feene in *Brereley*, and others; out of
whome I will heere name *Iewell* faying : *The
truth was vnknowne* (c) *at that tyme, and vnheard
of, when Martin Luther, and Vlderick Zuinglius
firſt came vnto the knowledge and preaching of the
Goſpell. Perkins* fayth : *We ſay, that* (d) *before the
dayes of Luther for the ſpace of many hundred yeares
an vniuerſall Apoſtaſy ouerſpread the whole face of
the earth, and that our* (Proteſtant) *Church was
not then viſible, to the world. Napier* vpon the *Reuelations* teacheth, that *from the yeare of* (e) *Chriſt
three hundred and ſixteene, the Antichriſtian and
papiſticall raigne hath begun, raigning vniuerſally,
and without any debatable contradiction one thouſand
two hundred ſixty yeares* (that is, till *Luthers* tyme :) And that, *from the yeare of* (f) *Chriſt three
hundred and ſixteen, God hath withdrawne his viſible Church from open Aſſemblies, to the hearts of
particular godly men &c. during the ſpace of one
thouſand two hundred threeſcore yeares:* And that,
the (g) *Pope and Clergy haue poſſeſſed the outward
viſible Church of Chriſtians, euen one thouſand two
hundred threeſcore yeares.* And that, *the* (h) *true
Church aboad latent, and inuiſible.* And Brocard
(i) vpon the *Reuelations*, profeſſeth to ioyne in
opinion with Napier . *Fulke* affirmeth, that *in
the* (k) *tyme of Boniface the third*, which was the
yeare 607. *the Church was inuiſible, and fled into
the wilernes, there to remaine a long ſeaſon. Luther*
fayth : *Primò ſolus eram : At the fiſt* (l) *I was a-
lone. Iacob Hailbronerus* one of the Diſputants for

the

(c) *Apolog.
part. 4. cap.
4. diuiſ.* 2.
*And in his
defèce prin-
ted Ann.*
1571. *pag.*
426.
(d) *Jn his
expoſition
vpon the
Creed pag.*
400.
(e) *Propoſ.*
37. *pag.* 68.
(f) *Ibid. in
cap.* 12. *pag.*
161. *col.* 3.
(g) *Ibid. in
cap.* 11. *pag.*
145.
(h) *Ibid. pag.*
191.
(i) *fol.* 110.
& 123.
(k) *Anſwere
to a counter-
fait Cath.
pag.* 16.
(l) *Jn præfat.
operum ſuo-
rum.*

the Proteſtant party in the Conference at Ra-
tisbone, affirmeth (m) that the true Church
was interrupted by Apoſtaſy from the true
Fayth. Caluin ſayth : *It is abſurd in the very (n)*
beginning to breake one from another, after we
haue beene forced to make a ſeparation from the
whole world. It were ouerlong to alledge the wordes of *Ioannes Regius, Daniel Chamierus, Beza,*
Ochimus, Caſtalio, and others to the ſame purpoſe. The reaſon which caſt them vpon this
wicked doctrine, was a deſperate voluntary
neceſſity : becauſe they being reſolued not to ac-
knowledg the Romā Church to be Chriſts true
Church, & yet being conuinced by all manner
of euidence, for that diuers Ages before *Luther*
there was no other Congregation of Chriſtians, which conld be the Church of Chriſt ;
there was no remedy but to affirme, that vpon
earth Chriſt had no viſible Church : which they
would neuer haue auouched, if they had known
how to auoyd the foreſayd inconuenience (as
they apprehended it) of ſubmitting themſelues
to the *Roman* Church.

10. Agaynſt theſe exterminating ſpirits,
D. Potter, and other more moderate Proteſtants,
profeſſe, that Chriſt alwayes had, and alwayes
will haue vpon earth a viſible Church : other-
therwiſe (ſayth he) *our Lords (o) promiſe of her*
ſtable (p) edification ſhould be of no value. And in
another place, hauing affirmed that Proteſtāts
haue not left the Church of Rome, but her corruptions,

(m) In ſuo
Acacatholi-
co volum. 4.
15.cap. 9. p.
479.
(n) Ep.141.

(o) pag. 154
(p) Matt.16
14.

ruptions, and acknowledging her still to be a member of Christs body, he seeketh to cleere himselfe and others from *Schisme,* becaufe (faith he) *the property* (q) *of Schifme is (witnesse the Donatists and Luciferians) to cut off from the Body of Christ, & the hope of saluation, the Church frō which it separates. And if any Zelotes amongst vs haue proceeded to heauier cenfures, their zeale may be excused, but their Charity and wifedome cannot be iustifyed.* And elfwhere he acknowledgeth, that the Roman Church hath *thofe maine, and* (r) *essentiall truths, which giue her the name and essence of a Church.*

(q) *pag.* 76.

(r) *Pag.* 83.

11. It being therefore granted by D. Potter, and the chiefest and best learned English Proteftants, that Chrifts vifible Church cannot perifh, it will be needles for me in this occafion to proue it. *S. Augustine* doubted not to fay: *The Prophets* (s) *spoke more obfcurely of Christ, then of the Church : becaufe, as I thinke, they did forefee in spirit, that men were to make parties ngaynst the Church, and that they were not to haue fo great strife concerning Christ : therefore that was more plainely foretold & more openly prophecyed about which greater contentions were to rife, that it might turne to the condemnation of them, who haue feen it, and yet gone forth.* And in another place he fayth : *How doe we confide* (t) *to haue reccaued manifestly Christ himfelfe from holy Scriptures, if we haue alfo manifestly receaued the Church from them?* And indeed to what Gongregatiō fhall a man haue recourfe

(s) *In Pfalm. 30. Com.* 2.

(t) *epist.* 48.

for

for the affaires of his foule, if vpon earth there
be no vifible Church of Chrift? Befides, to imagine a company of men belieuing one thing in
their hart, and with their mouth profeffing
the contrary, (as they muft be fuppofed to doe;
for if they had profeffed what they belieued,
they would haue become vifible) is to dreame
of a damned crew of diffembling Sycophants,
but not to conceiue a right notiō of the Church
of Chrift our Lord. And therefore *S. Auguftine*
fayth : *We cannot be faued, vnles labouring alfo for*
the (u) *faluation of others, we profeffe with our*
mouths, the fame fayth which we beare in our harts.
And if any man hold it lawfull to diffemble, &
deny matters of fayth, we cannot be affured,
but that they actually diffemble, and hide A-
nabaptifme, Arianifme, yea Turcifme, & euen
Atheifme, or any other falfe beliefe, vnder the
outward profeffion of Caluinifme. Doe not
Proteftants teach that, preaching of the word,
and adminiftration of Sacraments (which cānot but make a Church vifible) are infeparable
notes of the true Church? And therfore they
muft eyther grant a vifible Church, or none at
all. No wonder then if *S. Auguftine* account
this Herefy fo groffe, that he fayth againft thofe
who in his tyme defended the like errour : *But*
this Church which (w) hath beene of all Nations is
no more, (fhe hath perished; fo fay they that are not
in her. O impudent fpeach ! And afterward. This
voyce fo abominable, fo detestable, fo full of prefump-
                                                    tion

(u) *S. Aug.*
de fide &
Symbolo c. 1.

(w) *In Pfal.*
101.

tion and fallhood, which is sufteined with no truth, enlightned with no wifdome, feafoned with no falt, vaine, rafh, heady, pernicious, the Holy Ghoft forefaw &c. And, *Peraduenture fome* (x) *one may fay, there are other Sheepe I know not where, with which I am not acquainted, yet God hath care of them. But he is too abfurd in humane fenfe, that can imagine fuch things.* And thefe men do not confider, that while they deny the perpetuity of a vifible Church, they deftroy their owne prefent Church, according to the argument which *S. Auguftine* vrged againft the *Donatifts* in thefe words : *If the Church were loft in Cyprians* (we may fay in Gregories)*time, from whence did Donatus* (Luther)*appeare? From what earth did he fpring? from what fea is he come? From what heauen did he drop?* And in another place : *How can they vaunt* (z) *to haue any Church, if he haue ceafed euer fince thofe times?* And all Deuines by defining *Schifme* to be a diuifion from the true Church, fuppofe, that there muft be a knowne Church, from which it is poffible for men depart. But enough of this in thefe few words.

(x) De ouib. cap. 1.

(y)De Bapt. cont. Donat.

(z) Lib. 3. cont. Parm.

12. Let vs now come to the fourth, and chiefeft Point, which was, to examine whether *Luther, Caluin,* and the reft did not depart from the externall Communion of Chrifts vifible Church, and by that feparation became guilty of Schifme. And that they are properly Schifmatiques cleerely followeth from the grounds which we haue layed, concerning the nature of

4. Point.

Luther and all that follow him are Schifmatiques.

Schifme,

Schifme, which confifts in leauing the externall Cummunion of the vifible Church of
Chrift our Lord:and it is cleere by euidence of
fact, that *Luther* and his followers forfooke the
Communion of that Ancient Church. For they
did not fo much as pretend to ioyne with any
Congregation which had a being before their
time;for they would needs conceiue that no vifible Company was free from errours in doctrine,and corruption in practife: And therfore
they oppofed the doctrine;they withdrew their
obedience from the Prelates;they left partici-
pation in Sacraments; they changed the Liturgy of publique feruice of whatfoeuer Church
then extant. And thefe things they pretended
to do out of a perfwafion,that they were bound
(forfooth)in confcience fo to do, vnleffe they
would participate with errors, corruptions, &
fuperftitions. *We dare not (* fayth *D. Potter)com-*
municate (a) *with Rome either in her publique Li-*
turgy, which is manifeftly polluted with groffe fuper-
ftition &c. or in thofe corrupt and vngrounded opi-
nions, which fhe hath added to the Fayth of Catho-
liques. But now let *D.Potter* tell me with what
vifible Church extant before *Luther*, he would
haue aduentured to communicate in her publique *Liturgy* and *Doctrine*, fince he durft not
communicate with *Rome?* He will not be able
to affigne any, euen with any litle colour of
common fenfe. If then they departed from all
vifible Communities profeffing Chrift, it fol-
                                        loweth

(a) *pag.* 68.

loweth that they also left the Communion of the true visible Church, which soeuer it was, whether that of *Rome*, or any other; of which Point I do not for the present dispute. Yea this the *Lutherans* do not only acknowledge, but proue, and brag of. If (sayth a learned *Lutheran*) there had been right (b) *belieuers which went before Luther in his office, there had then been no need of a Lutheran Reformation.* Another affirmeth it to be ridiculous, to thynke that *in the time* (c) *before Lu ther, any had the purity of Doctrine; and that Luther should receiue it from them, and not they from Lu ther.* Another speaketh roundly, and sayth it is impudency to say, that *many learned men* (d) *in Germany before Luther, did hold the Doctrine of the Gospell.* And I add: That far *greater impudency,* it were to affirme that *Germany* did not agree with the rest of Europe, and other Christian Catho- lique Nations, and consequently, that it is the greatest *impudency* to deny, that he departed from the Communion of the visible Catholi- que Church, spread ouer the whole world. We haue heard *Caluin* saying of Protestants in ge- nerall; *We were, euen, forced* (e) *to make a separa- tion from the whole world.* And, *Luther* of himself in particular: *In the beginning* (f) *I was alone.* *Ergo* (say I, by your good leaue) you were at least a *Schismatique,* deuided from the Ancient Church, and a member of no new Church. For no sole man can constitute a Church; & thogh he could, yet such a Church could not be that

glo-

(b) *Georgius Milius in Augustan. Confess. art. 7. de Eccles. pag. 157.*
(c) *Benedict. Morgestern.*
tract de Ec- clef. pag. 145.
(d) *Conrad. Schlusselb. in Theolog. Cal- uinist. lib. 2. fol. 130.*

(e) *Ep. 141.*
(f) *In praefat. operum sua- rum.*

glorious company, of whofe number , great-
neſſe, and amplitude, ſo much hath been ſpoken both in the old Teſtament , & in the New.

13.   *D. Potter* endeauours to auoide this e-
uident Argumēt by diuers euaſions ; but by the
confutation thereof I will (with Gods holy
aſſiſtance) take occaſion, euen out of his owne
Anſwers and grounds , to bring vnanſwerable
reaſons to conuince them of *Schiſme.*

14.   His chiefe Anſwere is : That they haue
not left the *Church,* but her *Corruptions.*

15.   I reply. This anſwere may be giuen eyther by thoſe furious people , who teach that
thoſe abuſes , and corruptions in the Church
were ſo enormous , that they could not ſtand
with the nature , or being of a true Church of
Chriſt : Or elſe by thoſe other more calme Proteſtants, who affirme that thoſe errours did not
deſtroy the *being,* but only deforme the *beauty*
of the Church. Againſt both theſe ſorts of men,
I may fitly vſe that vnanſwerable Dilemma ,
which S. *Auguſtine* brings againſt the *Dona-*
tiſts in theſe concluding words : *Tell me whether*
the (g) *Church at that tyme when you ſay ſhe enter-*
tayned thoſe who were guilty of all crimes, by the con-
tagion of thoſe ſinnefull perſons, periſhed, or periſhed
not ? Anſwere ; whether the Church periſhed , or pe-
riſhed not? Make choyce of what you thinke. If then
ſhe periſhed, what Church brought forth Donatus?
(we may ſay Luther.) *But if ſhe could not periſh,*
becauſe ſo many were incorporated into her (without
Bap-

(g) Lib. 2.
cont. epiſt.
Gaudent. c.

Baptifme (that is, *without* a fecõd baptifme, or rebaptization, & I may fay, without Luthers reformation) *anfwere me I pray you, what madnes did
moue the Sect of Donatus to feparate themfelues from
her vpõ pretence to auoid theCõmunion of bad men?* I
befeech theReader to põder euery one of *S. Auguftine* words: & to confider whether any thing
could haue been fpoken more directly againft
Luther, & his followers of what fort foeuer.

16.   And now to anfwere more in particular; I fay to thofe who teach, that the vifible
Church of Chrift perifhed for many Ages, that
I can eafily affoard them the courtefy, to free
them from meere *Schifme*: but all men touched
with any fparke of zeale to vindicate the wifedome, and Goodnes of our Sauiour from blaf-
phemous iniury, cannotchoofe but belieue and
proclaime them to be fuperlatiue Arch-heretiques. Neuertheles, if they will needs haue the
honour of Singularity, and defire to be both
formall Heretiques, & *properly Schifmatiques*, I will
tell them, that while they dreame of an inuifible Church of men, which agreed with them in
Fayth, they will vpon due reflection find themfelues to beSchifmatiques, from thofe corporeal
Angels, or inuifible men, becaufe *they* held external Communion with the vifilbe Church of
thofe times, the outward Cõmunion of wch vifibleChurch *thefe* moderne hot-fpurs forfaking,
were therby diuided frõ the outward Communion of their hidden Brethren, & fo are Separa-

tifts from the external *Communion* of them, with whome they agree in *fayth*, which is Schifme in the moft formall, and proper fignification thereof. Moreouer according to *D. Potter*, thefe boyfterous Creatures are properly Schifmatiques. For, the reafon why he thinks himfelfe, and fuch as he is, to be cleared from Schifme, notwithftanding their diuifion from the *Roman* Church, is becaufe (according to his Diuinity) the property of (h) *Schifme, is (witneffe the Donatifts and Luciferians) to cut off from the Body of Chrift, and the hope of Saluation, the Church from which it feparats:* But thofe Proteftants of whome we now fpeake, *cut off from the Body of Chrift, and the hope of Saluation,* the Church from which they feparated themfelues; and they doe it directly as the Donatifts (in whome you exéplify)did by affirming that the true Church had perifhed: and therefore they cannot be cleared from *Schifme*, if you may be their Iudge. Confider, I pray you, how many prime Proteftants both domefticall and forraine, you haue at one blow ftrucke off from hope of Saluation, and condemned to the loweft pit, for the grieuous finne of *Schifme.* And withall it imports you to confider, that you alfo inuolue your felfe, and other moderate Proteftants in the felfe fame crime and punifhment, while you communicate with thofe, who, according to your owne principles, are properly, and formally *Schifmatiques.* For if you held your felfe

obli-

(h) Pag.76.

obliged vnder paine of damnation to forſake
the Communion of the *Roman* Church, by reaſon of her Errors and Corruptions, which yet
you confeſſe were *not fundamentall* ; ſhall it not
be much more damnable for you, to liue in
Communion and Confraternity, with thoſe
who defend an errour of the fayling of the
Church, which in the *Donatiſts* you confeſſe (i)
to haue been *properly hereticall againſt the Article* (i) *pag.* 12*.*
of our Creed ; I beleeue the Church? And I deſire
the Reader, heer to apply an authority of *S. Cyprian* (*ep.* 76.) which he ſhall find alledged in
the next number. And this may ſuffice for confutation of the aforeſaid Anſwere, as it might
haue relation to the rigid Caluiniſts.

17. For Confutation of thoſe Proteſtants,
who hold that the Church of Chriſt had alwayes a being, and cannot erre in points fundamentall, and yet teach, that ſhe may erre in
matters of leſſe moment, wherin if they forſake her, they would be accounted not to leaue
the Church, but only her corruptions; I muſt
ſay, that they change the ſtate of our preſent
Queſtion, not diſtinguiſhing between *internall*
Fayth, and *externall Communion*, nor between
Schiſme, and *Hereſy.* This I demonſtrate out of
D. Potter himſelfe, who in expreſſe words teacheth, that the promiſes which *our Lord hath*
made (k) *vnto his Church for his aſſiſtance, are in* (k) *pa.*151*.*
tended, not to any particular Perſons or Churches, but
only to the Church Catholique: and they are to be ex-

Z 2 *tended*

tended not to euery parcel,or particularity of truth,but only to points of Faith,or fundamentall. And afterwards speaking of the *Vniuerfall Church* , he

(l) pag. 155. sayth : *It's comfort* (l) *inough for the Church , that the Lord in mercy will secure her from all capitall dangers, and conserue her on earth against all enemies ; but she may not hope to triumph ouer all sinne and errour , till she be in heauen.* Out of which words I obserue,that,according to *D.Potter,*the selfe same Church , which is the Vniuerfall Church, remayning the vniuerfall true Church of Chrift, may fall into errors and corruptions: from whence it cleerely followeth that it is impoſſible to leaue the *Externall communion* of the Church so corrupted,and retaine *externall* communion with the Catholique Church; since the Church Catholique, and the Church so corrupted is the selfe same one Church, or company of men. And the contrary imagination talkes in a dreame, as if the errors and infections of the Catholique Church were not inherent in her, but were feparate from her, like to *Accidents* without any *Subiect,*or rather indeed,as if they were not *Accidents*, but *Hypoſtaſes,* or *Perſons* subsisting by themselues. For men cannot be said to liue,in, or out of the Communion of any dead creature , but with Perſons , endued with life and reaſon;and much leſſe can men be said to liue in the Communion of Accidents,as errors and corruptions are,and therfore it is an abſurd thing to affirme,that Proteſtants diuided them-

théfelues from the corruptions of the Church,
but not from the Church herfelfe, feing the
corruptions of the Church were inherent in
the Church. All this is made more cleere, if we
confider, that when *Luther* appeared, there were
not two diftinct vifible true Catholique Churches, holding contrary Doctrines, and diuided
in externall Communion; one of the which
two Churches did *triumph ouer all error*, and corruption in doctrine and practife; but the other
was ftained with both. For to faigne this diuerfity of two Churches cannot ftand with record
of hiftories, which are filent of any fuch matter. It is againft *D. Potters* owne grounds, that
the Church may erre in points not fundamentall, which were not true, if you will imagine a
certaine vifible Catholique Church free from
error euen in points not fundamentall. It con-
tradicteth the words in which he faid, the
Church *may not hope to triumph ouer all error, till
fhe be in heauen.* It euacuateth the brag of Proteftants, that *Luther* reformed the whole Church:
and laftly it maketh *Luther* a Schifmatique, for
leauing the Cómunion of all vifible Churches,
feeing (vpon this fuppofition) there was a vifible Church of Chrift free from al corruption,
which therefore could not be forfaken without
iuft imputation of *Schifme.* We muft therefore
truly affirme, that fince there was but one vifible Church of Chrift, which was truly Catholique, and yet was (according to Proteftants)

ftai-

ftained with corruption; when *Luther* left the
external Cōmunion of that corrupted Church,
he could not remaine in the Communion of
the Catholique Church, no more then it is poffible to keep company with *Chriſtopher Potter*,
and not keepe company with the Prouoſt of
Queenes Colledge in Oxford , if *D. Potter* and
the Prouoſt be one, and the felfe fame man: For
fo one ſhould be, and not be with him at the
fame time. This very argument drawne from
the Vnity of God's Church , *S. Cyprian* vrgeth
to conuince, that *Nouatianus* was cut off from

the Church in thefe words: *The Church* is (m)
*One, which being One cannot be both within and with-
out . If ſhe be with Nouatianus, ſhe was net with Cornelius. But if she were with Cornelius , who ſuccecded
Fabianus, by laſtfull ordination, Nouatianus is not in
the Church.* I purpofely heere fpeak only of *externall Cōmunion* with the Catholique Church.
For in this point there is great difference between *internall acts* of our Vnderſtanding , and
will ; and of *externall deeds.* Our Vnderſtanding
and Will are faculties (as Philofophers fpeake)
abſtractiue, and able to diſtinguiſh , and as it
were, to part things, though in themfelues they
be really conioyned. But reall externall deeds do
take things in groſſe as they find them , not fe-
parating things which in reality are ioyned together. Thus, one may confider and loue a finner as he is a man, frĩed, benefactor, or the like;
and at the fame time not confider him, nor loue
him

him as he is a finner; becaufe thefe are acts of our
Vnderftanding, and Will, which may refpect
their obiects vnder fome one formality, or confideration, without reference to other things
contained in the felfe fame obiects. But if one
fhould ftrike, or kill a finnefull man, he will not
be excufed, by alledging, that he killed him, not
as a man, but as a finner; becaufe the felfe fame
perfon being a man, and the finner, the *externall*
act of murder fell iointly vpon the man, & the
finner. And for the fame reafon one cannot
auoide the company of a finner, and at the
fame time be really prefent with that man who
is a finner. And this is our cafe: and in this our
Aduerfaries are egregiously, and many of them
affectedly, miftaken. For one may in fome
points belieue as the Church belieueth, and difagree from her in other. One may loue the truth
which fhe holds, and deteft her (pretended) corruptions. But it is impoffible that a man fhould
really feparate himfelfe from her externall
Communion, as fhe is corrupted, and be really
within the fame externall Communion as fhe
is found; becaufe fhe is the felfe fame Church
which is fuppofed to be found in fome things,
and to erre in others. Now, our queftion for the
prefent doth concerne only this point of *externall Communion:* becaufe *Schifme*, as it is diftin-
gui hed from *Herefy*, is committed when one di-
ui es himfelfe from the *Externall Communion*
of that Church with which he agrees in *Fayth*;
Wheras

Wheras Herefy doth neceflarily imply a difference in matter of *Fayth*, and beliefe : and therfore to fay, that they left not the vifibleChurch,
but her errors, can only excufe them from *Herefy* (which fhall be tried in the next Chapter)
but not from *Schifme*, as long as they are really
diuided from the *Externall Communion* of the
felfe fame vifible Church; which, notwithftanding thofe errors wherin they do in iudgment
diflent from her, doth ftill remaine the true Catholique Church of Chrift; and therfore while
they forfake the corrupted Church, they forfake the Catholique Church. Thus then it remaineth cleere, that their chiefeft Anfwere
changeth the very ftate of the Queftion ; con-
foundeth internall acts of the Vnderftanding
with *externall Deeds* ; doth not diftinguifh between *Schifme* and *Herefy* ; and leaues this demonftrated againft them : That they diuided
themfelues from the Communion of the vifible Catholique Church, becaufe they concea-
ued that fhe needed Reformation. But whether
this pretence of Reformation will acquit them
of *Schifme*, I refer to the vnpartiall Iudges here-
(n) *Num. 8.* tofore (n) alledged; as to *S. Irenæus* who plainely fayth: *They cannot make any fo important R E-
FORMATION, as the Euill of the Schifme is
pernicious.* To *S. Denis* of *Alexandria*, faying:
*Certainely all things fhould be indured rather then to
confent to the diuifion of the Church of God : thofe
Martyrs being no leffe glorious that expofe themfel-*
ues

nes to hinder the dismembring of the Church, then *those that suffer rather then they will offer sacrifice to Idols.* To *S. Augustine,* who tels vs : That not to heare the Church, *is a more grieuous thing then if he were striken with the sword, consumed with flames, exposed to wild beasts.* And to conclude all in few wordes, he giueth this generall prescription : *There is no iust necessity, to diuide Vnity.* And *D. Potter* may remember his owne words : *There neither was (s) nor can be any iust cause to depart from the Church of Christ; no more then from Christ himselfe.* But I haue shewed that *Luther,* and the rest departed from the Church of Christ (if Christ had any Church vpon earth:) Therfore there could be no iust cause (of *Reformation,* or what else soeuer)to do as they did; and therfore they must be contented to be held for *Schisma-tiques.*

(s) *pag.* 75.

18   Moreouer ; I demaund whether those corruptions which moued them to forsake the Communion of the visible Church , were in manners, or doctrine? Corruption in manners yields no sufficient cause to leaue the Church , otherwise men must go not onely out of the Church , but out of the world, as the Apostle (t) sayth. Our blessed Sauiour foretold that there would be in the Church tares with choice corne , & sinners with iust men. If then Protestants waxe zealous, with the *Seruants* to plucke vp the weeds, let them first harken to the wisdome of the *Maister : Let both grow vp.*

(t) *1.Cor.* 5. 10,

A a   And

And they ought to imitate them , who as *S.*
Auguſtine ſaith : *tolerate for the (u)good of Vni-* (u) *Ep.162.*
ty , that which they deteſt for the good of equity. And
to whome the more frequent , and foule ſuch
ſcandals are; by ſo much the more is the merit
of their perſeuerance in the Communion of
the Church , and the Martyrdome of their patience, as the ſame Saint cals it. If they were offended with the life of ſome Eccleſiaſticall perſons , muſt they therefore deny obedience to
their Paſtours , and finally breake with Gods
Church ? The Paſtour of Paſtours, teacheth vs
another leſſon : *Vpon the Chaire of Moyſes* (w) (w) *Mat.33.*
haue ſitten the Scribes & Phariſes. All thinges there-
fore whatſoeuer they ſhall ſay to you , obſerue yee , &
doe yee : but according to their workes do yee not. Muſt
people except agaynſt lawes , and reuolt from
Magiſtrates , becauſe ſome are negligent , or
corrupt in the execution of the ſame lawes, and
performance of their office ? If they intended
Reformation of manners, they vſed a ſtrange
meanes for the achieuing of ſuch an end, by denying the neceſſity of Confeſſion , laughing at
auſterity of pennance, condemning the vowes
of Chaſtity, pouerty, obedience, breaking faſts,
&c. And no leſſe vnfit were the *Men* , then the
Meanes. I loue not recrimination. But it is well
knowne to how great crimes , *Luther* , *Caluin* ,
Zwinglius , *Beza.*, and other of the prime Reformers were notoriouſly obnoxious ; as might be
eaſily demonſtrated by the only tranſcribing of
what

what others haue deliuered vpon that fubiect ;
whereby it would appeare,that they were very
farre from being any fuch Apoftolicall men as
God is wont to vfe in fo great a worke . And
whereas they were wont, efpecially in the beginning of their reuolt, malicioufly to exagge-
rate the faults of fomeClergy men,*Erafmus* faid
well (*Epift ad fratres inferioris Germaniæ,*) *Let*
the riot , luft , ambition , auarice of Prieſts , and
whatfoeuer other crimes be gathered together, Herefy
*alone doth exceed all this filthy lake of vices.*Befides,
nothing at all was omitted by the facred Councell of *Trent* which might tend to reformation
of manners. And finally the vices of others are
not hurtfull to any but fuch as imitate,and confent to them;according to the faying of *S. Augu-*
ftine: *We conferue* (y) *innocency,not by knowing the*
ill deeds of men,but by not yielding confent to fuch as
We know, and by not iudging rafhly of fuch faults as
*we know not.*If you anfwere;that,not corruption
in manners,but the approbation of them, doth
yield fufficient caufe to leaue the Church; I reply with *S. Auguſtine*; That the Church doth
(as the pretended Reformers ought to haue
done)tolerate or beare with fcandals and corruptions, but neither doth, nor can approue
them. *The Church* (fayth he) *being placed* (z) *be-*
twixt much chaffe and cockle , doth beare with many
things; but doth not approue,nor diffemble , nor act
thofe things which are againſt fayth, and good life.
But becaufe to approue corruption in manners

(y) *De unit.*
Ecclef.c.2.

(z) *Ep.* 116.

as lawfull, were an errour againſt Fayth, it belongs to corruption in doctrine, which was the
ſecond part of my demaund.

19. Now then, that corruptions in doctrine
(I ſtill ſpeake vpon the vntrue ſuppoſition of
our Aduerſaries) could not affoard any ſufficiēt
cauſe, or colourable neceſſity to depart from
that viſible Church, which was extant when
Luther roſe, I demonſtrate out of *D. Potters* own
confeſſion ; that the Catholique Church neither hath, nor can erre in points *fundamentall*, as
we ſhewed out of his owne expreſſe words,
which he alſo of ſet purpoſe deliuereth in diuers
other places ; and all they are obliged to maintaine the ſame who teach that Chriſt had alwayes a viſible Church vpon earth : becauſe
any one *fundamentall* error ouerthrowes the *being* of a true Church. Now (as Schoolemen
ſpeake)it is, *implicatio in terminis* (a contradiction ſo plaine, that one word deſtroyeth the o-
ther, as if one ſhould ſay, a liuing dead man) to
affirme that the Church doth not erre in points
neceſſary to ſaluation, or damnably; & yet that
it is damnable to remaine in her Communion
becauſe ſhe teacheth errors which are confeſſed
not to be damnable. For if the error be not damnable, nor againſt any fundamentall Article of
Fayth, the beliefe therof cannot be damnable.
But *D. Potter* teacheth, that the Catholique
Church *cannot*, and that the *Roman* Church *hath
not* erred againſt any fundamentall Article of
Fayth;

Fayth. Therfore, it cannot be damnable to remaine in her Communion; and so the pretended corruptions in her doctrine could not induce any obligation to depart from her Communion, nor could excuse them from Schisme,
who vpon prece of necessity in point of conscience, forsooke her. And *D Potter* will neuer
be able to salue a manifest contradiction in these
his words: *To depart from the Church (a) of Rome* (a) *Pag.75.*
in some Doctrine, and practises, there might be neces-
sary cause, though she wanted nothing necessary to sal-
uation. For if, notwithstanding these doctrines
and practises, *she wanted nothing necessary to sal-*
uation; how could it be *necessary to saluation* to
forsake her? And therfore we must still cóclude
that to forsake her, was properly an act of
Schisme.

20. From the selfe same ground of the infallibility of the Church in all fundamentall
points, I argue after this manner. The visible
Church cannot be forsaken, without damnation, vpon pretence that it is damnable to remaine in her Communion, by reason of corruption in doctrine; as long as, for the truth of
her Fayth and beliefe, she performeth the duty
which she oweth to God, and her Neighbour:
As long as she performeth what our Sauiour
exacts at her hands; as long as she doth, as much
as lies in her power to do. But (euen according
to *D Potters* Assertions) the Church performeth
all these things, as long as she erreth not in

points

points fundamentall, although fhe were fuppofed to erre in other points not fundamentall. Therefore, the Communion of the Vifible Church cannot be forfaken without damnatió, vpon pretence that it is damnable to remaine in her Communion, by reafon of corruption in doctrine. The *Maior*, or firft Propofition of it felfe is euident. The *Minor*, or fecond Propofition doth neceffarily follow out of *D. Potters* owne doctrine aboue rehearfed, That, the *promifes of our Lord made to his Church for his afsi-*
(b)*Pag.151.* *stance, are to be* (b) *extended only to points of Fayth, or fundamentall:* (Let me note heer by the way that by his (Or,) he feemes to exclude from Fayth all points which are not fundamentall, & fo we may deny innumerable Texts of Scri-
(c)*pag. 155.* pture:) That, *It is* (c) *comfort inough for the Church, that the Lord in mercy will fecure her from all capitall dangers &c.* but *she may not hope to triumph ouer all finne and error, till she be in heauen.* For it is euident, that the Church (for as much as concernes the truth of her doctrines and beliefe)owes no more duty to God and her Neighbour; neither doth our Sauiour exact more at her hands, nor is it in her power to do more then God doth affift her to doe; which affiftáce is promifed only for points fundamentall; and confequently as long as fhe teacheth no fundamentall error, her Cómunion cannot without damnation be forfake: And we may fitly apply againft *D. Potter* a Concionatory declamation
which

which he makes againſt vs, where he ſayth: *May* (d) *pag. 221.* *the Church of after-Ages make the narrow way to heauen, narrowier then our Sauiour left it &c?* ſince he himſelfe obligeth men vnder paine of damnation to forſake the Church, by reaſon of errours againſt which our Sauiour thought it needles to promiſe his aſſiſtance, and for which he neither denieth his grace in this life, or glory in the next. Will *D.Potter* oblige the Church to do more then ſhe *may* euen hope for? or to performe on earth that which is proper to heauen alone?

21. And as from your owne doctrine concerning the infallibility of the Church in fundamentall points, we haue proued that it was a grieuous ſinne to forſake her : ſo doe we take a ſtrong argument from the fallibility of any who dare pretend to reforme the Church, which any man in his wits will belieue to be indued with at laſt as much infallibility as priuate men can challenge : and *D. Potter* expreſſely affirmeth that Chriſts promiſes of his aſſiſtance *are not intended*(e *) to any par-* (e) *Pag. 151.* *ticuler perſons or Churches* : and therefore to leaue the Church by reaſon of errours, was at the beſt hand but to flit from one erring company to another, without any new ʼope of triumphing ouer errours, and without neceſſity, or vtility to forſake that Communion of which *S. Augu-* (f) *Ep.cont.* *ſtine* ſayth, *There is* (f) *no iuſt neceſsity to diuide V- ʼParmen.lib.* *nity.* Which will appeare to be much more eui- 2. *cap. 11.* dent

dent if we cōsider that though the Church had maintained some false doctrines, yet to leaue her Communion to remedy the old, were but to add a new increase of errors, arising from the innumerable disagreements of Sectaries, which must needs bring with it a mighty masse of falshoods, because the truth is but one, & indiuisible. And this reason is yet stronger, if we still remember that euen according to *D. Potter* the visible Church hath a blessing not to erre in points fundamentall, in which any priuate *Reformer* may faile: and therfore they could not pretend any necessity to forsake that Church, out of whose Communion they were exposed to danger of falling into many more, and euen into damnable errors. Remember I pray you, what your selfe affirmes (*Pag.* 69.) where speaking of our Church and yours, you say: *All the difference is from the weeds, which remaine there, and heere are taken away ; Yet neither heere perfectly, nor euery where alike* Behold a faire cōfession of corruptiōs, still remayning in your Church, which you can only excuse by saying they are not fundamētal, as likewise those in the *Roman* Church are confessed to be not fundamentall. What man of iudgment wilbe a Protestant, since that Church is confessedly a corrupt One?

22.　I still proceed to impugne you expresly vpon your grounds. You say: *that it is comfort inough for the Church, that the Lord in mercy will secure her from all capitall dangers : but she may not*
hope

*hope to triumph ouer all sinne, and errour till she
be in heauen.* Now if it be comfort *inough* to be
secured from all capital dagers, which can arise
only from errour in fundamentall points: why
were not your first Reformers content with
Inough, but would needs dismeber the Church,
out of a pernicious greedines of more then *Inough?* For, this *Inough,* which according to you
is attained by not erring in points not funda-
metal was enioyed before *Luthers* reformation,
vnlesse you will now against your selfe affirme,
that long before *Luther* there was no Church free
from errour in fundamental points. Moreouer
if (as you say) no Church may hope *to triumph
ouer all errour till she be in heauen*; You must eyther grant that errours not fundamentall cannot yield sufficiet cause to forsake the Church,
or els you must affirme that all Communities
may, & ought to be forsaken, & so there wilbe
no end of Schismes : or rather indeed there can
be no such thinge as Schisme, because according to you, all Communities are subiect to
errours not fundamentall, for which if they
may be lawfully forsaken, it followeth cleerely that it is not Schisme to forsake them. Lastly,
since it is not lawfull to leaue the Communion
of the Church for abuses in life and manners,
because such miseries cannot be auoided in this
world of temptation : and since according to
your Assertion no *Church may hope to triumph o-
uer all sinne and errour*; You must grant, that as
B b she

she ought not to be left by reason of sinne; so
neyther by reason of errours not fundamental,
because both *sinne*, & *errour* are (according to
you)impossible to be auoided til she be in heauē.

23.   Furthermore, I aske whether it be the
Quantity or *Number*; or *Quality*, and *Greatnes*
of doctrinall errours that may yield sufficient
cause to relinquish the Churches Communion?
I proue that neyther. Not the *Quaiy*, which is
supposed to be beneath the degree of points
fundamentall,or necessary to saluation. Not the
Quantity or Number : For the foundation is
strong inough to support all such *vnnecessary ad-*
ditions, as you terme them. And if they once
weighed so heauy as to ouerthrow the foundation, they should grow to fundamentall errors, into which your selfe teach the Church
cannot fall. *Hay and stubble (* say you *) and such*
(g)pag.155. *(g) vnprofitable stuff, laid on the roofe, destroies not*
the house, whilest the maine pillars are standing on
the foundation. And tell vs, I pray you, the pre-
cise number of errors which cannot be tolerated? I know you cannot do it; and therfore being *vncertaine*,whether or no you haue cause to
leaue the Church,you are *certaincly* obliged not
to forsake her. Our blessed Sauiour hath declared his will, that we forgiue a priuate offender
seauenty seauen times,that is, without limitation of quantity of time,or quality of trespasses;
and why then dare you alledge his commaund,
that you must not pardon his Church for errors,

rors, acknowledged to be not fundamentall?
What excuse can you faigne to your selues, who
for points not necessary to saluation, haue been
occasions, causes, and authors of so many mis-
chiefes, as could not but vnauoydably accom-
pany so huge a breach in kingdomes, in Common wealths, in priuate persons, in publique
Magistrates, in body, in soule, in goods, in life,
in Church, in the state, by Schismes, by rebel-
lions, by war, by famine, by plague, by bloud-
shed, by all sorts of imaginable calamities vpon
the whole face of the Earth, wherin as in a map
of Desolation, the heauines of your crime appeares, vnder which the world doth pant?

24. To say for your excuse, that you left
not the Church, but her errors, doth not extenuate, but aggrauate your sinne. For by this
deuise you sow seeds of endles Schismes, & put
into the mouth of all Separatists, a ready answere how to auoide the note of *Schisme* from
your Protestant Church of England, or from
any other Church whatsoeuer. They will, I say,
answere, as you do prompt, that your Church
may be forsaken, if she fall into errors, though
they be not fundamentall: And further that no
Church must hope to be free from such errors;
which two grounds being once laid, it will not
be hard to infer the consequence, that she may
be forsaken.

25. From some other words of *D. Potter* I
likewise proue, that for Errors not fundamen-

tall,

tall, the Church ought not to be forsaken. *There*
(h) *Pag. 75.* *neither was (*sayth he*) nor can be* (h) *any iust cause*
to depart from the Church of Christ, no more then
from Christ himselfe. To depart from a particular
Church, & namely from the Church of Rome, in some
doctrines and practises, there might be iust and neces-
sary cause, though the Church of Rome wanted no-
thing necessary to saluation. Marke his doctrine,
that there *can be no iust cause to depart from the*
Church of Christ; and yet he teacheth that the
Church of Christ may erre in points not fundamentall; Therfore (say I) we cannot forsake
the *Roman* Church for points not fundamental,
for then we might also forsake the Church of
Christ, which your selfe deny : and I pray you
consider whether you do not plainely contradict your selfe, while in the words aboue recited, you say there can be no *iust cause to forsake*
the Catholique Church; and yet that there may
be necessary cause to depart from the Church
of Rome, since you grant that the Church of
Christ may erre in points not fundamentall; &
that the *Roman* Church hath erred only in such
points; as by and by we shall see more in particular. And thus much be said to disproue their
chiefest Answere, that they left not the *Church*,
but her *Corruptions*.

26.   Another euasion *D. Potter* bringeth, to
auoid the imputation of *Schisme*, and it is because they still acknowledge the Church of
Rome to be a *Member of the body of Christ*, and
not

not *cut off from the hope of faluation. And this* (fayth
he *) cleares vs from* (1) *the imputation of Schifme,* (i) *pag.76.*
whofe property it is, to cut of from the Body of Chrift,
and the hope of faluation , the Church from which it
feparates.

27. This is an Anfwere which perhaps you
may get fome one to approue, if firft you can
put him out of his wits. For what prodigious
doctrines are thefe? Thofe Proteftants who belieue that the Church erred in points neceffary
to faluation, and for that caufe left her, cannot
be excufed from damnable *Schifme :* But others
who belieued that fhe had no damnable errors,
did very well, yea were obliged to forfake her:
and (which is more miraculous, or rather mon-
ftrous) they did well to forfake her formally
and precifely , *becaufe* they *iudged,* that fhe retained all meanes neceffary to faluation. I fay,
becaufe they fo *iudged.* For the very reafon for
which he acquitteth himfelfe, and condemneth
thofe others as Schifmatiques, is becaufe he holdeth that the Church which both of them forfooke, is not cut of from the *Body of Chrift , and*
the hope of faluation ; whereas thofe other Zea-
lots deny her to be a member of Chrifts Body,
or capable of faluation, wherin alone they difagree from *D. Potter :* for in the effect of feparation they agree, only they do it vpon a different
motiue or reafon. Were it not a ftrang excufe if
a man would thinke to cloake his rebellion, by
alledging that he held the perfon againft whom

he

he rebelled to be his lawfull Soueraygne? And *D. Potter* thinkes himfelfe free from Schifme, becaufe he forfooke the Church of *Rome*, but yet fo, as that ftil he held her to be the true Church, and to haue all neceffary meanes to Saluation. But I will no further vrge this moft folemne foppery, and doe much more willingly put all Catholiques in mind, what an vnfpeakeable comfort it is, that our Aduerfaries are forced to confeffe, that they cannot cleere themfelues from *Schifme*, otherwife then by acknowledging that they do not, nor cannot *cut off from the Hope of faluation* our Church. Which is as much as if they fhould in plaine termes fay: They muft be damned, vnleffe we may be faued. Moreouer this euafion doth indeed condemne your zealous Brethren of *Herefy*, for denying the Churches perpetuity, but doth not cleere your felfe from *Schifme*, which confifts in being diuided from that true Church, with which a man agreeth in all points of fayth, as you muft profeffe your felfe to agree with the Church of Rome in all fundamentall Articles. For otherwife you fhould cut her off from the hope of faluation, and fo condemne your felfe of *Schifme*. And laftly euen according to this your owne definition of *Schifme*, you cannot cleere your felfe from that crime, vnleffe you be content to acknowledge a manifeft contradiction in your owne Affertions. For if you do not cut vs off *from the Body of Chrift, and the Hope*

of

of saluation; how come you to say in another place that you iudge a *reconciliation* with vs *to be* (k) *damnable?* That to depart *from the Church of Rome, there might be iust and necessary* (l) *cause?* That, *they that haue the vnderstanding and meanes to discouer their error, and neglect to vse them* (m) *we dare not flatter them* (say you) *with so easy a censure,* of hope of saluation? If then it be (as you say) a property of *Schisme,* to cut off from the hope of saluation the Church from which it separates: how wil you cleere your selfe from *Schisme,* who dare not flatter vs with so easy a censure? and who affirme that a reconciliation with vs is *damnable?* But the truth is, there is no constancy in your Assertions, by reason of difficulties which presse you on all sides. For, you are loath to affirme cleerly that we may be saued, least such a grant might be occasion (as in all reason it ought to be) of the conuersion of Protestants to the *Roman* Church: And on the other side, if you affirme that our Church erred in points fundamentall, or necessary to saluation, you know not how, nor where, nor amōg what Company of men, to find a perpetuall visible Church of Christ before *Luther:* And therfore your best shift is to say, and vnsay as your occasions command. I do not examine your Assertion that it is the property of Schisme *to cut of from the Body of Christ, and the hope of saluation, the Church from which it separates;* wherin you are mightily mistaken, as appeares by
your

(k) *pag.* 20.

(l) *pag.* 75.

(n) *pag.* 79.

your owne example of the *Donatists*, who were
moſt formall and proper *Heretiques*, and not
Schiſmatiques, as *Schiſme* is a vice diſtinct from
Hereſy. Beſides although the *Donatists*, & *Luciferians* (whom you alſo alledg) had byn meere
Schiſmatiques, yet it were againſt all good Logick, from a particular to inter a generall Rule,
to determine what is the property of *Schiſme*.

28.   A third deuiſe I find in *D. Potter* to
cleere his Brethren from Schiſme. *There is* ſayth
(n) *Pag.75.* he) *great difference betweene* (n) *a Schiſme from
them, and a Reformation of our ſelues.*

29.   This I confeſſe is a quaint ſubtility, by
which all Schiſme, and Sinne may be as well
excuſed. For what diuell incarnate could meerly pretend a ſeparation, and not rather ſome o-
ther motiue of vertue, truth, profit, or pleaſure?
But now ſince their pretended *Reformation* con-
ſiſted, as they gaue out, in forſaking the corruptions of the Church, the *Reformation* of thé-
ſelues, and their *diuiſion* from vs, falls out to
be one, and the ſelfe ſame thing. Nay, we ſee
that although they infinitly diſagree in the particulars of their reformation, yet they ſymbo-
lize, and conſent in the generall point of forſaking our pretended corruptions : An euident ſigne, that the thinge, vpon which their
thoughts firſt pitched, was not any particuler
Modell, or Idæa of Religion, but a ſetled reſo-
lution to forſake the Church of *Rome*. Wherefore this Metaphyſicall ſpeculation, that they
inten-

intended only to reforme themfelues , cannot
poſſibly excufe them from *Schifme*, vnleſſe firſt
they be able to proue,that they were obliged to
depart from vs. Yet for as much as concernes
the fact it felfe; it is cleere, that *Luthers* reuolt
did not proceed from any zeale of Reformation : The motiues which put him vpon fo wretched , and vnfortunate a worke , were Couetoufnes, Ambition , Luſt , Pride , Enuy , and
grudging that the promulgation of Indulgences was not committed to himfelfe , or fuch as
he deſired. He himſelfe taketh God to witneſſe,
that he *fell into theſe troubles caſually, and* (o) *a-*
gainſt his will(not vpon any intention of Reformation) not fo much as *dreaming or ſuſpecting a-*
ny change which might (p) *happen.* And he *began*
to preach (againſt Indulgences) *when he knew not*
what (q) *the matter meant.* For (fayth he) *I ſcar-*
cely vnderſtood (r) *then what the name of Indul-*
gences meät. In fo much as afterwards *Luther* did
much miſlike of his owne vndertaken courfe ,
oftentymes (fayth he) *wiſhing* (s) *that I had ne-*
uer begunne that buſines. And *Fox* fayth: *It is appa-*
rent that (t) *Luther promiſed Cardinall Caietan to*
keepe ſilence, prouided alſo his aduerſaries would do
the like. M.*Cowper* reporteth further, that *Luther*
by his letter ſubmitted (u) *himſelfe to the Pope, ſo*
that he might not be compelled to recant. With much
more, which may be feene in (w)*Brerdley* . But
this is fufficient to ſhew,that *Luther* was far i-
nough from intending any Reformation . And

(o) *Caſu nô*
voluntate in
has turbas
incidi Deum
ipſum teſtor.
(p) *Act. Ex*
mon. p.404.
(q) *Sleidan*
lib.16.fol.
232.
(r)*Sleid.lib.*
13.fol. 177.
(s) *Luth. in*
colloq. men-
ſal.
(t)*Act. mon.*
pag.404.
(u) *Cowp.in*
his Cronicle.
(w)*Tract.2:*
cap. 2. Sect.
11.*ſubd.*2.

if he iudged a *Reformation* to be neceſſary, what a huge wickednes was it in him, to promiſe *ſilence if his aduerſaries would do the like?* Or to ſubmit *himſelfe to the Pope, ſo that he might not be compelled to recant?* Or if the Reformation were not indeed *intended* by him, nor iudged to be *neceſſary,* how can he be excuſed from damnable. *Schiſme?* And this is the true manner of *Luthers* reuolt, taken from his owne acknowledgmēts, and the words of the more ancient Proteſtants themſelues, wherby D. *Potters* faltring, & mincing the matter is cleerly diſcouered, and confuted. Vpon what motiues our Countrey was diuided from the Roman Church by king *Henry* the Eight, and how the Schiſme was continued by Queene *Elizabeth,* I haue no hart to rip vp. The world knoweth, it was not vpon any zeale of *Reformation.*

30.　But you will proue your former euaſion by a couple of ſimilitudes: *If a Monaſtery* (x) *ſhould reforme it ſelfe, and ſhould reduce into practiſe, ancient good diſcipline, when others would not; in this caſe could it in reaſon be charged with Schiſme from others, or with Apoſtacy from its rule and order? Or as in a ſociety of men vniuerſally infected with ſome diſeaſe, they that ſhould free themſelues from the common diſeaſe, could not be therfore ſaid to ſeparate from the ſociety: ſo neither can the reformed Churches be truly accuſed for making a Schiſme from the Church, ſeing all they did was to reforme themſelues.*

(x) pag. 81. 82.

31. I was very glad to find you in a Monaſtery, but ſorry when I perceiued that you were inuenting wayes how to forſake your Vocation, and to maintaine the lawfulnes of Schiſme from the Church, and Apoſtaſy from a Religious Order. Yet before you make your finall reſolutiō heare a word of aduiſe. Put caſe; That a Monaſtery did confeſſedly obſerue their ſubſtantiall vowes, and all principall Statutes, or Conſtitutions of the Order, though with ſome neglect of leſſer Monaſticall Obſeruances: And that a Reformation were vndertaken, not by authority of lawfull Superiours, but by ſome One, or very few in compariſon of the reſt: And thoſe few knowne to be led, not with any ſpirit of Reformation, but by ſome other ſiniſter intention: And that the Statutes of the howſe were euen by thoſe buſy-fellowes confeſſed, to haue been time out of mind vnderſtood, and practiſed as now they were: And further that the pretended Reformers acknowledged that themſelues as ſoone as they were gone out of their Monaſtery, muſt not hope to be free from thoſe or the like errors and corruptions, for which they left their Brethren: And (which is more) that they might fall into more enormous crimes then they *did*, or *could* do in their Monaſtery, which we ſuppoſe to be *ſecured* from all ſubſtantiall corruptions, for the auoyding of which they haue an infallible aſſiſtance. Put (I ſay) together all theſe my *And's*,

and then come with your *If's, if a Monastery should reforme it selfe &c.* and tell me, if you could excuse such Reformers from Schisme, Sedition, Rebellion, Apostasy, &c ? What would you say of such Reformers in your Colledge? or tumultuous persons in a kingdome? Remember now your owne Tenets, and then reflect how fit a similitude you haue picked out, to proue your selfe a *Schismatique*. You teach that the Church may erre in points not fundamentall, but that for all fundamentall points she is *secured* from error : You teach that no particular person, or Church hath any promise of assistance in points fundamentall : You, and the whole world can witnes that when *Luther* began, he being but only *One*, opposed himselfe *to All*, as well subiects as superiours; and that euen then, when he himselfe confessed that he had no intention of Reformation : You cannot be ignorant but that many chiefe learned Protestants are forced to confesse the Antiquity of our doctrine and practise, and do in seuerall, and many Controuersies, acknowledge that the Ancient Fathers stood on our side : Consider I say these points, and see whether your similitude do not condemne your Progenitors of *Schisme* from God's visible *Church*, yea and of *Apostasy* also from their Religious *Orders*, if they were vowed Regulars, as *Luther*, and diuers of them were.

32. From the Monastery you are fled into an Hospitall *of persons vniuersally infected with*

fome difeafe, where you find to be true what I
fuppofed,that after your departure from your
Brethren you might fall into greater inconueniences , and more *infectious difeafes,* then
thofe for which you left *them*. But you are alfo vpon the point to abandon thefe miferab'e
needy perfons , in whofe behalfe for Charities
fake , let me fet before you thefe confiderati-
ons . If the difeafe neyther *were* , nor *could* be
mortall,becaufe in that Company of men God
had placed a Tree of life : If going thence , the
fick man might by curious tafting the Tree of
Knowledge eate poyfon vnder pretence of bet-
tering his health: If he could not hope therby to
auoid other difeafes like thofe for which he
had quitted the company of the firft infected
men:If by his departure innumerable mifchiefs
were to enfue; could fuch a man without fence-
leneffe be excufed by faying, that he fought *to
free himfeife from the common difeafe,* but not forfooth *to feparate from the fociety?* Now your felfe
côpare the Church to a man deformed with(y) (y) *Pag.155.*
fuperfluous fingers and toes, but yet who hath not
loft any *vitall part*: you acknowledge that out of
her fociety no man is fecured from damnable
errour, and the world can beare witnes what
vnfpeakeable mifchiefes and calamities enfued
Luthers reuolt from the Church . Pronounce
then concerning thê , the fame fentence which
euen now I haue fhewed them to deferue who
in the manner aforefayd fhould *feparate from*
C c 3 per-

perſons *vniuerſally* infected with ſome diſeaſe.

33. But alas, to what paſſe hath Hereſy brought men, who terme theſelues Chriſtians, & yet bluſh not to compare the beloued Spouſe of our Lord, the one Doue, the purchaſe of our Sauiours moſt precious bloud, the holy Catho-lique Church, I meane that viſible Church of Chriſt which *Luther* found ſpread ouer the whole world; to a Monaſtery ſo diſordered that it muſt be forſaken ; to the *Gyant in Gath much deformed with ſuperfluous fingers and toes* ; to a *ſociety of men vniuerſally infected with ſome diſeaſe?* And yet all theſe compariſons, & much worſe, are neyther iniurious, nor vndeſerued, if once it be graunted, or can be proued, that the viſible Church of Chriſt may erre in any one point of Fayth, although not fundamentall .

34. Before I part from theſe ſimilitudes, one thing I muſt obſerue againſt the euaſion of *D. Potter*, that they left not the *Church*, but her Corruptions. For as thoſe Reformers of the Mo-naſtery, or thoſe other who left the company of men vniuerſally infected with ſome diſeaſe, would deny themſelues to be *Schiſmatiques*, or any way blame-worthy, but could not deny, but that they left the ſayd Communities : So *Luther* and the reſt cannot ſo much as pretend, not to haue left the viſible Church, which ac-cording to them was infected with many diſea-ſes, but can only pretend that they did not ſinne in leauing her . And you ſpeake very ſtrangely
when

when you fay : *In a Society of men vniuerfally infe-*
cted with some difeafe , they that should free themselues
from the Common difeafe, could not be therefore said
to feparate from the Society. For if they doe not
feparate themfelues from the Society of the infected perfons ; how do they free themfelues &
depart from the common difeafe ? Do they at
the fame tyme remaine *in the company* , and yet
depart *from* thofe infected creatures ? We muft
then fay, that they *feparate* themfelues from the
perfons, though it be by occafion of the difeafe:
Or if you fay , they free their owne perfons frō
the common difeafe , yet fo, that they remaine
ftill in the Company infected , fubiect to the
Superiours and Gouernours thereof, eating &
drinking & keeping publique Affemblies with
them ; you cannot but know , that *Luther* and
your Reformers the firft pretended free perfons
from the fuppofed common infectiō of the Roman Church, did not fo : for they endeauoured
to force the Society whereof they were parts ,
to be healed and reformed as they were : and if
it refufed,they did,when they had forces, driue
them away , euen their Superiours both fpirituall and temporall, as is notorious. Or if they
had not power to expell that fuppofed infected
Community, or Church of that place , they
departed from them corporally , whome men-
tally they had forfaken before. So that you cannot deny, but *Luther* forfooke the external Cōmunion , and Company of the Catholique
Church,

(z) *Pag.*75.

Church, for which as your felfe (z) confeffe, *There neyther was nor can be any iuſt cauſe, no more then to depart from Chriſt himſelfe*. We do therfore inferre, that *Luther* and the reſt who forſooke that vifible Church which they found vpon earth, were truly, and *properly Schifmatiques*.

35.   Moreouer, it is euident that there was a diuifion betweene *Luther* and that Church which was Vifible when he arofe : but that Church cannot be fayed to haue deuided her felfe from him, before whofe tyme ſhe was, & in comparifon of whome ſhe was a *Whole*, and he but a *part* : therefore we muſt fay, that he deuided himfelfe & went out of her ; which is to be a *Schifmatique*, or *Heretique*, or both . By this argument, *Optatus Meliuitanus* proueth, that not *Cæcilianus*, but *Parmenianus* was a Schif-

(a) *Lib.* 1.
cont. *Parm.*

matique, faying : *For, Cæcilianus went* (a) *not out of Maiorinus thy Grandfather, but Maiorinus from Cæcilianus: neyther did Cæcilianus depart from the Chayre of Peter, or Cyprian, but Maiorinus, in whofe Chaire thou ſitteſt, which had no beginning before Maiorinus. Since it manifeſtly appeareth that theſe things were acted in this manuer, it is cleere that you are heyres both of the deliuerers vp (* of the holy Bible to be burned) *and alſo of Schifmatiques*. The whole argument of this holy Father makes directly both againſt *Luther*, and all thoſe who continue the diuifion which he begun ; and proues : That, *going out*, conuinceth thoſe

who

who go out to be Scifmatiques ; but not thofe from whome they depart : That to forfake the Chaire of Peter is *Schifme*; yea, that it is *Schifme* to erect a Chaire which had no origen, or as it were predeceffour, before it felfe : That to continue in a diuifion begun by others, is to be *Heires of Schifmatiques*: and laftly; that to depart from the Communion of a particuler Church (as that of *S. Cyprian* was) is fufficient to make a man incurre the guilt of *Schifme*, and confequently, that although Proteftants, who deny the Pope to be fupreme Head of the Church, do thinke by that *Herefy* to cleere *Luther* frō Schifme, in difobeying the Pope : Yet that will not ferue to free him from *Schifme*, as it importeth a diuifion from the obedience, or Communion of the particular Bifhop, Dioceffe, Church, & Countrey, where he liued.

36. But it is not the herefy of Proteftants, or any other Sectaries, that can depriue *S. Peter*, and his Succeffours, of the authority which Chrift our Lord conferred vpon them ouer his whole militant Church : which is a point confeffed by learned Proteftants to be of great Antiquity, and for which the iudgement of diuers moft ancient holy Fathers is reproued by them, as may be feen at large in *Brerelcy*(b) exactly citing the places of fuch chiefe Proteftants. And we muft fay with *S Cyprian*: *Herefies* (c) *haue fprung, and Schifmes been bred from no other caufe then for that the Prieſt of God is not obeyed, nor one*

(b)*Tract. 1.* *Sect.3. fubd.* 10.

(c) *Epiſt·55.*

D d   *Prieſt*

Prieſt and Iudge is cōſidered to be for the time in the Church of God. Which words do plainely condemne *Luther* , whether he will vnderſtand them as ſpoken of the *Vniuerſall*, or of euery *particular* Church. For he withdrew himſelfe both from the obedience of the Pope, and of all particular Biſhops, and Churches. And no leſſe cleere is the.ſayd *Optatus Meliuitanus*, ſaying :

(d) *Lib* 2. *cont.Parm.*

Thou canſt not deny (d *) but that thou knoweſt, that in the Citty of Rome, there was firſt an Epiſcopall Chaire placed for Peter, wherin Peter the head of all the Apoſtes ſat, wherof alſo he was called Cephas ; in which one Chaire ,Vnity was to be kept by all, leaſt the other Apoſtles might attribute to themſelues , ech one his particular Chaire ; and that he ſhould be a Schiſmatique and ſinner, who againſt that one ſingle Chaire ſhould erect another.* Many other Authorities of Fathers might be alledged to this purpoſe, which I omit, my intention being not to handle particular controuerſies.

37. Now, the arguments which hitherto I haue brought, proue that *Luther* , and his followers were Schiſmatiques, without examining (for as much as belonges to this point) whether or no the Church can erre in any one thing great or ſmall , becauſe it is vniuerſally true, that there can be no iuſt cauſe to forſake the Communion of the Viſible Church of Chriſt, according to *S. Auguſtine* , ſaying : *It is*

(e) *Ep*. 48. *not poſsible (* e *) that any may haue iuſt cauſe to ſeparate their Communion, from the Commnnion of the whole*

*Whole world, and call themselues the Church of Christ,
as if they had separated themselues from the Communion of all Nations vpon iust cause.* But since indeed the Church cannot erre in any one point
of doctrine, nor can approue any corruption in
manners; they cannot with any colour auoid
the iust imputation of *eminent* Schisme, according to the verdict of the same holy Father in
these words : *The most manifest (f) sacriledge of* (f) *De Bapt.*
Schisme is eminent, when there was no cause of sepa- *Lib. 5.c.1.*
ration .

38.   Lastly, I proue that Protestants cannot
auoid the note of Schisme, at least by reason of
their mutuall separation from one another. For
most certaine it is that there is very great difference, for the outward face of a Church, and
profession of a different fayth, between the *Lu-*
therans, the rigid *Caluinists,* and the *Protestants*
of England So that if *Luther* were in the right,
those other Protestants who inuented Doctrines far different from his, and diuided themselues from him, must be reputed *Schismatiques:* &
the like argument may proportionably be applied to their further diuisions, and subdiui-
sions. Which reason I yet vrge more strongly
out of *D.Potter,(g)* who affirmes, that to him & (g) *pag.* 20.
to such as are conuicted in conscience of the er-
rors of the *Roman* Church , a reconciliation is
impossible, and *damnable* : And yet he teacheth,
that their difference from the *Roman* Church,
is not in fundamentall points. Now, since a-

mong Proteſtants there is ſuch diuerſity of beliefe, that one denieth what the other affirmeth, they muſt be côuicted in conſcience that
one part is in error (at leaſt not fundamétall.)
and, if *D.Potter* will ſpeake conſequently, that
a reconciliation between them is *impoſsible:*and
what greater diuiſion,or *Schiſme* can there be,
then when one part muſt iudge a reconciliation
with the other to be *impoſsible,*and *damnable?*

39.   Out of all which premiſes, this *Concluſion* followes: That, *Luther* & his followers
were *Schiſmatiques*; from the vniuerſail viſible
Church; from the Pope Chriſts Vicar on earth,
and Succeſſour to *S. Peter*; from the particular
Dioceſſe in which they receiued Baptiſme;
from the Countrey or Nation to which they
belonged; from the Biſhop vnder whom they
liued; many of them from the Religious Order
in which they were Profeſſed; from one another; And laſtly from a mans ſelfe (as much as
is poſſible)becauſe the ſelfe ſame Proteſtant to
day *is conuicted in conſcience,* that his yeſterday's
Opinion was an error (as *D. Potter* knowes a
man in the world who from a Puritan was turned to a moderate Proteſtant)with whom therfore a reconciliation, according to *D. Potters*
grounds, is both *impoſsible*, and *damnable.*

40.   It ſeemes *D. Potters* laſt refuge to excuſe himſelfe and his Brethren from Schiſme,is
becauſe they proceeded according to their conſcience, dictating an obligation vnder damnation

tion to forfake the errors maintayned by the
Church of Rome. His words are: *Although we*
confeffe the (h) *Church of Rome to be* (*in fome fenfe*) (h) *Pag.* 81.
a true Church, and her errors to fome men not dam-
nable: yet for vs who are conuinced in confcience, that
fhe erres in many things, a necefsity lyes vpon vs, euen
vnder paine of damnation, to forfake her in thofe er-
rors.

41.   I anfwere : It is very ftrang, that you
iudge vs extremely Vncharitable , in faying,
Proteftáts cannot be faued ; while your felfe a-
uouch the fame of all learned Catholiques,
whom ignorance cannot excufe. If this your
pretence of confcience may ferue, what Schifmatique in the Church, what popular feditious
braine in a kingdome , may not alledge the di-
&amen of confcience to free themfelues from
Schifme, or *Sedition* ? No man wifhes them to do
any thing againft their confcience, but we fay,
that they may, and ought to re&ifie, and depofe
fuch a confcience, which is *eafy* for them to do,
euen according to your owne affirmation ; that
we Catholiques want no meanes neceffary to
faluation. Eafy to do ? Nay not to do fo , to any
man in his right wits muft feeme *impofsible*. For
how can thefe two apprehenfions ftand together: In the Roman Church I enioy all meanes
neceffary to faluation, and yet I cannot hope to
be faued in that Church? or, who can conioine
in one braine (not crack't) thefe affertions ?
After due examination I iudge the Roman er-

rors not to be in themselues fundamentall, or damnable; and yet I iudge that according to true reafon, it is damnable to hold them? I fay *according to true reafon*. For if you grant your confcience to be *erroneous*, in iudging that you cannot be faued in the *Roman* Church, by reafon of her errors; there is no other remedy, but that you muft rectify your erring confcience, by your other Iudgment, that her errours are not fundamentall, nor damnable. And this is no more Charity, then you daily affoard to fuch other Proteftants as you terme Brethren, whom you cannot deny to be in fome errors, (vnles you will hold, That of contradictory propofitions both may be true) & yet you do not iudge it damnable to liue in their Communion, becaufe you hold their errours not to be fundamentall. You ought to know, that according to the doctrine of all Deuines, there is great difference betwixt a fpeculatiue perfwafion, and a practicall dictamen of confcience; and therfore although they had in fpeculation conceiued the vifible Church to erre in fome doctrines, of themfelues not damnable; yet with that fpeculatiue iudgement they might, & ought to haue entertayned this practicall dictamen, that for points not fubftantiall to fayth, they neyther were bound, nor lawfully could breake the bond of Charity, by breaking vnity in Gods Church. You fay that, *hay & ftubble (1) and fuch vnprofitable ftuffe* (as are Corruptions in points

(4) *Pag. 155.*

not

not fundamental) *layd on the roofe, destroyes not the houfe, whilst the maine pillars are standing on the foundation.* And you would thinke him a madman who to be rid of fuch ftuffe, would fet his houfe on fire, that fo he might walk in the light, as you teach that *Luther* was obliged to forfake the houfe of God, for an vnneceffary light, not without a combuftion formidable to the whole Chriftian world ; rather then beare with fome errours, which did not deftroy the foundation of faith. And as for others who entred in at the breach firft made by *Luther*, they might, & ought to haue guided their confciences by that moft reafonable rule of *Vincētius Lyrinenfis,* deliuered in thefe words. *Indeed it is a matter of great* (k) *moment, and both most profitable to be learned, & neceffary to be remembred, & which we ought againe and againe to illustrate, and inculcate with weighty heapes of examples, that almost all Catholiques may know, that they ought to receiue the Doctours with the Church, and not forfake the fayth of the Church with the Doctours:* And much leffe fhould they forfake the fayth of the Church to follow *Luther, Caluin,* and fuch other Nouelifts. Moreouer though your firft Reformers had conceiued their owne opinions to be *true* ; yet they might, and ought to haue doubted, whether they were *certaine* : becaufe your felfe affirme, that infallibility was not promifed to any particular Perfons, or Churches. And fince in cafes of *vncertainties,* we are not to leaue our Superiour, nor caft off

his

(k) *Aduerf. haref. c.27.*

his obedience, or publiquely oppofe his decrees;
your Reformers might eafily haue found a fafe
way to fatisfy their zealous confcience, without a publique breach: efpecially if with this
their *vncertainty*, we call to mind the peaceable
poffeffion, and prefcription which by the confeffion of your owne Brethren, the Church, &
Pope of *Rome* did for many ages enioy. I wifh
you would examine the workes of your Brethren, by the words your felfe fets downe to
free *S. Cyprian* from *Schifme* : euery fyllable of
which words conuinceth *Luther*, and his Cō-
partners to be guilty of that crime, and fheweth
in what manner they might with great eafe, &
quietnes haue rectified their confcience about
the pretended errours of the Church. *S. Cyprian*
(l) Pag. 124. (fay you) *was a peaceable (*l*) and modeſt man; dif-
fented from others in his iudgement, but without any
breach of Charity; condemned no man (much leſſe
any Church) for the contrary opinion. He belieued
his owne opinion to be true, but belieued not, that it
was neceſſary, and therefore did not proceed rashly
and peremptorily to cenfure others, but left them to
their liberty.* Did your Reformers imitate this
manner of proceeding? Did they *cenfure no man,
much leſſe any Church?* S. *Cyprian belieued his owne
Opinion to be true, but belieued not that it was neceffary, and* THEREFORE *did not proceed raſhly,
and peremptorily to cenfure others.* You belieue the
points wherin *Luther* differs from vs not to be
fundamentall, or *neceſſary* ; and why do you not
thence

thence infer the like THEREFORE, he
fhould not haue *proceeded to cenfure others?* In a
word, fince their difagreement from vs concerned only points which were not fundamentall, they fhould haue belieued that they might
haue been deceaued, as well as the whole vifible Church, which you fay may erre in fuch
points; and therefore their doctrines being not
certainely *true,* and certainely *not neceffary,* they
could not giue fufficient caufe to depart from
the Communion of the Church.

42. In other places you write fo much,
as may ferue vs to proue that *Luther,* and his
followers ought to haue depofed, and rectified
their confciences: As for example, when you
fay: *When the Church (* m *) hath declared her felfe* (m) *pag.* 105.
in any matter of opinion, or of Rites, her declarati-
on obliges all her children to peace, and externall obe-
dience. Nor is it fit, or lawfull for any priuate man
to oppofe his iudgement to the publique; (as *Luther*
and his fellowes did) *He may offer his opinion to*
be confidered of, fo he do it with euidence, or great
probability of Scripture, or reafon, and very modeftly,
ftill contayning himfelfe within the dutifull refpect
which he oweth: but if he will factioufly aduāce his own
conceyts (his owne conceyts? and yet grounded
vpō euidence of Scripture) *& defpife the Church*
fo farre as to cut of her Communion; he may be iuftly
branded and condemned for a Schifmatique, yea and
an Heretique alfo in fome degree, & in foro exteriori,
though his opinion were true, and much more if it be

E e   *falfe.*

falfe. Could any man, euen for a Fee, haue fpoken more home to condemne your Predeceflors
of *Schifme*, or Herefy ? Could they haue ftron-
ger Motiues to oppofe the doctrine of the
Church, and leaue her Communion, then euidence of Scripture? And yet, according to your
owne words, they fhould haue anfwered, and
rectifyed their confcience, by your doctrine,
that though their opinion *were true*, and grounded vpon euidence of *Scripture, or reafon*; yet it
was not lawfull for any *priuate man to oppofe his
iudgment to the publique*, which obligeth all
Chriftians *to peace and externall obedience :* and if
they caft of the communion of the Church for
maintayning their owne *Conceits*, *they may be
branded for Schifmatiques, and Heretiques in fome
degree, and in foro exteriori,* that is; all other Chriftians ought fo *to efteeme* of them, (and why
then are we accounted vncharitable for iudging fo of you ?) and they alfo are obliged to
behaue themfelues *in the face of all Chriftian Churches*, as if indeed they were not Reformers, but
Schifmatiques, and *Heretiques*, or as Pagans, and
Publicans. I thanke you for your ingenuous
confeffion, in recompence wherof I will do a
deed of Charity by putting you in mind, into
what labyrinths you are brought, by teaching
that the Church may erre in fome points of
fayth, and yet that it is not lawfull for any man
to oppofe his iudgment, or leaue her Communion, though he haue euidence of Scripture a-
gainft

gainſt her. Will you haue ſuch a man diſſemble
againſt his conſcience, or externally deny a
truth knowne to be contained in holy Scripture? How much more coherently do Catholiques proceed, who belieue the vniuerſall infallibility of the Church, and from thence are
aſſured that there can be no euidence of Scripture, or reaſon againſt her definitions, nor any
iuſt cauſe to forſake her Cōmunion? M. Hooker
eſteemed by many Proteſtants an incompara-
ble man, yields as much as we haue alledged out
of you. *The will of God is* (ſayth he) *to haue* (n)
them do whatſoeuer the ſentence of iudiciall and fi-
nall deciſion ſhall determine, yea though it ſeeme in
their priuate opinion, to ſwarue vtterly from that
which is right. Doth not this man tell *Luther*
what the will of God was, which he tranſgreſ-
ſing muſt of neceſſity be guilty of *Schiſme?* And
muſt not *M. Hooker* either acknowledge the v-
niuerſall infallibility of the Church, or elſe
driue men into the perplexities and labyrinths
of diſſembling againſt their conſcience, wherof
now I ſpake? Not vnlike to this, is your doctrine
deliuered elſewhere. *Before the Nicene Councell*
(ſay you *) many* (o) *good Catholique Biſhops were of*
the ſame opinion with the Donatiſts, that the Bap-
tiſme of Heretiques was ineffectuall; and with the
Nouatians, that the Church ought not to aſſolue ſome
grieuous ſinners. Theſe errors therfore (if they had
gone no further) were not in themſelues Hereticall,
eſpecially in the proper, and moſt heauy, or bitter

ſenſe

(n) *In his*
Preface to
his bookes of
Eccleſiaſtical
policy. Sect.
6. pag. 28.

(o) *pag.* 131.

fenfe of that word; neither was it in the Churches in-
tention (or in her power) to make them fuch by her
declaration. Her intention was to filence all difputes,
and to fettle peace and Vnity in her gouernment : to
which all wife and peaceable men fubmitted, whatfoe-
uer their opinion was. And thofe factious people , for
their vnreafonable and vncharitable oppofition, were
very iuſtly branded for Schifmatiques. For vs , the
Miſtaker *will neuer proue that we oppofe any declara-*
tion of the Catholique Church &c. and therfore he
doth vniuſtly charge vs either with Schifme, or He-
refy . Thefe words manifeſtly condemne your
Reformers who oppofed the vifible Church in
many of her declarations, Doctrines, and Commaunds impofed vpon them, for filencing all
difputes, *and fetling peace and Vnity in the gouern-*
ment, and therfore they ſtill remayning obſtina-
tely difobedient , are iuſtly *charged with Schifme,*
and Herefy. And it is to be obferued that you
grant the *Donatiſts* to haue been *very iuſtly bran-*
ded for Schifmatiques, although their oppofition
againſt the Church did concerne (as you hold)
a point not fundamentall to the Fayth , and
which according to *S.Auguſtine* cannot be proued out of Scripture alone ; and therfore either
doth euidently conuince that the Church is v-
niuerfally infallible, euen in points not fundamentall, or elfe that it is *Schifme* to oppofe her
declarations in thofe very things wherin fhe
may erre; and confequently that *Luther,* and his
fellowes were *Schifmatiques,* by oppofing the vifible

ſible Church for points not fundamentall, though it were (vntruly) ſuppoſed that ſhe erred in ſuch points. But by the way, how come you on the ſuddaine to hold the determination of a Generall Councell (of *Nice*) to be the declaration of the Catholique Church, ſeeing you teach, That Generall Councels may erre euen fundamentally ? And do you now ſay, with vs, that to oppoſe the declaration of the Church is ſufficient that one may be branded with *Hereſy*, which is a point ſo often impugned by you ?

43. It is therfore moſt euident, that no pretended ſcruple of *conſcience* could excuſe *Luther*, which he might, and ought to haue rectified by meanes inowe, if Pride, Ambition, Obſtinacy &c. had giuen him leaue. I grant he was touched with ſcruple of conſcience, but it was becauſe he had forſaken the viſible Church of Chriſt ; and I beſeech all Proteſtants for the loue they beare to that ſacred ranſome of their ſoules, the Bloud of our bleſſed Sauiour, attentiuely to ponder, and vnpartially to apply to *their* owne *Conſcience,* what this Man ſpoke concerning the feelings, and remorſe of his. *How often* (ſayth he) *did my trembling heart* (p) *beate within me, and reprehending me, obiect against me that moſt ſtrong argument; Art thou only wiſe? Do ſo many worlds erre? Were ſo many ages ignorant? What if thou erreſt, and draweſt ſo many into hell to be damned eternally with thee ?* And in another place he ſayth : *Doſt thou who art but One, and of no* (q)

(p) *Tom.* 2. *Germ Jen. fol* 9. *& tom* 2. *Witt. of anno* 1562 *de abrog. Miſſ. priuat. fol.* 244. (q) *Tom.* 5. *Annot. breuiſſ.*

ac-

account, take vpon thee so great matters? What, if thou, being but one, offendest? If God permit such, so many, and all to erre, why may he not permit thee to erre? To this belong those arguments, the Church, the Church, the Fathers, the Fathers, the Councels, the Customes, the multitudes and greatnes of wise men: *Whom do not these Mountaines of arguments, these clouds, yea these seas of Examples ouerthrow?* And these thoughts wrought so deepe in his soule, that he *often wished and desired that he had* (r) *neuer begun this businesse*: wishing yet further that his *Writings were burned, and buried* (s) *in eternall obliuion.* Behold what remorse *Luther* felt, and how he wanted no strength of malice to crosse his owne conscience: and therfore it was no scruple, or conceiued obligation of conscience, but some other motiues which induced him to oppose the Church. And if yet you doubt of his courage to encounter, and strength to maister all reluctations of conscience, heare an example or two for that purpose. Of Communion vnder both kinds, thus he sayth: *If the Councell* (t) *should in any case decree this, least of all would we then vse both kinds, yea rather in aspight of the Councell, and that Decree, we would vse either but one kind only, or neither, and in no case both.* Was not *Luther* perswaded in *Conscience*, that to vse neither kind was against our Sauiours commaund? Is this only to *offer his opinion to be considered of,* as you said all men ought to do? And that you may be sure that he spoke from his heart,

(r) Colloq. mensal. fol. 158.
(s) Præfat. in tom. German. Ien.

(t) De formula missæ.

heart, and if occasion had been offered, would haue been as good as his word; marke what he sayth of the Eleuation of the Sacrament: *I did know* (u) *the Eleuation of the Sacrament to be Idolatricall; yet neuerthelesse I did retaine it in the Church at Wittemberge, to the end I might vex the diuell Carolostadius.* Was not this a conscience large and capacious inough, that could swallow Idolatry? Why would he not tolerate Idolatry in the Church of Rome (as these men are wont to blaspheme) if he could retaine it in his owne Church at Wittemberge? If *Carolostadius*, *Luthers* of-spring, was the Diuel who but himselfe must be his damme? Is Almighty God wont to send such furies to preach the Ghospell? And yet further (which makes most directly to the point in hand) *Luther* in his Booke of abrogating *the Priuate Masse*, exhorts the *Augustines* Friars of *Wittemberg*, who first abrogated the Masse, that euen against their conscience accusing them, they should persist in what they had begun, acknowledging that in some things he himselfe had done the like. And *Ioannes Mathesius* a Lutheran Preacher sayth: *Antonius Musa the Parish Priest* (w) *of Rocklitz, recounted to me that on a time he hartily moaned himselfe to the Doctor* (he meanes *Luther*) *that he himselfe could not beleeue what he preached to others: And that D. Luther answered; praise and thankes be to God, that this happens also to others, for I had thought it had happened only to me.* Are not these conscionable, and

(u) *In parua Confeß.*

Vid. Tan. tom. 2. disput. 1. q. 2° dub. 4. n. 108.

(w) *In orat. Germ. de Lath.*

fit Reformers ? And can they be excufed from *Schifme* vnder pretence that they held themfel-ues obliged to forfake the Roman Church ? If then it be damnable to proceed againft ones confcience, what will become of *Luther,* who a-gainft his confcience perfifted in his diuifion from the *Roman* Church ?

44. Some are faid to flatter themfelues with another pernicious conceit, that they (for-footh)are not guilty of finne; Becaufe they were not the *firft Authors,* but only are the *con-tinuers* of the *Schifme,* which was already be-gunne.

45. But it is hard to belieue, that any man of iudgment, can thinke this excufe will fubfift, when he fhall come to giue vp his finall accopt. For according to this reafon, no Schifme wil be damnable, but only to the Beginners : Wheras contrarily, the longer it continues, the worfe it growes to be, and at length degenerates to *He-refy* as wine by long keeping growes to be Vi-negar, but not by continuance returnes againe to his former nature of wine. Thus *S. Auguftine* faith, that *Herefy is* (x) *Schifme inueterate.* And in another place : *We obiect to you only the* (y) *crime of Schifme, which you haue alfo made to become Here-fy by euill perfeuering therin.* And *S. Hierom* fayth: *Though Schifme* (z) *in the beginning may be in fome fort vnderftood to be differet from herefy ; yet there is no Schifme which doth not faigne to it feife fome He-refy, that it may feeme to haue departed from the*

> Church

Church vpon iuſt cauſe. And ſo indeed it falleth
oūt. For men may beginne vpon paſſion, but afterward by inſtinſt of corrupt nature ſeeking to
maintaine their Schiſme as lawfull, they fall into ſome Hereſy, without which their Separation
could not be iuſtified with any colour, as in our
preſent caſe the very affirming that it is lawfull
to continue a Schiſme vnlawfully begunne, is
an error againſt the maine principle of Chriſtianity, that it is not lawfull for any Chriſtian to liue out of God's Church, within which
alone Saluation can be had ; Or, that it is not
damnable to diſobey her Decrees, according to
the words of our Sauiour : *If he ſhall not heare*
(a) the Church, let him be to thee as a Pagan or Pu-   (a) *Matt.*18.
blican. And, *He (b) that deſpiſeth you, deſpiſeth me.*   (b) *Luc.* 10,
We heard aboue *Optatus Mileuitanus* ſaying to   16.
Parmenianus, that both he, and all thoſe other
who cōtinued in the Schiſme begun by *Maiori-*
nus, did inherite their Forefathers Schiſme; and
yet *Parmenianus* was the third Biſhop after *Ma-*
iorinus in his Sea, and did not *begin*, but only *con-*
tinue the Schiſme. *For (* ſayth this holy Father *)*
Cæcilianus (c) *went not out of Maiorinus thy Grand-*   (c) *Lib.* 1.
Father, but Maiorinus from Cæcilianus : neither did   *cont. Parm.*
Cæcilianus depart from the Chaire of Peter, or Cy-
prian, but Maiorinus, in whoſe Chaire thou ſitteſt,
which before Maiorinus (Luther *) had no beginning.*
Seing it is euident that theſe things paſſed in this
manner (that, for example, Luther departed
from the Church, and not the Church from
F f   Lu-

Luther) *it is cleere that you be* HEIRES *both of the giuers vp of the Bible to be burned, and of* SCHISMATIQVES. And the Regall Power, or example of *Henry* the Eight could not excuse his Subiects from Schisme according to what we haue heard out of *S. Chryfostome* say-

(d) *Hom* 11. *in ep ft . ad Ephef.*

ing : *Nothing doth fo much prouoke* (d) *the wrath of Almighty God, as that the Church fhould be diuided. Although we fhould do innumerable good deeds, if we diuide the full Ecclefiasticall Congregation, we fhall be punifhed no leffe, then they who did rend his (*naturall*) Body; for that was done to the gaine of the whole world, though not with that intention: but this hath no good in it at all, but that the greateft hurt rifeth from it. Thefe things are fpoken not only to thofe who be are office, but to fuch alfo as are gouerned by them.* Behold therfore, how liable both *Subiects,* and *Superiours* are to the finne of *Schifme*, if they breake the vnity of God's Church. The words of *S. Paul* can in no occafion be verified more then in this of which we fpeake. *They who do fuch*

(e) *Rom.* 1. 32.

*things (*e*) are worthy of death: and not only they that do them, but they alfo that confent with the doers.* In things which are indifferent of their owne nature, Cuftome may be occafion, that fome act not well begun, may in time come to be lawfully cōtinued. But no length of Time, no Quality of Perfons, no Circumftance of Neceffity can legitimate actions which are of their owne nature vnlawfull : and therfore diuifion from Chrifts myfticall Body, being of the number of
thofe

thofe actions, which Deuines teach to be *intrin-fece malas, euill of their owne nature and effence,* no difference of Perfons or Time can euer make it lawfull. *D. Potter* fayth : *There neither was, nor can be any caufe to depart from the Church of Chrift, no more then from Chrift himfelfe.* And who dares fay, that it is not damnable to *continue* a Separation from Chrift ? *Prefcription* cannot in confcience runne, when the firft beginner, and his Succeffours are confcious that the thing to be *prefcribed,* for example goods or lands, were vninftly poffeffed at the firft. Chriftians are not like ftrayes, that after a certaine time of wandring from their right home, fall from their owner to the Lord of the Soile; but as long as they retaine the *indeleble Character* of Baptifme, and liue vpon earth, they are obliged to acknowledge fubiection to God's Church. Human Lawes may come to nothing by difcontinuance of Time, but the Law of God, commaunding vs to conferue Vnity in his Church, doth ftill remaine. The continued difobedience of Children cannot depriue Parents of their paternall right, nor can the Grand-child be vndutifull to his Grand-Father, becaufe his Father was vnnaturall to his owne Parent. The longer God's Church is difobeyed; the profeffion of her Doctrine denyed, her Sacraments neglected; her Liturgy condemned; her Vnity violated; the more grieuous the fault growes to be : as the longer a man with-holds a due debt, or retaines

his

his Neighbours goods, the greater iniuftice he commits. Conftancy in euill doth not extenuate, but aggrauate the fame, which by extenfion of Time, receiueth increafe of ftrength, & addition of greater malice. If thefe mens conceits were true, the Church might come to be wholy diuided by wicked Schifmes, and yet after fome fpace of time, none could be accufed of Schifme, nor be obliged to returne to the vifible Church of Chrift: and fo there fhould remaine no *One* true vifible Church. Let therfore thefe men who pretend to honour, reuerence, & belieue the Doctrine, and practife of the vifible Church, and to condemne their forefathers who fofooke her, and fay they would not haue done fo, if they had liued in the dayes of their Fathers, and yet follow their example in remaining diuided from her Communion; confider, how truly thefe words of our Sauiour fall vpon them. *Wo be to you, becaufe you build* (f) *the Prophets fepulchers, and garnifh the monuments of iuft men, and fay: If we had been in our Fathers dayes, we had not been their fellowes in the bloud of the Prophets. Therfore you are a teftimony to your owne felues, that you are the fonnes of them that killed the Prophets; and fill vp the meafure of your Fathers.*

(f) *Matt.*23. v. 29. &c.

46. And thus hauing demonftrated that *Luther*, his Affociates, and all that continue in the Schifme by them begunne, are guilty of *Schifme*, by departing from the vifible true Church of Chrift; it remaineth that we examine what in

par-

particular was that Vifible true Church, from
which they departed, that fo they may know
to what Church in particular they ought to returne: and then we fhall haue performed what
was propofed to be handled in the fifth Point.

47. ' That the *Roman* Church (I fpeake not
for the prefent, of the particular Diocefle of
Rome, but of all vifible Churches difperfed
throughout the whole world, agreeing in faith
with the Chaire of *Peter*, whether that Sea were
fuppofed to be in the Citty of *Rome* or in any o-
ther place:)That (I fay) the Church of *Rome*, in
this fenfe, was the vifible Catholique Church
out of which *Luther* departed, is prouedby your
owne Confeffion, who affigne for notes of the
Church, the true Preaching of Gods Church,
and due Adminiftration of Sacraments, both
which for the fubftance you cannot deny to the
Roman Church, fince you confefle that fhe wa-
ted nothing fundamentall, or necefIary to faluation; and for that very caufe you thinke to
cleare your felfe from Schifme, *whofe property*, as
you fay, is *to cut off from the* (g) *Body of Chrift and*
the Hope of Saluation, the Church from which it fe-
parates. Now that *Luther* and his fellowes were
borne and baptized in the *Roman* Church, and
that fhe was the Church out of which they departed, is notorioufly knowne: And therefore
you canno: cut her off *from the Body of Chrift, &*
Hope of Saluation, vnles you will acknowledge
your felfe to deferue the iuft imputatio of *Schif-*

5. Point.

Luther &
the reft de-
parted frō
the Roman
Church.

(g) *pag.* 78.

me. Neyther can you deny her to be truly Catholique by reason of (pretended) corruptions, not fundamentall. For your felfe auouch, and endeauour to proue, that the true Catholique Church may erre in fuch points. Moreouer, I hope you will not fo much as go about to proue, that when *Luther* rofe, there was any other true vifible Church, *difagreeing* from the *Roman*, & *agreeing* with Proteftants in their particular do-ctrines: and you cannot deny but that England in thofe dayes agreed with *Rome*, and other Na-tions with England : And therefore eyther Chrift had no vifible Church vpon Earth, or elfe you muft grant that it was the Church of *Rome*. A truth fo manifeft, that thofe Proteftats who affirme the Roman Church to haue loft the Nature & being of a true Church, do by ineui-table Confequence grant, that for diuers Ages Chrift had no vifible Church on Earth : from which errour, becaufe *D. Potter*, difclaymeth, he muft of neceffity maintaine, that the *Roman* Church is free from fundamentall, and damna-ble errour, and that *fhe is not cut off from the Body of Chrift, and the Hope of Saluation* : And if (faith he) *any Zelots amongft vs haue proceeded* (h) *to hea-nier cenfures, their zeale may be excufed, but their Charity and wifedome cannot be iuftifyed.*

(h) *Ibid.*

48. And to touch particulars which per-haps fome may obiect. No man is ignorant that the Grecians, euen the Schifmaticall Grecians, do in moft points agree with *Roman* Catholi-ques,

ques, & disagree from the Proteſtant Reformation. They teach Tranſubſtantiation (which
point *D. Potter* alſo (i) confeſſeth ;) Inuocation
of Saints, and Angels; veneration of Reliques,
and Images; Auricular Confeſſion; enioyned
Satisfaction ; Confirmation with Chriſme ;
Extreme-vnction; All the ſeauen Sacraments ;
Prayer, Sacrifice, Almes for the dead; Mona-
chiſme; That Prieſts may not marry after their
Ordination. In which points that the Grecians agree with the Roman Church appeareth
by a Treatiſe publiſhed by the Proteſtant Deuines of Wittemberg, intituled, *Acta Theologorum*
Wuttembergenſium, & Ieremiæ Patriarchæ Conſtan-
tinop. de Auguſtana Confeſsione &c. Wittembergæ
anno 1584 by the Proteſtant (k) *Criſpinus* , & by
Syr Edwin Sands in the Relation of the State of
Religion of the Weſt· And I wonder with what
colour of truth (to ſay no worſe) *D. Potter* could
affirme that the Doctrines *debated betweene the*
Proteſtāts (l) *& Rome, are only the partiall & particu-*
lar fancies of the Roman Church ; vnleſſe happily the
opinion of Tranſubſtātiation may be excepted, wherin
the latter Grecians ſeeme to agree with the Romaniſts.
Beſide the Proteſtant Authors already cited ,
Petrus Arcudius a Grecian and a learned Catholique Writer, hath publiſhed a large Volume,
the Argument and Title wherof is: *Of the agree-*
ment of the Roman, and Greeke Church in the ſeauen
Sacraments As for the Hereſy of the Grecians,
that the Holy Ghoſt proceeds not from the

Sonne

(i) *Pag.* 225.

(k) *De ſta-
tu Eccleſ.
pag.* 253.

(l) *pag.* 225;

Sonne, I fuppofe that Proteftants difauow them in that errour, as we doe.

49. *D. Potter* will not (I thinke) fo much wrong his reputation, as to tell vs, that the *Waldenfes*, *Wiccliffe*, *Huffe*, or the like were Proteftants, becaufe in fome things they difagreed from Catholiques. For he well knowes that the example of fuch men is fubiect to thefe manifeft exceptions. They were not of all Ages, nor in all Countries, but confined to certaine places, and were interrupted in Time, againft the notion and nature of the word *Cathelique*. They had no Ecclefiafticall Hierarchy, nor Succeffion of Bifhops, Priefts, and Paftours. They differed among themfelues, and from Proteftants alfo. They agreed in diuers things with vs againft Proteftants. They held doctrines manifeftly abfurd and damnable herefies.

50. The *Waldenfes* begun not before the yeare 1218. fo far were they from Vniuerfality of all Ages. For their doctrine: firft, they denied all Iudgments which extended to the drawing of bloud, and the Sabbaoth, for which caufe they were called In-fabbatifts. Secondly, they taught that Lay men, and women might confecrate the Sacrament, and preach (no doubt but by this meanes to make their Maifter, *Waldo*, a meere lay man, capable of fuch functions.) Thirdly, that Clergy men ought to haue no poffeffions, or proprieties. Fourthly, that there fhould be no diuifion of Parifhes, nor Churches,

●hes, for a walled Church they reputed as a
barne. Fiftly, that men ought not to take an
oath in any cafe. Sixtly, that thofe perfons fin-
ned mortally, who accompanied without hope
of iffue. Seauenthly, they held all things done a-
boue the girdle, by kiffing, touching, words,
compreffion of the breafts, &c. to be done in
Charity, and not againft Continency. Eightly,
that neither Prieft, nor ciuill Magiftrate, being
guilty of mortall finne did enioy their dignity,
or were to be obeyed. Ninthly, they condemned Princes, and Iudges. Tenthly, they affirmed finging in the Church to be an hellifh cla-
mor. Eleauenthly, they taught that men might
diffemble their Religion, and fo accordingly
they went to Catholique Churches, diffembling their Fayth, and made Offertories, confeffions, and communions after a diffembling   (m) *Act.*
manner. *Waldo* was fo *vnlearned,* that (fayth (m) *Mon. pag.*
Fox) he gaue rewards to certaine learned men 628.
to tranflate the holy Scripture for him, and being thus holpen did (as the fame *Fox* there reporteth) *confer the forme of religion in his time to*
the infallible word of God. A godly example, for
fuch as muft needs haue the Scripture in Englifh, to be read by euery fimple body, with fuch
fruit of godly doctrine, as we haue feen in the
forefaid groffe herefies of *Waldo.* The followers
of *Waldo,* were like their Maifter, fo vnlearned, (n) *Ibid.*
that *fome of them* (fayth (n) *Fox*) expounded the
words, Ioan. 1. *Sui eum non receperunt : Swyne did*

not receiue him. And to conclude, they agreed in diuers things with Catholiques againſt Proteſtants, as may be ſeene in *(o) Brereley.*

(o) Tract 2. cap. 2. ſect. ſubd. 3.

51. Neither can it be pretended, that theſe are ſlanders, forged by Catholiques. For, beſides that the ſame things are teſtified by Proteſtant Writers, as *Illyricus, Cowper,* & others, our Authours cannot be ſuſpected of partiality in disfauour of Proteſtants, vnles you will ſay perhaps, that they were Prophets, and ſome hundred yeares agoe, did both foreſee that there were to be Proteſtants in the world, and that ſuch Proteſtants were to be like the *Waldenſes.* Beſides, from whence, but from our Hiſtories are Proteſtants come to know, that there were any ſuch men as the *Waldenſes?* and that in ſome points they agreed with the Proteſtants, and diſagreed from them in others? And vpon what ground can they belieue our Authours for that part wherin the *Waldenſes* were like to Proteſtants, and imagine they lyed in the reſt?

52. Neither could *Wicliffe* continue a Church neuer interrupted from the time of the *Waldenſes,* after whom he liued more then one hundred and fifty yeares, to wit, the yeare 1371. He agreed with Catholiques about the worſhipping of Reliques, and Images: and about the Interceſſion of our bleſſed Lady, the euer-Immaculate Mother of God, he went ſo far as to ſay, *It ſeemes to me* (p) *impoſsible, that we ſhould be rewarded without the interceſsion of the Virgin Mary.*

(p) In ſerm. de Aſſump. Mariæ.

He

He held feauen Sacraments, Purgatory, and o-
ther points. And againft both Catholiques and
Proteftants he maintained fundry damnable doctrines, as diuers Proteftant Writers relate. As
firft: If a Bifhop or Prieft be in deadly finne, he
doth not indeed either giue Orders, Confecrate, or Baptize. Secondly, That Ecclefiafticall
Minifters ought not to haue any temporall poffeffions, nor propriety in any thing, but fhould
beg; and yet he himfelfe brake into herefy becaufe he had been depriued by the Archbifhop
of Canterbury of a certaine Benefice; as all
Schifmes, & herefies begin vpon paffion, which
they feeke to couer with the cloake of Reformation. Thirdly, he condemned lawfull Oaths,
like the Anabaptifts. Fourthly, he taught that
all things came to paffe by abfolute neceffity.
Fiftly, he defended human merits as the wicked
Pelagians did, namely, as proceeding from naturall forces, without the neceffary help of God's
grace. Sixtly, that no man is a Ciuill Magiftrate, while he is in mortall finne; and that the
people may at their pleafure correct Princes,
when they offend: by which doctrine he proues
himfelfe both an Heretique, and a Traytour.

53. As for *Huffe*, his chiefeft Doctrines
were: That Lay people muft receiue in *both
kinds*; and That Ciuill Lords, Prelates, and Bifhops loofe all right, and authority, while they
are in mortall finne For other things he wholy
agreed with Catholiques againft Proteftants;

and the *Bohemians* his followers being demaunded, in what points they difagreed from the
Church of *Rome*, propounded only thefe : *The
necefsity of Communion vnder both kinds*; That *all
ciuill Dominion was forbidden to the Clergy*; That
Preaching of the word, was free for all men, and in
all *places*; That *open Crimes were in no wife to be permitted for auoyding of greater euill*. By thefe particulars, it is apparant, that *Huffe* agreed with
Proteftants againft vs, in one only point of *both
Kinds*, which according to *Luther* is a thing indifferent; becaufe he teacheth that *Chrift in this
matter* (q) *commaunded nothing as neceffary*. And
he fayth further: *If thou come to a place* (r) *where
one only kind is adminiftred, vfe one kind only, as o-
thers do*. *Melancthon* likewife holds it a thing
(s) indifferent : and the fame is the opinion of
fome other Proteftants. All which confidered,
it is cleer that Proteftants cannot challenge the
Waldenfes, *Wiccliffe*, and *Huffe* for members of
their Church : & although they could, yet that
would aduatage them litle towards the finding
out a perpetuall vifible Church of theirs, for
the reafons aboue (t) fpecifyed.

54.   If *D. Potter*, would go fo farre off, as to
fetch the *Mufcouites*, *Armenians*, *Georgians*, *Æ-
thiopians*, or *Abifsines* into his Church, they
would proue ouer deare bought : For they eyther hold the damnable herefy of *Eutiches*, or
vfe Circumcifion, or agree with the *Greeke*, or
Roman Church. And it is moft certayne that
they

*(q) In epift.
ad Bohemos.
(r) De vtra-
que fpecie
Sacram.
(s) In Cent.
epift. Theol.
pag. 225.*

(t) Num.49

they haue nothing to do with the doctrine of
Proteſtants.

55. It being therefore granted that Chriſt
had a viſible Church in all ages , and that there
can be none aſſigned but the Church of *Rome*; it
followes that ſhe is the true Cath. Church; and
that thoſe pretended Corruptions for which
they forſooke her, are indeed diuine truths, deliuered by the viſible Catholique Church of
Chriſt: And, that *Luther* and his followers departed from her, and conſequently are guily of
Schiſme, by diuiding themſelues from the *Communion of the Roman Church* . Which is cleerely
conuinced out of *D*. *Potter* himſelfe, although
the *Roman* Church were but a particular (u) *Pag. 76.*
Church. For he ſayth : *Whoſoeuer profeſſes* (u)
*himſelfe to forſake the Communion of any one mēber
of the body of Chriſt, muſt confeſſe himſelfe conſequently to forſake the whole* . Since therefore in
the ſame place he expreſſely acknowledges the
Church of Rome to be a member of the Body of Chriſt,
and that it is cleere they haue forſaken her ; it
euidently followes, that they haue forſaken the
whole, and therefore are moſt properly *Schiſmatiques* .

56. And laſtly, ſince the crime of *Schiſme* is ſo
grieuous, that according to the doctrine of holy
Fathers rehearſed aboue, no multitude of good
workes, no morall honeſty of life , no cruell
death endured euen for the profeſſion of ſome
Article of faith can excuſe any one who is guil-

ty

ty of that finne from damnation ; I leaue it to
be confidered, whether it be not true Charity
to fpeake as we belieue, and to belieue as all
Antiquity hath taught vs, That whofoeuer eyther *beginnes,,* or *continues* a diuifion for the *Ro-*
wan Church, which we haue proued to be
Chrifts true *Militant* Church on earth, cannot
without effectuall repentance hope to be a méber of his Triumphant Church in heauen. And
fo I conclude with thefe words of bleffed *Saint*
*Auguftine : It is common (*w *) to all Heretiques to*
be vnable to fee that thing which in the world is the
moft manifeft, and placed in the light of all Nations;
out of whofe Vnity whatfoener they worke , though
they feeme to doe it with great care and diligence, can
no more auaile them againft the wrath of God , then
the Spiders web agaynft the extremity of cold. But
now it is high tyme that we treat of the other
fort of *Diuifion* from the Church, which is by
Herefy.

(w) *Cont.*
Parm.lib.2:
cap.3.

CHAP.

CHAP. VI.

That Luther ; and the reſt of Pro-
teſtants, haue added Hereſy vnto
Schiſme .

ECAVSE Vice is beſt
knowne by the contrary Vertue, we cannot well determine what *Hereſy* is , nor who
be *Heretiques* , but by the oppoſite vertue of *Fayth*, whoſe
Nature being once vnderſtood
as farre as belongs to our preſent purpoſe , we
ſhall paſſe on with eaſe to the definition of *He-*
reſy , and ſo be able to diſcerne who be *Here-*
tiques. And this I intend to do, not by entring
into ſuch particular Queſtions as are controuerted betweene Catholiques and Proteſtants,
but only by applying ſome generall grounds ,
eyther already proued , or els yielded to , on
all ſides.

2. Almighty God hauing ordayned Man
to a ſupernaturall End of Beatitude by *ſuperna-*
turall meanes; it was requiſite that his Vnderſtanding ſhould be enabled to apprehend that *End* ,

and

and *Meanes* by a *supernaturall* knowledge. And becaufe if fuch a knowledge were no more then *probable*,it could not be able fufficiently to ouer-beare our Will, & encounter with human probabilities, being backed with the ftrēgth of flefh and bloud; It was further neceffary, that this fupernatural knowledge fhould be moft *certaine* and infallible; and that *Fayth* fhould belieue nothing more *certainely* then that it felfe is a moft *certaine* Beliefe, and fo be able to beate downe all gay *probabilities* of humane *Opinion*. And becaufe the aforefayd *Meanes* and *End of Beatificall Vifion*, do farre exceed the reach of naturall wit, the *certainty* of fayth could not alwayes be ioyned with fuch *euidence* of reafon, as is wont to be found in the *Principles*, or *Conclufions* of humane naturall *Sciences*: that fo all flefh might not glory in the arme of flefh, but that he, *whe glories, fhould glory (a) in our Lord*. Moreouer, it was expedient that our beliefe, or affent to diuine truths, fhould not only be vnknowne, or *ineuident* by any humane difcourfe,but that abfolutely alfo it fhould be obfcure in it felfe, and (ordinarily fpeaking) be void euen of fupernaturall euidence; that fo we might haue occafion to actuate,and teftifie the obedience which we owe to our God, not only by fubmitting our *Will* to his *Will* and *Commaunds*,but by fubiecting alfo our *Vnderftanding* to his *Wifdome* & *Words*,captiuating(as the Apoftle fpeakes)the fame *Vnderftanding* (b) to the Obedience of Fayth:

(a) 2. Cor. 10

(b) 2. Cor. 10 5.

Fayth : Which occasion had been wanting, if
Almighty God had made *cleere* to vs, the truths
which now are *certainely,* but *not euidently* presented to our minds. For where Truth doth
manifestly open it selfe; not *obedience,* but *necefsity* comaunds our assent. For this reason, Deuines teach, that the Obiects of Fayth being not
euident to humane reason, it is in mans power
not only to abstaine from belieuing, by sus-
pending our Iudgement, or exercising no act
one way or other; but also to disbelieue, that is,
to belieue the contrary of that which Fayth
propoeth; as the examples of innumerable
Arch-heretiques can beare witnes. This obscurity of fayth we learne from holy Scripture, according to those words of the Apostle. *Fayth is
the* (c) *substance of things to be hoped for, the argu-* (c)Heb. 11.
ment of things not appearing. And, *We see by a glasse*
(d) *in a darke manner : but then face to face.* And,
accordingly S. *Peter* sayth : *Which you do well at-* (d) *1. Cor.*
tending vnto, as to (e) *a Candle shining in a darke* 13.*v. 12.*
place. (e) *2. Pet.*
3. Fayth being then *obscure* (wherby it dif- 1.*v.19.*
fereth from naturall *Sciences*) and yet being
most *certaine* and *infallible* (wherin it surpaf-
feth humane Opinion) it must rely vpon some
motiue and ground, which may be able to giue
it *certainty*, and yet not releafe it from *obscurity.*
For if this *motiue, ground,* or *formall Obiect* of
Fayth, were any thing euidently presented to
our vnderstanding, and if also we did euidently
H h know,

know, that it had a neceſſary conneꝭion with
the Articles which we belieue, our aſſent to
ſuch Articles could not be *obſcure*, but *euident*;
which, as we ſaid, is againſt the nature of our
Fayth. If likewiſe the motiue or ground of our
fayth were *obſcurely propounded* to *vs*, but were
not in it ſelfe *infallible*, it would leaue our aſſent in *obſcurity*, but could not endue it with
certainty. We muſt therfore for the ground of
our Fayth, find out a motiue obſcure to *vs*, but
moſt certaine *in it ſelfe*, that the act of fayth
may remaine both *obſcure*, and *certaine*. Such a
motiue as this, can be no other but the diuine Authority of almighty God, reuealing, or ſpeaking
thoſe truths which our fayth belieues. For it is
manifeſt, that God's infallible teſtimony may
transfuſe *Certainty* to our fayth, and yet not
draw it out of *Obſcurity*; becauſe no humane diſcourſe, or demonſtration can euince, that God
reuealeth any ſupernaturall Truth, ſince God
had been no leſſe perfeꝭ then he is, although he
had neuer reuealed any of thoſe obiects which
we now belieue.

4. Neuertheles, becauſe Almighty God out
of his infinite wiſdome and ſweetnes, doth concur with his Creatures in ſuch ſort as may befit
the temper, and exigence of their natures; and
becauſe Man is a Creature endued with *reaſon*,
God doth not exaꝭ of his Will or Vnderſtan-
(f) *Rom. 12.* ding any other then, as the Apoſtle ſayth, *ratio-*
v. 1. *nabile (f) Obſequium*, an Obedience, ſweetned
with

with good reafon; which could not fo appeare,
if our Vnderftanding were fummoued to belieue with *certainty,* things no way reprefented
as infallible and *certaine.* And therfore Almighty God obliging vs vnder paine of eternal damnation to believe with greateft certainty diuers
verities, not knowne by the light of naturall
reafon, cannot faile to furnifh our Vnderftanding, with fuch inducements, motiues, and arguments as may fufficiently perfuade any mind
which is not partiall or paffionate, that the ob-
ieds which we believe, proceed from an Authority fo *Wife,* that it cannot be deceiued, and
fo *Good* that it cannot deceiue; according to the
words of *Dauid: Thy Teftimonies are made(g)cre-*
dible exceedingly. Thefe inducements are by De- (g) *Pfal.*92.
uines, called *argumenta credibilitatis, arguments of*
credibility, which though they cannot make vs
euidently fee what we believe, yet they *euidently*
conuince that in true wifdome, and prudence,
the obiects of fayth deferue credit, and ought
to be accepted as things reuealed by God. For
without fuch reafons & inducements our iudgment of fayth could not be conceiued prudent,
holy Scripture telling vs, that, *he who foone* (h) (h) *Ecclef.*19
believes, is light of hart. By thefe arguments and 4.
inducements our Vnderftanding is both fatif
fied with *euidence of credibility,* and the obiects of
fayth retaine their *obfcurity:* becaufe it is a different thing to be euidently *credible,* and euidently *true;* as thofe who were prefent at the

Mi-

Miracles wrought by our bleſſed Sauiour,& his Apoſtles, did not euidently ſee their doctrine to be true (for then it had not beene *Fayth* but *Science*, and all had been neceſſitated to belieue, which we ſee fell out otherwiſe) but they were euidently conuinced, that the things confirmed by ſuch Mira cles, were *moſt credible*, and wor-thy to be imbraced as truths reuealed by God.

5. Theſe euident Arguments of Credibility are in great aboundance found in the Viſible Church of Chriſt, perpetualy exiſting on earth. For, that there hath been a company of men profeſſing ſuch and ſuch doctrines , we haue from our next Predeceſſors, and theſe from theirs vpward, till we come to the Apoſtles, & our Bleſſed Sauiour; which gradation is known by euidence of ſenſe, by reading bookes, or hea-ring what one man deliuers to another. And it is euident that there was neither cauſe, nor poſ-ſibility, that men ſo diſtant in place, ſo different in temper, ſo repugnant in priuate ends, did, or could agree to tell one and the ſelfe ſame thing, if it had been but a fiction inuented by them-ſelues, as ancient *Tertullian* well ſayth: *How is it likely that ſo many (i) & ſo great Churches ſhould erre in one fayth? Among many euents there is not one iſſue, the error of the Churches muſt needs haue va-ried. But that which among many is found to be One, is not miſtaken, but deliuered. Dare then any body ſay, that they erred who deliuered it ?* With this neuer interrupted exiſtence of the Church are ioy-ned

(i) *Præſcript.* *cap.* 28.

ned the many and great miracles wrought by
men of that Congregation or Church; the fan-
&ity of the perfons ; the renowned victories
ouer fo many perfecutions, both of all forts of
men, and of the infernall fpirits; and laftly, the
perpetuall exiftence of fo holy a Church, being
brought vp to the *Apoſtles* themſelues, *ſhe* comes
to partake of the fame affurance of truth, which
They by fo many powerfull wayes, did communicate to their Doctrine, and to the Church of
their times, together with the diuine Certainty
which *they* receiued from our Bleſſed Sauiour
himſelfe, reuealing to Mankind what he heard
from his Father; and fo we conclude with *Ter-*
tullian: We receiue it *from the Churches, the Chur-*
ches (k) *from the Apoſtles, the Apoſtles from Chriſt,*
Chriſt from his Father. And if we once interrupt
this line of fucceffion , moft certainly made
knowne by meanes of holy *Tradition* , we cannot conioyne the prefent Church , & doctrine,
with the Church , and doctrine of the Apoſtles, but muft inuent fome new meanes, and arguments fufficient of themfelues to find out ,
and proue a true Church, and fayth indepen-
dently of the *preaching,* and *writing* of the Apoſtles; neither of which can be knowne but by
Tradition, as is truly obferued by *Tertullian* faying : *I will preſcribe, that* (l) *there is no meanes to*
proue what the Apoſtles preached , but by the fame
Churches which they founded.

6. Thus then we are to proceed: By euidéce

(k) *Preſc.* c.
21. *&* 37.

(l) *Preſc.* c.
21.

of

of manifeft and incorrupt Tradition, I know
that there hath alwayes been a neuer interrupted Succeffion of men from the Apoftles tyme,
belieuing, profeffing, and practifing fuch and
fuch doctrines: By euident arguments of credibility, as Miracles, Sanctity, Vnity &c. and
by all thofe wayes whereby the Apoftles, and
our Blefleed Sauiour himfelfe confirmed their
doctrine, we are affured that what the fayd neuer interrupted Church propofeth, doth deferue to be accepted & aknowledged as a diuine
truth: By euidence of Senfe, we fee that the fame Church propofeth fuch and fuch doctrines
as diuine truths, that is, as reuealed and teftifyed by Almighty God. By this diuine Teftimony we are infallibly affured of what we belieue: and fo the laft period, ground, motiue,
and *formall obiect* of our Fayth, is the infallible
teftimony of that fupreme Verity, which neyther can deceyue, nor be deceiued.

7. By this orderly deduction our Faith com-
meth to be endued with thefe qualities which
we faid were requifite thereto; namely *Certainly*, *Obfcurity*, and *Prudence*. *Certainty* proceeds
from the *infallible* Teftimony of God propounded & conueied to our vnderftanding by fuch a
meane, as is infallible in it felfe, and to vs is euidently knowne that it propofeth this point or
that, and which can manifeftly declare in what
fenfe it propofeth them, which meanes we haue
proued to be only the vifible Church of Chrift.

Ob-

Obfcurity from the māner in which God fpeakes
to Mankind, which ordinarily is fuch, that it
doth not manifeftly fhew the perfon who fpeakes, nor the truth of the thing fpoken. *Prudence*
is not wanting, becaufe our fayth is accompanied with fo many arguments of *Credibility*, that
euery wel difpofed *Vnderstanding*, may & ought
to iudge, that the doctrines fo cōfirmed deferue
to be belieued, as proceeding from Authority.

8.　And thus from what hath been faid, we
may eafily gather the particular nature, or definition of *Fayth*. For, *it is a voluntary, or free,
infallible obfcure aſſent to fome truth, becaufe it is te-
Stifyed by God, & is fufficiently propounded to vs for
fuch*: which propofal is ordinarily made by the
viſible Church of Chrift. I fay, *Sufficiently propofed by the Church*; not that I purpofe to difpute
whether the propofall of the Church enter into
the *formall Obiect*, or *motiue* of Fayth : or whether an error be any herefy, *formally and precifely*, becaufe it is againft the propofition of the
Church, as if fuch propofall were the formall
Obiect of fayth, which *D. Potter* to no purpofe
at all, labours fo very hard to difproue : But I
only affirme, that when the Church propoūds
any Truth, as reuealed by God, we are affured
that it is fuch indeed ; & fo it inftantly growes,
to be a fit Obiect for Chriftian fayth, which
enclines and enables vs, to belieue whatfoeuer
is duely prefented, as a thing reuealed by Almighty God. And in the fame manner we are
　　　　　　　　　　　　　　　　　fure,

fure that whofoeuer oppofeth any doctrine propofed by the Church, doth thereby contradict a
truth, which is teftified by God : As when any
lawfull Superiour , notifies his will, by the
meanes,and as it were propofall of fome faithfull meffenger, the fubiect of fuch a Superiour
in performing, or neglecting what is deliuered
by the meffenger, is faid to obey, or difobey his
owne lawfull Superiour. And therfore becaufe
the teftimony of God is notified by the Church,
we may,and we do moft truly fay, that not to
belieue what the Church propofeth, is to deny
God's holy word or teftimony, fignified to vs
by the Church, according to that faying of *S.*
Irenæus. We need not goe (m *) to any other to feeke*
the truth, which we may eafily receiue from the
Church .

(m) *Lib. 3.*
cont. heref.
cap. 4.

9. From this definition of fayth we may alfo know what *Herefy* is, by taking the contrary
termes, as *Herefy* is contrary to *Fayth*, and faying: *Herefy is a voluntary error againft that which*
God hath reuealed, and the Church hath propofed for
fuch. Neither doth it import, whether the error
concerne points in themfelues great or fmall,
fundamentall or not fundamentall. For more
being required to an act of Vertue, then of
Vice, if any truth though neuer fo fmall may be
belieued by *Fayth* affoone as we know it to be
teftified by diuine reuelation; much more will it
be a formall *Herefy* to deny any leaft point fufficiently propoūded as a thing witneffed by God.

10. This

10. This diuine Fayth is diuided into *Actuall,* and *Habituall.* *Actuall* fayth, or fayth actuated is when we are in act of confideration, and beliefe of fome myftery of Fayth; for example, that our Sauiour Chrift, is true God, and Man, &c. *Habituall* fayth, is that from which we are denominated *Faithfull,* or *Beliewers,* as by *actuall* fayth they are ftiled, *Beliewing.* This *Habit* of fayth is a *Quality,* enabling vs moft firmely to belieue Obiects aboue human difcourfe, and it remaineth permanently in our Soule, euen when we are fleeping, or not thinking of any Myftery of Fayth. This is the firft among the three *Theologicall* Vertues. For *Charity* vnites vs to God, as he is infinitely *Good in' himfelfe;* *Hope* ties vs to him, as he is vnfpeakably *Good to vs.* *Fayth* ioynes vs to him, as he is the *Supreme immoueable Verity.* *Charity* relies on his *Goodnes;* *Hope* on his *Power;* *Fayth* on his diuine *Wifedome.* From hence it followeth, that *Fayth* being one of the Vertues which Deuines terme *Infufed* (that is, which cannot be acquired by human wit, or induftry, but are in their Nature & Effence, fupernaturall) it hath this property; that it is not deftroied by little and little, (contrarily to the *Habits,* called *acquifiti,* that is, gotten by human endeuour, which as they are fuccef-fiuely produced, fo alfo are they loft fucceffiuely, or by little and little) but it muft either be conferued entire, or wholy deftroied: And fince it cannot ftand entire with any one act which

is directly contrary, it muſt be totally ouerthrowne,and as it were demoliſhed, and razed
by euery ſuch act. Wherfore, as *Charity* or the
Loue of God is expelled from our ſoule by any
one act of *Hatred*, or any other mortall ſinne
againſt his diuine Maieſty: and as *Hope* is deſtroied by any one act of voluntary *Deſperation*:
ſo *Fayth* muſt periſh by any one act of *Hereſy*;
becauſe euery ſuch act is directly, and formally
oppoſite therunto. I know that ſome ſinnes
which (as Deuines ſpeake) are *ex genere ſuo*, in
in their kind, grieuous and *mortall*, may be much
leſſened,and fall to be *veniall, ob leuitatem mate-
ria*, becauſe they may happen to be exerciſed in
a matter of ſmall conſideration; as for example, to ſteale a penny, is veniall, although theft
in his *kind* be a deadly ſinne. But it is likewiſe
true, that this Rule is not generall for all ſorts
of ſinnes; there being ſome ſo inexcuſably wicked of their owne nature, that no ſmalnes of
matter, nor paucity in number, can defend
them from being deadly ſinnes. For, to giue an
inſtance, what Blaſphemy againſt God, or voluntary falſe Oath is not a deadly ſinne? Certainely, none at all, although the ſaluation of
the whole world ſhould depend vpon ſwearing
ſuch a falſhood. The like hapneth in our preſent caſe of Hereſy, the iniquity wherof redoun-
ding to the iniury of God's ſupreme wiſdom &
Goodnes, is alwayes great, & enormous. They

were no precious ſtones which *Dauid* (n) pickt

out

out of the water, to encounter *Golias*; and yet if
a man take from the number but one, and say
they were but foure, againft the Scripture affirming them to haue been fiue; he is inftantly
guilty of a damnable finne. Why? Becaufe by
this fubtraction of *One*, he doth depriue Gods
word and Teftimony of *all* credit and infallibility. For if either he could deceiue, or be deceiued in any *one* thing, it were but wifdome
to fufpect him in *all.* And feing euery *Herefy* oppofeth fome Truth reuealed by God; it is no
wonder that no one can be excufed from deadly, and damnable finne. For if voluntary *Blaf-*
phemy, and *Periury,* which are oppofite only to
the *infufed Morall* Vertue of *Religion*, can neuer be excufed from mortall finne: much leffe
can *Herefy* be excufed, which oppofeth the
Theologicall Vertue of *Fayth.*

11. If any obiect, that *Schifme* may feeme
to be a greater finne then *Herefy*; becaufe the
Vertue of *Charity* (to which Schifme is oppofite) is greater then Fayth, according to the A-
poftle, faying: *Now there remaine* (o) *Fayth, Hope,* (o) *1. Cor.*
Charity; but the greater of thefe is Charity. S. Tho- 13. 13.
mas anfweres in thefe words: *Charity hath two*
Obiects: one principal, to wit, the Diuine (p) *Goodnes;* (p) 2.2. *q.*
& another fecondary, namely the good of our Neigh- 39. *ar.* 2. *in*
bour; But Schifme and other finnes which are com *corp. & ad*
mitted against our Neighbour, are oppofite to Chari- 3.
ty in refpect of this fecondary good, which is leffe, then
the obiect of Fayth, which is God; as he is the Prime
Ve-

Verity, on Which *Fayth doth rely ; and therfore thefe finnes are leffe then Infidelity.* He takes *Infidelity* after a generall manner, as it comprehends *Herefy,* and other vices againft Fayth.

12. Hauing therfore fufficiently declared, wherin *Herefy* confifts ; Let vs come to proue that which we propofed in this Chapter. Where I defire, it be ftill remembred : That the vifible Catholique Church cannot erre damnably ,as *D.Potter* confeffeth: And, that when *Luther* appeared, there was no other vifible true Church of Chrift difagreeing from the *Roman ,* as we haue demonftrated in the next precedent Chapter.

13. Now , that *Luther* & his followers cannot be excufed from formall *Herefy,* I proue by thefe reafons. To oppofe any truth propounded by the vifible true Church as reuealed by God, is formall *Herefy,* as we haue fhewed out of the definition of *Herefy*: But *Luther, Caluin,* and the reft did oppofe diuers truths propounded by the vifible Church as reuealed by God; yea they did *therfore* oppofe her, becaufe fhe propounded as diuine reuealed truths , things which they iudged either to be falfe, or human inuentions : Therfore they committed formall *Herefy.*

14. Moreouer , euery Errour agaynft any doctrine reuealed by God , is damnable Herefy, whether the matter in it felfe be great or fmall, as I proued before : and therefore eyther the Proteftants, or the *Roman* Church muft be guil-

ty

ty of formall Herefy; becaule one of them muft erre againft the word & teftimony of God : but you grant (perforce) that the *Roman* Church doth not erre damnably ; & I add that fhe cannot erre damnably , becaule fhe is the truly Catholique Church , which you confeffe cannot erre damnably : Therefore Proteftants muft be guilty of formall *Herefy* .

15. Befides , we haue fhewed that the vifible Church , is Iudge of Controuerfies & therfore muft be infallible in all her Propofalls ; which being once fuppofed , it manifeftly followeth , that to oppofe what fhe deliuereth as reuealed by God , is not fo much to oppofe *her* , as *God* himfelfe ; and therefore cannot be excufed from grieuous Herefy .

16. Agayne , If *Luther* were an *Heretique* for thofe points wherin he difagreed from the *Roman* Church ; All they who agree with him in thofe very points , muft likewife be Heretiques. Now , that *Luther* was a formall Heretique I demonftrate in this manner . To fay , that Gods vifible true Church is not vniuerfal , but confined to one onely place or corner of the world , is according to your owne expreffe words *(* q *) properly* Herefy , *agaynft that* ⌐*Article* (q) *Pag.* *of the Creed , wherein we profeffe to belieue the holy* 126. *Catholique Church* : And you brand *Donatus* with herefy , becaule he limited the vniuerfal Church to *Africa* . But it is manifeft , and acknowledged by *Luther* himfelfe , and other chiefe Proteftants

that _Luthers_ Reformation when it firſt begaa
(and much more for diuers Ages before) was
not _Vniuerſall_, nor ſpread ouer the world, but
was confiñed to that compaſſe of grouud
which did containe _Luthers_ body . Therefore
his Reformation cannot be excuſed from formall Hereſy. If _S. Auguſtine_ in thoſe times ſayd
to the Donatiſts , _There are innumerable teſtimo-_
nies (r) _of holy Scripture in which it appeareth that_
the Church of Chriſt is not onely in Africa , as theſe
men with moſt impudēt vanity do raue, but that ſhe is
ſpred ouer the whole earth : much more may it be
ſayd ; It appeareth by innumerable teſtimonies
of holy Scripture that the Church of Chriſt cã-
not be confined to the Citty of _Wittemberg_ , or
to the place where _Luthers_ feet ſtood , but muſt
be ſpread ouer the whole world. It is therefore
muſt impudent vanity, and dotage to limit her to
Luthers Reformation. In another place alſo this
holy Father writes no leiſe effectually agaynſt
Luther then againſt the _Donatiſts._ For hauing out
of thoſe words, _In thy ſeed all Nations ſhall be bleſ-_
ſed, proued that Gods Church muſt be _vniuerſal,_
he ſayth : _Why (s) doe you ſuperadde, by ſaying that_
Chriſt remaines heire in no part of the earth , except
where he may haue Donatus for his Coheyre . Giue
me this (Vniuerſall) Church if it be among you :
ſhew your ſelues to all Nations, which we already ſhew
to be bleſſed in this Seed: Giue vs this (Church)
or elſe laying aſide all fury, receyue her from vs . But
it is euident, that _Luther_ could not , when he
he

he said, *At the beginning I was alone*, giue vs an *vniuersall* Church. Therfore happy had he been, if he had then, and his followers would now, *receiue her from vs.* And therfore we must con-clude with the same holy Father, saying in ano-ther place of the vniuersall Church : *She hath this (t) most certaine marke, that she cannot be hid-den: She is then knowne to all Nations. The Sect of* *Donatus is vnknown to many Nations; therfore that* *cannot be she. The Sect of Luther* (at least when he *began*, and much more before his beginning) *was vnknowne to many Nations, therfore that cannot be she.*

(t) *Cont. lit. Petil. lib.* 1. *cap.* 104.

17. And that it may yet further appeare how perfectly *Luther* agreed with the *Donatists:* It is to be noted, that they neuer taught, that the Catholique Church ought not to extend it selfe further then that part of *Africa*, where their faction raigned, but only that in fact it was so confined, becaufe all the rest of the Church was prophaned, by communicating with *Cæcilianus*, whom they falsly affirmed to haue been ordained Bishop by thofe who were *Traditours*, or giuers vp of the Bible to the Perfe-cutors to be burned: yea at that very time they had some of their Sect residing in *Rome*, and sent thither one *Victor*, a Bishop, vnder colour to take care of their Brethren in that Citty, but indeed as *Baronius* (u) obserueth, that the world might account them Catholiques, by communicating with the Bishop of *Rome*, to communicate with

(u) *Anno* 321. *nu.* 2. *Spond.*

whom

whom was euen taken by the Ancient Fathers
as an aſſured ſigne of being a true Catholique.
They had alſo, as *S. Auguſtine* witneſſeth, a pretended (w) Church in the howſe and territory
of a Spaniſh Lady called *Lucilla*, who went flying out of the Catholique Church, becauſe ſhe
had been iuſtly checked by *Cæcilianus*. And the
ſame *Saint* ſpeaking of the conference he had
with *Fortunius* the Donatiſt, ſayth: *Heere did he*
firſt (x) attempt to affirme that his Communion was
ſpread ouer the whole Earth &c. but becauſe the thing
was euidently falſe, they got out of this diſcourſe by
confuſion of language : wherby neuertheles they
ſufficiently declared, that they did not hold, that
the true Church ought neceſſarily to be confined to one place, but only by meere neceſſity
were forced to yield that it was ſo in fact, becauſe their Sect which they held to be the only
true Church was not ſpread ouer the world: In
which point *Fortunius*, and the reſt were more
modeſt, then he who ſhould affirme that *Lu-*
ther's reformation in the very beginning was
ſpead ouer the whole Earth ; being at that time by
many degrees not ſo far diffuſed as the Sect of
the *Donatiſts*. I haue no deſire to proſecute the
ſimilitude of Proteſtants with *Donatiſts*, by re-
membring that the Sect of theſe men was began and promoted by the paſſion of *Lucilla*; and
who is ignorant what influence two women,
the Mother and Daughter, miniſtred to Proteſtancy in England ? Nor will I ſtand to obſerue
their

(w) *De Vni.*
Eccleſ. c. 3.

(x) *Ep.* 163.

their very likenes of phrafe with the *Donatifts,*
who called the Chaire of *Rome*, the Chaire of
peftilence, and the *Roman* Church an Harlot,
which is *D.Potter's* owne phrafe, wherin he is
leffe excufable then they, becaufe he maintai-
neth her to be a true Church of Chrift: & therfore let him duely ponder thefe words of *S. Auguftine* againft the *Donatifts. If I perfecute him iuftly who detracts* (y *)from his Neighbour, why fhould
I not perfecute him who detracts from the Church
of Chrift, and fayth, this is not fhe, but this is an Harlot ?* And leaft of all, will I confider, whether
you may not be well compared to one *Ticonius*
a *Donatift,* who wrote againft *Parmenianus* likewife a *Donatist*, who blafphemed, that the
Church of Chrift had perifhed(as you do e-
uen in this your Booke write againft fome of
your Proteftant Brethren, or as you call them
Zelots among you, who hold the very fame or
rather a worfe Herefy)and yet remained among
them, euen after *Parmenianus* had excommunicated him, (as thofe your Zealous Brethren
would proceed agaynft you if it were in their
power) and yet like *Ticonius* you remaine in
their Communion, and come not into that
Church which is, hath been, and fhall euer be
vniuerfall: For which very caufe *S. Auguftin*
complaines of *Ticonius,* that although he wrote
againft the Donatifts, yet he was of *an hart* (z)
fo extremely abfurd, as not to forfake them alto
gether. And fpeaking of the fame thing in ano-

(y) *Cone. fæ-*
per geft. cum
Emerit.

(z) *De doctr.*
Chrift. lib. 3.
cap. 30.

K k   ther

ther place he obferues, that although *Ticonius*
did manifeftly confute them who affirmed that
the Church had perifhed ; yet, *he faw not* (fayth
this holy Father) *that which in good confequence*

(a) *he fhould haue feene, that thofe Christians of A-
frica belonged to the Church fpread ouer the whole
world, who remained vnited, not with them who were
diuided from the communion and vnity of the fame
world , but with fuch as did communicate with the
whole world.* But *Parmenianus , and the rest of the
Donatists faw that confequence, and refolued rather
to fettle their mind in obftinacy against the most manifest truth which Ticonius maintained , then by yielding therto, to be ouercome by thofe Churches in A-
frica , which enioyed the communion of that vnity
which Ticonius defended , from which they had diuided themfelues .* How fitly thefe words agree
to Catholiques in England in refpect of the
Proteftants, 1 defire the Reader to confider.
But thefe and the like refemblances of Proteftants to the *Donatiftes*, 1 willingly let paffe ,
and onely vrge the maine point: That fince
Luthers Reformed Church was not in being
for diuers Centuries before *Luther* , and yet
was (becaufe fo forfooth they will needs haue
it) in the Apoftles time, they muft of neceffity affirme heretically with the *Donatifts*, that
the true and vnfpotted Church of Chrift perifhed ; & that fhe which remained on earth was
(O blafphemy !) an Harlot. Moreouer the fame herely followes out of the doctrine of *D*.

Potter

Potter, and other Proteftants, that the Church may erre in points not fundamentall; becaufe we haue fhewed that euery errour againft any one reuealed truth, is *Herefy* and *damnable*, whether the matter be otherwife of it felfe, great or fmall. And how can the Church more truly be fayd to perifh, then when fhe is permitted to maintaine a *damnable Herefy*? Befides, we will heereafter proue, that by any act of Herefy all diuine fayth is loft; & to imagine a true Church of faithfull perfons without any fayth, is as much as to fancy a liuing man without life. It is therefore cleere, that Donatift-like they hold that the Church of Chrift perifhed: yea they are worfe then the *Donatifts*, who faid, that the Church remained at leaft in *Africa*; whereas Proteftants muft of neceffity be forced to grant, that for a long fpace before *Luther*, fhe was no where at all. But let vs goe forward to other reafons.

18. The holy Scripture, and Ancient Fathers do affigne Separation from the Vifible Church as a marke of *Herefy*; according to that of *S. Iohn: They went ous* (b) *from vs.* And, *Some who* (c) *went out from vs.* And, *Our of you fhall* (d) *arife men fpeaking peruerfe things.* And accordingly *Vincentius Lyrinenfis* fayth: *Who euer* (e) *began herefies, who did not firft feparate himfelfe from the Vniuerfality, Antiquity, and Confent of the Catholique Church?* But it is manifeft, that when *Luther* appeared, there was no vifible Church

di-

(b) 2. *Ioan.* 19.
(c) *Act.* 15. 21.
(d) *Act.* 20; 30.
(e) *Lib. aduerfus hær.* cap. 34.

diftinct from the *Roman*, out of which fhe could
depart, as it is likewife well knowne that *Luther*, & his followers departed out of *her*: Therfore fhe is no way lyable to this Marke of *Herefy*, but Proteftants cannot poffibly auoid it. To
this purpofe *S. Profper* hath thefe pithy words:
A Chriftian communicating (f) with the vniuerfall Church *is a Catholique, and he who is diuided from her, is an Heretique, and Antichrift.* But
Luther in his firft Reformation could not communicate with the vifible Catholique Church
of thofe times, becaufe he began his Reformation by oppofing the fuppofed Errors of the
then vifible Church: we muft therfore fay with
S. Profper, that he was an *Heretique* &c. Which
likewife is no leffe cleerly proued out of *S. Cyprian,* faying: *Not we* (g) *departed from them, but
they from vs, and fince Herefies and Schifmes are
bred afterwards, while they make to themfelues diuers
Conuenticles, they haue forfaken the head and origen
of Truth.*

19, And that we might not remaine doubtfull what feparation it is, which is the marke of
Herefy, the ancient Fathers tel vs more in particular, that it is from the Church of *Rome,* as it is
the Sea of *Peter.* And therfore *D. Potter* need not
to be fo hot with vs, becaufe we fay & writ that
the Church of *Rome,* in that fenfe as fhe is the
Mother Church of all others, and with which
all the reft agree, is truly callled the *Catholique
Church. S. Hierome* writing to Pope *Damafus*
fayth:

(f) *Dimid.
temp. cap.5.*

(g) *Lib. de
Vnit. Eclef.*

sayth : *I am in the Communion* (h) *of the Chayre of Peter; I know that the Church is built vpon that Rocke. Whosoeuer shall eate the Labe out of this house he is profane. If any shall not be in the Arke of Noe, he shall perish in the tyme of the deluge : Whosoeuer doth not gather with thee, doth scatter, that is, he that is not of Christ is of Antichrist.* And elswheres *Which doth he* (i) *call his fayth? That of the Roman Church? Or that which is contained in the Bookes of Origen; If he answere, the Roman, then we are Catholiques, who haue translated nothing of the error of Origen.* And yet further : *Know thou, that the* (k) *Roman fayth commended by the voyce of the Apostle doth not receiue these delusions, though an Angell should denounce otherwise, then it hath once been preached.* S. *Ambrose* recounting how his Brother *Satyrus* inquiring for a Church wherin to giue thanks for his deliuery from Shipwrack, sayth: *he called vnto him* (l) *the Bishop, neither did he esteeme any fauour to be true, except that of the true fayth, and he asked of him whether he agreed with the Catholique Bishops; that is, with the Roman Church.* And hauing vnderstood that he was a *Schismatique,* that is, separated from the *Roman* Church, he abstained from communicating with him. Where we see the priuiledge of the *Roman* Church confirmed both by word and deed, by doctrine and practise. And the same Saint sayth of the Roman Church : *From thence the Rights* (m) *of Venerable Communion do flow to all.* S. *Cyprian* sayth: *They are bold* (n) *to saile to the*

(h) *Ep.* 57. *ad Damas.*

(i) *Lib.* 1. *Apolog.*

(k) *Jbid. lib.* 3.

(l) *De obitu Satyris fratri.*

(m) *lib.* 1. *ep.* 4. *ad Impe-ratores.*

(n) *Epist.* 55. *ad Cornel.*

Chaire

Chaire of Peter, and to the principall Church, from
whence Priestly Vnity hath sprung. Neither do they
consider, that they are Romans, whose Fayth was commended by the preaching of the Apostle, to whom falshood cannot haue accesse. Where we see this holy
Father ioynes together the principall Church, and
the Chaire of Peter; and affirmeth that falshood
not only hath not had, but cannot haue accesse to
that Sea. And else where : Thou wrotest that I
should send (o) a Coppy of the same letters to Cornelius our Collegue, that laying aside all solicitude, he
might now be assured that thou didst Communicate
with him, that is, with the Catholique Church. What
thinke you M. Doctor of these words? Is it so
strang a thing to take for one and the same
thing, to communicate with the Church & Pope
of Rome, and to communicate with the Catholique Church? S. Irenæus sayth. Because it were long
to number the successions of all Churches, (p) we declaring the Tradition (and fayth preached to men,
and comming to vs by Tradition) of the most
great, most ancient, and most knowne Church, founded by the two most glorious Apostles Peter and Paul;
which Tradition it hath from the Apostles, comming
to vs by succession of Bishops ; We confound all those
who any way either by euill complacence of themselues, or vaine glory, or by blindnes, or ill Opinion do gather otherwise then they ought. For to this Church for
a more powerfull Principality, it is necessary that all
Churches resort, that is, all faythfull people of what
place soeuer: in which (Roman Church) the Tradition

(o) Epist.52.

(p) Lib.3.
cont.her.c.
3.

dition which is from the Apostles hath alwayes been conserued from those who are euery where. S. Augustin sayth : *It grieues vs* (q) *to see you so to ly cut off. Number the Priests euen from the Sea of Peter ; and consider in that order of Fathers who succeeded to whome. She is the Rock which the proud Gates of Hell do not ou rcome.* And in another place , speaking of *Cæcilianus* he sayth : *He might contemne the conspiring* (r) *multitude of his Enemies , because he knew himselfe to be vnited , by Communicatory letters both to the Roman Church in which the Principality of the Sea Apostolique did alwayes florish ; and to other Countreys from whence the Gospell came first into Africa.* Ancient *Tertullian* sayth : *If thou be neere Italy , thou hast Rome whose* (s) *Authority is neere at hand to vs: a happy Church ,into which the Apostles haue powred all Doctrine, together with their bloud* S. *Basill* in a letter to the Bishop of *Rome* sayth. *In very deed that which was giuen* (t) *by our Lord to thy Piety , is worthy of that most excellent voyce which proclaymed thee Blessed, to wit, that thou maist discerne betwixt that which is counterfeit, and that which is lawfull and pure , and without any diminution mayest preach the Fayth of our Ancestors.* *Maximianus* Bishop of Constantinople about twelue hundred yeares agoe, said : *All the bounds of the earth who haue sincerely acknowledged our Lord, and Catholiques through the whole world professing the true Faith, looke vpon the power of the Bishop of Rome, as vpon the sunne &c. For the Creator of the world, amongst all men of the world elected him*

(q) *In psal. cont. partem Donati.*

(r) *Ep. 162.*

(s) *Prescr. cap. 36.*

(t) *Epist. ad Pont. Rom.*

(he

(he speakes of *S. Peter*) *to whom he granted the Chaire of Doctour to be principally possessed by a perpetuall right of Priuiledge; that whosoeuer is desirous to know any diuine and profound thing, may haue recourse to the Oracle, and Doctrine of this instruction.* Iohn Patriarck of *Constantinople*, more then eleauen hundred yeares agoe in an Epistle to Pope *Hormisda*, writeth thus: *Because* (u)*the beginning of saluation is to conserue the rule of right Fayth, & in no wise to swarue from the tradition of our for-Fathers; because the words of our Lord cannot faile, saying: Thou art Peter, and vpon this Rocke I will build my Church; the proofes of deeds haue made good those words, because in the Sea Apostolicall the Catholique Religion is alwayes conserued inuiolable.* And a-gaine: *We promise heerafter not to recite in the sacred Mysteries the names of them who are excluded from the Communion of the Catholique Church, that is to say, who consent not fully with the Sea Apostolique.* Many other Authorities of the ancient Fathers might be produced to this purpose, but these may serue to shew, that both the *Latin*, & *Greeke* Fathers held for a Note of being a Catholique, or an Heretique, to haue been vnited, or diuided from the Sea of *Rome*. And I haue purposely alledged only such Authorities of Fathers, as speake of the priuiledges of the Sea of *Rome*, as of things permament, and depending on our *Sauiours* promise to *S. Peter*, from which a generall rule, and ground ought to be taken for all Ages, becaule *Heauen and Earth*

shall

shall (w) *paße*, *but the word of our Lord shall re-*
maine for euer. So that I heere conclude, that feing it is manifeſt that *Luther* and his followers
diuided themſelues from the Sea of *Rome*, they
beare the inſeparable Marke of *Hereſy.*

20. And though my meaning be not to
treate the point of Ordination, or Succeſſion
in the Proteſtants Church, becauſe the Fathers
alledged in the laſt reaſon, aſſigne Succeſſion
as one marke of the true Church; I muſt not o-
mit to ſay, that according to the grounds of
Proteſtants themſelues, they can neyther pretend *perſonall Succeſsion* of Biſhops, nor *Succeſsion of doctrine.* For whereas Succeſſion of Biſhops
ſignifies a neuer - interrupted line of Perſons,
endued with an indeleble *Quality*, which Deuines call a *Character*, which cānot be taken away
by *depoſition, degradation* or other meanes whatſoeuer; and endued alſo with Iuriſdiction and
Authority to teach, to preach, to gouerne the
Church by lawes, precepts, cenſures, &c. Proteſtāts cannot pretend Succeſſiō in either of theſe.
For (beſids that there was neuer Proteſtant Biſhop before *Luther*, and that there can be no
continuance of *Succeſsion*, where there was no
beginning to ſucceed) they cōmonly acknowledge no *Character*, & conſequently muſt affirme
that when their pretended Biſhops or Prieſts
are depriued of Iuriſdiction, or degraded, they
remaine meere lay Perſons as before their Ordination; fulfilling what *Tertullian* obiects as a

(x)*Prefer.*
*cap.*41.
marke of Herefy : *To day a Priest, to morrow (x) a
Lay-man.* For if there be no immoueable *Character*, their power of *Order* muft confift onely in
Iurifdiction, and authority, or in a kind of morall deputation to fome function, which therefore may be taken away by the fame power, by
which it was giuen. Neither can they pretend
Succeffion in Authority, or Iurifdiction. For
all the Authority, or Iurifdiction which they
had, was conferred by the Church of *Rome*,
that is, by the Pope : Becaufe the whole Church
collectiuely doth not meet to ordayne Bifhops
or Priefts, or to giue them Authority. But according to their owne doctrine, they belieue
that the Pope neyther *hath, or ought to haue any
Iurifdiction, Power, Superiority, Preheminence, or
Authority Ecclefiafticall, or Spirituall within this
Realme*, which they fweare euen when they are
ordained Bifhops, Priefts, and Deacons : How
then can the Pope giue Iurifdiction where they
fweare he neyther *hath, nor O V G H T to haue a-
ny* ? Or if yet he had, how could they without
Schifme withdraw themfelues from his obedience ? Befides, the *Roman* Church neuer gaue
them Authority, to oppofe Her, by whome it
was giuen. But grant, their firft Bifhops had
fuch Authority from the Church of *Rome*: after
the deceafe of thofe men, who gaue Authority
to their pretended Succeffours ? The Primate
of England? But from whome had he fuch Authority ? And after his deceafe, who fhall conferre

ferre Authority vpon his Succeſſours ? The
temporall Magiſtrate? King *Henry*, neyther a
Catholique , nor a Proteſtant ? King *Edward* , a
Child ? Queene *Elizabeth* , a Woman? An Infant of one houres Age , is true King in caſe of
his Predeceſſours deceaſe: But ſhal your Church
lye fallow till that Infant - King, and greene
Head of the Church come to yeares of diſcre-
tion ? Doe your Biſhops , your Hierarchy, your
Succeſſion, your Sacraments , your being or
not being Heretiques for want of Succeſſion,
depēd on this new-found Supremacy-doctrine
brought in by ſuch a man meerely vpon baſe
occaſions , and for ſhamefull ends; impugned
by *Caluin* , and his followers ; derided by the
Chriſtian world; & euen by chiefe Proteſtants
as *D. Andrewes* , *Wotton &c.* not held for any
neceſſary point of fayth ? And from whome I
pray you, had Biſhops their Authority , when
there were no Chriſtian Kinges ? Muſt the
Greeke Patriarks receiue ſpirituall Iuriſdiction
from the Greeke Turke . Did the Pope , by the
Baptiſme of Princes , looſe the ſpirituall Power
he formerly had of conferring ſpirituall Iuriſdiction vpon Biſhops ? Hath the temporall Magiſtrate authority to preach, to aſſoile from ſinnes , to inflict excommunications , and other
Cenſures? Why hath he not Power to excommunicate, as well as to diſpenſe in Irregularity,
as our late Soueraigne Lord King *Iames* , either
diſpenſed with the late *Archbiſhop* of *Canter-*
bury,

bury, or els gaue commiſſion to ſome Biſhops to
doe it? and ſince they were ſubiect to their Primate, and not he to them, it is cleere, that they
had no Power to diſpenſe with him, but that
power muſt proceed from the Prince, as Superiour to them all, and head of the Proteſtants
Church in England. If he haue no ſuch authority, how can he giue to others what himſelfe
hath not? Your Ordination, or Conſecration
of Biſhops and Prieſts imprinting no *Character*,
can only conſiſt in giuing a Power, Authority,
Iuriſdiction, or (as I ſaid before) ſome kind of
Deputation to exerciſe Epiſcopall, or Prieſtly
functions: If then, the temporall Magiſtrate
confers this Power &c. he can, nay he cannot
chuſe but Ordaine, and conſecrate Biſhops, and
Prieſts, as often as he confers Authority or Iuriſdiction: and your Biſhops as ſoone as they
are deſigned and confirmed by the King, muſt
ipſo facto be Ordained and Conſecrated by him
without interuention of *Biſhops*, or *Matter* and
Forme of *Ordination:* Which abſurdities you will
be more vnwilling to grant, then well able to
auoid, if you will be true to your owne doctrines. The Pope from whom originally you muſt
beg your Succeſſion of Biſhops, neuer receiued,
nor will, nor can acknowledge to receiue any
Spirituall Iuriſdiction from any Temporall
Prince, and therfore if Iuriſdiction muſt be deriued from Princes, he hath none at all: and yet
either you muſt acknowledge, that he hath true
ſpiri-

fpirituall Iurifdiction, or that your Selues can receiue none from him.

21. Moreouer, this new Reformation, or Reformed Church of Proteftants, will by them be pretended to be *Catholique*, or *Vniuerfall*, and not confined to *England* alone, as the Sect of the *Donatifts* was to *Africa:* and therfore it muft comprehend all the Reformed Churches in *Germany, Holland, Scotland, France &c.* In which number, they of *Germany*, *Holland*, and *France*, are not gouerned by Bifhops, nor regard any perfonall Succeffiō, vnles of fuch fat-beneficed Bifhops as *Nicolaus Amsfordius*, who was con-fecrated by *Luther*, (though *Luther* himfelfe was neuer Bifhop) as witneffeth (y) *Dreſſerus*. (y) *In Mille-* And though *Scotland* hath of late admitted fome *nario fexto* Bifhops, I much doubt whether they hold them *pag.187.* to be neceffary, or of diuine Inftitution; and fo their enforced admitting of them, doth not fo much furnifh that kingdome with *perfonall Suc-cefsion* of Bifhops, as it doth conuince them to want *Succefsion of Doctrine*; fince in this their neglect of Bifhops they difagree both from the milder Proteftants of England, and the true Catholique Church : And by this want of a cō-tinued perfonall Succeffion of Bifhops, they re-taine the note of *Schifme*, & *Herefy*. So that the Church of Proteftants, muft either not be *vni-uerfall*, as being confined to England ; Or if you will needs comprehend all thofe Churches which want Succeffion, you muft confeffe,

Ll 3   that

that your Church doth not only communicate
with *Schifmaticall* and *Hereticall* Churches, but
is alfo compounded of fuch Churches; & your
felues cannot auoid the note of Schifmatiques,
or Heretiques, if it were but for participating
with fuch hereticall Churches. For it is impoffible to retaine Communion with the true Catholique Church, and yet agree with them who
are diuided from her by Schifme, or Herefy; becaufe that were to affirme, that for the felfe fame time, they could be *within*, and *without* the
Catholique Church, as proportionably I dif-
courfed in the next precedent Chapter, concerning the Communicating of moderate Proteftants with thofe who maintaine that Herefy of
the Latency and Inuifibility of Gods Church,
where I brought a place of *S. Cyprian* to this
purpofe, which the Reader may be pleafed to
reuiew in the *Fifth Chapter*, and 17.*Number*.

22. But befides this defect in the perfonall
Succeffion of Proteftant Bifhops, there is another of great moment; which is, that they wāt
the right *Forme* of ordaining *Bifhops*, and *Priefts*,
becaufe the manner which they vfe is fo much
different from that of the *Roman* Church (at
leaft according to the common opinion of Deuines) that it cannot be fufficient for the *Effence*
of *Ordination*; as I could demonftrate if this
were the proper place of fuch a Treatife, and
will not fayle to doe if *D. Potter* giue me occafion. In the meane time the Reader may be plea-
led

fed to read the Authour (z) cited heere in the
margent, & then compare the forme of our Ordination with that of Proteſtants; and to remēber that if the forme which they vſe eyther in
Conſecrating Biſhops, or in Ordayning Prieſts
be *at leaſt* douvtfull, they can neyther haue *vn-*
doubtcd Prieſts, nor Biſhops. For *Prieſts* cannot
be ordayned but by true *Biſhops*, nor can any
be a true *Biſhop*, vnles he firſt be *Prieſt*. I ſay,
their Ordination is *at leaſt* doubtfull; becauſe
that ſufficeth for my preſent purpoſe. For Biſhops and Prieſts, whoſe Ordination is *noto-*
riouſly knowne to be but doubtfull, are not to be
eſteemed Biſhops, or Prieſts: and no man without Sacriledge can receiue Sacraments from
them; all which they adminiſter vnlawfully:
And (if we except Baptiſme, with manifeſt
danger of inualidity, and with obligation to
be at leaſt conditionally repeated) ſo Proteſtants muſt remaine doubtfull of Remiſſion
of ſinnes, of their Eccleſiaſticall Hierarchy, and
may not pretend to be a true Church, which
cannot ſubſiſt without *vndoubted* true Biſhops,
and Prieſts, nor without due adminiſtration of
Sacraments, which (according to Proteſtants)
is an eſſentiall note of the true Church. And
it is a world to obſerue the proceeding of Engliſh Proteſtants in this point of their *Ordinati-*
ons. For firſt, *Ann. 3. Edw. 6. cap. 2.* when he
was a *Child* about twelue yeares of age, *It was*
enacted, that ſuch (a) *forme of making, and conſe-*
crating

(z) *See A-*
damum Tā-
nerum tom.
4. diſp. 7.
quæſt. 2.
dub. 3. & 4.

(a) *Dyer fol.*
234. term.
Mich. 6. &
7. Eliz.

crating of Bifhops and Priefts , as by fix Prelates,and
fix other to be appointed by the King,fhould be deui-
fed (marke this word *, deuifed) and fet forth vn-*
der the great Seale ; *fhould be vfed , and none other.*
But after, this Act was repealed 1. *Mar. Seff.* 2.
in fo much as that when afterward *An.* 6. *&* 7.
Reg. Eliz. Bifhop *Bonner* being endicted vpon
a certifitate made by *D. Horne* a Proteftant Bifhop of *Winchefter,* for his refufal of the Oath of
Supremacy ; and he excepting agaynft the en-
dictment becaufe *D. Horne* was no Bifhop; all
the Iudges refolued that his exceptiō was good,
if indeed *D. Horne* was not Bifhop ; and they
were all at a ftand, till *An.* 8. *Eliz.cap.* 1. the act
of *Edw.* 6. was renewed and confirmed, with a
particular *prouifo,* that no man fhould be impe-
ched or molefted by meanes of any certificate
by any Bifhop or Archbifhop made before this
laft Act . Whereby it is cleere , that they made
fome doubt of their owne ordination ; and that
there is nothing but vncertainty in the whole
bufines of their Ordination , which (forfooth)
muft depend vpon fix Prelats , the great Seale ,
Acts of Parlaments being contrary one to another, and the like.

23.   But though they want Perfonall Succeffion ; yet at leaft they haue Succeffion of doctrine as they fay, & pretend to proue , becaufe
they belieue as the *Apoftles* belieued . This is
to begg the Queftion, and to take what they
may be fure , will neuer be graunted . For if
                                                        they

they want Perſonall Succeſſion, and ſleight
Eccleſiaſticall Tradition, how will they perſwade any man, that they agree with the doctrine of the Apoſtles? We haue heard *Tertulliæ*
ſaying: *I will preſcribe* (b) *againſt all Heretiques)
that there is no meanes to proue what the Apoſtles
preached, but by the ſame Churches which they founded.* And *S. Irenæus* tels vs that, *We may* (c) *behold
the Tradition of the Apoſtles in euery Church , if
men be deſirous to heare the truth; and we can number them who were made Biſhops by the Apoſtles in
Churches, and their Succeſſors, euen to vs.* And the
ſame Father in another place ſayth : *We ought to
obey (d) thoſe Prieſts who are in the Church , who
haue Succeſsion from the Apoſtles, and who together
with Succeſsion in their Biſhoprickes haue receiued the
certaine guift of truth. S. Auguſtin* ſayth: *I am kept
in the Church* (e) *by the Succeſsion of Prieſts from
the very Sea of Peter the Apoſtle , to whom our Sauiour after his Reſurrection committed his Sheep to
be fed , euen to the preſent Biſhop. Origen* to this
purpoſe giueth vs a good and wholeſome Rule
(happy, if himſelfe had followed the ſame) in
theſe excellent words : *Since there be many who
thinke* (f) *they belieue the things which are of Chriſt,
and ſome are of different opinion from thoſe who went
before them; let the preaching of the Church be kept,
which is deliuered by the Apoſtles by order of Succeſsion, and remaines in the Church to this very day;
that only is to be belieued for truth , which in nothing
diſagrees from the Tradition of the Church.* In vaine

(b) *Sap.* æ.
5.

(c) L. 3. 4.

(d) L. 4. 4.
43.

(e) *Contr.
epiſt. Fun-
dam. cap. 4.*

(f) *Præf. ad
lib. Periar-
chon.*

M m   then

then do thefe men brag of the doctrine of the
Apoftles, vnles firft they can demonftrate that
they enioy a continued Succeffion of Bifhops
from the Apoftles, and can fhew vs a Church
which according to *S. Auguftin* is deduced *by*
vndoubted S V C C E S S I O N from the Sea (g) of
the Apoftles, euen to the prefent Bishops.

23.   But yet neuerthelefe, fuppofe it were
granted, that they agreed with the doctrine of
the Apoftles; this were not fufficient to proue a
Succefsion in *Doctrine.* For *Succefsion*, befides a-
greement or fimilitude, doth alfo require a neuer-interrupted conueying of fuch doctrine,
from the time of the Apoftles, till the dayes of
thofe perfons who challenge fuch a *Succefsion.*
And fo *S. Auguftine* fayth : We are to belieue
that Gofpell which from the time of the Apoftles, *the* (h) *Church* hath brought downe to our
dayes *by a neuer-interrupted courfe of times, and by*
vndoubted fuccefsion of connection. Now, that the
Reformation begun by *Luther*, was interrupted
for diuers Ages before him, is manifeft out of
Hiftory, and by his endeauouring a Reformation, which muft prefuppofe abufes. He cannot
therfore pretend a continued Succeffion of that
Doctrine which he fought to reuiue, and reduce
to the knowledge, and practife of men. And
they ought not to proue that they haue Succeffion of doctrine, becaufe they agree with the
doctrine of the Apoftles ; but contrarily we
muft infer, that they agree not with the Apo-
                                                      ftles,

(g) *Cont.*
Fauft.cap.
2.

(h) *Lib.*28.
cont.Fauft.
*c.*2.

ftles, becaufe they cannot pretend a neuer-interrupted Succeffion of doctrine from the times of the Apoftles, till *Luther.* And heere it is not amifle to note, that although the *Waidenfes, Wicliffe &c.* had agreed with Proteftants in all points of doctrine; yet they could not brag of Succeffion from them, becaufe their doctrine hath not beene free from *interruption,* which neceffarily croffeth *Succefsion.*

24. And as Want of Succeffion of Perfons and *Doctrine,* cannot ftand with that *Vniuerfality of Time,* which is infeparable from the *Catholique* Church; fo likewife the difagreeing Sects which are difperfed throughout diuers Countreys, and Nations, cannot help towards that *Vniuerfality* of *Place,* wherwith the true Church muft be endued: but rather fuch locall multiplication, doth more and more lay open their diuifion, and want of Succeffion in Doctrine. For the excellent Obferuation of *S. Auguftine* doth punctually agree with all moderne Heretiques; wherein this holy Father hauing cited thefe words out of the Prophet *Ezechiel,* (i) *My flockes are difperfed vpon the whole face of the Earth;* he adds this remarkable fentence: *Not all Heretiques* (k) *are fpred ouer the face of the Earth, and yet there are Heretiques fpred ouer the whole face of the Earth, fome heere fome there, yet they are wanting in no place, they know not one another. One Sect for example in Africa, another Herefy in the Eaft, another in Egypt, another in Mefopotamia. In diuers*

(i) *Cap.* 24.

(k) *Lib de Paftorib. c. 8.*

Mm 2   *places*

places they are diuers : *one Mother Pride hath begot*
them all , as our one Mother the Catholique Church
hath brought forth all faithfull people difperfed throu-
ghout the whole world. No wonder then , if Pride
breed Diffention , and Charity Vnion. And in another place, applying to Heretiques thofe words
of the Canticles: *If thou know not* (l *) thy felfe, goe*

(l) *Cant.* 1.   *forth,and fol'ow after the steps of the flocks,and feed*
(m) *Ep.*48.   *thy kids,*he layth: *If thou know not thy felfe,goe(m)*
thou forth,I do not cast thee out , but goe thou out,
that it may be faid of thee : They went from vs , but
they were not of vs. Goe thou out in the steps of the
flocks; not in my steps , but in the steps of the flocks,
nor of one flocke , but of diuers and wandring flocks ;
And feed thy Kids,not as Peter,to whom is faid,Feed
my sheep:but feed thy Kids in the Tabernacles of the
Pastors, not in the Tabernacle of the Pastor , where
there is One flock , and one Pastor. In which words
this holy Father doth let downe the Markes of
Herely, to wit, *going out* from the Church, and
Want of Vnity among themlelues, which proceed from not acknowledging one fupreme Vifible Paftor and Head vnder Chrift. And fo it
being proued that Proteftants hauing neither
fuccellion of *Perfons,* nor *Doctrine,* nor *Vniuerfa-*
lity of *Time,*or *Place,* cannot auoid the iuft note
of *Herely.*

25.   Hitherto we haue brought arguments
to proue , that *Luther ,* and all Proteftants are
guilty of *Herefy* againft the *Negatiue* Precept
of *fayth,*which obligeth vs vnder paine of damnation,

nation, not to imbrace any one error, contrary
to any truth fufficiently propounded,as teftified
or reuealed by Almighty God ▪ Which were
inough to make good, that among Perfons who
difagree in any one point of fayth,one part only can be faued ▪ Yet we will now proue that
whofoeuer erreth in any one point, doth alfo
breake the *Affirmatiue* Precept of *Fayth*, wherby
we are obliged pofitiuely, to belieue fome reuealed truth with an *infallible*, and *fupernaturall*
Fayth, which is neceffary to faluation, euen *ne-*
ceffitate finis, or *medij*, as Deuines fpeake; that is,
fo neceffary that not any, after he is come to
the vfe of Reafon, was or can be faued without
it, according to the words of the Apoftle:*With-*
out Fayth (n) *it is impofsible to pleafe God.*

(n)*Hebr.11.*
6.

26. In the beginning of this Chapter I
fhewed, that to Chriftian Catholique fayth are
required *Certainty, Obfcurity, Prudence,* and *Su-*
pernaturality : All which Conditions we will
proue to be wanting in the beliefe of Proteftants, euen in thofe points which are true in
themfelues, and to which they yield affent, as
hapneth in all thofe particulars, wherin they a-
gree with vs; from whence it will follow, that
they wanting true *Diuine Fayth*, want meanes
abfolutely neceffary to faluation.

27. And firft, that their beliefe wanteth
Certainty, I proue, becaufe they denying the
Vniuerfall infallibility of the Church, can haue
no certaine ground to know what Obiects are

The fayth
of Prote-
ftants wan-
teth Cer-
tainty.

Mm   reuea-

reuealed, or teftifyed by God. Holy Scripture is
in it felfe moft true and infallible : but without
the direction & declaration of the Church , we
can neyther haue certaine meanes to know
what Scripture is Canonicall ; nor what Tranflations be faythfull ; nor what is the true meaning of Scripture. Euery Proteftant , as I fuppofe , is perfuaded that his owne opinions , be
true , and that he hath vfed fuch meanes as are
wont to be prefcribed for vnderftanding the
Scripture , as Prayer , Conferring of diuers
Texts &c. and yet their difagreements fhew
that fome of them are deceiued : And therefore
it is cleer that they haue no one certaine ground
whereon to relye for vnderftanding of Scripture. And feeing they hold all the Articles of
Fayth , euen concerning fundamentall points,
vpon the felfe fame ground of Scripture , interpreted , not by the Churches Author ty , but
according to fome other Rules , which as experience of their contradictions teach , do fome-
tymes fayle; it is cleere that the ground of their
fayth is infallible in no point at all. And albeit
fometyme it chance to hit on the truth , yet it is
likewife apt to leade them to errour : As all
Arch - heretiques belieuing fome truths , and
withall diuers errours vpon the fame ground
and motiue , haue indeed no true diuine infallible fayth , but only a fallible humane opinion ,
and perfuafion. For if the ground vpon which
they rely were certaine , it could neuer produce
any

any errour.

28. Another caufe of Vncertainty in the fayth of Proteftants, muft rife from their diftinction of points fundamentall, and not fundamentall. For fince they acknowledge, that euery errour in fundamentall points deftroieth the fubftance of fayth, and yet cannot determine what points be fundamentall: it followeth that they muft remaine vncertayne whether or no they be not in fome fundamentall errrour, & fo want the fubftance of fayth, without which there can be no hope of Saluation.

24. And that he who erreth againft any one reuealed truth (as certainly fome Proteftants muft doe, becaufe contradictory Propofitions cannot both be true) doth loofe all *Diuine fayth*; is a very true doctrine deliuered by Catholique Deuines, with fo generall a confent, that the contrary is wont to be cenfured as temerarious. The Angelicall Doctour *S. Thomas* propofeth this Queftion: *Whether (o) he who denyeth one Article of fayth, may retayne fayth of other Articles?* and refolueth that he canot: which he proueth, (*Argumenta fed contra*) becaufe ; *As deadly finne is oppofite to Charity ; fo to deny one Article of fayth is oppofite to fayth : But Charity doth not remaine with any one deadly finne; therefore faith doth not remaine after the denyall of any one Article of fayth.* Whereof he giues this further reafon : *Becaufe* (fayth he) *the nature of euery habit doth depend vpon the formall Motiue & Obiect ther-*
of,

(o) 2.2. q.5. ar.3. in corp.

*of, which Motiue being taken away the nature of the
habit cannot remayne. But the formall Obiect of faith
is the supreme truth as it is manifested in Scriptures,
and in the doctrine of the Church, which procceds frō
the same supreme verity. Whosoeuer therefore doth
not rely vpon the doctrine of the Church (which proceeds from the supreme Verity manifested in Scriptures) as vpon an infallible Rule , he hath not the
habit of fayth , but belieues those things which belong
to fayth, by some other meanes then by fayth: as if one
:hould remember some Conclusion , and not know the
reason of that demonstration, it is cleere that he hath
not certaine knowledge, but only Opinion. Now it is
manifest , that he who relies on the doctrine of the
Church, as vpon an infallible Rule , will yield his af-
sent to all , that the Church teacheth. For if among
those things, which she teacheth, he hold what he will,
and doth not hold what he will not, he doth not rely v-
pon the doctrine of the Church, as vpon an infallible
Rule, but only vpon his owne will. And so it is cleere
that an Heretique, who with pertinacity denieth one
Article of fayth, is not ready to follow the doctrine of
the Church in all things : And therfore it is manifest, that whosoeuer is an Heretique in any one Article of fayth, concerning other Articles , hath not
fayth, but a kind of Opinion, or his owne will.* Thus
far S. *Thomas.* And afterward: *A man doth belieue*

(q) Ad 2: *(*q*) all the Articles of fayth for one and the selfe same
reason, to wit, for the Prime Verity proposed to vs in
the Scripture, vnderstood aright according to the Doctrine of the Church : and therfore whosoeuer fals*
from

from this reason or motiue, is totally depriued of fayth. From this true doctrine we are to infer, that to retaine, or want the substance of fayth, doth not consist in the matter, or multitude of the Articles, but in the opposition against Gods diuine Testimony, which is inuolued in euery least error against Fayth. And since some Protestants must needs erre, and that they haue no certaine Rule to know , why rather one then another; it manifestly followes that none of them haue any Certainty for the substance of their faith in any one point. Moreouer *D. Potter*, being forced to confesse that the Roman Church wants not the substance of fayth ; it followes that she doth not erre in any one point against fayth, becaufe as we haue seen out of *S. Thomas*, euery such error destroyes the substance of fayth. Now if the Roman Church did not erre in any one point of fayth, it is manifest that Protestants erre in all those points wherin they are contrary to her. And this may suffice to proue that the fayth of Protestants wants Infallibility .

30. And now for the second Condition of fayth, I say : If Protestants haue *Certainty*, they want *Obscurity*, and so haue not that fayth which, as the Apostle faith, is of things *not appearing*, or not necessitating our Vnderstanding to an assent. For the whole edifice of the fayth of Protestants, is setled on these two Principles: These particular Bookes are Canonicall Scripture:

They want the second Condition of Fayth; Obscurity.

pture : And, the fenſe and meaning of theſe
Canonicall Scriptures, is cleere and euident,
at leaſt in all points neceſſary to Saluation.
Now, theſe Principles being once ſuppoſed, it
cleerly followeth, that what Proteſtants belieue
as neceſſary to Saluation, is euidently knowne
by them to be *true*, by this argument: It is *certayne* and *euident*, that whatſoeuer is contayned
in the word of God, is true. But it is *certaine*
and *euident*, that theſe Bookes in particular are
the word of God: Therefore it is *certaine* and
euident, that whatſoeuer is contayned in theſe
Bookes is true. Which *Concluſion* I take for a
Maior in a ſecond Argument, and ſay thus :
It is *certaine* and *euident* that whatſouer is contayned in theſe Bookes is true : but it is *certayne*
and *euident*, that ſuch particular Articles (for
example, the Trinity, Incarnation, Originall
ſinne &c.) are cōtained in theſe Bookes: Therfore it is *certaine* and *euident*, that theſe particular Obiects are true. Neyther will it auaile
you to ſay, that the ſayd Principles are not euident by naturall diſcourſe, but only to *the eye
of reaſon cleered by grace*, as you ſpeake. For ſupernaturall euidence, no leſſe (yea rather
more) drawes and excludes *obſcurity*, then naturall euidence doth : neyther can the party ſo
enlightned be ſayd voluntarily to captiuate his
vnderſtanding to that light, but rather his vnderſtanding is by a neceſſity made captiue, and
forced not to diſbelieued, what is preſented by

ſo

to cleere a light: And therefore your imaginary fayth is not the true fayth defined by the Apostle, but an inuention of your owne.

31. That the fayth of Protestants wanteth the third Condition which was *Prudence*, is deduced from all that hitherto hath beene sayd. What wisdome was it, to forsake a Church confessedly very ancient, and besids which, there could be demonstrated no other visible Church of Christ vpon earth? A Church acknowledged to want nothing necessary to Saluatiō; endued with Succession of Bishops, with *Visibility* and Vniuersality of *Tyme* and *Place*; A Church which if it be not the true Church, her enemies cannot pretend to haue any Church, Ordination, Scriptures, Succession, &c. and are forced for their owne sake, to maintaine her perpetuall Existence, and Being? To leaue, I say, such a Church, & frame a Community, without eyther Vnity, or meanes to procure it; a Church which at *Luthers* first reuolt had no larger extent then where his body was; A Church without *Vniuersality* of *place* or *Tyme*; A Church which can pretend no *Visibility*, or *Being*, except only in that former Church which it opposeth; A Church void of Succession of *Persons* or *Doctrine*? What wisdome was it to follow such men as *Luther*, in an opposition against the visible Church of Christ, begun vpon meere passion? What wisdome is it to receiue from *Vs*, a Church, Ordination, Scriptures, Personall

Their faith wants Prudence.

Suc-

Succeſſion, and not Succeſſion of Doctrine? Is not this to verify the name of *Hereſy*, which ſignifieth *Election* or *Choyce*? Wherby they cannot auoid that note of Imprudency, (or as *S. Auguſtine* cals it) Fooliſhnes, ſet downe by him againſt the *Manichees*, and by me recited before.

(r) Cont. ep. Fund. c. 5.

I would not (ſayth he) belieue (r) the Goſpell, vnles the Authority of the Church did moue me. Thoſe therfore whom I obeyed, ſaying, Belieue the Goſpell, why ſhould I not obey the ſame men ſaying to me, Do not belieue Manichæus (Luther, Caluin, &c. *) Chuſe What thou pleaſeſt: If thou ſay, Belieue the Catholiques; they Warne me, not to belieue thee. Wherfore if I belieue them, I cannot belieue thee. If thou ſay, Do not belieue the Catholiques; thou ſhalt not do well, in forcing me to the fayth of Manichæus, becauſe by the Preaching of Catholiques, I belieued the Goſpell it ſelfe. If thou ſay; you did Well to belieue them (* Catholiques *) commending the Goſpell, but you did not well to belieue them, diſcommending Manichæus; doſt thou thinke me ſo very F O O L I S H, that without any reaſon at all, I should belieue What thou wilt, and not belieue, What thou wilt not?* Nay this holy Father is not content to call it *Foolishnes*, but meere *Madnes*, in theſe words: *Why should I not*

(s) Lib. de vtil. Cred. c. 14.

moſt diligently enquire (s) What Chriſt commaunded of thoſe before all others, by Whoſe Authority I was moued to belieue, that Chriſt commaunded any good thing? Canſt thou better declare to me, What he ſaid, Whom I would not haue thought to haue been, or to be, if the Beliefe therof had been recommended by thee to me?

*me? This therfore I belieued by fame, ſtrengthned
with Celebrity, Conſent, Antiquity. But euery one
may ſee that you, ſo feW, ſo turbulent, ſo neW, can produce nothing Which deſerues Authority. What
MADNES is this? Belieue them* (Catholiques)
*that We ought to belieue Chriſt; but learne of vs, What
Chriſt ſaid. Why I beſeech thee? Surely if they* (Catholiques) *were not at all, and could not teach me
any thing, I Would more eaſily perſWade my ſelfe, that
I Were not to belieue Chriſt, then I ſhould learne any
thing concerning him from any other then thoſe, by
Whom I belieued him.* Laſtly, I aske what wiſdome it could be to leaue all viſible Churches,
and conſequently the true Catholique Church
of Chriſt, which you confeſſe cannot erre in
points neceſſary to ſaluation, and the *Roman*
Church which you grant doth not erre in fundamentalls, and follow priuate men who may
erre euen in points neceſſary to ſaluation? Eſpecially if we add, that when *Luther* roſe there
was no viſible true Catholique Church beſides
that of *Rome,* and them who agreed with her; in
which ſenſe, ſhe was, & is, the only true Church
of Chriſt, and not capable of any Error in
fayth. Nay, euen *Luther,* who firſt oppoſed the
Roman Church yet comming to diſpute againſt
other Heretiques, he is forced to giue the Lye
both to his owne words and deeds, in ſaying:
We freely confeſſe (t) *that in the Papacy there are
many good things, worthy the name of Chriſtian,
Which haue come from them to vs. Namely, we confeſſe,*

(t) *In epiſt.
cont. Anab.
ad duos Pa-
rochos. to. 2.
Germ. Witt.
fol.* 229. *&*
230.

feſſe, that in the Papacy there is true Scripture, true Baptiſme, the true Sacrament of the Aultar, the true keyes for remiſsion of ſinnes, the true Office of Preaching, true Catechiſme, as our Lords Prayer, Ten Commandements, Articles of fayth &c. And afterward : I auouch, that vnder the Papacy there is true Chriſtianity, yea the Kernel and Marrow of Chriſtianity, and many pious and great Saints. And againe he affirmeth, that the Church of Rome hath the true Spirit, Goſpells, Fayth, Baptiſme, Sacraments, the Keyes, the Office of Preaching, Prayer, Holy Scripture, and whatſoeuer Chriſtianity ought to haue. And a litle before : I heare and ſee that they bring in Anabaptiſme onely to this end, that they may ſpight the Pope, as men that will receiue nothing from Antichriſt; no otherwiſe then the Sacramentaries doe, who therefore belieue only Bread and Wine to be in the Sacrament, meerely in hatred againſt the Biſhop of Rome; and they thinke that by this meanes they shall ouercome the Papacy. Verily theſe men rely vpon a weake ground, for by this meanes they muſt deny the whole Scripture, and the Office of Preaching. For we haue all theſe things from the Pope; otherwiſe we muſt goe make a new Scripture. O Truth, more forcible (as S. Auguſtine ſayes) to wring out (x) Confeſsion, then is any racke, or torment ! And ſo we may truly ſay with Moyſes: Inimici noſtri ſunt Iudices : Our very Enemies giue (y) ſentence for vs.

(x) Contra Donat.poſt collat.cap. 24.
(y) Deut. c. 32.31.

32.   Laſtly, ſince your fayth wanteth Certainty, and Prudence, it is eaſy to inferre that it
wants

wants the fourth Condition, *Supernaturality*. For being but an *Humane* perſuaſion, or Opinion, it is not in nature, or Eſſence *Supernaturall*. And being *imprudent*, and raſh, it cannot proceed from diuine Motion and Grace ; and therefore it is neyther ſupernaturall in *it ſelfe*, or in the *Cauſe* from which it procedeth.

Their faith wants Supernaturality.

33. Since therefore we haue proued, that whoſoeuer erres agaynſt any one point of faith, looſeth all diuine fayth, euen concerning thoſe other Articles wherein he doth not erre; and that although he could ſtill retayne true fayth for ſome points, yet any one errour in whatſoeuer other matter concerning fayth, is a grieuous ſinne; it cleerely followes, that when two or more hold different doctrines concerning fayth and Religion, there can be but one part ſaued. For declaring of which truth, if Catholiques be charged with *Want* of *Charity*, and *Modeſty*, and be accuſed of raſhnes, ambition, and fury, as *D. Potter* is very free in this kind; I deſire euery one to ponder the words of *S. Chryſoſtome*, who teacheth, that euery leaſt errour ouerthrowes all fayth, and whoſoeuer is guilty therof, is in the *Church*, like one, who in the *Common-wealth* forgeth falſe Coyne: *Let them beare* (ſayth this holy Father) *what S. Paul ſayth: Namely, that they who brought in ſome ſmall errour* (z) *had ouerthrowne the Ghoſpell. For, to ſhew how a ſmall thing ill mingled doth corrupt the whole, he ſayd, that the Ghoſpell was ſubuerted. For as he who*

(z) *Galat.* 5. 7.

clips

clips a litle of the stamp from the Kings money, makes the whole piece of no value: so whosoeuer takes away the least particle of sound fayth, is wholy corrupted, alwayes going from that beginning to worse thinges. Where then are they, who condemne vs as contentious persons, because we cannot agree with Heretiques, and doe often say, that there is no difference betwixt vs and them, but that our disagreement proceeds frō Ambition to dominiere? And thus hauing shewed that Protestants want true *Fayth*, it remayneth that, according to my first designe, I examine whether they do not also want *Charity*, as it respects a mans selfe.

CHAP.

CHAP. VII.

In regard of the Precept of Charity touvards ones selfe, Proteſtants are in ſtate of Sinne, as long as they remaine ſeparated from the Roman Church.

HAT, due *Order* is to be obſerued in the Theologicall Vertue of *Charity*, whereby we are directed to preferre ſome Objects before others; is a truth taught by all Deuines, and declared in theſe words of holy Scripture: *He hath ordered (a) Charity in me.* The reaſon whereof is; becauſe the infinite Goodnes of God, which is the *formall Object*, or Motiue of *Charity*, & for which all other things are loued, is differently participated by different Objects; and therefore the loue we beare to them for Gods ſake, muſt accordingly be vnequall. In the vertue of *Fayth*, the caſe is farre otherwiſe; becauſe all the Objects, or points which we belieue, do equally participate the diuine

(a) *Cant.2.4*

O o

uine Teſtimony, or Reuelation, for which we
belieue alike all things propounded for ſuch.
For it is as impoſſible for God, to ſpeake an vntruth, in a ſmall, as in a great matter. And this
is the ground for which we haue ſo often affirmed, that any leaſt errour againſt *Fayth*, is iniurious to God, and deſtructiue of Saluation.

2. This order in Charity may be conſidered ; Towards God ; Our owne ſoule ; The
ſoule of our Neyghbour ; Our owne life, or
Goods; and the life or goods of our Neighbour.
God is to be beloued aboue all things, both *ob-
iectiuè* (as the Deuines ſpeake) that is, we muſt
wiſh or deſire to God, a Good more great, perfect, and noble then to any, or all other things:
namely, all that indeed He is, a Nature Infinite,
Independent, Immenſe &c. and alſo *appretia-
tiuè*, that is, we muſt ſooner looſe what good
ſoeuer, then leaue, and abandon Him. In the o-
ther Obiects of Charity, of which I ſpake,
this *Order* is to be kept. We may, but are not
bound, to preferre the life and goods of our
Neyghbour before our owne : we are bound to
prefer the ſoule of our Neyghbour before our
owne temporall goods or life, if he happen to
be in extreme ſpirituall neceſſity, and that we
by our aſſiſtance can ſuccour him, according to
the ſaying of S. *Iohn* : *In this we haue knowne* (b.)
*the Charity of God, becauſe he hath yielded his life
for vs: and we ought to yield our life for our Brethren*.
And S. *Auguſtine* likewiſe ſayth : *A Chriſtian
will*

will not doubt (c) *to loose his owne temporall life, for* (c) *De men-*
the eternall life of his Neighbour. Laſtly we are to *dac. cap. 6.*
prefer the *ſpirituall* good of our owne ſoule, be-
fore both the ſpirituall and temporall good of
our Neighbour, becauſe as Charity doth of its
owne Nature, chiefly encline the perſon in
whom it reſides, to loue God, and to be vnited
with him : ſo of it ſelfe it enclines him, to procure thoſe things wherby the ſaid Vnion with
God is effected, rather to himſelfe then to o-
thers. And from hēce it followes, that in things
neceſſary to ſaluation, no man ought in any
caſe, or in any reſpect whatſoeuer, to prefer the
ſpirituall good, either of any particular perſon,
or of the whole world before his owne ſoule;
according to thoſe words of our Bleſſed Sa-
uiour : *What doth it* (d) *auaile a man, if he gaine* (d) *Matt. 6.*
the whole world, and ſuſtaine the domage of his owne
ſoule? And therfore (to come to our preſent
purpoſe) it is directly againſt the *Order* of Charity, or againſt Charity as it hath a reference to
our ſelues, which Deuines call *Charitas propria,*
to aduenture either the *omitting* of any meanes
neceſſary to ſaluation, or the committing of
any thing repugnant to it, for whatſoeuer reſpect, & conſequently, if by liuing out of the *Ro-*
man Church we put our ſelues in hazard, either to want ſome thing neceſſarily required
to ſaluation, or elſe to performe ſome act a-
gainſt it, we commit a moſt grieuous ſinne, a-
gainſt the vertue *of Charity,* as it reſpects our
ſelues,

felues, and fo cannot hope for faluation, without repentance.

3. Now, of things neceffary to faluation, there are two forrs, according to the doctrine of all Diuines. Some things (ſay they) are neceffary to faluation, *necefsitate præcepti*, neceffary only becaufe they are commaunded; For : *If thou wilt* (e) *enter into life, keep the Commandements.* In which kind of things, as probable ignorance of the Law, or of the Commandement doth excufe the party from all faulty breach therof; fo likewife doth it not exclude faluation in cafe of ignorance. Some other things are ſaid to be neceffary to faluation *necefsitate medij*, *finis*, or *falutis*; becaufe they are Meanes appointed by God to attaine our *End* of eternall *faluation*, in fo ſtrict a manner, that it were *prefumption* to *hope* for Saluation without them. And as the former meanes are ſaid to be *neceffary*, becaufe they are *commaunded*; ſo the later are commonly ſaid to be *commaunded*, becaufe they are *neceffary*, that is: Although there were no other ſpeciall precept concerning them; yet ſuppofing they be once appointed as meanes abſolutely neceffary to faluation, there cannot but rife an obligation of procuring to haue them, in vertue of that vniuerſall precept of Charity, which obligeth euery man to procure the faluation of his owne foule. In this ſort *diuine infallible Fayth* is neceffary to faluation; as likewife repentance of euery deadly finne, and in the doctrine of

Catho-

(e) *Matt.* 19. 17.

Catholiques, Baptifme *in re*, that is, in *act* to Children, and for thofe who are come to the vfe of reafon, *in voto*, or *harty defyre*, when they cannot haue it in act. And as Baptifme is neceffary for remiffion of *Originall*, and *actuall* finne committed before it : fo the Sacrament of *Confefsion*, or Penance is neceffary *in re*, or *in voto*, in *act*, or *defire*, for the remiffion of mortall finnes, comitted after Baptifme . The Minifter of which Sacrament of Penance being neceffarily a true Prieft, true Ordination is necefsary in the Church of God for remifsion of finnes by this Sacrament, as alfo for other ends not belonging to our prefent purpofe. From hence it rifeth, that no ignorance, or impofsibility can fupply the want of thofe meanes which are abfolutely neceffary to faluation. As if, for example, a finner depart this world without repenting himfelfe of all deadly finnes , although he dye fuddenly , or vnexpectedly fall out of his wits, and fo commit no new finne by omifsion of repentance; yet he fhall be eternally punifhed for his former finnes committed, and neuer repented. If an Infant dye without Baptifme , he canrot be faued, not by reafon of any actuall finne committed by him in omitting Baptifme, but for Originall finne , not forgiuen by the meanes which God hath ordained to that purpofe. Which doctrine , all, or moft Proteftants will (for ought I know) grant to be true , in the Children of Infidels , yea not only *Luthe-*

r.ins, but allo some other Proteftants as *M. Bil-*
fon late of *Winchefter* (f) and others hold it to
be true, euen in the Children of the faithfull.
And if Proteftants in generall difagree from
Catholiques in this point, it cannot be denyed
but that our difagreement is in a point very
fundamentall. And the like I fay of the Sacrament of Penance, which they deny to be neceffary to faluation, either in act, or in defire; which
error is likewife fundamentall, becaufe it concernes (as I fayd) a thing necefsary to faluation: And for the fame reafon, if their Prieft-
hood and Ordination be doubtfull, as certainly
it is, they are in danger to want a meanes without which they cannot be faued. Neither ought
this rigour to feeme ftrang, or vniuft : For Almighty God hauing of his owne *Goodnes*, without our *merit*, firft ordained Man to a *fupernatu-*
rall end of eternall felicity; and then, after our
fall in *Adam* vouchfafed to reduce vs to the attayning of that End, if his blefsed *Will* be pleafed to limit the attayning of that End, to fome
meanes which in his infinite Wifedome he
thinkes moft fit ; who can fay, why doft thou
fo ? Or who can *hope* for that *End*, without
fuch *meanes* ? Blefsed be his diuine Maiefty, for
vouchfafing to ordaine vs, bafe creatures, to fo
fublime an End, by any *meanes* at all.

4. Out of the forefayd difference followeth another, that (generally fpeaking) in things
neceffary only, becaufe they are commaunded,

(f) *In his*
true differen-
ce &c. part.
4 *pag. 368.*
& 369.

it is fufficient for auoydnng finne , that we
proceed prudently, and by the conduct of fome
probable opinion , maturely weighed and approued by men of vertue, learning, & wifdom.
Neyther are we alwayes obliged to follow the
moft ftrict, and feuere , or fecure part, as long
as the doctrine which we imbrace , proceeds
vpon fuch reafoos, as may warrant it to be truly probable, and prudent , though the contrary part want not alfo probable grounds. For in
humane affaires , and difcourfe , euidence and
certainty cannot be alwayes expected . But
when we treate not precifely of auoyding fin ,
but moreouer of procuring fome thing without
which I can not be faued ; I am obliged by the
Law, & *Order* of *Charity* to procure as great certainty as morally I am able ; and am not to follow euery probable Opinion , or dictamen, but
tutiorem partem , the fafer part , becaufe if my *probability* proue falfe , I fhall not *probably ,* but *certainly* come fhort of Saluation. Nay in fuch cafe,
I fhall incurre a new finne againft the *Vertue* of
Charity towards *my felfe ,* which obligeth euery
one not to expofe his foule to the hazard of eternall perdition , when it is in his power , with
the affiftance of Gods grace, to make the matter fure. From this very ground it is , that although fome Deuines be of opiniõ, that it is not
a finne to vfe fome *Matter,* or *Forme* of Sacraments, onely probable, if we refpect precifely
the reuerence or refpect which is due to Sacraments

ments, as they belong to the *Morall infufed* Vertue of *Religion* ; yet when they are fuch Sacraments, as the inualidity therof may endanger
the faluation of foules, all doe with one confent agree, that it is a grieuous offence to vfe a
doubtfull, or onely probable *Matter* or *Forme*,
when it is in our power to procure certainty. If
therefore it may appeare, that though it were
not certaine that Proteftancy vnrepented deftroyes Saluation (as we haue proued to be very certayne) yet at leaft that is *probable*, & with
all, that there is a way more fafe; it will follow
out of the grounds already layd, that they are
obliged by the law of Charity to imbrace that
fafe way.

5. Now, that Proteftants haue reafon at leaft
to doubt in what cafe they ftand, is deduced frō
what we haue fayd, and proued about the vniuerfall infallibility of the Church, and of her
being Iudge of Controuerfies, to whome all
Chriftians ought to fubmit their Iudgment (as
euen fome Proteftants grant,) and whome to
oppofe in any one of her definitions, is a grieuous finne : As alfo from what we haue fayd
of the *Vnity* , *Vniuerfality* , and *Vifibility* of the
Church, and of Succeffion of Perfons, and Doctrine ; Of the Conditions of Diuine Fayth,
Certainty, *Obfcurity*, *Prudence* , and *Supernaturali-*
ty , which are wanting in the fayth of Proteftants ; Of the friuolous diftinction of points
fundamentall and not fundamentall, (the cō-
futation

futation wherof proueth that *Heretiques* difagreeing among themfelues in any leaft point, cannot haue the fame fayth, nor be of the fame Church:) Of Schifme ; of Herefy ; of the Perfons who firft reuolted from *Rome*, and of their Motiues ; of the Nature of Fayth, which is deftroyed by any leaft errour, & it is certaine that fome of them muft be in errour, and want the fubftance of true fayth ; and fince all pretend the like certainty , it is cleere that none of them haue any certainty at all , but that they want true fayth, which is a meanes *moſt abſolutly neceſſary* to Saluation . Moreouer , as I fayd heertofore , fince it is granted that euery Errour in fundamentall points is damnable , & that they cannot tell in particular, what points be fundamentall ; it followes that none of them knowes whether he , or his Brethren do not erre danably, it being certayne that amongft fo many difagreeing perfons fome muft erre . Vpõ the fame gioũd of not being able to affigne what points be fundamentall , I fay , they cannot be fure whether the difference among them be fundamentall or no , and confequently whether they agree in the fubftance of fayth and hope of Saluation . I omit to add that you want the Sacrament of Pennance , inftituted for remiffion of finnes , or at leaft you muft confeffe that you hold it not neceffary ; and yet your owne Brethren , for example, the *Century Writers* doe (g) acknowledge , that in the tymes of *Cyprian*,

(g) *Cent. 3, cap. 6. col.* 127.

Pp   and

and *Tertulian, Priuate Confefsion* euen of *Thoghts*
was *vfed*; and that, it was then *commanded, and
thought necefʃary*. The like, I fay , concerning
your Ordination , which at leaft is very doub-
full, & confequently all that depends thereon.

6. On the other fide, that the *Roman* Church
is the fafer way to Heauen (not to repeat what
hath been already fayd vpon diuers occafions)
I will againe put you in mynd , that vnles the
Roman Church was the true Church, there was
no vifible true Church vpon Earth . A thing fo
manifeft , that Proteftants themfelues confeffe
that more then one thoufand ye ares the *Roman*
Church poffeffed the whole world , as we haue
ſhewed heertofore, out of their own (h) words:
from whence it followes, that vnleffe Ours be
the true Church , you cannot pretend to any
perpetuall vifible Church of your Owne ; but
Ours doth not depend on yours , before which
it was. And heere I wiſh you to confider with
feare and trembling , how all *Roman* Catholiques, not one excepted; that is , thofe very men
whom you muft hold not to erre damnably in
their beliefe, vnleffe you wil deftroy your owne
Church , and faluation , do with vnanimous
confent belieue , and profefse that Proteftancy
vnrepented, deftroies Saluation ; and then tell
me, as you will anfwere at the laft day, whether
it be not more fafe, to liue & die in that Church,
which euen your felues are forced to acknowledge *not to be cut off from hope of faluatiō* (which

*(h) Chap. 5.
num. 9.*

are

are your owne words)then to liue in a Church, which the fayd confefsedly true Church doth firmely belieue, and conftantly profefse not to be capable of faluation. And therfore I conclude that by the moft ftrict obligation of *Charity* towards your owne foule, you are bound to place it in fafety, by returning to that Church, from which your Progenitors Schifmatically departed ; leaft too late you find that faying of the holy Ghoft verified in your felues : *He that loues* (1) *the danger, fhall perifh therin.*   (i) *Ecclef.* 3. 27.

7.   Againft this laft argument of the greater fecurity of the Roman Church drawne from your owne confeffion, you bring an Obiection; which in the end will be found to make for vs, againft your felfe. It is taken from the words of the Donatifts , fpeaking to Catholiques in this manner : *Your felues confeffe* (k) *our* (k) *pag.* 112. *Baptifme, Sacraments, and Fayth* (heer you put an Explication of your owne, and fay *, for the moft part,* as if any fmall error in fayth did not deftroy all Faith) *to be good , and auayleable. We deny yours to be fo, and fay there is no Church, no faluation amongft you. Therfore it is fafeft for all to ioyne with vs.*

8.   By your leaue our Argument is not (as you fay) for fimple people alone, but for all them who haue care to faue their foules. Neither is it grounded vpon your *Charitable Iudgment* (as you (l) fpeake)but vpon an ineuitable (l) *Pag.* 81. necceffity for you , either to grant faluation, to

our Church, or to entaile certaine damnation
vpon your owne: becaufe yours can haue no being till *Luther,* vnles ours be fuppofed to haue
been the true Church of Chrift. And fince you
terme this Argument a Charme, take heed you
be none of thofe, who according to the Prophet
Dauid , do not heare *the voyce of him (* m *) who*
charmeth wi*fely.* But to come to the purpofe: Catholiques neuer granted that the Donatifts had
a true Church, or might be faued: And therfore
you hauing cited out of *S.* u*Auguftin,* the words
of the Catholiques, that the Donatifts had true
Baptifme, when you come to the cotrary words
of the *Donatifts,* you add, *No Church , No Salua-*
tion; making the Argument to haue *quinque ter-*
minos ; without which Addition you did fee, it
made nothing againft vs: For, as I faid, the Catholiques neuer yielded, that among the Donatifts there was a true Church, or hope of faluation. And your felfe a few leaues after acknowledge that the Donatifts *maintained an errour ,*
which, *was in the Matter and Nature of it properly*
hereticall, againft that Article of the Creed, wherin
we profeffe to belieue the holy (n *) Catholique Church:*
and confequently , you cannot allow faluation
to them, as you do, and muft do to vs. And therfore the *Donatifts* could not make the like argument againft Catholiques , as Catholiques
make againft you , who grant vs Saluation,
which we deny to you. But at leaft (you will
fay) this Argument for the Certainty of their
Bap-

(m) *Pfal.*
y. 6.

(a) *pag. 126.*

Baptifme, was like to Ours touching the Security and Certainty of our faluation; & therfore
that Catholiqnes fhould haue efteemed the
Baptifme of the Donatifts, more Certaine then
their owne, and fo haue allowed Rebaptization
of fuch as were baptized by Heretiques, or finners, as the Donatifts efteemed all Catholiques
to be. I anfwere, no. Becaufe it being a matter of
fayth, that Baptifme adminiftred by Heretiques, obferuing due Matter, Forme &c. is va-
lide; to rebaptize any fo baptized, had beene
both a facriledge in reitering a Sacrament not
reiterable, and a profeffion alfo of a damnable
Herefy, and therfore had not been more *fafe,*
but certainly *damnable.* But you confefse that in
the doctrine or practife of the *Roman* Church,
there is no beliefe, or profeffion of any damnable errour, which if there were, euen your
Church fhould certainly be no Church. To belieue therfore and profefse as we do, cannot exclude Saluation, as Rebaptization muft haue
done. But if the *Donatists* could haue affirmed
with truth, that in the opinion both of Catholiques and themfelues, their Baptifme was good,
yea and good in fuch fort as that vnles theirs
was good, that of the Catholiques could not be
fuch; but theirs might be good, though that of
the Catholiques were not: and further that it
was no damnable error to belieue, that Baptifme adminiftred by the Catholiques was not
good, nor that it was any Sacriledge to reite-

rate the fame Baptifme of Catholiques: If, I
fay, they could haue truly affirmed thefe things,
they had faid fomewhat, which at leaft had feemed to the purpofe. But thefe things they could
not fay with any colour of truth, and therfore
their argument was fond, and impious. But we
with truth fay to Proteftants: You cannot but
confeffe that our doctrine containes no damnable error, and that our Church is fo certainely a true Church, that vnlefse ours be true you
cannot pretend any; Yea you grant, that you
fhould be guilty of Schifme, if you did cut off
our Church from the Body of Chrift, and the
hope of faluation: But we neither do, nor can
grant that yours is a true Church, or that within it there is hope of faluation: *Therfore it is fafeft* for you, *to ioyne with vs.* And now againft
whom hath your Obiection greateft force?

9. But I wonder not a little, and fo I thinke
will euery body elfe, what the reafon may be,
that you do not fo much as goe about to anfwere the argument of the *Donatifts,* which you
fay is all one with Ours, but refer vs to *S. Auguftin* there to read it; as if euery one caried with
him a Library, or were able to examine the places in *S. Auguftine:* and yet you might be fure
your Reader would be greedy to fee fome folid
anfwere to an Argument fo often vrged by vs,
and which indeed, vnles you can confute it,
ought alone to moue euery one who hath care
of his foule, to take the fafeft way, by incorpo-
rating

rating himfelfe in our Church. But we may eafily imagine the true reafon of your filence. For
the anfwere which *S. Auguftine* giues to the
*Donatifts,*is directly againft your felfe, and the
fame which I haue giuen. Namely, that Catholiques (o) approue the Baptifme of Donarifts,
but abhor their herefy of Reoaptization . And
that as gold is good (which is the fimilitude v-
fed by (p) *S. Auguftin*) yet not to be fought in
company of theeues ; fo though Baptifme be
good,yet it muft not be fought for in the Con-
uenticle of *Donatifts.* But you free vs from damnable herefy , and yield vs faluation , which I
hope is to be imbraced in whatfoeuer Company it is found, or rather that Company is to be
imbraced before all other, in which all fides a-
gree, that faluation may be found. We therfore
muft infer, that it is fafeft for you to feeke faluation among vs.You had good reafon to conceale *S. Auguftins* anfwere to the *Donatifts.*

(o) *Ad lit. Petil. lib. 2. cap.* 108.
(p) *Contra Crefc lib.* 1. *cap.* 21.

10. You frame another argument in our
behalfe, & make vs fpeake thus : If Proteftants
*belieue the (*q*) Religion* of Catholiques *, to be a
fafe way to Heauen, why do they not follow it?* Which
wife argument of your owne , you anfwere at
large, and confirme your anfwere by this inftance : *The Iefuits and Dominicans hold different
Opinions touching Predetermination , and the Immaculate Conception of the Bleffed Virgin :Yet fo, that
the Iefuits hold the Dominicans Way fafe, that is , his
errour not damnable , and the Dominicans hold the*
fame

(q) *pag.* 79.

same of the Iesuits. *Yet neither of them with good* Consequence can presse *the other to belieue his opinion* ,because by his owne Confession it is no damnable error.

11. But what Catholique maketh such a wife demaund, as you put into our mouths? If our Religion be a safe way to heauen, that is, not danable; why do you not follow it? As if euery thing that is good, must be of necessity imbraced by euery body But what thinke you of the Argument framed thus? Our Religion is safe, euen by your Confession, therfore you ought to grant that all *may* imbrace it. And yet further, thus : Among different Religions and *contrary* wayes to heauen, one only can be safe : But Ours, by your owne Confession, is safe, wheras we hold that in yours there is no hope of saluation : Therfore you *may*, and *ought* to imbrace ours. This is our Argument. And if the Dominicans and Iesuits did say one to another as we say to you; then one of them might with good consequence prelse *the other to belieue his opinion*. You haue still the hard fortune to be beaten with your owne weapon.

12. It remaineth then, that both in regard of *Fayth*, and *Charity*, Proteftants are obliged to vnite themfelues with the Church of Rome. And I may add alfo, in regard of the *Theologicall* Vertue of *Hope*, without which none can hope to be faued, and which you want, either by excefse of *Confidence*, or defect by *Defpaire*, not

vnlike

vnlike to your *Fayth*, which I shewed to be either deficient in *Certainty*, or excessiue in *Euidence*; as likewise according to the rigid Caluinists, it is either so strong, that once had, it can neuer be lost; or so more then weake, and so much nothing; that it can neuer be gotten. For the true Theologicall *Hope* of Christians, is a *Hope* which keepes a meane betweene *Presumption*, and *Desperation*; which moues vs to worke our saluation with feare, and trembling; which conducts vs to make sure our saluation by good workes, as holy Scripture aduiseth But contrarily, Protestants do either exclude *Hope* by *Despaire*, with the Doctrine that our Sauiour died not for all, and that such want grace sufficient to saluation; or else by vaine *Presumption* grounded vpon a fantasticall persuasion, that they are Predestinate; which Fayth must exclude all feare, and trembling. Neither can they make their Calling *certaine by good workes*, who do certainly belieue that before any good workes they are iustified, and iustified euen by Fayth alone, and by that Faith wherby they certainly belieue that they are iustifyed. Which points some Protestants do expresly affirme to be *the soule of the Church*; *the principall Origen of saluatiō*; *Of all other points of Doctrine the chiefest and weightiest*; as already I haue noted *Chap.* 3. *n.* 19. And if some Protestants do now relent from the rigour of the aforesaid doctrine, we must affirme, that at least some of them want the Theologi-

call

call Vertue of *Hope*; yea that none of them can haue true *Hope*, while they hope to be faued in the Communion of thofe, who defend fuch doctrines, as doe directly ouerthrow all true Chriftian *Hope*. And for as much as concernes *Fayth*, we muft alfo infer, that they want *Vnity* therin (and confequently haue none at all) by their difagreement about *the foule of the Church* ; *the principall Origen of faluation* ; *of all other points of Doctrine the chiefeft and weightieft*. And if you want true *Fayth*, you muft by confequence want *Hope*, or if you hold that this *point* is not to be fo indiuifible on either fide, but that it hath latitude fufficient to imbrace all parties, without preiudice to their faluation; notwithftanding that your Brethren hold it to be *the foule of the Church &c*. I muft repeate what I haue faid heertofore, that, euen by this Example, it is cleere, you cannot agree what points be *fundamentall:* And fo (to whatfoeuer anfwere you fly) I preffe you in the fame manner, and fay, that you haue no Certainty whether you agree in fundamentall points, or Vnity and fubftance of Fayth, which cannot ftand with difference in fundamentall. And fo vpon the whole matter, I leaue it to be confidered, whether, *Want of Charity can be iuftly charged* on vs, becaufe we affirme, that they cannot (without repentance) be faued, who want of all other the moft neceffary meanes to faluation, which are, the three *Theologicall* Vertues, *F A I T H, H O P E, and*

C H A-

CHARITY.

13. And now I end this *firft Part*, hauing as I conceiue, complyed with my firft defigne (in that meafure , which Tyme, Commodity, fcarcity of Bookes , and my owne fmall Abilities could affoard) which was to fhew , that *A-mongft men of different Religions , one fide onely can be faued*. For fince there muft be fome *infallible Meanes* to decide all Controuerfies concerning Religion , and to propound truth reuealed by Almighty God ; and this *Meanes* can be no other , but the *Vifible Church of Chrift* , which at the tyme of *Luthers* appearance was only the Church of *Rome* , and fuch as agreed with *her* : We muft conclude , that whofoeuer oppofeth himfelf to her definitions, or forfaketh her Cō-munion, doth refift God himfelfe, whofe fpoufe fhe is , and whofe diuine truth fhe propounds ; and therefore becomes guilty of *Schifme* , and *Herefy*, which fince *Luther* , his Affociates, and Proteftants haue done , and ftill continue to doe ; it is not *Want* of *Charity* , but aboundance of euident caufe , that forceth vs to declare this neceffary Truth, *PROTESTANCY VN-REPENTED DESTROYES SALVA-TION.*

The End *of the*
firſt Part.

THE
SECOND PART.

THE PREAMBLE.

 IN CE *I haue hand-led the subfance of our prefent Controuerfy, &* *anfvvered the chiefe grounds of* D. Potter *in the* Firſt Part; *I may vvell in this* Second *be more briefe, referring the Reader to thofe feueral places, vvher-in his reafons are confuted, and his ob-*

Qq 3   *iecti-*

iections anſvvered. ℰ*And becauſe in euery* Section, *he handleth ſo many different points, that they cannot be ranged vnder one* Title, *or* Argument; *my* Chapters *muſt according- ly haue no particular* Title *as they had in the* Firſt Part; *but the Reader may be pleaſed to conceiue, and yet do me no more then Iuſtice therein, that the* Argument *of euery one of my* ſeauen Chapters, *is an* Anſvvere *to his* Sea- uen Sections, *as they lye in order.* But *let vs novv addreſſe our ſpeach to* D. Potter.

CHAP.

CHAP. I.

YOV pretend, and profeſſe in your Preface to the Reader, that you haue not omitted without Anſwer *any one thing of moment in all the Diſcourſe* of *Charity Miſtaken* : and yet you omit that, which very much imported to the Queſtion in hand, namely the moderate Explication of our doctrine, that *Proteſtancy vnrepented deſtroyes Saluation*; and that you muſt ſay the ſame of vs, if you belieue your owne Religion to be true, and Ours to be falſe : which points are prudently deliuered by *Charity Miſtaken* in his *ſecond Chapter*; which togeather with his *Firſt*, you vndertake to anſwere in this your *Firſt Section*. And wheras he ſhewed by diuers arguments that it is improbable that the Church ſhould want *Charity*, your Anſwere to that point is ſuperficiall, and vntrue in ſome things, and none at all in others, as will eaſily appeare to any that ſhal reade *Charity Miſtaken* in his firſt Chapter.

2. You tell vs in very confident manner, that *hardly* (a) *any Age in former times may compare* (a) Pag. 33.
with

with this of Ours (since this Church was happily pur-
ged from Popery) for publike exprefsions of Charity ;
but you doe it in fo generall termes , as if you
were afrayd of being confuted . For I befeech
you, *D. Potter* , are the Churches which Proteftants haue built , any thing comparable to the
which haue been erected by Catholiques ? Doe
your Hofpitalls fo much deferue as to be named ? Haue you any thing of that kind in effect
of particular note, fauing the few meane Nur-
feries of idle beggars and debauched people, except perhaps *Suttons Hofpitall*, which (as I haue
beene informed) was to take no profit at all
till he was dead ? He who (as I haue alfo vnderftood) dyed fo without any Children , or Brothers , or Sifters , or knowne kindred , as that
peraduenture it might haue efchetead to the
King ? He who liued a wretched and penu-
rious life , and drew that maſſe of wealth together by Vfury , in which cafe according to
good confcience, his eftate without asking him
leaue, was by the Law of God obnoxious to
reftitution , and ought to haue been applyed to
pious vfes ? Whereas both anciently in this
Countrey , and at all tymes , and fpecially in
this laft age , men fee aboundance of heroicall
actions of this kind performed in forrayne
parts . And if it were not for feare of noting
many other great Citties , as if there were any
want of moft munificent Hofpitalls in them ,
wherein they abound ; I could tell you of one
cal-

called the *Annunciata* in the Citty of *Naples*, which spends three hundred thousand Crownes *per annum*, which comes to about fourescore thousand pounds sterling by the yeare, which euer feeds, and cures a thousand sicke persons, and payes for the nursing and entertayning of three thousand sucking children of poore people, and hath fourteene other distinct Hospitals vnder it, where the persons of those poore creatures are kept, and where they are defrayed of all their necessary charges euery weeke. I could allo tell you of an Hospitall in *Rome* called *S. Spirito* of huge reuenewes, but it is not my meaning to enter into particulars, which would proue endles. In the meane time it is prety entertainment for you to belieue no more then you see, which is not much, and to talke in generall termes, by comparing that which comes in your way, with those which are in other Countries, wherof you seeme to know very little. And where I pray you can you verify that which *Charity Mistaken* sayth of our Church in these words. (*pag.* 7.) *Persons sicke of all diseases are serued and attended (after the example of Christ our Lord) by the owne hands of great Princes and Prelates, and of choyce and delicate Ladies and Queenes, in the Communion of the holy Catholique Church?* Would to God the first Head of your Church had not destroyed those innumerable glorious monumēts of Charity which he found! But because our present question a-

R r   bout

bout the Saueablenes of Proteſtants belongeth
rather to Faith then Charity, out of your owne
hyperbolicall affirmation, I will infer: That ſeeing the Monuments of Charitable workes performed by Catholiques, do incomparably exceed thoſe of yours ; and yet, that time for time
your Charity (as you affirme) ſurpaſseth ours;
it followes very cleerly , that our Fayth and
Church is far more ancient then yours, and
conſequently that yours cannot be *Catholique*
for all Ages. So that by exaggeration of your
Charity, you haue ouerthrowne your *Fayth* and
Charity alſo, which cannot ſubſiſt without true
Catholique Fayth.

3.   But yet you are ſo ingenuous, that you
do not ſo much as pretend to compare your
Charity in conuerting ſoules, to that of the Catholiques: nor do you ſo much as once venture
to inſinuate that the Proteſtant Miniſters leaue
their Countrey and Commodities , and the
howſes of rich and louing friends, to tranſport
themſelues into barbarous Nations , with the
ſufferance of all cruell inconueniences, and very many times of death it ſelfe, for the conuer-
ſion of ſoules to Chriſt our Lord. For of this
you were expreſſely tould , and conſequently
how improbable it was, that Catholiques ſhould
feare the daungerous ſtate of Proteſtants ,
through meere want of Charity; wheras yet for
the only exerciſe of that vertue, they were conſent with ſo much courage and ioy to caſt away
their

their liues; & that therfore when we made that
iudgment of you, it was rather through our
zeale and cordiall defire of your good, and feare
of your loffe, then for want of charity, or com-
paffion. But of this, as I was faying, you were
fo wife as not to fpeake a word. For that glorious marke of the Dilatation and Amplitude
of Gods Church, by the Conuerfion of Nations, Kings, and Kingdomes, fo manifeftly
foretold by the holy Prophets, and ordained in
the Gofpell, when our Sauiour bid the Apoftles
preach to all Nations, and yet neuer performed
by Proteftants, by euidence of fact, and by the
confeffion of our Aduerfaries, doth fhine moft
bright in the Church of *Rome*.

4. But I cannot fay, that you omitted to
raile againft the Iefuites, whom I will not dif-
honour fo much, as to defend them againft that
which you offer fo impertinently, vulgarly, and
meanely againft them, and particularly becaufe
in defence of a common caufe I will not be di-
uerted by the confideration of particular perfons, though by reafon of the Eminency of the
perfon of Cardinall *D'offat*, I cannot forbeare
to tell you, that you falfify him, when you make
him fay in his eight Epiftle, that he *coll.cted
from their wicked doctrine and practifes, that they belieue neither in Iefus Chrift, nor the Pope*. For the
Cardinall fpeakes not thofe words of any doctrine or practifes of the Iefuites: And in the
funerall Oration which was pronounced at the

Exe-

Exequyes of the faid *Cardinall*, and is prefixed before the Booke which you alleadge, it is affirmed, that he of his owne accord, and without being dealt with to that purpofe, did negociate the readmiffion of the Iefuites into *France.* So far was he from *collecting from their doctrine & practifes, that they belieue neither in Iefus Chrift, nor in the Pope.* And as for our doctrine, which concernes the incompatibility of Proteftancy with faluation, as proper to the Iefuites, it is an idle fpeach, void of all colour of truth. For it is fo far from being proper to them, that it is common to all Roman Catholiques in the world, and you fhall neuer be able to fhew me any one of an entire fame, who holds the contrary.

5.   And wheras you aske: Why may not a Proteftant be faued fince he belieues *entirely the Scriptures, the Catholique Creeds, and whatfoeuer the Catholique Church in all ages hath belieued as neceffary to faluation?* You may take the anfwere out of my *Firft Part*, where I haue fhewed, that he neither keepes the Commaundments, nor belieues *all* things neceffary to faluation, yea and belieues not *any one* point with diuine and fupernaturall fayth, who difobeyes, and difagrees from the vifible Church of Chrift, in any one thing, propounded by her as a *Diuine truth.*

6.   You tell vs, that you are *no further departed from the prefent Roman Church, then fhe is departed from herfelfe.* But no wife man will belieue this, till you can informe him, what vifible

ble Church at,or before *Luthers* appearance remained pure, *out* of which the *Roman* Church
had formerly departed;or els you muſt confeſſe
that the whole Church of Chriſt was corrupted. Which becauſe you will neuer be able to
doe,with truth you muſt be forced to confeſſe,
that ſhe ſtill kept her integrity , without any
ſpot of erroneous doctrine , and therfore that
your departure *out* of her , cannot be excuſed
from *Schiſme*,and *Hereſy.*

7. You ſay *truly,* That it is *meerly impoſsible*
(b)the Catholique Church ſhould want Charity , be- (b) *Pag.* 10.
cauſe the good ſpirit of Truth and Loue euer aſsiſts
and animates that great Body. But you ſpeake not
conſequently to your owne Aſſertion , that the
Catholique Church may erre in points of fayth
not fundamentall.For if the *good ſpirit of Truth,*
may faile to aſſiſt her fayth: why may not the
good Spirit of Loue , faile to direct her Charity?
Nay if we obſerue it well, the Want of Charity
which you impute to vs,is reſolued into this doctrinall point, *Proteſtancy vnrepented deſtroies ſal-*
uation : Which Doctrine and Aſſertion , if you
hold to be a fundamentall errour , you depriue
vs,of ſaluation, and become as vncharitable to
vs as you ſay we are to you. If it be not a fundamentall point, then(according to your principles)the Church may erre therin, and ſo want
Charity, by iudging that Proteſtants cannot be
ſaued .

8. What we vnderſtand by the *Roman* Ca-
R r 3   tho-

tholique Church, I haue explained heertofore,
to wit, all Chriftians vnited with the Church
of *Rome*, as it is the fea of *Peter*. In which fenfe
it is not a part, but comprehendeth all the Catholique Church (which heertofore I proued
out of the Fathers;) as, in fome proportion, we
do not vnderftand the Tribe of *Iuva* alone by
the *Iewifh Church*, though the other Tribes were
called by the name of the *Iewifh* People and
Church, from that principall Tribe of *Iuda*. So
that your marginall quotations to proue that
the Church of Rome is a particular Church, are
emploied to proue that which no man denies,
if we fpeake of the particular *Dioceffe* of *Rome*,
and not as it is the Sea of *Peter*, to which all
Chriftian Catholiques difperfed throughout
the whole world are vnited: Which Sea of *Peter*
fetled in *Rome*, being the Roote, the Center, the
Fountaine, the Idæa of all Ecclefiafticall Vnion
in all Chriftian Churches, giueth them the denomination of *Roman Catholiques*; which doth
no more limit the whole *Catholique* Church,
then the name of *Iewifh* Church, did limit the
whole Sinagogue to the Tribe of *Iuda* alone.
And therfore your thred-bare Obiection, that
(c) *Pag.* 11. *Catholique Roman* (c) *are termes repugnant*, figni-
fying *vniuerfall particular*, vanifheth vtterly a-
way by this different acception of the *Roman*
Church, and ferues only to conuince by your
owne obiection, that *D. Potter*, or the *Church of
England* cannot ftile themfelues *Catholique*, becauſe

caufe *Catholique* fignifieth *Vniuerfall*, and *D. Potter and the Church of England*, are things *particular*. And I would gladly know what your Brethren meane , when they affirme the *Roman*
Church , for diuers Ages to haue poſſeſſed the
whole world ? Do they thinke that the particular Dioceſſe of *Rome* was lifted ouer the Al-
pes? Or when your Prelates demaund, whether
we be *Roman* Catholiques , do they demaund
whether we dwell in the Citty , or Dioceſſe of
Rome ? And heer I note in a word , what now
cometh to my mind, that I wonder *D. Andrewes*,
a man ſo highly eſteemed among Proteſtants,
would tell vs that the *Roman* Church is *indiuiduum (*d*)* as the Logicians call it , and that Catholique is *Genus* , or a generall kind . For to
omit that the thing it ſelfe is ridiculous , it
maketh directly for vs;becauſe euery *indiuiduum*
containes in it ſelfe the *Genus*, as *Peter (* for
example) is a ſubſtance,a ſenſible creature &c.
and ſo if the *Roman* Church be *indiuiduum*, it
muſt containe *Catholique* in it ſelfe ; and ſo the
Roman Church muſt of neceſſity be affirmed to
be a *Catholique Church*. Before I leaue this point
I muſt tell you , that you corrupt *Innocentius
Tertius*,to proue (e)that the *Roman* Church was
anciently eſteemed a *Topical*, or *particular Church*
diſtinct from others, and in, & vnder the vniuerſal,
in theſe words : *It is called the Vniuerfall Church*
which conſiſts of all Churches : where you put an
&c. and then add, *Eccleſia Romana ſic non eſt vni-*
uerſalis

(d) *Jn Reſp.
ad Apolog.
Card. Bel-
lar.ad ça. 5,*

(e) *Pag.* 12.

uerſalis Ecclesia, ſed pars vniuerſalis Ecclesiæ : The Roman Church is not thus the vniuerſall Church, but part of the vniuerſall Church , where you breake off. But *Inncentius* his words are theſe : *The Vniuerſall Church is ſaid to be that which conſiſts of all Churches, which of the Greeke word is called Catholique : and according to this acception of the Word, the Roman Church is not the Vniuerſall Church, but part of the Vniuerſall Church : Yet the first and chiefe part, as the head in the body; becauſe in her, fulnes of power doth exist , but only a part of fulnes is deriued to others . And that One Church, which containes vnder it ſeife all Churches , is ſaid to be the Vniuerſall Church. And according to this ſignification of the Word, only the Roman Church is called the Vniuerſall Church, becauſe ſhe alone is preferred before the reſt by priuiledge of ſinguler dignity. As God is called the vniuerſall Lord , not becauſe he is diuided into ſpecies &c. but becauſe all things are contained vnder his Dominion : For there is One generall Church of which Truth it ſelfe ſaid to Peter ; Thou art Peter and vpon this Rocke &c. And the many particular Churches, of which the Apoſtle ſayth, Inſtantia mea &c. One doth conſiſt of all, as the generall of particulars, & One hath the preeminence before all, becauſe ſeing there is one Body of the Church, of which the Apoſtle ſayth ; We are all one Body in Christ : ſhe excels the reſt, as the Head excels the other members of the body.* Thus far *Innocentius* ; who as you ſee teacheth that the *Roman* Church is the Head of all others : That although the *Roman* Church in one

ſenſe

fenfe be a particular Church, yet in another fenfe it both is, and ought to be called the Vniuerfall Church; and finally that your Obieſtiō about the repugnance betwixt the terme *Vniuerfall* and *particular* is friuolous, as he explicates very well by the example of Almighty God, who is faid to be an *Vniuerfall* Caufe, and yet had neyther *genus*, nor *fpecies*, and befids whom there are other particular Caufes. Is this to affirme, as you fay, that the Roman Church is a *topycall, or particular Church in, and vnder the Vniuerfall? Or that fhe is onely Topicall, or particular, as you would make the Reader belieue?*

9. Your preaching, rather then prouing the *Charity* of your Church, *Adminiftration of Sacraments &c.* muft rely vpon a voluntary begging of the Queftion, that your Religion is true; otherwife the good deeds you mention are not expreffions of *Charity*, but profeffions of *Herefy*; The learned Cardinall *Hofius* faying: *Whofocuer belieues* (f) *the Article of the Catholique Church, belieues all things neceffary to Saluation,* fayes no more then you will fay, that whofoeuer belieues the whole Canon of Scripture, belieues all things neceffary to Saluation. And you cannot but fpeake againft your owne confcience, when you fay of the Roman Church, (*pag.* 16.) *She tells them it is Creed inough for them to belieue onely in the Catholike Church:* For your felfe (*pag.* 198.) affirme, that *the beft aduifed of Catholique Deuines yield there are fome points ne-*

(f) *Hofius in Confefs. Petricon. cap.* 14.

Sf   ceffary

ceſſary to be knowne of all ſorts., neceſsitate medii, in
which points implicite fayth doth not ſuffice, & you
cite ſome of our Authors to this purpoſe *(Chap.*
71. *&* 141.*)* and referre vs to a great many
more. What conſcionable dealing is this ? I
will not ſtand to note, that *Hoſius* euen as he is
cited by you in Latin, doth not ſay, that we belieue *in the Church*, as you make him ſpeake in
your text, but that, *we belieue the Church* . But
inough of this .

10.   In your Firſt *Edition,* I find theſe wor-
(g) *Pag. 13.*   des : *Neuer did* (g*) any Church affoard more plenti-
fully the meanes of grace, nor more abound with all
helps and aduantages of Piety, then this of ours.* But
in your ſecond *Edition* you ſay: *No Church of this
Age doth affoard &c.* Whereby you acknowledge
that at firſt you did ouerlaſh, & ſo do you now.
But it comes to you by kind. *Beza* makes bold
to ſay : *When I compare, euen the tymes which were*
(h) *In epiſt.*   *next to the Apoſtles* (h) *with ours, I am wont to*
Theol. epiſt.   *ſay, and in my opinion not without cauſe, that they*
1. *pag. 5.*   *had more conſcience and leſſe knowledge; and contrarily we haue more knowledge and leſſe conſcience.*
And *M. Whitgift* your once Archbiſhop of *Canterbury* ſayth : *The doctrine taught and profeſſed*
(i) *In his*   (i*) by our Biſhops at this day, is more perfect and
defēce of the   ſounder then commonly was in any Age after the A-
anſwer &c.*   *poſtles &c. How greatly were almoſt all the Biſhops*
pag. 472. &   *and learned Writers of the Greeke Church, and La-
473.*   *tins alſo for the moſt part, ſpotted with doctrines of*
FreeWill, of Merits, of Inuocation of Saints., and
ſuch

such like. Surely you are not able to reckon in any Age, since the Apostles times, any Company of Bishops, that taught and held so found and perfect doctrine in all points, as the Bishops of England do at this day. And will not the *Puritanes* fay, that they are more pure then *Protestants,* and *Anabaptists* accompt themselues more vnſpotted then *Puritanes &c?* In the meane time your own Archbiſhop grants that, *Almost all the Bishops & learned Writers of the Greeke Church, and Latins alſo, were for the moſt part ſpotted with doctrines,* which now you call *Popish Superstitions.*

11. The reſt of this Section contaynes nothing but rayling, and vntruths, continually vttered by euery Miniſter, and often anſwered by our Writers. In Catholique Countreys there may be good reaſon for not mentioning the needles praiſes of condemned *Heretiques,* leſt the eſtimation of their morall parts, which they abuſe againſt Gods Church, breed a liking, and add authority to their peſtiferous errors. If *D. Stapleton,* or any other ſpeaking of Heretiques in generall, compare them to *Magicians* &c. (as *Tertullian* alſo doth) what is that to you, vnles you be reſolued to proclaime your ſelfe an Heretique? Such ſayings are not directed to their Perſons, which we loue; but fall vpon their ſinne : which conſidered in it ſelfe, cannot, I hope, be ouerwronged by ill language. *S. Policarpe* called an Heretique the firſt begotten of the Diuell. *S. Paul* giues them the name of (k) (k)*Philip.3.* 2.

* *Ep.* 2. 7. Dogs. *S. Iohn* * termes them *Antichrists,* as your Ministers are wont to call the Pope. *Charity Mistaken* compares you not with Iewes, or Turkes for impossibility to be saued . Euery deadly sinne excludes saluation ; yet some are more grieuous, and further from pardon then others.

12. *I hope the Mistaker* (1) *would not wish vs* (1) *Pag.* 19. *conuerted from our Creed.* No : But we wish you conuerted , *from* Erroneous Interpretations therof, *to* the Catholique Church, which we professe in our Creed. In the meane time these are learned arguments which may serue both sides. Protestants belieue the Creed , *Ergo* , they need not be couuerted . Catholiques belieue the Creed , *Ergo* they need not be conuerted . You tell vs of a *Cenfure of the Creed,* written by some Catholique. And in your first *Edition* you put, *Cenfura Symboli Apostolici, ad inftar Cenfura Parifienfis.* But in your second *Edition* , being as it seemes, sory for your former sincerity, you say absolutely , *Cenfura Symboli Apostolici,* with an &c. which helpes you in diuers occasions, both to deceiue the Reader, and yet to saue your selfe when you shall be told of corrupting the sentence by leauing out words, as in this particular the Reader will conceiue, that it was an absolute *Cenfure of the Apostles Creed*; wheras contrarily, it suppofeth that the Creed , as a thing most facred, cannot be cenfured, and out of that suppofition, taxeth a certaine *Cenfure* framed , as he thinkes, in fuch manner that the Creed it selfe

felfe could not be free from mens Cenfure, if fuch a forme of Cenfure might paffe for cur-rant. This I fay, is the drift of that Cenfure, and not to cenfure the Creed: which thing I touch, but to anfwere you, who infer that *fome* Catho-liques *feeme very meanely to efteeme* the Creed. But my intention is not to medle any way with that *Cenfure* of the Creed, (whofe Authour in very deed is vnknowne to me) or with any *Bookes,* or *Cenfures* in that kind , wholy leauing thofe affaires to the Vicar of Chrift, the Succef-four of *S.Peter*; which is a great happines proper to Catholiques, who though they may difagree as men, yet as Catholiques , they haue meanes to end all Controuerfies , by recourfe and fub-miffion to one fupreme Authority.

CHAP. II.

OVR *Second Section* treates principally of two points : *The Vnity of the Church,* where-*in it confifts*; and; *The Commu-nion of the Church, how farre neceffary* . Both thefe points haue been handled in the *firft* *Part*; where I proued that Difference in any one

point

point of fayth deftroyeth the *Being* and *Vnity* of *Fayth*, and of the *Church*. And; That, Communion with the true Vifible Church is fo far necefsary, that all voluntary error againft her definitions, as *Herefy* is, and all diuifion from her outward Society, which is *Schifme*, excludes faluation. By thefe Rules, we can certainly know what is damnable *Schifme*, and *Herefy*; whereas *you*, placing the Vnity of *Fayth*, and truth of a Church in the beliefe of points, which you call *fundamentall*, although it be ioyned with difference in a thoufand other points, and yet *not knowing* what Articles in particular be *fundamentall*, muft giue this finall refolution : The Vnity of fayth, and of the Church confifts in, *We know not what.* Moreouer, if you meafure the Nature, and Vnity of fayth, not by the *formall motiue*, for which we belieue, to wit, the Word, or Reuelation of God, but by the weight of the particular obiects which are belieued, you will not be able to fhew, that he who erreth in fome one, or more fundamentall points, doth loofe diuine infallible fayth in refpect of thofe other truths which he belieues : and by this meanes, Perfons difagreeinge, euen in *Fundamentall* points, may retaine the fame fubftance or effence of fayth, and be of the felfe fame true Church; which is moft abfurd, & makes a faire way to affirme, that Iewes, and Turkes are of the fame Church with Chriftians, becaufe they all agree in the beliefe of one God. And thus we

haue

haue anfwered the fubftance of your *Section*.
Yet becaufe you interpofe many other vnneceffary points we muft follow your wädrings ,
left els you may be thought to haue faid fomewhat to vs which is vnanfwerable.

2. After an vnprofitable oftentation of
Erudition (which yet required no deeper learning, then to read fome of our Catholique In-
terpreters) about the place *Deut.* 17. you come
in the end to grant, that the High Prieft *in cafes
of moment had an abfolutely infallible direction, &c.*
And will you giue greater priuiledge of infallibility to the Type, then to the Thing fignified,
to wit, the true Church of Chrift, of which the
Synagogue was but a figure? You cite fome Catholique Authours , as affirming that by the
Iudge is meant the Ciuill Magiftrate, and by the
Prieft, not the *High* Prieft alone. Of which Catholique Authours, I haue at the prefent only
the *Dowifts* (as you are pleafed to call them) in
their Marginall Note on the 2. *Chro.* 19. *Verf.* 1.
whom I find you to falfify. For their words are
only thefe : *A moft plaine diftinction of fpirituall
and temporall authority and offices, not inftituted by
Iofaphat, nor any other King , but by God himfelfe.*
And vpon the words of *Deut.* 17. *Verf.* 9. *Thou
fhalt come to the Prieft of the Leuiticall Stocke, and
to the Iudge that fhall be at that time* ; they fay : *In
the Councell of Priefts one fupreme Iudge , which
was the High Prieft. verf.* 12. And further they fay:
*There were not many Prefidents at once , but in Suc-
cefsion;*

cefsion,one after another. Is this to affirme, that
by the Prieft, is meant *not the high Prieft* alone?
Do they not fay the quite contrary? And as for
your Obiectiós againft our Argument drawne
from the Synagogue, to proue the infallibility

(m) 1. *Part.* of the Church, I haue anfwered them (m) heer-
Chap. 2. n. tofore.
23.

3. That *Core, Dathan, and Abiron* , *with all*
(n) *Pag.29.* *their Company defcended aliue into the pit of Hell;*
you fay, *is rafhly, and* (n) *uncharitably faid by Cha-*
rity Miftaken. But you falfify his words which
are : *The ground* (o) *opened it felfe and fwallowed*
(o) *Pag. 16.* *them aliue, with all their goods into the profound pit*
of Hell. Are (*goods*) and (*company*) two words
of one fignification? And yet in your *fecond E-*
dition, you cite (*with all their company* &c.) in a
differét letter, as the words of your Aduerfarie.
But fuppofe he had faid , as you alledge him
(*with all their company &c.*) what great crime
had he committed? The holy Scripture fayth of
them, and their Complices, without limitation

(p) *Num.16.* or diftinction:*The Earth* (p) *brake in funder vnder*
v. 31.32.33. *their feete ; and opening her mouth , deuoured them*
with their Tabernacles , and all their fubftance , and
they went downe into Hell quicke , couered with the
ground, and perifhed out of the midft of the multi-
tude. You fee the Scripture fpeakes indefinitely,
and fo doth *Charity Miftaken* , without adding
any *Vniuerfall* particle, as *All, Euery one,* or the
like, except when he fayth, *with all their Goods,*
which are the very words of Scripture. Nay
since

ſince the Scripture ſayth: *They went downe into Hell quicke, and periſhed out of the midſt of the multitude*; by what authority will you affirme, that *all* periſhed out of the midſt of the multitude, but *not all* went downe into Hell quicke?

4. Though it were granted that thoſe wordes *Math .* 18.17. *If thy Brother offend thee , tell the Church*, are meant of priuate wrongs: yet it is cleere , that from thence is inferred *à fortiori,* that all Chriſtians are obliged to obey the Catholique Church in her decrees. And no man is ſo ignorant as not to know , that the holy Fathers do euery where apply thoſe words againſt *Schiſmatiques* and *Heretiques ,* as appeareth by *S. Auguſtine* whome heertofore (p) I cited , and *S. Cyprian* (q) and others . And I pray you , if one vtter ſome *Hereſy* , in preſence of his brother ; doth he not in a very high degree offend his Brother? and conſequently , is he not comprehended in thoſe words of our Sauiour , *If thy Brother offend thee &c.?* Now , if the Church were *fallible ,* how could we be obliged vnder payne of being reckoned *Pagans* and *Publicans ,* to obey her *Decrees* and *Declarations* concerning matters of fayth , which is a Vertue , that neceſſarily inuolues *infallibility?* But when did you euer heare any Catholique ſay what you impoſe vpon *Charity Miſtaken ,* that *abſolute obedience is due vnto the Church , no appeale being allowed, no not* (r) *to Scriptures though expounded in a Catholike ſenſe , and conſonantly to the iudgment of the*

(p) *1.part. cap.* 5. *num.* 7.

(q) *Lib.* 1: *epiſt.* 3. *& Ibid. ep. 6:*

(r) *pag.* 28.

T t

the most ancient and famous members of the Church?
With what face can you vtter fuch ftuffe ?
You know we belieue, that the Church cannot
oppofe Scripture.

5. As for thofe corruptions of the Text of
S. Cyprian in his Booke *de vnitate Ecclefiæ*, which
you charge *Pamelius* to haue committed in fauour of *S. Peters Primacy*; it is but an old obiection borrowed of others, and purpofely anfwered by *Pamelius* in his notes vpon that Booke: where, for his iuftification he cites diuers
ancient Copies, and one more then nine hundred yeares old. And as for the phrafe & maine
point it felfe, that *Chrift built the Church vpon
Peter*, it is expreifely affirmed by *S. Cyprian* in
many other places, which I quote in the (s)
Margent: whereby it manifeftly appeareth
what *S. Cyprian* belieued about the Authority
of *Saint Peter*: and how much his Booke *de Vnitate Ecclefiæ* maketh for the Roman Church:
neyther can you in all *S. Cyprians* workes, or in
this place in particular, fhew any thing to the
contrary, as you are pleafed to (t) affirme. To
proue that our vnworthy fafhion is, to alter &
raze many records and Monuments of Antiquity, you cite *a moderne English Writer*, & *Sixtus Senenfis*. But both of them are alledged after your fafhion: for the firft fpeakes onely of
Bookes writen in fauour of the Popes Power
in temporall things, wherein neuertheles we
can in no wife allow of his faying, nor is he in
this

(s) *De ex-
hort. Mart.
c. 11. ep.55.
69.73.which
laft is cited
by S. Augu-
ftin de Bapt.
lib 3. c. 17.
as he cites
the like wor-
des out of
epift. 71. ad
Quint.*
(t) *Pag. 30.*

this point a competent witnes; and the second
directly falsifyed. For you say, he highly com-
mends (u) Pope *Pius the fifth* for the care which (u) *Epist. de.*
he had to *extinguish all dangerous Bookes*; and, *to die. ad Pium*
purge the writings of all Catholique Authours, *es.* 5.
pecially of the Ancient Fathers, from the filth and
poyson of Heresy; & there you end the sentence.
But *Sixtus Senensis* hath *faecibus haereticorum aeta-*
tis nostrae : *from the dregs of the Heretiques of our*
tymes, vnderstanding nothing else, but that
the sayd holy *Pope* caused the false Annotations
Glosses, Marginall notes &c. of *Erasmus*, and
moderne Heretiques to be blotted, or taken out
of the Bookes of the holy Fathers. Is not this
playne falsification ? And so much lesse excusable, because it could not be done but wittingly, and willingly; for that in the Margent you
cite the Latin, & when you come to those wordes, *especially of the ancient Father*s, you breake
off with an *&c.* leauing out that which did
directly ouerthrow the purpose for which
you alledged those wordes. For want of better matter, you tell vs of an Edition of *Isido-*
rus Pelusiotes his Greeke Epistles approued,
because they contayned nothing contrary to the Ca-
tholique Roman Religion : wherein what great
harme is there ? If the *Approbator* had left out
Roman, would you haue made this obiection ?
To vs, *Catholique* and *Roman* are all one, as heertofore I explicated. But it *seemes* (say you)
that they had not passed, but vpon that Condition.

This

This is but a poore Confequence in Logicke: For, one effect may be produced by fome caufe, yet in fuch manner, as that the effect would follow, though that caufe were taken away; & accordingly you grant that the aforefayd claufe of *Approbation* is left out in another *Edition*. Neyther can you be ignorant that Catholiques do print, and reprint the writings of ancient Authours, although they contayne *Herefies*; as the workes of *Tertullian*, *Origen &c* And ther-fore you are leffe excufable both for making this Obiection in generall, and alfo for fallify-ing *Sixtus Senenfis* in particular.

6. The places alledged by you out of *S. Augu-ftin* againft the *Donatists*, come far fhort of pro-uing, that (u) Scripture alone is the *Iudge*, or ra-ther (as you correct your felfe) *Rule* of Cötro-uerfies : & your bringing thé to that purpofe is directly againft *S. Auguftins* ᵂords & *meaning*, as will appeare by what now I am about to fay. Two Queftions were debated between the Ca-tholiques, & Donatifts. the one concerning the Church, whether or no fhe were confined to that corner of the world, where the faction of *Donatus* did refide: The other, whether fuch as were baptized by Heretiques ought to be reba-ptized. We grant that *S Auguftine* in the former Queftion, preffed the *Donatifts* with manifeft Scripture to proue the exeternall apparant No-tes, or Markes of the Church, as Vifibility, per-petuity, Amplitude, Vniuerfality &c. And no

(u) *pag. 32.*

wonder

wonder that he appealed to Scripture. For that very Queſtió being, whether the Catholiques, or Donatiſts, were the true Church; to ſuppoſe the Catholiques to be the true Church, and vpon that ſuppoſition to alledge their Authority againſt the Donatiſts, had been but to beg the Queſtion : as if there were Controuerſy, whether ſome particular Booke were *Canonical Scripture*, or no, it were an idle thing to alledge that very writing in queſtion, to proue it ſelfe *Canonicall* : and on the other ſide, both the Catholikes and Donatiſts did acknowledge & belieue the ſame Scriptures, which as *S. Auguſtine* is wont to ſay, ſpeake more *cleerely* of the Church, then of Chriſt himſelfe: and therfore he had good reaſon to try that Queſtion concerning the Church by *cleer*, & not *doubtfull* Teſtimonies of holy Writ; wheras the *Donatiſts* had recourſe eyther to obſcure Texts, as that of the Canticles, *Shew me where thou feedeſt, where thou lieſt in the midday*, to proue that the Church was cófined to *Africa*; or els to *humane* Teſtimonies as Acts of Notaries or Scriueners, to proue that the Catholiques had been *Traditores*, that is had giué vp the holy Bible to be burned. Or that they had ſacrificed to Idols. Or had been cauſe of perſecution againſt Chriſtians ; and that either for theſe crimes, or for communicating with ſuch as had committed them, the Church had periſhed from among Catholiques : Or els they produced their owne bare affirmation, or mock-

mock-Miracles, & falſe Councels of *T H E I R*
O W N E : All which proofes being very partiall, inſufficient, and impertinent, *S. Auguſtin*
had reaſon to ſay : *Let theſe fictions* (w) *of lying*
men, or fantaſticall wonders of deceiptfull Spirits, be
remoued. And: *Let vs* (x) *not heare; Theſe things I*
ſay; Theſe things thou ſaiſt; but let vs heare; Theſe
things our Lord ſayth. And: *What are our words* (y)
wherin we muſt not ſeeke her &c. All that we obiect
one againſt another of the giuing vp of the holy
Bookes, of the Sacrificing to Idols, and of the perſecu-
tion, are our words. (theſe words you fraudulently conceale, although you cite other in the ſelfe
ſame Chapter, becauſe they plainly ſhew what
S. *Auguſtin* vnderſtands by *Humane Teſtimo-*
nies, & they anſwere all your Obiections:) And:
The Queſtion betweene vs (z) *is, where the Body of*
Chriſt, that is, the Church is? What then are we to do?
Shall we ſeeke her in our words, or in the words of our
Lord Ieſus-Chriſt her head? Surely we ought rather
to ſeeke her in his words who is Truth, and beſt knowes
his owne Body. And : *Let this Head* (a) *of which we*
agree, ſhew vs his Body, of which we diſagree, that
our diſſentions may by his words be ended. Which
words plainely declare the reaſon why he appealed to Scriptures, becauſe both parts agreed
about *them,* but diſagreed concerning the
Church. And: *That we are in the* (b) *True Church*
of Chriſt, and that this Church is vniuerſally ſpread
ouer the earth, we proue not by O V R Doctours, or
Councels, or Miracles, but by the diuine Scriptures.

The

(w) De vnit.
Eccleſ. cap.
19.
(x) cap. 3.
(y) cap. 2.

(z) cap. 2.

(a) cap. 4.

(b) cap. 19.

The Scriptures are the only (this word *only* put by
you in a different letter, as if it were *S. Auguſtines*, is your owne addition : *) Document, and
foundation of our cauſe.* Theſe are the places by
you alleaged ſo vnfaithfully . And will you in
good earneſt infer from them, that we muſt reiect all Councels, neuer ſo lawfull;all Doctors,
neuer ſo Orthodox; all Miracles, neuer ſo authenticall, euen thoſe which were wrought in
the Primitiue Church, & particularly in *S. Au-* (c) *De ciuit.*
guſtines time, which he himſelfe publiſhed *(c)* *Dei lib. 22.*
approued, and admired? And aboue all, will you *cap. 8.*
infer, that after we haue found out the true
Church by Markes ſet downe in Scripture, her
voyce for other particular points of doctrine is
not to be heard, but to be eſteemed a meere *humane teſtimony* of Notaries &c. as *S. Auguſtine*
vnderſtood *humane* Teſtimony when he writ a-
gainſt the Donatiſts? Or will you infer that we
muſt learne from Scripture all that which we
are obliged to belieue ? This you pretend, but
with ſuch ſucceſſe as you are wont ; that is, to
plead for your Aduerſary againſt your ſelfe.
Which is manifeſtly proued by the other Queſtion of *Rebaptization*, controuerted with the
Donatiſts,for which they were properly and formally *Heretiques*:and yet *S. Auguſtine* confeſſeth
that for this point of beliefe, he could not produce Scripture,as appeares by his words, which
I cited in the *firſt* (d) *Part* , and deſire the Rea- (d)*Chap.* 3,
der to ſaue me the labour of repeating them *num.* 16.
heere:

heere: and then he will eaſily ſee, that there is
great difference betwixt the *generall* queſtion of
the Church, and Queſtions concerning *parti-*
cular Doctrines deliuered by the Church; in
which this holy Father ſayth not we muſt haue
recourſe to *Scripture*. alone, but that we ought
to belieue the Church, which is recommended
to vs by *Scripture* And this he teacheth in that
very booke *De vnitate Ecclesiæ,* out of which
you brought the aforeſaid places, to proue that
all Controuerſies muſt be decided by Scripture.
With what modeſty then do you ſay, *The Miſta-*
(e) *pag. 33.* *ker was ill aduiſed to ſend vs to this* (e) *Treatiſe,*
which both in the generall ayme, and in the quality of
the Arguments and proofes is ſo contrary to his pre-
tenſions?

(f) *pag. 33.* 7. You leaue (f) a paſſage taken out of *S.*
Auguſtine to *Charity Miſtaken* to ruminate v-
(g) *S. Aug.* pon: *Whoſoeuer* (g) *will belieue aright in Chriſt the*
de vnit. Ec-
cleſ. cap. 4. *Head, but yet doth ſo diſſent from his Body the*
Church, that their Communion is not with the whole
wherſoeuer diffuſed, but with themſelues ſeuerall in
ſome part; it is manifeſt that ſuch are not in the Ca-
tholique Church. Well; ſuppoſe all were done as
you deſire; what other thing could be concluded, then this? But when *Luther* appeared,
Proteſtantiſme was not with the whole wherſoeuer diffuſed, but with himſelfe alone: *What*
will follow from hence, you haue *ſo much Logicke*
that you *cannot Miſtake.* Wherefore at this day,
and for euer, we muſt ſay of the Catholique
Church,

Church, as *Saint Augustine* fayd : *Euery one of thofe* (he fpeakes of Heretiques) *is not* (g) *to be found where fhe is to be found; but fhe who is ouer All, is to be found in the felfe fame places, where the others are.*

(g) *De Vnit. Ecclef. c. 3.*

8. You made an ill choyce of *S. Epiphanius*, to proue by his example that the Fathers were wont to confute Herefies by the only Euidence of Scripture. For he not only approues Traditions as neceffary, but alfo proues them out of Scripture. *We ought* (fayth he) *to vfe alfo* (h) *Tradition, for all things cannot be taken from the holy Scripture: the holy Apoftles therfore deliuered fome things in writing, and fome things by Tradition , as the holy Apoftle fayth: As I deliuered to you.* And in another place : *So I teach , and fo I deliuered in the Churches.* And the fame Father, as we fhall fee anon, doth moft cleerly approue Traditiós, yea and confutes *Aërius* by Tradition alone without any Scripture. It is then no wonder, if you corrupt *S. Epiphanius* to make men belieue that he fpeakes of *Herefies* in generall, whereas his words concerne fome few in particular, as the *Samofatenians, Arians &c.* His wordes as you tranflate them are thefe : *The Diuine* (k) *Goodnes hath forewarned vs agaynft Herefies by his Truth, for God forefeeing the Madnes , Impiety, & Fraude of the Samofatenians, Arians , Manichees, and other Heretiques, hath fecured vs by his diuine Word againft all their fubtilities.* But the true Tranflation of *S. Epiphanius* is this : *Therfore the*

(h) *Heref. 61.*

(k) *Heref. 65.*

V u   *holy*

holy Scripture doth make vs fecure of ι uery ϒ*ord*:
That is,hath fecured vs how we are to fpeake,
or what ϒ*ords* to vfe againft the deceipts of the
Samofatenians, Arians,and of other Herefies concerning the bleffed Trinity , as it is cleere by
thefe words immediatly following *(*which you
thought fitteft to conceale : *) For he doth not fay
the Father is the Only-begotten.For* ho*ϒ can he be the
Only-begotten,*ϒ*ho is not Begotten? But he calls the
Sonne the only begotten, that the Sonne may not be
thought to be the Father* &*c.* Where you fee he
fpeakes of *Words*, or manner of fpeaking , and
concerning particular *Herefies*, which yet is
made more cleere by the words immediatly
precedent to the fentence by you cited, which
words you alfo thought good to leaue out. For
he firft proues out of Scripture that the *Word* is
begotten of the *Father*, but that the Father is
not Begotten, and therfore the Only-Begotten
is the *Sonne*. And then he comes to the words by
you cited , and teacheth , that holy Scripture
hath warned vs , what words and manner of
fpeach , or phrafe we ought to vfe in fpeaking
of the Perfons of the Bleffed Trinity , which
Schoole Deuines cal *Proprietates Perfonarum.* Yet
that your Corruption might not be void of art
(or rather a double fraud)in your Margent you
put in Greeke *S. Epiphanius* his words, that fo to
fuch as vnderftood not Greeke, nor perceiue
your miftranflation,your fraud might paffe for
honeft dealing,and deceiue your Reader; an

ot

others, you might anſwere, if need were, that in your Margent, *S. Epiphanius* was rightly alleaged.

9.　Theſe words of *Charity Miſtaken* (*I muſt needs obſerue, that (* m *) he (* that is, *S. Auguſtin) recounts diuers Hereſies, which are held by the Proteſtant Church at this day, and particularly that of denying Prayers, and Sacrifices for the dead)* you corruptly compendiate when you ſay: *The Miſtaker muſt needs obſerue, that the Proteſtants hold diuers ancient Hereſies, and particularly (* n *) that of denying Prayers for the dead.* Where you omit the words (*Saint Auguſtine recounts diuers Hereſies, and in particular, that &c. (* to make men belieue that it was but a bare affirmation of *Charity Miſtaken,* and not collected out of *S. Auguſtine :* As likewiſe you conceale) *Sacrifices)* left the world might belieue *S. Auguſtine* was a Papiſt; who neuertheles both in this Treatiſe *de hæreſibus ad Quod-vult-Deum, hær.* 35. cited by *Charity Miſtaken,* and elſewhere, teacheth that the dead are holpen by the holy (o) *Sacrifice.* After this you ſay: *He is very much (* p *) miſtaken in his Obſeruation. The Commemoration of the deceaſed in the ancient Church , which Aërius without reaſon diſallowed, was a thing much differing from thoſe Prayers for the dead , which are now in vſe in the Church of Rome.* Thus hauing ſubſtituted *Commemoration of the deceaſed,* inſteed of *Prayers and Sacrifices for the dead ,* you add, with your wonted ſincerity: *Our Roman Catholiques belieue (at leaſt they ſay ſo)*

(n) *Pag.* 33.

(o) *De verb. Apoſt. ſerm.* 34.

(p) *Pag.* 35.

　that

that some soules of the faithfull after their departure hence, are detained in a certaine fire bordering vpon Hell till they be throughly purged: and their Prayers for them are, that they may be released, or eased of those tormeāts. But you are ſtill like your ſelfe. You may read in (q) *Bellarmine,* that concerning the Queſtion, *Vbi ſit Purgatorium, Where Purgatory is, the Church hath defined nothing.* And to the other point: *Whether in Purgatory there be true corporeall fire,* he anſwers ; (r) *That it is the common Opinion of Deuines that properly there is true fire, & of the same nature with our fire. Which Doctrine is not indeed a matter of fayth, becauſe it is no where defined by the Church, yea in the Councell of Florence the Grecians openly profeſs't, that they did not hold there was fire in Purgatory ; neuertheles in the definition which was made in the laſt Seſſ. it was defined that there is a Purgatory, without making any mention of fire: Neuertheles it is a moſt probable Opinion, by reason of the agreement of the Schoole -Deuines, which cannot be reiected without raſhnes.* Thus Bellarmine.

10.   Now for the maine point : That *Aërius* was put in the liſt of *Heretiques,* for denying Prayers for the Dead, which are offered to releaſe, or eaſe them of their paine, I proue out of *Aërius* his owne words ; Out of *S. Epiphanius* whom you ſeeme to alledge in your behalfe; Out of the ancient Fathers, Greeke, and Latine ; & out of Proteſtants themſelues ; both in regard that they confeſſe the Doctrine of Purgatory

(q)*De Purg. lib. 2.cap.6.*

(r)*Ib. ç.11.*

gatory and Prayer for the dead, euen as Catholiques belieue them, to haue been belieued by
the Ancient Fathers; and alſo in regard, they
directly acknowledge, that *Aërius* was condemned by the Fathers for denying Prayer for
the Dead, as we belieue, and practiſe it.

11.   Heare then your Progenitor *Aërius* te-
ſtifying with his owne mouth the practiſe of
Catholiques in thoſe ancient dayes. *How* (ſaith
he to Catholiques) *doe you* (*) *after Death name,*   (*) *Apud*
the names of the dead? For if the liuing pray &c. what   *Epiph. hæ-*
will it profit the dead? Or if the prayers of them who   *ref. 75.*
are heere, be for thoſe who are there, then let no man
be vertuous, nor let him doe any good worke, but let
him get friends by what meanes he will, eyther by mo-
ney, or leauing that charge to his friends at his death,
& let them pray for him that he may not S V F F E R
any thing there. and that, irremediable ſinnes com-
mitted by him may not be layd to his charge. Is it not
cleere inough by theſe wordes, that this *Here-*
tique taketh Prayers offered for the dead, to releaſe or leſſen their paynes after this life, & not
only for a bare *Commemoration,* or *Thankeſ-giuing,*
or the like? And that any man may yet further
conſider, eſpecially if he continue to be of as
Puritanicall a ſpirit, as he was who moſt re-
ſembles the ſpirit of this *Aërius*; let vs, by the
way, add theſe words of his: *Neyther ought* (s)   (s) *Ibid.*
there to be any appointed faſt, for theſe things are
Iudaicall, and vnder the yoake of ſeruitude. For there
is no law appointed for the iuſt man, but for *Mur-*
therers

therers of their Fathers and Mothers, and such like. But if I be refolued to faft, I will choofe my felfe any day, and I will faft with freedome.

12.   Let vs now fee what *S. Epiphanius* in the fame place fayth for your *Commemoration of the deceafed: As for pronouncing the names of the Dead* (fayth he) *What can be more profitable, good, and admirable? Becaufe the liuing belieue that the deceafed liue, and are not extinct, but haue a being, and liue with our Lord: And, that I may vtter a moft pious doctrine, that there is hope in thofe who pray for their Brethren, as for thofe who are trauailed to another Countrey.* Thefe words you recite out of *S. Epiphanius,* but leaue out thofe words which immediatly follow, and are directly againft the doctrine which you will proue out of him in that very place. For thus he faith: *But the Praiers which are made for them do profit them, although they do not releafe the whole fin; in regard as long as we are in this world, we faile, and erre both voluntarily and againft our will, to the end that, that alfo may be mentioned which is more perfect, we remember both the Iuft, & Sinners: For Sinners, imploring the mercy of God: But for the Iuft, Fathers, Patriarches, Prophets, Apoftles, Euangelifts, Martyres, Confeffors, Bifhops, and Anchorites &c. that we may put a difference betwixt our Lord Iefus Chrift, and all Orders of men, by that honour which we giue to him, and that to him we may giue adoration.* You fee that *S. Epiphanius* fpeakes of forgiuenes of finnes, & that he makes a difference betweene Prayers offered

for

for deceaſed *Sinners,* and the Commemoration of *Saints,* who by way of Thankes-giuing, are remembred as *holy men;* wheras to our *Sauiour Chriſt* higheſt adoration is exhibited as to *God;* Or (as *Bellarmine* (t) ſayth,) we diſtinguiſh (t)*De Purg.* *Saints* from *Christ,* becauſe we offer Sacrifice of *lib.1.cap. 9.* Thankes-giuing for Saints, but we do not offer Sacrifice for Chriſt, but to him, together with the *Father,* and the *holy Ghost.* You likewiſe falſi-fy *S. Epiphanius,* while you ſay out of him; That the liuing haue hope for the deceaſed, as for thoſe which be from home in another Coun-trey, and that, *at length they ſhall attaine the state which is more perfect.* Which laſt words are not in *S. Epiphanius,* who neuer taught, that we offer Prayers for Saints, that they may attaine a ſtate which is more perfect. And when *S. Epiphanius* ſayth, that thoſe who pray for their Brethren haue hope of them as of thoſe who are in ano-ther Countrey; you leaue out *Praying,* and on-ly put in *Hope.* And that you may be aſſured how contrary *S. Epiphanius* is to you; not only in the doctrine of Prayer for the dead, but alſo in the ground and reaſon, for which he belieues it, namely *Tradition;* marke his wordes : *The Church* (ſayth he in the ſame place) *doth neceſſa-rily pract. ſe this by Tradition receiued from our An-cestors. And who can breake the Ordination of his Mother, and the Law of his Father? as Salomo ſayth: Heare O Sonne the words of thy Father, and reiect not the Ordination of thy Mother: Shewing by this, that*

God

God the Father, the Sonne , and the holy Ghost haue taught both by writing , and without writing, (behold diuine Traditions) and our Mother the Church, *hath alfo in herfelfe Ordinances inuiolable which cannot be broken* : (behold Ecclefiafticall Traditions. *) Since therfore there be Ordinances fet downe in the Church, and that all be right, and admirable , this Seducer* (Aërius *) remaines confuted.* And together with him all thofe that follow his herefy . And let vs yet heare *S. Epiphanius* fpeaking a little before of another point , thus: *But who knowes moft of thefe thinges ? Whether this deluded fellow* (Aërius *) who is yet aliue &c. or thofe who before vs haue yielded Teftimony, and haue had the Tradition of the Church, which alfo was deliuered from their Fore- Fathers; as they likewife learned of thofe who were before them , in which manner the Church doth ftill conferue the true Fayth receiued from their Fore-Fathers, and alfo Traditions?* Confider now with what reafon you alleaged *S.Epiphanius,* as one who fayth that all Herefy is to be confuted by euidence of Scripture ; wheras he doth cleerly auouch *Tradition* in *generall,* and doth in *particular* confute the Herefy of *Aërius,* without alleaging fo much as one Text of Scripture .

13.   And though *S. Epiphanius* alone , might fuffice both to affure vs what was the *Herefy* of *Aërius* in whofe time he liued ; and alfo to witnes for all the reft of the Greeke Fathers , yea & for the whole Church , (becaufe he auouched

Prayer

Prayer for the dead to come from the Traditiō
of Gods Church) yet I will add some more of
the Greeke Church, as *S. Dionyſius Areopagita*,
who ſaith: *Then the Venerable (* u *) Biſhop doth pray* (u) *Ecclef.*
ouer the dead party, that the diuine Goodnes would Hierarch.
pardon all his ſinnes committed by humane frailty, cap.7.
and transferre him to light, and the Countrey of the
liuing. I wonder then how in your *Text* your
could tel vs, that (w) *conformably* to your *Opini-*
on ; *The ancient Church in her Liturgy remembred* (w) *Pag.37.*
all thoſe that ſlept in hope of the Reſurrectiō of euer-
laſting lyfe, and particularly the Patriarchs, Prophets,
Apoſtles, Martyrs &c. beſeeching God to giue thē reſt,
and to bring them (you put in a parenthesis at the
Reſurrectiō)*to the place where the light of his coun-*
tenance ſhould ſhine vpon them for euermore. And in
your *Margent*, you cite *S. Dionyſius* as fauouring
you, who neuertheles in the very Chapter wch
you cite for your Opinion, is directly agaynſt
you in the words euen now alledged . The like
ſincerity you ſhew in the very ſame Margent in
citing *S. Cyril,* who doth cleerly affirme, that in
the Sacrifice we remēber ſome that they would
pray for vs, and others that they may be re-
lieued by our Prayers and Sacrifices, in theſe (x) *Catech.*
words: *When we offer this Sacrifice (* x)*we make mē-* 5.
tion of thoſe who are deceaſed, of Patriarchs &c. that
God would receyue our prayers by their interceſsion .
And: *we pray for al who are deceaſed, belieuing that*
it is a moſt great help to thoſe for whom the obſecratiō
of that holy and dreadfull Sacrifice is offered. S. Gre-
X x

gory

(y)*In Orat.* gory *Nyſſen* faith: *He cannot after his departure* (y)
pro mortuis. *from the body be made partaker of the Diuinity, vnles*
the purging fire shall cleanſe the ſtaynes of his ſoule.

14.   Among the Latin Fathers, Proteſtants
pretend to eſteeme none more then *S. Augu-*
ſtine, and yet none can ſpeake more plainely a-
gainſt them in this point then he doth, who
befids that he rankes *Aërius* among the Hereti-

(z) *In Pſal.* ques, in another place, he ſayth: *Purge me* (z)
17. *in this lyfe, in ſuch ſort, as that I may not need the*
correcting, or amending fire. And afterward : *It is*
ſayd he ſhall be ſaued as if it were by fire, and becauſe
it is ſayd, he shall be ſaued, that fire growes to be
contemned. But ſo it is ; though he shall be ſaued, yet
the paine of that fire is more grieuous, then what-
ſoeuer a man can ſuffer in this life. And elſwhere;

(a) *De ciuit.* *Some ſuffer* (a) *temporall punishments, only in this*
lib. 21.c.13. *life, others after death, others both now and then.* Of
which place, *Fulke* is enforced to ſay : *Auguſtine*
concludes very cleerly, (b) *that ſome ſuffer Tempo-*
(b *Confut.* *rall paines after this life, this may not be denied.* And
of Purg.pag. in another place, *S. Auguſtine* ſayth : *We ought*
110. *not* (c) *to doubt, but that the dead are holpen by the*
(c)*De verbis* *Prayers of the holy Church, and by the holeſome Sa-*
Apoſt.ſerm. *crifice, and by Almes giuen for their ſoules, that our*
34. *Lord would deale with them more mercifully then*
their ſinnes haue deſerued. For the whole Church ob-
ſerues this, as deliuered from our Fathers. Neither
can you auoide theſe Authorities by flying to
the *Requeſts of Gods mercy that they may haue their*
(d)*Pag. 39.* (d)*perfect Conſummation in body and ſoule, in the*
king-

kingdome of God *at the laſt Iudgment* , as you
ſpeake. For (beſides that all they who depart
this life in Gods fauour are moſt aſſured of **a**
perfect Conſummation independantly of our
Almes-deeds,Prayers &c.) *S.Auguſtine* as you
haue heard ſpeakes of a *Purging fire*, of *Temporall
Puniſhments*, after this life &c. And doth elſewhere write as if he had purpoſely intended to
preuent this your Euaſion , ſaying: *At the Altar
(e)* we *do not remember Martyrs, as* we *do other deceaſed* who reſt *in peace, by praying for them* ; *but rather that they would pray for* vs. Which difference
between Martyrs, and other deceaſed , cannot
ſtand with your meere *Commemoration* of *Than-
keſgiuing* , or your *Requeſt* for a *perfect Conſummation*, both which according to your doctrine
concerne Martyrs, no leſſe then others . The
ſame difference is expreſſed by *S. Cyprian* , ſaying: *It is one thing to be purged ,* (f) *after long torment for ones ſinnes,and to be long cleanſed with the
fire*,and another thing to haue wiped away all
the ſinnes by ſuffering. *S.Hierome* ſayth*: If Origen affirme that* (g) *all Creatures endued with reaſon*,*are not to be loſt, and granteth repentance to the
Diuell*; what *belongs that to* vs , who *affirme that the
Diuell, and all his Officers ,and all ſinneful and* wicked
men do eternally periſh; *and that Chriſtians,if they be
taken away in ſinne* , *are to be ſaued after puniſhments ?* More Fathers may be ſeen in *Bellarmine*
and other Catholique Writers. Theſe may ſuffice to ſhew, what was that Beliefe & Practiſe of

(e) Tract.84
in Joan.

(f) *Lib.* 4:
ep. 2. *alias
epiſt.*52.

(g) *Lib.* 1.
*cont. Pela-
gianos* .

the Church, which *Aërius* oppoſed in his time, as you do at this day.

15.   Laſtly, your owne Brethren beare wit-nes thus againſt you. *Caluin* ſayth: *More then a thouſand three hundred* (h) *yeares ago, it was a Cuſtome to pray for the dead: But I confeſſe they were all driuen into Error.* Bucer his words are: *Becauſe* (i) *almoſt from the beginning of the Church, Prayers and Almes-deeds were offered for the dead, that opinion which S. Auguſtine ſets downe in his Enchiridio cap.* 110. *crept in by little & little: Neither ought we to deny, that ſoules are releaſed by the piety of their liuing friends, when the Sacrifice of our Mediatour is offered for them &c.* Therfore I doubt not, but that from hence aroſe that duty of *Praying*, and *offering Sacrifice for them. Fulke* ſpeaketh plainely: *Aërius* taught, that *Prayer for the dead* (k) *was vnprofitable, as witneſſeth both Epiphanius, and Auguſtine, which they count for an Errour.* He likewiſe acknowledgeth, that *Ambroſe, Chryſoſtome, & Auguſtine allowed Prayer for the dead:* That, *Tertullian, Auguſtine, Cyprian, Hierome, and a great many more do witnes, that Prayer for the dead is the Tradition of the Apoſtles.* And that *Fulke* vnderſtands theſe Fathers in the ſenſe of ſatisfying for Temporall paines after this life, I hope you will not deny. For it is cleere by what we ſaid out of him aboue; Nay, euen in the *Communion Booke* allowed, and eſtabliſhed by Act of *Parlament* in the ſecond yeare of *Edward* the *Sixth*, and printed in London by *Edward Whitchurch* Anno 1549. there

(h) *Inſtit. l. 3. c. 5. Sect. 11.*

(i) *In his enarrat. in ſacra quatuor Euang. printed Baſil. 1536. in Matt. c. 12.*

(k) *In his anſwer to a counterfeyt Cath. pag. 44.*

there is Prayer for the dead : and in the yeare
1547. the firſt yeare of *Edward* the *Sixth* his
raigne, *Stow* recounts, that *on the* 19. *of Iune a
Dirige was ſung in euery pariſh Church in London for
the French King late deceaſed; and a Dirige was alſo
ſung in the Church of S. Paul in the ſame Citty, & on
the next morrow the Archbiſhop of Canterbury, aſsi-
ſted of eight Biſhops, all in rich miters, & other their
Pontificalls, did ſing a Maſſe of Requiem.* And (to
ſay this by the way) there is in the ſame Communion Booke offering vp of our Prayers by
Angels : as likewiſe in the firſt yeare of that
Kings raigne, Communion in *One Kind,* in time
of Neceſſity, is approued, as alſo in the *Collection
in Engliſh of Statutes &c.* the reaſon heerof is added, becauſe at that time *the opinion of the Reall
preſence (as* the *Collector* ſayth *) was not remoued
from vs* Which ingenuous confeſſion ſuppoſes
that Communion in one kind cannot be diſallowed, if we belieue the reall preſence, becauſe
indeed the Body and Bloud of our Sauiour
Chriſt is both vnder the ſpecies of bread, and
vnder the ſpecies of wine.

16.   You ſay, the *Ancient Church* (n) *in her* (n) ᴾᵃᵍ.37.
*Liturgies remembred all thoſe that ſlept in hope of the
Reſurrection of euerlaſting lyfe, and particularly the
Patriarchs, Prophets, Apoſtles &c. beſeeching God
to giue vnto them reſt, and to bring them, (at the
Reſurrection,* as you add *) to the place where the
light of his countenance ſhould ſhine vpon them for
euermore .*

(o)*DePurg.*
lib. 1. cap. 9.

17.   But reade (o) *Bellarmine*, and you shall find a farre different thing in the *Greeke* Liturgy, of which *S. Epiphanius* makes mention, whome you also cite in your Margent : *We offer Sacrifice to thee, O Lord, for all the Patriarchs, Apostles, Martyrs, and especially for the most Blessed Mother of God.* And that the Sacrifice was offered for those Saints onely in Thankes-giuing, the words following doe shew : *By whose Prayers O God, looke vpon vs.* But for other faythfull deceased, the speach is altered, thus : *And be mindfull of all the faythfull deceased who haue slept in hope of the Resurrection, and grant them to rest where the light of thy Countenance is seene.* Which last words you vntruly applyed to *Patriarches* &c. and added *at the Resurrection* ; wheras they are referred only to other faithfull people, for whom Sacrifice is offered, that they may come to see the light of Gods Countenance, euen before the Resurrection; that is, as soone as they haue satisfied for their sinnes. And now how many wayes is the Greeke Liturgy repugnant to you? It speakes of *Sacrifice*, which you turne to *Remembrance*; It speakes of some persons whom we intreate to pray for vs, & others for whom we pray: It teacheth Prayers to Saints : It teacheth that Saints do already enioy the Beatificall Vision, and therfore that Sacrifice only of Thankes-giuing is offered for them And as for the latter Schismaticall, and Hereticall *Grecians*, although their Authority weigh not much ; yet

euen

euen they profeffed in the *Councell* of *Florence,*
that they belieued a Purgatory , & only denied
that the foules were there tormented by fire;
teaching neuertheles that it was a darke place,
and full of paine. And your owne *(*q*)* Brethren
Sparke,*Ofiander*,and *Crifpinus* affirme; that about
Prayer for the dead they conformed themfelues
to Rome. And *S*ᵗ. *Edwin (*r*) Sands* faith ;that the
Greeke Church doth concur with *Rome* in the
opinion of Tranfubftantiation , in Praying to
Saints,in offering Sacrifices,and Prayer for the
dead, Purgatory, &c. And a Treatife publifhed
by the Proteftant Diuines of Wittemberge Anno 1584. intituled *Acta Theologorum Wittember-*
genfium &c. affirmeth that the Greeke Church
at this day belieues Inuocation of Saints , and
Prayer for the dead , as heertofore I noted. All
which confidered, with what Modefty can you
fay : *The generall opinion of (*t*) the Ancient Do-*
ctors Greeke and Latin , downe almoft to thefe laft
Ages, was (and is the opinion of the Greeke Church
at this day) that all the fpirits of the Righteous de-
ceafed, are in Abrahams bofome , or in fome outward
Court of heauen &c. And to mend the matter you
alleage in your Margent , for what you fay a-
bout the Greeke Church at this day,the Councell of (u) *Florence*; wheras indeed it is affirmed
in the *Councell,* that *Declaratum fuit &c.It was at*
length declared,that the Saints haue both attained ,
and not attained Perfect Beatitude ;that is , that the
foules as Soules haue attained perfect Beatitude , yet

*(*q*) Vid. A-*
pol. Prot.
tract.1.Sect.
7. fubd. 12.
at 11.
*(*r*)In his re-*
lation &c.

*(*t*) Pag.36.*

*(*u*)Graei*
in Conc.
Flor.ante
Seff.1.in
Quaft. de
Purgat.

that

that they shall receiue some perfection with their bo-
dies, when they shall shine as the sunne. And it is to
be noted that before this declaration was made,
the Greeke Emperour came into the Councell,
and so it was done with the common consent
of the Grecians.

18.   And heere let me put you in mind, that
if the *Heresy* of *Aërius* , (whether you take it in
our, or your owne sense) were *not fundamentall*,
then you may learne that to make an *Heresy*, or
Heretique it is sufficient that the error consist in
any point, though the same be not fundamentall. If you hold it to be *fundamentall*; then it followes, that Tradition , and Custome of the
Church extends it selfe euen to *fundamentall*
points, in such sort, as to oppose such Tradition
is a fundamentall error. For as we haue seene
before, *S. Epiphanius* , and *S. Augustine* proue
Prayer for the dead by Tradition , though I
grant we want not Scripture for it: but you who
both deny the *Machabees*, and also turne Prayer
for the Dead, into a bare Commemoration &c.
will find no Scripture, wherby to refute *Aërius.*
Moreouer wheras you are wont to impugne a
third place distinct from Heauen and Hell , by
those words of Scripture: *If the Tree shall fall to*
the South (w) *or the North , in what place soeuer it*
shall fall, there shall it be : and such like Arguments ; how come you now to admit a third
Temporary place, and so be forced to solue your
owne obiections?

(w) *Eccle-*
siast. cap.
11. 3.

19.   **Now,**

19. Now, I wifh you to confider, that eyther the *Grecians* did belieue that the Saints enioy the *Beatificall Vifion*, & are not (as you teach)
in fome outward Court; or els they thought
that *Inuocation of Saints* may well be defended,
though they doe not fee the face of God; which
two points you (x) deny, can ftand togeather. (x)*Pag.* 36.
For you haue heard both out of the Greeke *Li-*
turgy, and your Proteftant Writers, that the
Grecians belieue *Inuocation of Saints*. True it is,
if Saints doe not enioy the *Beatificall Vifion*, they
cannot heare, or fee our Prayers *in verbo*, or in
the *Diuine Effence*, but yet they may behold vs
and our Prayers by particular Reuelation, as
fome Catholique Deuines teach *de facto*, of the
bleffed foules, and Angels.

20. Yet if you will needs fuppofe that *In-*
uocation of Saints cannot be defended, vnleffe
they enioy the *Beatificall Vifion*; you fhould not
in true reafon deny *Inuocation* becaufe they are
not Bleffed; but contrarily you ought to belieue
that they are in Bliffe, becaufe it hath alwayes
beene the practife of the Ancient Church to
inuocate them. Nor ought Proteftants in geuerall, to deny prayers to Saints, becaufe they
cannot heare vs; but they ought on the other
fide to belieue that they cā heare vs, becaufe the
Church both Greeke, and Latin hath alwayes (y)*In his de-*
practifed, and allowed Prayers to them. *M*. *fence of the*
Whitgift, as I fayd already, confeffeth; that al- *anfwer.pag.*
moft all the Bishops and Writers (y) *of the Greeke* 473.
　　　　Y y　　　　　　　*Church*

Church and Latin alfo, for the moſt part, were ſpotted with the doctrines of Freewill, of Merit, of Inuocation of Saints, and ſuch like. In particular, the
Saints, *Ambroſe, Auguſtine, Hierome, Nazan-*
zen, Baſill, Nyſſen, Chryſoſtome, are taxed by
your Brethren for holding Inuocatiõ of Saints.
And your *Centuriſts* not only charge ancient *O-*
rigen for praying for himſelfe to holy *Iob* : but
they alſo lay that there are manifeſt ſteps of In-

(z) Vid. A- uocatiõ of Saints in the Doctors of that ancient
pol Prot
traȧ 1. eſt (z) Age. And *D. Couel* affirmeth that *diuers both*
3 ſuba 7 of the Greeke (a) and Latin Church, were ſpotted
(a in his E- with errours about Freewill, Merits, Inuocation of
xamination
&c pag. 120. *Saits &c.* That *Vigilantius* was condemned as
an Heretike for denying Prayers to Saints, may
(b) Cont. be ſeen in (b) S. *Hierome*, and is confeſſed by
Vigilant. c. (c) *Fulke*. Thus then we ſee what the Ancient
2. & 3
(c) in his Church held concerning *Inuocation of Saints*,
anſwer to a & conſequently they belieued that they heare
counterfeyt our Prayers .
Cath. pag.
46. 21. Your ſaying, that we inuocate Saints
(d) pag. 36. as *Commiſſioners* (d) *vnder God, to whome he hath*
delegated the power of conferring ſundry benefits, de-
poſited in their hands, & to be beſtowed at their plea-
ſure; I let paſſe as a very vulgar ſlaunder, vn-
(e) Seſs 22. worthy of a particular anſwere. *For* (as the ſa-
cap. 3. cred Councell of *Trent* ſpeaketh) *we implore* (e)
(f) De San- *their aſsiſtance, that they would vouchſafe to pray*
ȧorum Bea- *for vs in heauen, whoſe memory we keep on earth* .
titud lib. 1.
cap. 2. 3. 4. Which wordes are alſo in the Maſſe.
s. 6.
22. But how ſolidly *Bellarmine* (f) proues

that

that the Saints enioy the fight of God , may be
feen by weighing his Arguments drawne fiom
Scriptures, Councels, Fathers, both Greeke and
Latin, and Reafons grounded on Scripture:
And your affirming , that , *It may be* (g) *thought* (g) *pag. 36.*
he fpake againft his knowledge, & confcience, comes
very vnfeafonably, befides the groffe vntruth,
and great folly of it, in a Treatife wherin you
tax others for *want* of *Charity*. But I remember
that *S. Thomas* among the caufes of fufpition,
putteth the firft of them to proceed from this:
That a man is (h) *ill himfelfe , and therfore being*
confcious of his owne finne, he eafily conceiues ill of o- (h) *2. 2. q.*
thers; according to that *Ecclef. 10. The foolifh man* *60. art. 3.*
walking by the way, he himfelfe being foolifh, doth ac- *in corp.*
count all to be Fooles. Did your prime Brethren
fpeake againft their confcience, who affirme fo
many Ancient Fathers to haue beene fpotted
with the *Inuocation of Saints*, which you fay
cannot ftand with their want of Beatitude?

23.   You fay; *The Roman Writers vtterly con-*
demne the (i) *former doctrine, and practife of Anti-* (i) *pag. 38.*
quity. One of them feares not to cenfure it as abfurd
and impious: for which laft words you cite in
your (k) Margent, *Azor*. But it is an egregious (k *Azor.*
vntruth, and falfification. For we do both ad- *Jnftit Mo-*
mit and practife Thankes-giuing for the hap- *ral. tom. 1.*
pines of Saints. And your further *Requefts of* *cap. 20. lib.*
Gods mercy that they may haue their perfect Confum- *8. § Neque*
mation both in body and foule in the kingdome of *vero.*
God at the laft Iudgmēt, are wholy needles at left,

becaufe without any dependance, or reference to our Prayers, they are moft affured therof by the immutable decree of God. And you might in the fame manner make *Requefts*, that they may not loofe their happines in body & foule, when they fhall once haue attained it, after the generall Refurrection, which were a *Requeft* fauouring of Infidelity, as if the Saints could be depriued of Beatitude once enioyed. Now as for *Azor*, he proues in the place cited by you, that the Grecians do not altogether take away fome kind of Purging fire, but only feeme to deny a certaine determinate punifhment of corporall fire, *Becaufe (* fayth he *) they do truly offer Sacrifice and Prayers to God for the dead , furely not for the Bleffed, nor for thofe which be damned in Hell, which were plainely abfurd and impious: it muſt therfore be for them, who are deceafed with fayth and Piety, but haue not fully fatisfied for the temporall punifhment due to their finnes.* Is this to condemne the doctrine of Antiquity as abfurd, and impious? Did Antiquity offer Sacrifice, and Prayers for the damned Ghofts, or for the Saints to fatisfy for the paine due to their finnes, as *Azor* meanes & fpeakes, and therfore doth truly fay, it were abfurd and impious? Is not this to corrupt Authors?

24. Wherfore vpon the whole matter we muft conclude, that *Aërius* was condemned by the Church, and was reckoned among Heretiques, and particularly by S. *Epiphanius* , and S.

Augu-

Augustine, for the selfe same Error which you maintaine. To which *Maior Proposition,* if we adde this *Minor,* (which *Charity Mistaken* expreffely notes (m) and you conceale:) But S. *Augustine* fayth, *Whosoeuer should hold any one of* (m)Pag.27. the Herefies by him recounted,(wherof this of *Aërius* is one) *were not a Christian Catholique;* The Conclufion will follow of it felfe.

25.   Would to God,your felfe,and all Proteftants did ferioufly confider,what accompt will be exacted at the laft day,of thofe who by their erroneous doctrine, and oppofition to the vifible Church of Chrift, depriue the foules of faythfull people deceafed,of the many Prayers, Sacrifices,and other good deeds, which in all rigour of *Iustice* are due to them by Title of founding Colledges, Chanonryes, Chantries, Hofpitals &c. Leffe cruelty had it been to rob them of their Temporall goods, or to bereaue them of their corporall liues, then to haue abandoned them to the Torment of a fier, which although as S. *Augustine* fayth (n) is fleighted (n)*Jn Pfal.* by worldly men, yet indeed is more grieuous 37. then whatfoeuer can be endured in this world. Confider I fay,whether this manifeft *Iniustice,* though it did not proceed (as it doth) from *hereticall* perfwafion, were not alone fufficient to exclude faluation. And fo much of this point concerning Prayer for the dead.

26.   The words of S.*Thomas,* whom you cite (*pag.* 40.) to ftrengthen your diftinction of

points

points fundamentall and not fundamentall, do directly ouerthrow that sense, and purpose for which you make vse of them. *For as much* (sayth

he) *as belongs to the prime* (o *) Obiects of Beliefe, which are the Articles of Fayth , a man bound explicitely to belieue them, as he is bound to haue Fayth. But as for other Obiects of fayth, a man is not bound to belieue them explicitely, but only implicitely , or in readines of mind, for as much as he is ready to belieue whatsoeuer the holy Scripture containes : But he is bound to belieue them explicitely, only when it appeares to him that it is contained in the doctrine of fayth.* Now our Queſtion is not about *nescience,* or *ignorance* of some points of fayth, but of diſagreeing concerning them, one denying what another affirmes: in which caſe, according to the aforesaid doctrine of *S.Thomas,* there is neither explicite , nor implicite Beliefe of such points, but poſitiue & direct error in them: and therfore such diſagreement cannot ſtand with Vnity of fayth. It is ſtrange Diuinity , to confound, as you do, points *secundary* or not fundamentall , with *probable* points . For how many millions of Truths are there contained in Scripture, which are not of their owne nature *prime* Articles ? Will you therfore infer that they are *but probable? Primary,* and *secundary* reſpect the matter which we belieue. *Probable ,* and *certaine* are deriued from the formall reaſon, or *motiue* for which we belieue . Let two diſagree in some points euen fundamentall, yet not ſufficiently

pro-

propounded as reuealed Truths, they ftill retaine the fame fayth; and contrarily, put cafe
that two agree in all fundamentall points, if
they difagree in any fecundary point fufficiently applied to their vnderftanding as a reuealed
truth, then the one muft be an Heretique, and
differ from the other, in the very nature, and
fubftance of fayth. *For as in a Muficall Confort
(* fay you *) a difcord (* p *) now and then (fo it be in
the Defcant, and depart not from the ground) fwee-
tens the Harmony :* fo fay I (retorting your own
fweet fimilitude) becaufe euery leaft error oppofing a reuealed Truth is not *in the Defcant,* but
departs from the *ground* of fayth, which is the
atteftation of God, it doth not *fweeten the Harmony,* but deftroyes the *fubftance* of Fayth. And
heerafter it fhalbe fhewed, that you wrong *Stapleton,* no leffe (q) then you do S. *Thomas.*

   27. That, *Variety of Opinions or Rites in
parts of the Church doth rather commend then preiudice the Vnity of the whole,* you pretend to proue
out of (s) *Firmilianus* in an Epiftle to S. *Cyprian;*
which doctrine though it be true in fome fenfe,
yet according to your application, it is pernicious: as if it were fufficient to Vnity of Fayth,
that men agree in certaine fundamentall
points, though they vary in other matters concerning fayth. And you fhould haue obferued,
that *Firmilianus* (who wrote that Epiftle in fauour of S. *Cyprians* error about Rebaptization)
fpeakes in that place of the Cuftome of keeping

(p) *pag.* 40.

(q) *Infra
chap.*5 *num.*
17.

(s) *Epift.* 75.
apud Cypr.

ping Eaſter: which point after it was once defined, remained no more indifferent, but grew
to be a neceſſary Obiect of Beliefe, in ſo much
that the Heretiques called *Quartadecimani* were
for that point condemned, and anathematized
by the Vniuerſall Church in the Councels of
Nice, Conſtantinople, and *Epheſus.* Wherby it is e-
uident that though ſome point be not in it ſelfe
fundamentall; yet if it be once defined by the
Church, the *Errour* degenerates into Hereſy.
Your *Charity* is alwayes *Miſtaken*, aduantaging
your Aduerſary by your owne Arguments.

28. I ſaid already that to be ſeparate from
the Church for *Hereſy,* or *Schiſme* deſtroies Saluation, becauſe perſons lyable to thoſe crimes
are in the Church neither *in re* nor *in voto*; neither *in fact*, nor in effectuall deſire; as *Cathecu-
mens* are, and as *Excommunicate* perſons may be,
if repenting their former Obſtinacy, they cannot by reaſon of ſome extrinſecall impediment, obtaine Abſolution from the Cenſure.

29. You extend your Charity ſo far to Infidels, as to forget fidelity in relating what Catholique Deuines teach concerning them, not
telling whether they require ſome ſupernaturall
fayth at leſt, for ſome Obiect; and quoting Authors with ſo great affected confuſion, that a
man would thinke them to maintaine the opinion which they expreſſely condemne as erroneous, or in the next degree to Hereſy. But becauſe it were a vanity to muſter a number of
Writers

Writers in a queſtion impertinent to our preſent deſigne, which is only againſt *Hereſy* or *Schiſme*, both which exclude inuincible ignorance; I hold it beſt to paſſe them ouer in ſilence.

30. Your ſaying, that *A man may be a true viſible member* (t) *of the holy Catholique Church, who is not actually (otherwiſe then in vow) a member of any true viſible Church*; deſtroyes it ſelfe. For in the ſame manner and degree, neyther more nor leſſe, a man is a viſible member in act, or in deſire of the viſible Church, as he is a member of the true Catholique Church, which is viſible. And *Bellarmine,* whome you cite for your ſelfe, is directly agaynſt you. For he teacheth that *a man may* (u) *be in the Church in deſire, which is ſufficient for Saluation* (when he is inuoluntarily hindred from being actually of the Church) *and yet not in the Church by externall Comunion, which properly maketh him to be of the viſible Church*; which is directly to deny what you affirmed. I might reflect what a pretty connection you make in ſaying: *who is not actually otherwiſ then in vow &c.* you might as well haue ſayd, who is not *actually*, otherwiſe then *not in act &c.* But ſuch ſmall matters as theſe I willingly diſſemble. The poore man in the Ghoſpell was caſt out of the Synagogue by notorious inſuſtice, and therefore ſtill remayned a member of the Iewiſh Church, not only in deſire, but alſo in act. You ſay, *Athanaſius ſtood ſingle* ...

(t) *Pag.* 47.

(u) *de Eccleſ. milit. cap.* 6. *Reſponſio.*

defenſe of diuine Truth , all his Brethren the other
Patriarchs(not he of Rome excepted)hauing ſubſcribed to Arianiſme , and caſt him out of their Communion . And you referre vs to *Baronius* cited in
your Margent,to what purpoſe I know not,ex-
cept to diſplay your owne bad proceeding. For
Baronius in the place by you alledged (w) doth
(not incidently , or only by the way , but) in-
duſtriouſly , and of ſet purpoſe cleere Pope *Li-
berius* from hauing euer ſubſcribed to *Arianiſme*.
He ſubſcribed indeed to the condemnation of
S. Athanaſius, which was not for matter of faith
but of fact, to wit,for certayne crimes obiected
agaynſt him, as *Bellarmine* (x) affirmeth,which
being falſe , *S. Athanaſius* did not therefore ceaſe
to be a member of the Catholike Church.If the
errours of *Tertullian* were in themſelues ſo ſmal,
as you would make them , it may ſerue for an
example , that not ſo much the matter , as the
manner , and obſtinacy is that which makes an
Heretique ; which ouerthrowes your diſtinction
of points fundamentall &c.

31.   The proofes which you bring from the
Africans , and others , that Communion with
the *Roman* Church was not alwayes held neceſſary to Saluation , haue been a thouſand tymes
anſwered by Catholique Writers ; and they are
ſuch as you could not haue choſen any more
diſaduantagious to your cauſe . Heertofore I
ſhewed, that Communion with the *Roman*
Church, was by Antiquity iudged to be the
marke

(w) *Anno*
357.*num*.44.
apud Spond.

(x) *De Rom.*
*Pont.lib.*4.
cap. 9.

marke of a true Belieuer. And indeed feing you speake of thofe times wherin *Rome* ftood in her purity (as you fay) how could any be diuided from her fayth, and yet belieue aright? Do not your felfe fay: *Whofoeuer profeffeth himfelfe to for-**fake* (y) *the Communion of any one member of the Body of Chrift, muft confeffe himfelfe confequently to forfake the whole?* How then could any diuide themfelues from the *Romane* Church while fhe was in her purity? Euen *S. Cyprian,* whofe exam-ple you alleage, fayth: *They* (z) *prefume to faile to the Roman Church, which is the Chaire of Peter, and to the principall Chaire, from whence Prieftly Vnity hath fprung. Neither do they confider that they are Romans, whofe fayth was commended by the prea-ching of the Apoftle, to whom falfhood cannot haue ac-ceffe. Optatus Mileuitanus,* alfo an *African,* faith: *At Rome hath been conftituted to Peter* (a) *the E-pifcopall Chaire, that in this only Chaire, the Vnity of all might be preferued.* And *S. Auguftine,* likewife an *African,* affirmeth, that *Cacilianus might def-pife* (b) *the confpiring multitude of his enemies,* (that is, of feauenty Bifhops of *Africa* affembled in *Numidia*) *becaufe he faw himfelfe vnited by let-ters Communicatory with the Roman Church, in which the Principality of the Sea Apoftolique had al-wayes flourifhed.* And after *Pelagius* had been iud-ged in the Eaft by the Bifhops of *Paleftine,* and *Celeftius* his Difciple had been excommunicated for the fame caufe in *Africa* by the African Bi-fhops; the *Mileuitan* Councell referred them

(y) Pag. 76.
(z) Ad Cor-nel. ep. 55.

(a) Contra Parm. lib. 2.

(b) Epift. 62

(c)*Ep.Conc.
Milen. ad
Innocent.
inter epift.
Aug.epift.92*

finally to the Pope, faying: *We hope by the* (c)
*mercy of our Lord Iefus-Chrift,who vouchfafe to go-
uerne thee confulting with him, and to heare thee
praying to him,that thofe who hold thefe Doctrines fo
peruerfe and pernicious, will more eafily yield to the
authority of thy Holynes, drawne out of the holy Scriptures.* Behold the Popes prerogatiue drawne
out of the holy Scriptures.And it is very ftrang
that you will alleage the Authority of *S. Cyprian,*and other Bifhops of *Africa,*againft Pope
Stephen, who oppofed himfelfe to them in the
Queftion of *Rebaptization,* wherin they agreed
with the Herefy of the *Donatifts,* which was
condemned not only by the Pope, but by the
whole Church,yea by thofe very Bifhops who
once adhered to *S.Cyprian,*as *S. Hierome* witnef-

(d) *Contra
Lucifer.*

feth, faying: *Finally they who had been* (d) *of the
fame opinion,fet forth a new decree, faying : What
fhall we do? So hath it been deliuered to them by their
Aucestors and ours.*And *Vincentius Lyrinenfis* fpeaking of *Stephen* his oppofing *S. Cyprian,* fayth :

(e) *In Com.
part.* 1.

Then (e) *the bleffed Stephen refifted, together with,
but yet before his Collegues; iudging it as I conceiue
to be a thing worthy of him,to excell them as much in
Fayth,as he did in the authority of his place .*

　　32.   Neither are you more fortunate in the

(f) *Contra
Ruff.Apol.*1.

example of Pope *Victor,*then in the other of *Stephen* For although *Eufebius (* whom *S. Hierome*
(f)ftiles the Enfigne-bearer of the *Arian* Sect,

(g)*Hist.Ec-
clef.lib.*5.*c.*
24.

and who was a profeft Enemy of the *Roman*
Church) doth relate that *S. Irenæus* (g) repre-
　　　　　　　　　　　　　　　　hended

hended *Victor*, for hauing excommunicated the Churches of *Asia*, for the queſtion about keeping Eaſter: yet euen he dare not ſay, that *Irenæus* blamed the Pope for want of Power, but for miſapplying it; which ſuppoſeth a Power to do it, if the cauſe had been ſufficient. And the ſucceſſe ſhewed, that euen in the vſe of his Power, Pope *Victor* was in the right. For after his death, the Councels of *Nice*, *Conſtantinople*, and *Epheſus* (which you receiue as lawfull Generall Councels) excommunicated thoſe who held the ſame Cuſtome with the Prouinces which *Victor* had excommunicated: and ſo they came to be ranked among Heretiques vnder the name of *Quartadecimini*. You may know what opinion S. *Irenæus* had of Popes by theſe words: *Euery Church ought to haue recourſe* (h) *to Rome, by reaſon of her more powerfull Principality.* And euen in this your inſtance, *Euſebius* doth only ſay, that *Irenæus* did *fitly exhort* Pope *Victor*, that *he ſhould not cut off all the Churches of God, which held this ancient Tradition.* Which exhortation doth neceſſarily imply, that Pope *Victor* had Power to do it, as I ſaid already. And now I pray you, reflect vpon your precipitation in ſaying of *Victor* and *Stephen: Their Cenſures* (i) *were much ſleighted, and their Pride and Schiſme in troubling the peace of the Church much condemned.* For they did nothing which was not approued by the vniuerſall Church of God; and the Doctrines which they condemned were no leſſe then here

(h) *Aduerſ. Hæreſ. lib.* 3. *cap.* 3.

(i) *Pag.* 50.

hereticall. And therfore (to anſwere alſo to what you obiect *pag.* 52.) *If the Britiſh and Scotiſh Biſhops did adhere to the Churches* of *Aſia in their Celebration of Eaſter ,* after the matter was knowne to be defined by the Church , their example can only be approued by ſuch, as your ſelfe; nor can it either impeach the Authority, or darken the proceeding of the Pope. You cite *Baronius* (1) in the Margent, who directly a-gainſt you relates out of *Bede* ; that when our Apoſtle *S. Auguſtine* , could neither by Arguments, nor by Miracles wrought in their preſence, bow their ſtifnes, he prophefied that they ſhould periſh by the Engliſh , as afterwards it hapned. But you are a fit Champion for ſuch men , and they no leſſe fit examples to be alleaged againſt the Authority of the *Roman* Church .

(1)*Ann.604.*

33.   Your other example , that S. *Auguſtine* and diuers other Biſhops of *Africa* , and their *Succeſſours for one hundred yeares together were ſeuered from the Roman Communion ,* is manifeſtly vntrue in S. *Auguſtine,* and ſome other chiefe Biſhops. For when king *Thraſimundus* had baniſhed into *Sardinia* almoſt all the Biſhops, to wit, two hundred and twenty , Pope *Symmachus* maintained them at his owne charges , as perſons belonging to his Communion . To the Epiſtle of Boniface the ſecond to *Eulalius* Biſhop of *Alexandria* , and the Epiſtle of *Eulalius* to the ſame Boniface, recited by you, out of

which

which it is gathered, that after the fixt Councell of *Carthage* for the fpace of one hundred
yeares, the Bifhops of *Carthage* were feparated
from the Communion of the *Roman* Church,
& that in the end they were reconciled to her,
Eulalius fubmitting himfelfe to the *Apoſtolique*
Sea, and anathematizing his Predeceſſors; *Bellarmine* (m) anfwereth, that thefe Epiftles may
iuftly be fufpeﬁed to be Apochryphall for diuers reafons which he alleageth, and it feemeth
alfo by your owne words that you do doubt of
them: For you fay, *If their owne Records* (n) *be
true.* Yet if they be authenticall, their meaning
cannot be, that all the Predeceſſors of *Eulalius*
were for fo long fpace diuided from the *Roman*
Church; the contrary being moft manifeft not
only in S. *Auguſtine,* who kept moft ftriﬁ amity
with *Zozimus, Innocentius,* and *Celeſtinus* Popes,
but alfo in S. *Fulgentius* and others : but it muft
be vnderftood only of fome Bifhops of *Carthage,* and in particular of *Eulalius,* himfelfe, till
he being informed of the truth, fubmitted himfelfe to the *Roman* Church. And you ought rather to haue alleaged his fubmiſſion, and condemnation of his Predeceſſors to proue the Popes Authority ouer the *African* Church; then to
obieﬁ againſt it the example of fome of his
Predeceſſors, & of himfelfe who afterward repented, and condemned his owne faﬁ. You do
well, only to mention the *Pretenſions and forge-
ries of the fea of Rome in the matter of Appeales.* For

(m) *de Rom.
Pont. l. 2. c.
25.*

(n) *Pag.* 50;

you may know that *Bellarmine* (o) doth so fully
answere that point, as nothing can be more effectuall to proue the Popes Supremacy in *Africa*, then the right of *Appeales* from *Africa* to
Rome, in causes of greater moment.

34. Your last instance about three Chapters of the Councell of *Chalcedon, condemned by
the fifth Generall Councell, the Bishop of Rome at
length consenting, for which diuers Bishops of Italy,*
and also the Bishops of Ireland did ioyntly depart from the *Church of Rome,* is like to your former Obiections. For *Baronius* whome you cite
in your Margent hath these words as cōtrary to
your purpose as may be. *Hence was it, that the* (q)
Bishops of Venice & the adioyning Regions did gather
(q) *Ann.* *together a Councell at Aquileia agaynst the Fifit Sy-*
553. num.14. *noae; and the diuisions at length went as farre as Ire-*
apud Spond. *land: for all these relying on the Decree of Vigilius*
Pope, persuaded themselues that they might dee it.
Is this to depart from the Pope, or the *Roman*
Church; to oppose that which he is thought to
oppose,& formally, because he is thought to oppose it? Now, as for the thing it selfe, when *Vigilius* had afterward condēned the three Chapters, which at the first he refused to doe, and
had confirmed the *fifth Councell* which had cō-
demned them, whosoeuer opposed that Condemnation, were accounted Schismatiques by
the whole Catholique Church: which plainly
shewes the Popes Authority, and therefore
whatsoeuer Bishops had opposed *Vigilius*, their
exam-

example could proue no more, then the faction
of rebellious perſons can preiudice the right of
a lawfull King. And in fine , all this Controuerſy did nothing concerne any matter of *faith,*
but only in *fact*; and not *doctrine,* but *perſons,* as
may be ſeen at large in *Baronius* : Neither was it
betwixt Catholiques and Heretiques , but a-
mong Catholiques themſelues. The reſt of your
Section needs no anſwere at all: Only whereas
you ſay ; *Whoſoeuer willfully oppoſeth* (r) *any Ca-*   (r) *Pag.* 57.
tholique Verity maintayned by the Catholique Viſible
Church, as doe Heretiques ; or peruerſly diuides him-
ſelfe from the Catholique Communion, as doe Schiſ-
matiques ; the Condition of both them is damnable :
What vnderſtand you by *Catholique verities* of
the *Catholique* Church ? Are not all Verityes
mayntayned by the *Catholique* Church, *Catho-*
lique Verities ? or how do you now diſtinguiſh
Hereſy, and *Schiſme* from the Catholique Communion? You tells vs , *(pag 76.*) that it is the
property of Schiſme to cut off from the Body of Chriſt,
and the hope of Saluation , the Church from which
it ſeparats : and is it not an *Hereſy* to cut off from
the *Body* of Chriſt & *hope* of Saluation, the Catholike Church ? How then can one (according to your principles) be a *Schiſmatique* from
the *Catholique* Church , & not be iointly an *He-*
retique?

C H A P. III.

(a) *Pag.* 59.

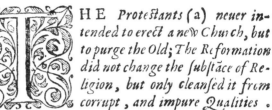

H E *Proteſtants (*a*) neuer intended to erect a new Church, but
to purge the Old; The Reformation
did not change the ſubſtāce of Religion, but only cleanſed it from
corrupt, and impure Qualities* .
Therfore (ſay we) the viſible Church extāt before thoſe your cleanſing dayes, had & ſtill hath
the ſubſtance of Religion; and ſo according to
your owne ground we are ſafe, if you can poſſibly be ſaued. But we haue no ſuch dependance vpon you. Nay, the ſame Confeſſion which
acquits vs , condemnes your ſelues. For while
you confeſſe a Reformatiō of the Old Church,
and neyther doe , nor can ſpecify any Viſible
Church , which in your opinion needed no Reformation ; you muſt affirme , that the Church
which you intended to reforme , was indeed
the Viſible Catholique Church; if ſo, then you
cannot deny but that you departed from the
Catholique Church, & are guilty of *Schiſme*, yea
and of *Hereſy*. For if the *Catholique* Church was
infected with erroneous doctrine which needed

ded Reformation ; it followes , that the errours
were *Vniuerſall*, and that the Reformation con-
ming after thoſe errours , muſt want *Vniuer-*
ſality of *Place* and *Tyme* , and therefore be branded with the marke of *Hereſy* . For in true Diuinity a *new*, and *no* Church are all one. Moreouer, the very *Nature*, & *Eſſence* of the Church
requiring true *fayth*,it is impoſſible to alter any
left point of fayth , without changing the ſubſtance of the Church , and Religion ; and therfore to reforme the Church in matters of faith,
is as if you ſhould reforme a man by depriuing
him of a reaſonable Soule , whereby he is a
man; And a *Reformed Catholique* are termes no
leſſe repugnant , then a reaſonable vnreaſonable creature,or a deſtroied exiſting thing.Wher-
fore to ſay , the *Reformation* did not *change the*
ſubſtance of Religion , but only *cleanſed it from*
corrupt and impure qualities, are meer wordes to
deceaue ſimple ſoules. And it is a lamentable
caſe, that you can neuer be brought from ſuch
ridiculous ſimilitudes , as heere you bring of
Naaman,who was ſtil the ſame man before and
after he was cured of his leproſy ; Of a field o-
uergrowne with weeds,thiſtles &c. (and your
Brethren are full of twenty ſuch childiſh pretended illuſtrations :) whereas euery body
knowes that leproſy is accidental to a man,and
weeds to a field , but Fayth is eſſentiall to the
Church; and that *Affirmation* , or *Negation* of
any one reuealed Truth whatſoeuer , are diffe-

rences no leſſe eſſentiall in fayth , then *reaſonable* and *vnreaſonable* in liuing Creatures. And
Fayth it ſelfe being an *accident* and *quality* conſiſting in *Affirmation*, or *Negation* ; to cleanſe it
from the *corrupt* and *impure quality* of *affirming* ,
or *denying* ; is to cleanſe it from its own *Nature* ,
and *Eſſence* ; which is not to *reforme* , but to *deſtroy* it . Laſtly , from this your forced Confeſſion, not to *erect a new Church, but to purge the Old,*
we muſt inferre that the *Roman* Church, which
you ſought to *purge,* was the *Old* Church , and
the Catholike Church of Chriſt . For if you
found any other Old viſible Catholike Church,
which needed no Reformation , then you neyther intended to erect a *new Church* , nor to *purge
the Old* .

(b) *Pag.* 61.   **2.**   You ſay, *the things which Proteſtants* (b)
*belieue on their part, and wherin they iudge the life
and ſubſtance of Religion to be comprized, are moſt,
if not all of them, ſo euidently and indiſputably true,
that their Aduerſaries themſelues do auow, and receiue them as well as they.* IF this be true, and that
the ſaid Verities *make vp the fayth of Proteſtants*
(as you ſpeake) then what needed you a Reformation to teach men the fayth of Proteſtants, which they belieued before Proteſtants
appeared ? Or how can you be excuſed from
Schiſme, who diuided your ſelues from that viſible Church , which belieued thoſe verities
(c) *pag.* 61.   which *make vp your fayth ?* You ſay , *If all other*
62.   *Chriſtians could be content* (c) *to keepe within theſe*

gene-

generall bounds, the wofull Schismes and ruptures of Christendome might be more easily healed. O words moſt powerfull to condemne your ſelues, who were not content to keep within thoſe generall bounds, which you confeſſe we belieued, but would attempt new Reformations, although with ſo wofull Schiſmes and Ruptures of Chriſtendome, as you hold worthy to be lamented with teares of bloud! If our errors were not fundamentall, your Reformation could not be neceſſary to ſaluation; as when the wound or diſeaſe is knowne not to be deadly, the cure cannot be neceſſary to the conſeruation of life.

3. The Reformation which zealous Catholiques did deſire, and with whoſe words you vainely load your Margent, were not in fayth but manners. For which if it be lawfull to forſake a Church, no Church ſhall remaine vnforſaken. But of this I haue ſpoken in the *Firſt Part. Luther* was iuſtly cut of by *Excommunication,* as a pernicious member: which yet was not done, till the Pope had vſed all meanes to reclaime him. Prouincial or Nationall Synods may ſeeke to reforme abuſes in manners, and endeauour that the fayth already eſtabliſhed be conſerued: but if they go about to reforme the Catholique Church in any one point, they deſerue the name of Conuenticles, and not of Councels.

4. What meane you when you ſay; that you *left the* (e) *Church of Rome in nothing ſhe holds*

of

(e) *pag.* 67,

of Christ, or of Apostolique Tradition? Do you admit *Traditions?* Are they fallible or infallible?
For if they be *infallible*, then may they be part
of the *Rule* of fayth. If *fallible*, they are not *Apostolique*.

5. You goe then about to proue, that our
doctrines are, First, *doubtfull and perplexed opinions*. 2. *Doctrines vnneceſſary, and forraine to the
fayth:* and 3. *Nouelties vnknowne to Antiquity.*

6. You pretend they are *doubtfull*, and ſay:
*The Roman Doctours doe not fully and abſolutly agree in any one point among themſelues, but only in
ſuch points wherin they agree with vs.* If a manifeſt
vntruth be a good proofe, your Argument conuinceth. If you thinke, that diſagreement in
matters not defined by the Church, argues difference in matters of fayth, you ſhew ſmall reading in our Deuines, who euen in all thoſe Articles wherein you agree with vs, haue many
different, and contrary Opinions concerning
points not defined : as about ſome ſpeculatiue
queſtions concerning the Deity, the Bleſſed Trinity, Incarnation; yea there are more diſputes about thoſe high Myſteries wherin you agree
with vs, then in others wherin we diſagree: and
yet you grant, that ſuch diſputes do not argue
thoſe maine points to be doubtfull. And ſo you
muſt anſwere your owne inſtance, by which
you might as well proue, that Philoſophers do
not agree whether there be ſuch things as *Time,
Motion, Quantity, Heauens, Elements, &c.* becauſe

cause in many particulars concerning those things, they cannot agree.

7.   In the second place you affirme our do-ctrines to be *vnnecessary and superfluous*: becauſe *a very ſmall meaſure of explicite knowledge is of ab-ſolute neceſsity.* But this is very cleerly nothing at all to the purpoſe. For our Queſtion is not what euery one is obliged *explicitely to belieue,* but whether euery one be not obliged, *not to diſ-belieue,* or deny any one point ſufficiently pro-pounded by the Church, as a diuine Truth. Nei-ther do we treate of *ignorance* of ſome points, but of plaine *oppoſition*, and *contradiction* both between you and vs, and alſo among your ſel-ues. You cite *Bellarmine*, ſaying : *The Apoſtles neuer vſed* (g) *to preach openly to the people, other things, then the Articles of the Apoſtles Creed, the Ten Commaundments, and ſome of the Sacraments, becauſe theſe are ſimply neceſſary, and profitable for all men : the reſt beſides, ſuch as a man may be ſaued without them.* Heere you ſtop, leauing out the words immediately following, which are dire-ctly againſt you . *So that* (ſayth *Bellarmine*) *he haue* (h) *a will ready to imbrace and belieue them, whenſoeuer they ſhall be ſufficiently propounded to him by the Church.* Beſides, you falſifie *Bellarmine* when you make him ſay, *that the Apoſtles neuer vſed to preach to the people other things then the Ar-ticles of the Apoſtles Creed, the commandments, and ſome of the Sacraments, becauſe theſe are ſimply ne-ceſſary, and profitable for all men;* But he ſayth dire-

ctly

(g) *De verbo Dei lib. 4. cap.* 11.

(h) *Ibid.*

&ly the contrary, namely ; that the Apoftles preached to all, fome things which were not *neceſſary*, but only *profitable* to *all* (and therfore not *ſuperfluous* as you ſay;) whereas yet he ex-preſſely affirmes the knowledge of the Creed, commandments, and fome ſacraments to be *ne-ceſſary* to *all.* I wonder what pleaſure you can take in corrupting Authors, to your owne diſ-credit ? Now fince we muſt haue , as *Bellar-mine* rightly teacheth , *a will ready to imbrace whatſoeuer is propounded by the Church* ; it fol-loweth , that notwithſtanding your Confi-dence to the contrary , we *cannot* but *except* againſt your publique Seruice, or Liturgy. I haue neither will nor leiſure to examine parti-culars : but Exceptions jnough offer themſelues to any mans firſt Conſideration. The very oc-caſion and end for which it was framed, pro-ceeded out of an *Hereticall* ſpirit, to oppoſe the true Viſible Church: It was turned into Engliſh vpon an hereticall perſwaſion, and a popular inſinuation, and a crafty affectation to inueigle the humor of the people, that publique Prayers were vnlawfull in an vnknowne tongue. It lea-ueth out Prayers both *for* deceaſed finners, and *to* glorious Saints, blotting diuers of them out of their Calendar; and hath abrogated their fe-ſtiuall dayes : and the like they haue done con-cerning faſts , except thoſe few which they vouchſafe to like : It aboliſheth all memory of *S. Peters* Succeſsour: It treateth only of two Sa-

cra-

craments, excluding the reſt; and in the one it omitteth moſt of our Ceremonies, as ſuperſtitious: in the other it profeſſeth not to giue any thing but the ſubſtance of Bread and wine. It adminiſtreth to Lay people both kinds, as *neceſſary* by the *inſtitution* of Chriſt our Lord: Maſſe, or Sacrifice it hath none: It reades and belieues Scripture heretically tranſlated: It mentioneth no Reliques of Saints: And in a word, it is both in the whole Body, and deſigne, and in euery point a profeſſion of a Church, and fayth contrary to Catholiques, and implies a condemnation of our *Liturgy* as *ſuperſtitious*, & your ſelfe boldly ſay: *We cannot, we* (i) *dare not communicate with Rome in her publique Liturgy, which is manifeſtly polluted with groſſe ſuperſtitions*; and therefore *wee* Catholiques alſo can no more approue your *practiſe* and *Liturgy*, then we can imbrace your *Doctrine*, and *fayth* I ſaid that I had no deſire to examine the particulars of your Liturgy, neither is it needfull. For we may iudge of the reſt by the very firſt words, or Introite of your Seruice, beginning with a Text, for which you cite *Ezech.* 18. *At what time ſoeuer a ſinner doth repent him of his ſinnes from the bottome of his heart, I will put all his wickednes out of my remembrance, ſayth the Lord.* But there is no ſuch ſentence in *Ezechiel*, whoſe words are theſe, euen in the Bible of the Proteſtants: *But if the wicked will turne from all his ſinnes which he hath committed, and keep all my ſtatutes, and do that*

(i) *Pag.* 61.

Bbb   *which*

*which is lawfull and right, he shall surely liue, he shall
not die: All his Transgressions which he hath committed, they shall not be mentioned vnto him: in the
righteousnes which he hath done, he shall liue.*
Your firſt Reformers, the *foule* of whoſe Church
was *folifidian* Iuſtification, were loth to heare
of poſſibility to keep all the Commandments,
of working Righteouſnes, or liuing in the
Righteouſnes which he hath wrought; as alſo
they were vnwilling to particularize with the
Prophet, what is required to true *Repentance*,
knowing full well, the different opinions of
their firſt Progenitors about this point of *Repentance*, and therfore they thought beſt to corrupt this Text. And which is more ſtrange, in
your feruice-Booke tranſlated into Latin, and
printed in *London*, *Per aſsignationem Franciſci
Floræ*, the ſentence is cited at large as it is in the
Prophet, and therfore the corruption ſtill remayning in the Engliſh to deceiue the Vnlearned, is more inexcuſable. Neither (in the ſame
Introite) is the allegation of *Ioel. 2.* much more
truly made: *Rent your hearts, & not your garments,
and turne to the Lord your God &c.* Out of which
place, you know men are wont to declaime a-
gainſt our corporall Penance of Faſting, Wat-
ching, Hayre-cloth, Diſciplines &c. but, euen
according to your owne Tranſlation, the words
are: *Turne you euen to me with all your heart, and
with faſting, and with weeping, and with mourning;
And rent your hearts, and not your garments &c.*
                                                    where

where I belieue you will confeſſe, that your o-
miſſion was not vſed to no purpoſe.

8.   You ſpeake among other things of Images, & we grant that *God may be worſhipped without an Image.* But we ſay, that he cannot be truly
worſhipped by any one, who denieth worſhip
of Images, becauſe true worſhip of God cannot
ſtand with any one *Hereſy.* It is highly good, &
lawfull, and a moſt holy thing to pray to God;
but yet if one ſhould belieue, that we may not
alſo pray to liuing men, your ſelfe would I
thinke condemne him for an *Heretique,* becauſe
all Chriſtians intreate their Brethren to pray
for them: By which example all your inſtances
(*pag.* 72.) may be anſwered. Your ſaying out
of *Bellarminine* that the worſhip, and Inuocation of Saints was brought into the Church, *rather by cuſtom then any Precept*, is anſwered heerafter *n.* 12. And I would gladly know by what
authority your Church can inioyne ſecret Cõ-
feſſion in ſome caſe, as (heere *pag.* 72.) you ſay
ſhe doth, if Chriſt haue left it free? Can a humane law oblige men to reueale their ſecret ſinnes, in Confeſſion? eſpecially ſince they know
not whether your Miniſters will not thinke
themſelues obliged to acquaint ſome Officer
therewith, in caſe the Penitent diſcloſe any crime puniſhable by the Lawes of the Realme. To
which propoſe I could tell you ſtrange and true
ſtories: as contrarily becauſe Catholikes belieue
the Sacrament of Confeſſion to haue been inſti-

tuted by our Sauiour Chriſt, as neceſſary to Saluation, they conſequently teach, that the Seale
and Secret thereof is ſo ſacred and inuiolable,
that the Pope himſelfe cannot diſpenſe therein,
though it were to ſaue his owne life. And now,
to follow your wandrings, you may know that
we doe not hinder, but giue free leaue to vnlearned perſons to ſay their prayers in a knowne
language: but the Church doth celebrate publique Seruice in one of the learned Tongues,
for weighty reaſons, which haue been learned-
ly ſet downe by our Catholique Writers. And
if nothing muſt be read but what the People,
yea learned men vnderſtand, you muſt giue o-
uer reading in publique, euen in Engliſh, diuers Pſalmes of *Dauid*, the Prophets, the Apocalyps, and other parts of Scriptures, the ſenſe
and meaning wherof the people vnderſtand no
more, then if they were read in Hebrew. Nay,
to vnderſtand the words, and not the ſenſe, is
not free from danger, becauſe they may by the
conceaue ſome errour, as we daily ſee by the
exāple of Sectaries, & in that vngracious creature, who lately out of Scripture, as he thought,
murthered his Mother, and Brother, for being
cauſe of his Idolatry in kneeling at the Communion. Happy had it beene both for him,
and a thouſand more, if the ſacred Scriptures in Engliſh were not ſo common among
them, but were read with due circumſpection,
and not without approbation of ſuch as can

iudge

iudge better of them, then themfelues. And in very truth it feemes ftrange, & not only not fafe but euen fhametull, that, for example, the Bookes of *Leuiticus*, and the *Canticles*, befids many paffages in other Bookes, fhould he promifcuoufly made fubiect to the vulgar eyes of fenfual, and vnmortifyed people, who morally willbe fure to make no other vfe thereof, then to hurt themfelues, together with the abufing & prophaning fo holy a thing, as euery word of holy Scripture is in it felfe.

9. Now, to come to your other particulars; we acknowledge and profeffe all Merits to be the gift of God, and therfore they cannot withdraw vs from relying on him. You cite *Bellarmine*, faying: It is *fafeft*, not *to truft* (m) *to a mans owne Merits, but wholy and folely to caft himfelfe on the mercy of Iefus-Chrift*. But doth *Bellarmine* fay, that it is *fafeft* to relye on Gods Mercy alone, and to deny all Merits, as Proteftants do? This indeed were to your purpofe. But let vs heare *Bellarmine* rightly cited : It is (fayth he) *moft fafe to place* (n) *al our truft in the fole mercy & Benignity of God*. Heere you ftay. But *Bellarmine* goes on, and fayth: *I explicate my fayd Propofition : for it is not to be fo vnderftood as if a man with all his forces ought not to attend to good workes : Or that we ought not to confide in them, as if they were not true Iuftice, or could not vndergo the Iudgment of God (for no wonder if Gods owne gifts, as all our merits are, may endure his examination)*

(m) *Pag.* 73.

(n) *De Juftificat. lib.* 5. *c.*7. §. *Sit tertia propofitio.*

but we only say, that it is more safe, as it were to for-
get our former Merits, and to looke onely vpon the
mercy of God; Both becaufe no man can without a re-
nelation certaynely know that he hath true merits, or
that he is to perfeuere in them to the end : And alfo,
becaufe in this *place of Temptation nothing is more*
eafy then to conceyue Pride by the confideration of our
good workes. I leaue it therefore to any mans cõ-
fideration, what fincerity you haue vfed in alledging *Bellarmine*.

10   In the laft place you affirme, that our
(o) *Pag. 73.* doctrines *are confeffed* (o) *Nouelties*, and you go
about to proue it by a few inftances ; all which
being either nothing to the purpofe, or plainely
miftaken, or manifeftly vntrue, do excellently
proue againft your felfe, how ancient our Religion is. Your inftance about the Popes infallibility, is not to the purpofe of prouing that the
Roman Church teacheth any Nouelty. For *Bel-*
larmine, out of whom you cite a few Authours
who teach that the Popes Decrees without a
Councell are not infallible, fayth: That, *that Do-*
(p) *De Rom.* *ctrine* (p) *is yet tolerated by the Church*, though he
Pont. l. 4. c. affirme it to be erroneous, and the next degree
2. to Herefy. The fame Anfwere ferues for your o-
ther example concerning the Popes Authority
aboue that of a Generall Councell, of which
(q) *De Con-* *Bellarmine* fayth: *They are not properly Heretiques*
cil. l. 2. cap. *who hold the contrary ; but* (q) *they cannot be excufed*
37. Denique *Lateranen-* *from great temerity.* And you are not ignorãt, but
fe. that euen thofe who defend thefe doctrines do
vnani-

vnanimoufly confent againft you, that the Pope
is Head of the Church. But I pray you, what
Confequence is it? Some Authors deny, or
doubt of the Popes Infallibility, or his Authority ouer a Generall Councell: *Ergo*, thefe doctrines are Nouelties? May not priuate men be
miftaken, euen in doctrines which of themfelues are moft ancient; as is knowne by experience in many Truths, which both you and we
maintaine? For how many Bookes of Scripture
were once doubted of by fome, which now
your felues receiue as Canonicall? Are you therfore Nouelifts? You ouerlafh then, when you
fay: *Aboue a thoufand* (r) *yeares after Chrift, the*
Popes iudgment was not efteemed infallible, nor his
authority aboue that of a generall Councell: and efpecially when you cite *Bellarmine* to make good
your fayings. And your affirming out of *Bellar-*
mine (*de Indulg. l. 2. c.* 17.) that *Eugenius the* 3.
(*who began his Papacy* 1145.) *was* (s) *the firft that*
granted Indulgences, is a huge vntruth, and falfification of *Bellarmine*, who in that very place,
directly, exprefly, purpofely, proues that other
Popes before *Eugenius* granted Indulgences, &
names them in particular. Wheras you fay that
the Councels of *Conftance* and *Bafil*, decreed the
Councell to be aboue the Pope; you might haue
feene the Anfwere in *Bellarmine* in the fame
Booke which you (t) cite; that thefe two Councels at that time were not lawfull Councels, or
fufficient to define any matters of Fayth.

(r) *Pag.* 72.
Edit. 1.

(s) *Pag.* 72.
Edit. 1.

(t) *De Con-*
cil. l. 2. c. 19.

11. **You**

11. You fay, *Many of them* (meaning Catholique Doctours) *yield alfo , that Papall Indulgences are things vnknowne to all Antiquity.* And to proue this, you alledge *Bellarmine* , (u) who cites *Durand*, *S. Antoninus*, and *Roffenfis*. Neither do thefe three, which you by I know not what figure call *many*, fay as you do , that Indulgences are things vnknowne to all *Antiquity* ; but only for the firft fiue hundred yeares , as *Bellarmine* fayth in the place by you cited, & therfore you take to your felfe a ftrange priuiledge to multiply perfons, and enlarge tynes : and yet thefe Authors do not deny Indulgences. And as *Bellarmine* anfweres : *We ought not to fay that Indulgences are not indeed Ancient , becaufe two or three Catholiques haue not read of them in Ancient Authors.* And you may, with greater fhew, deny diuers Bookes of Scripture , which more then three Writers did not only fay, they were not receiued by Antiquity ; but did exprefly reiect them. As for the thing it felfe, *Bellarmine* fheweth, that Indulgences are no lefle ancient then the (y) beginning of the Church of Chrift . & that your owne Proteftants confefle , that it is hard to know when they began, which is a figne of *Antiquity*, not of *Nouelty*. But we can tell you , when, and who, firft began to oppofe Indulgences, namely the *Waldenfes*, who appeared about the yeare 1170. And therfore the marke of Nouelty, & Herefy muft fall not vpon the defenders, but the impugners of Indulgeces.

12. You

(u) *De Indulg.l. 2. c. 17.*

(y) *Vbi fu-pra.c.3.*

12. You fay out of *Bellarmine*, that *Leo the Third was the firſt that euer Canonized any Saint,* as before (*pag.*72.) you alleaged out of him, that the worſhip of Saints , *was brought into the Church rather by Cuſtome then by any Precept* ; and in your Margent you cite him in Latin faying: *Saints began to be* (z) *worshipped in the vniuerſall Church rather by Cuſtome then by Precept.*But *Bellarmine* doth not there treate in generall of worſhip of Saints, but only handling the Queſtion, *Cuius ſit* &c. *To whom doth it belong to Canonize Saints,*and prouing that it belongs to the Pope to Canonize them for the whole Church, and not for fome particular Dioceſſe alone ; in anſwere to an Obiection , that there are many worſhipped for Saints , who were not Canonized by the Pope, he hath theſe words : I anſwere, that *the Ancient Saints began to be worshipped in the Vniuerſall Church , not ſo much by any Law, as by Cuſtome*: Where you breake off. But *Bellarmine* goeth forward,and ſayth:*But as other Cuſtomes haue the force of a Law by the tacite Conſent of the Prince, without which they are of no force &c. So the Worship of any Saint generally introduced by the Cuſtome of the Churches, hath force from the tacite , or expreſſe Approbation of the Pope.*Firſt then, you conceale the Queſtion of which *Bellarmine* treated. Secondly, you leaue out (*Veteres*) Ancient Saints, and ſay only *Saints,* and yet (*Ancient*) ſheweth he ſpoke not of all Saints, but of ſome who were not expreſly Canoni-

(z) *De Sanctorum beat. lib.* 1. *cap.*8. § *vlt*,

C c c   zed,

zed, or Commaunded to be held for Saintes, wheras diuers others haue been Canonized by direct commaund to belieue that they are happy. Thirdly, in your Tranflation, you leaue out *Vniuerfall*, & only put *Church*; wheras *Bellarmine* §. *Primo modo*, exprefly teacheth: That in ancient time euery Bifhop might Canonize Saints for his particular Dioceffe, and *de facto*, they did command fome Feafts to be kept, as *Bellarmine* proues; which fhewes, that the worfhip of Saints was held both to be lawfull, and was to fome particular perfons cōmanded. Fourthly, you leaue out *Bellarmines words*; That the *Worfhip of fome Saint generally introduced by the cuftome of the Churches*, growes to haue the force of a Law, or Precept, by the tacite, or expreffe Approbation of the Pope; which is contrary to that, which you cited out of *Bellarmine*; The *Worfhip and Inuocation of Saints was brought into the Church, rather by Cuftome, then any Precpt*. And now to come to your former Obiection out of *Bellarmine*, what is it to your purpofe if he affirme that *Leo* the *third was the firft that euer Canonized any Saint*? Doth he affirme that *Leo* was the firft that taught *Worfhip, and Inuocation of Saints*? Or that fuch worfhip was not practifed by Cuftome, yea & by *Precept* before his Time, as we haue feeme out of his words it was? *Bellarmine* fpeakes only of fuch forme and folemnity of Canonization as afterwards was vfed: Which makes nothing for your purpofe, to

proue

proue that our doctrine of *Worſhip*, or *Inuocation of Saints*, is a *Nouelty* If one ſhould affirme that the ſolénity of Crowning Kings, was not vſed in all places, or tymes alike; ſhould he therfore deny the Antiquity of Kings, or that Obedience is due to them? You may ſee not onely the errour, but the danger alſo of ſuch diſcourſe.

13.　When one reades in your Booke theſe words in a different letter; *Not any one ancient Writer (b) reckons preciſely ſeauen Sacraments; the first Authour that mentions that number is* Peter Lombard, *and the first Councell, that of Florence:* and in your Margent, the names of *Valentia*, and *Bellarmine*; Who would not thinke that in the opinion of theſe Authors no ancient Writer before *Lombard* belieued that there were ſeauen Sacraments, neither more nor fewer? Which is moſt vntrûe, and againſt their formall words, & expreſſe intentiōs. For thus ſaith *Valentia* in the very ſame place which you (c) cite: *The ſame Aſſertion,* (that there are ſeauen Sacraments) *is proued by the Authority of Fathers. For although the more ancient Writers do not number ſeauen Sacraments, all together in one place: yet it may be eaſily ſhewed, eſpecially by the teſtimony of* S. Auguſtine *that they did acknowledge euery one of theſe Ceremonies to be a Sacrament.* Thus *Valentia* in generall, and then he proues euery one of the ſeauen Sacraments, out of particular places of *S. Auguſtine*, *S. Cyprian, S. Ambroſe, Innocentius the firſt, Chryſoſtome, Bede*, and *Dionyſius Areopagita.* Now

tell

(b) *Pag.* 73.

(c) *Tom.* 4. *diſp* 3. *q.* 6. *p.* 2. § Tertio probatur.

tell me, whether *Valentia* fay : *Not any one An-cient Writer reckons precifely feauen Sacraments?* Doth he not proue out of *S. Augufline* euery one of the feauen Sacraments in particular, as you could not but fee in the very place cited by you? Is it all one to fay : *Not any one Ancient Writer reckons precifely feauen Sacraments*, as you corrupt thefe Authors, and to fay; The Ancient Wri-ters do not number feauen Sacraments *all togea-ther in one place?* Neither is your falfifying of *Bellarmine* lefle remarkable, who hauing faid that the number of feauen Sacraments is pro-ued out of Scriptures, and ancient Fathers, pre-mifeth this Obferuation : That, *Our Aduerfaries ought not to require of vs, that* (d) *we fhew in Scri-ptures and Fathers the N A M E of feauen Sacra-ments: For neither can they fhew the Name of two, or three, or fower: for the Scriptures and Fathers did not write a Catechifme, as now we do, by reafon of the multitude of Herefies, but only deliuered the things themfelues in diuers places : Neither is this proper to Sacraments, but common to many other things. For the Scripture reckons the miracles of our Sauiour, but neuer reckons how many there be: It deliuers the Ar-ticles of Fayth, but neuer fayth how many they be: The Apoftles afterward publifhed the Creed of twelue Ar-ticles for fome particular caufes. In like manner they cannot know out of Scripture, how many Canonicall Brokes there be: But Councels afterward fet downe the Canon, and the particular number, which they had learned by Tradition.* And afterward he notes:

That

(d) *Bellarm. de Sacram. lib. 2, c. 25.*

*That it is sufficient if we can shew out of Fathers and
Scriptures, that the Definition of a Sacrament doth a-
gree neither to more nor fewer Rites, then seauen.* By
which words it is cleere, that when *Bellarmine*
sayth, *Lombard* was the firſt that named the
number of seauen Sacraméts, he only meaneth,
as he explicates himſelfe, of the *name* of *Seauen* ;
as Proteſtants will not find in all Antiquity the
name of two Sacraméts. So that from the words
of *Valentia* and *Bellarmine* , as they are indeed,
nothing can be gathered, except your very vn-
conſcionable Dealing.

14. What you cite out of *Bellarmine* , that
(e) *Scotus* teacheth *Tranſubſtantiation to haue been* (e) *De Eu-*
neyther named, nor made an Article of fayth before *char. lib. 3,*
the Councell of Lateran , doth not proue it to be a *cap. 23,*
Nouelty , but only that *Scotus* did thinke it was
not ſo expreſſely declared before that Councell ; which (ſayth *Bellarmine*) he affirmed becauſe he had not read the Councell of *Rome* vnder *Gregory* the *Seauenth* , nor had obſerued the
conſent of Fathers. It is a fond thing to ſay, that
euery Truth is a Nouelty, which the Church as
occaſion ſerueth doth declare more expreſſely
then before. And if all Truthes muſt be declared alike at all tymes , vnder payne of being accounted Nouelties ; what will become of *Lu-*
thers Reformation , wherby he pretended to
teach the world ſo many things which he falſly,
& impiouſly blaſphemed to haue been for ſo lõg
time buried in obliuion , and ouer-whelmed

with corruption?

(f) *Pag. 74.*

15.   You cite *Peter Lombard* and *S. Thomas*, as if they affirmed *Sacrifice in the* (f) *Eucharist to be no other, but the image or Commemoration of our Sauiours Sacrifice vpon the Crosse*. But your conscience cannot but tell you, that these Authors neuer doubted whether the *Masse* be a true *Sacrifice* or no, and therefore the Question which

(g) *S.Thom.*
3.p.q. 83 a.
1.in corp.

they propounded is, Whether Christ in the *Masse* be *immolated*, or (g) *killed?* and according to this sense they answere, that he is *immolated* in figure, becaufe the vnbloudy Oblation of the Eucharist, is a reprefentation of our Sauiours bloudy Oblation, or Immolation on the

(h) *Ad 3.*

ours bloudy Oblation, or Immolation on the Crosse. And that this is fo, you might haue feen in *S. Thomas* in that very place which you (h) cite, where he teacheth that in this manner of being killed, or immolated in figure, Christ might haue been fayd to haue been immolated in the figures of the Old Teftament, which did prefigure his death; and yet you will not acknowledge your felfe fo perfectly Zwinglianized, that you will from hence inferre, that there is no more in the Eucharist then in the empty figures of the Old Law: and though you did, yet it would not ferue your turne, for euen diuers of thofe figures were truly & properly Sacrifices; and therefore though the Eucharist

(i) *Panopl.*
lib. 4.part.2.
cap. 56. §.
Hunc igitur.

were but a Commemoration, yet it might be a true Sacrifice withall.

16.   You alledge *Lindanus*, that (i) *in for-*
mer

mer Ages, for 1200. *yeares, the holy Cup was ad-
ministred to the Laity*. But you deceiue your
Reader; for *Lindanus* plainely fayth ; That *both
kinds were giuen to the Laity almost euery where, but
yet not euery where*. Which is fufficient agaynst
you, who fay, it is agaynst the inftitution of
Chrift not to giue both kinds to the Laity. And
I fhewed before, that in the raigne of King *E-
dward* the *Sixth*, Communion in one kind was
permitted ; and that *Melanctbon* & *Luther* held
it as a thing indifferent. .

17. That diuine Sacrifice was celebrated for (k) *Ju* 1. *corp.*
diuers Ages in a known & vulgar Tongue, you *cap.* 14.
would proue out of (k) *Lyra*. But what is this
to proue our doctrine to be a Nouelty ? Do we
teach, that there is any diuine Law, eyther forbidding, or commanding publique Seruice in a
vulgar Tongue ? And *Lyra* in that place teacheth that in thefe tymes it is more conuenient
that it be not celebrated in a known language.

18. *That the Fathers generally condemned the
worfhip of Images for feare of Idolatry, and allowed,
yea exhorted the people with diligence, to read the
Scriptures* ; You feeke (l) to proue the former (l) *pag.* 74.
part out of *Polydore Virgil*, and the latter out of
Azor; but ftill with your wonted fincerity. For
how often haue you been told that *Polydore* (m) (m) *De Ju-
*fpeakes not of the Ancient Fathers of the New *nent lib.* 6,
Teftamēt, but of thofe of the Old, naming *Moy- *cap.* 13.
fes, Dauid*, and *Ezechias*, and he proueth at large,
that in the New Law, Images are worthily placed

ced in Churches, and worſhipped ; and concludes, demanding what man is ſo diſſolute, and ſo
brazen faced, that wil, or can doubt, or dreame
of the contrary? *Azor* grants, that in the (n)
times of *S. Chryſoſtome*, Lay-men were conuer-
ſant in Scripture, becauſe *then they vnderſtood
Greeke or Latin*, *in which language the Scriptures
were written*; whereas *now the common people for the
moſt part vnderſtand not the Latin Tongue; but ſuch
Lay people as vnderſtand Greeke or Latin*, *do with
good reaſon read the Scripture*. Who would euer
imagine, that in ſo ſhort a compaſſe you could
haue corrupted ſo many Authors?

19.   What you ſay in this your *Section*, to
excuſe your Brethren from *Schiſme*, we haue anſwered in the *Firſt Part*, and haue confuted all
your euaſions & ſimilitudes. And whereas you
ſay, that (o) although our errors be not damnable to him, who in *ſimplicity of heart belieueth
and profeſſeth them* ; yet that he, that *againſt fayth
and conſcience ſhall goe along with the ſtreame*, *to profeſſe and practiſe them, becauſe they are but little ones;
his caſe is dangerous*, *and without repentance deſperate* . I anſwere, that if our errors be not *fundamentall*, how can they be damnable: and if they
be but litle ones, that is, not *fundamentall* or *damnable*, how is it *damnable* to imbrace them, becauſe
they are litle ones, that is, becauſe they are, as indeed they are ? If they were indeed little ones, &
yet by an *erroneous* cóſciéce were eſteemed great
ones, to ſuch a man they ſhould indeed be damnable

*(n) Moral.
Inſtit. lib.8.
cap.26 part.
1. §. Reſpō-
deo.*

(o) Pag.77.

nable; but to one that knowes them to be little
ones, and with such a knowledge, or cōscience,
for some humane respect, of it selfe not damnable, doth yet imbrace them, they are not damnable. For still we suppose that he would not
imbrace them, if his Conscience told him, that
they were great ones. And who can without
smiling read these your words : *It is the* (p) *Do-* (p) *Pag. 7*
ctrine of the Romane Schoole, that veniall sinnes to
him that commits them, not of subreption, or of a sud-
den motion, but of presumption that the matter is not
of moment, change their kind and become mortall ? I
pray you what Schoole man teacheth that to
commit a veniall sinne, knowing it to be such,
makes it become mortall? For in this sense you
must alleage this doctrine, if it be to your purpose: and in this sense it being a false doctrine,
doth indeed ouerthrow that for which you alledge it; and proues that to imbrace errors not
fundamentall, knowing them to be such, cannot
be damnable; as it is not a mortall sinne, to do
that which one knowes to be but veniall. In the
meane time you do not reflect, that if your doctrine might passe for true, it would be impossible for both *Catholiques*, and *Protestants, Luthe-*
rans, and *Caluinists* to be saued. For all these differ at lest in points not *fundamentall*, and so you
grant vnawares that which chiefly we intend,
that of two differing in Religion, both cānot be
saued, whether their differēces be great, or smal.

    20.   I haue told you already, that the Au-
D d d   thour

thor of the *Moderate Examination* &c. is no Catholique. That other Treatise entituled, *Syllabus aliquot Synodorum &c.* I haue not seen, but if the Author pretend, as you say, that both *Hugenots*, and *Catholiques* may be saued, he can be no Catholique.

21. You would faine auoide the note *of Heretiques*, which is to be named by Moderne names, deriued for the most part from their first Sect-Maisters. You renounce the names of *Lutherans*, *Zwinglians*, or *Caluinists*, and to that purpose you make halfe a Sermon; But words will not serue your turne. For they are no iniurious Nick-names as you say, but names imposed by meere necessity, to distinguish you from those from whom you really differ, and to expresse the variety of your late Reformation. If we speake of *Christians*, or *Catholiques* without some addition, no man will dreame of *you*, but will thinke of *vs*, who had that Name before *Luther* appeared, and therefore it cannot expresse the latter Reformation. If you wilbe called the *Reformed Church*; still the doubt remaynes, whether you meane those who follow *Luther*, or *Caluin*, or *Zwinglius &c.* Neyther will the Reformed Church (if she be in her wits) make her selfe lyable to all errors of *Lutherans*, *Caluinists*, *Anabaptists*, *Puritans &c.* And in this, your prime man *D. Field* is more ingenious, while he acknowledgeth a necessity of the name of *Lutherans*, in these words: *Neyther was*

it

it pofsible (q) *that fo great an alteration fhould be effected, and not carry fome remembrance of them, by whome it was procured.* And *Whitaker* fayth: *For* 2. *cap. p. diftinctions fake we are inforced to vfe the* (r) *name of Proteftants.* And *Grauerus* giueth a reafon why thofe of the fame Sect with him be called *Luthe rans,* faying: *The only reafon(* s) *of it is, that we may be diftinguifhed frõ Caluinifts & Papifts, from whom we cannot be diftinguifhed by the generall name eyther of Chriftiãs, or of Orthodoxe, or of Catholiques.* And *Hofpinianus* likewife fayth: *I abhorre the Schif- maticall names* (t) *of Lutherans, Zwinglians, and Caluinift;* (marke, *the Shifmaticall names*) *yet for diftinction fake I will vfe thefe names in this Hifto- ry.* The vulgar Obiection which you bring, that amongft vs alfo there are *Francifcans, Domini- cãs, Scottftes Loyalifts &c.* is pertinent only to cõ- uince you of manifeft *Nouelty* : For thofe Na- mes are not impofed to fignify difference in *fayth,* as the Names of *Lutherans, Caluinifts,* are ; but eyther diuers Inftitutes of Religion, as *Dominicans, Francifcans &c.* or els diuerfity of opinions concerning fome points not defi- ned by the Church, as *Thomifts, Scotifts &c.* And for as much as thefe Names be argumēts of new and particular *Inftitutes,* and are deriued from particular men, they likewife proue that the names of *Lutherans, Caluinifts &c.* being giuen vpõ diuerfity in *fayth,* muft argue a new begin- ning, & a new Sect, and Sect-Maifters concer- ning *Fayth.* *D. Field* is full to our purpofe, fay-

Ddd 2   ing :

(q) *Of the Church lib.* 2. *cap. p. p.* 59.

(r) *Jn his anfwer to Reynolds Preface. pag.* 44.

(s) *In his Abfurda Ab- furdorũ &c. in Præfat.*

(t) *In his Prologome- na.*

ing: *We must obserue that they who professe the fayth of Christ* (u) *haue been somtymes in these latter ages of the Church called after the speciall names of such men as were the Authours, Beginners, and Deuisers of such courses of Monasticall Profession , as they made choyce to follow , as Benedictins, and such like.* And in his other words following , he answers your obiection of the *Scotists,* and *Thomists,* affirming *their differences to haue been in the Controuersies of Religion , not yet determined by consent of the Vniuersall Church.* What can be more cleere, that our differences concerne not matters of *Fayth* , and that the names which you mention of *Franciscans, Dominicans &c.* signify a Meanes of that for which they are imposed , and which they are appointed to signify , and therfore proue that the names of *Lutherans &c.* must signify a *Noueley* in fayth ?

(u) *Ubi sup.* *pag. 58.*

(w) *pag. 87.* 22.   But you say , that *the iarres and diuisions betweene* (w) *the Lutherans , and Caluinists doe little concerne the Church of England , which followeth none but Christ.* And doe not *Lutherans* and *Caluinists* pretend to follow Chrift as well as you? Who shall be Iudge among you ? But you may easily be well assured, that as long as you follow him by contrary wayes , you can neuer come where he is . And yet indeed , doe these iarres *little concerne the Church of England?* Haue you in your Church none of those who are commonly called *Lutherans , Zuinglians , Caluinists, Puritans &c.* Doth it not behooue you to

com-confider, whether your Congregation can be *One* true Church of Chrift, while you are in Communion with fo many difagreeing Sects? Doth it little concerne you, whether your firft Reformers *Lutherans*, *Caluinifts*, *Zwinglians*, *Puritanes* be Heretiques, or no? How can it be, but that the diuifions of *Lutherans*, and *Caluinifts* muft concerne the Church of England? For, your Church cannot agree with them all; & if you fide with one part, you muft iarre with the other. Or if you agree with none of them, you difagree with all, & fo make a greater diuifion.

23. And therfore, being really diftruftfull of this Anfwere, you come at length to your maine refuge, namely; that *their diffentions* (x) *are neither many, nor fo materiall, as to fhake, or touch the foundation.* But till you can once tell vs what points *will fhake the foundation*, you cannot be fure whether their diffentions be not fuch. You fay, their (y) difference about *Confubftantiation*, and *Vbiquity* is not *fundamentall*, becaufe both agree, that *Chrift is really, and truly exhibited to ech faithfull Communicant, and that in his whole Perfon he is euery where.* In this manner you may reconcile all herefies, and fay, the *Arians* or *Neftorians* belieued Chrift to be truly God; that is, by reall and true affection of *Charity*, as many among you fay, Chrift is really in the Sacrament, that is, by a reall figure, or by a reall act of *fayth*, as the *Neftorians* faid of a reall act of *Charity:* fhat euen according to them who deny the

(x) *Pag. 87,*

(y) *Pag. 90,*

Ddd 3　　　　　*Trans-*

Trinity, there is truly a *Father*, *Sonne*, and *holy Ghost*, as in God there is truly *Power*, *Vnderstanding*, and *Will* ; but whether thofe *Perfons* be really diftinct or no, that is (as you fay of *Confubstantiation* and *Vbiquity*) a *nicecity infcrutable to the wit of man:* and fo a man may goe difcourfing of all other *Herefies*, which haue been condemned by the Church. Is there not a maine difference of receiuing our Sauiours body in reall fubftance, and in figure alone? Or betwixt the *immenfity* of our Sauiours *Deity*, and the *Vbiquity* of his *Humanity*, which deftroies the Myfteries of his Natiuity Afcenfion, &c. for who can afcend to the place where he is already? You fpecify only the faid difference betwixt *Lutherans*, and *Caluinifts*, whereas you know there are many more, as about the Canon of Scripture &c. as alfo between *Proteftants* and *Puritans* &c. And I could put you in mind of your Brethren, who teach that for diuers Ages the vifible Church perifhed; and yet *S. Augustine* teacheth, that there is nothing more euident in Scripture, then the Vniuerfality of the Church : as alfo who deny that *Bifhops* are by *diuine Inftitution* ; who oppofe your whole Hierarchy as Antichriftian; who differ from you in the forme of Ordination of Minifters ; all which are fundamental points. But I will refer the Reader to the moft exact *Brercley*, who (z) reckons no fewer then feauenty feauen differences amóg you, punctually citing the Bookes, and

(z) *Tract. 3. Sect. 7. vnder gr.*

and pages where you may find them. And yet
for the prefent I will fet downe fome words of
Doctor *Willet*, teftifying your differences. *From*
this fountaine (fayth he *) haue fprung* (a) *forth*
thefe and fuch like whirle-points, and bubbles of new
doctrine: as for example, that the Scriptures are not
meanes concerning God of all that profitably we know:
That, *they are not alone complete to euerlasting felici-*
ty : That, *the word of God cannot pofsibly affure vs*
what is the word of God: That, *there are works of Su-*
pererogation : That, *the Church of Rome, as it now*
standeth, is the family of Christ : That, *Idolaters and*
wicked Heretiques are members of the vifible Church:
(let *D. Potter* heere remember what himfelfe
fayth of the *Roman* Church, and what he rela-
teth about the opinion of *M. Hooker* and *M.*
Morton, that among Heretiques there may be a
true Church:) That, *there is in Ordination giuen a*
indeleble Character : That, *they haue power to make*
Chrifts body: That, *Sacraments are neceffary in their*
place, and no leffe required then beliefe it felfe : That,
the foules of Infants dying without Baptifme are dam-
ned &c. Do you thinke, that the neceffity of
Baptifme and other Sacraments, the fufficiency
of fole Scripture, which your Englifh Clergy
profefleth at their Ordination, and thofe other
points are but fmall matters? But befides thefe,
and many more, there are two other maine, generall, & tranfcendent differences among you.
The one, whether you do not differ in maine
points, which though you deny, yet others af-
　　　　　　　　　　　　　　　　firme:

(a) *In his me-*
ditation vpõ
the 122. *Pfa.*
pag. 9ı.

firme: The other, what be maine or fundamentall points. Vpon which two differences, it will
neceſſarily follow, that you cannot know, whether you haue the ſame *ſubſtance of fayth*, and
hope of ſaluation, or no. But though your differences were all reduced to one, and that how
ſmall ſoeuer; that one were ſufficient to exclude Vnity of faith among you, as I haue often
ſaid, and proued. I haue no mind to ſpend time
in telling you how vn-ſcholler-like you ſay :
(b) Pag. 87. *Two brothers (b) in their choller may renounce ech
other, and diſclaime their amity; yet that heat cannot
diſſolue their inward, and eſſentiall relation*. For
when a mans Brother dyes, doth he looſe any
eſſentiall relation? I alwayes thought that *eſſentiall* relations were inſeparable from the *eſſence*
to which they belong, and the *eſſence* from
them; and a man who ſtill remaynes a *man*, may
yet ceaſe to be a *Brother*: It is therfore no *eſſentiall* relation.

24. I grant that Differences in Ceremonies,
or diſcipline, do not alwayes infer diuerſity of
fayth; yet when one part condemnes the Rites and diſcipline of the other as Antichriſtian,
or repugnant to Gods word (as it hapneth a-
mong Proteſtants,) then differences in Ceremonies redound to a diuerſity in fayth.

25. *Luther tempered by* (c) *mild Melancthon
(c) Pag. 93. (that honour of Germany) did much relent and re-
mit of his rigour agaynſt Zwinglius, and began to
approue the good Counſels of peace.* If inconſtancy
con-

concerning matters of Fayth be Mildnes, *Me-lancton* was, I grant, extremely mild, in which respect he was noted euen by Protestãts, & was disliked by *Luther*. How much *Luther* relented of his rigour agaynst *Zwinglius*, let himselfe declare in these words, which you could not but read *in Charity-Mistaken*. *I hauing now one of my feet* (d) *in the graue, will carry this testimony and glory to the Tribunall of God; That I will with all my heart condemne, and eschew Carolostadius, Zwinglius, Oecolampadius, and their disciples; nor will I haue familiarity with any of them eyther by letter, writing, words, nor deeds, accordingly as the Lord hath commanded.* If in *Polonia* the followers of *Luther*, and *Caluin* haue long liued together in concord, as you would haue vs belieue, the thing being really not true; they must thanke the good Catholique King vnder whome they liue, who is able, and apt to punish when there is great excesse. But if they had the raynes in their owne hand, what greater concord could be hoped for amongst them in that Kingdome, then is found in other places, where they haue more power? In *Polonia* there are many *Arians*, and *Trinitarians*, who liue in outward concord with the rest; But will you acknowledge them for Brethren to *Lutherans, Caluinists*, and your selfe? The answere will be hardly made, if you sticke to your owne grounds, and I may well passe on to the rest.

(d) *Tug.* 55.

CHAP. IIII.

OVR very beginning pro-
miſeth ſmall ſincerity in that
which followes . For you
make *Charity - Miſtaken* ſay,
that Proteſtants be *Hereti-*
ques at the leſt, if not *Infidels*;
wheras he only ſayth, & ſub-
ſtantially proueth, that whoſoeuer doth disbelieue any one *Article* of fayth, doth not aſſent to
all the reſt , by *diuine infallible fayth* , but by an
humane perſwaſion; which is a point of great conſideration, and of which it ſeemes you are very
loath to ſpeake.

2. You take much paines to proue what
we do not deny. For it maketh nothing to the
purpoſe, whether or no the Propoſition of the
Church belong to the formall Obiect of fayth,
as heertofore I haue told you . Nor do we deny
Scripture to containe all mattes of fayth , if it
be rightly vnderſtood; becauſe Scripture, a-
mong other Verities. doth alſo recommend vnto vs the Church & diuine Traditions, though
they be vnwritten. And you egregiouſly falſi-

fy

ſy (a) *Bellarmine,* as if he excluded the Authority of the Church, wheras in the place by you
cited *(de verb. Dei lib.*1.*c.* 2. *)* he only ſpeakes a-
gainſt the priuate ſpirit, and euen there proues
out of *S. Auguſtine,* that God will haue vs
learne of other men. We likewiſe teach that the
Church doth not make any new Articles of
fayth, but only propounds, and declares to vs
the old. Only I would haue you heere conſider
that whether or no Scripture be the ſole Rule of
fayth: or whether fayth be reſolued into diuine
Reuelation alone, or els partly into the Propoſition of the Church: all is one, for the maine
Queſtion, whether perſons of diuers Religions
can be ſaued. For this remaineth vndoubted,
that it cannot be but damnable to oppoſe any
truth, ſufficiently declared to be contained in
Scripture, or reuealed by God.

3.   No leſſe impertinent is your other diſcourſe concerning the difficulty to know what
is *Hereſy.* For we grant, that it is not alwayes eaſy to determine in particuler occaſions, whether
this or that doctrine be ſuch: Becauſe it may be
doubtfull, whether it be againſt any Scripture,
or diuine Tradition, or Definition of the
Church; and much more, whether the perſon
be an Heretique, which requireth certaine conditions (as Capacity, Pertinacy, ſufficient Propoſition &c.) which are not alwayes ſo eaſily
explicated, and diſcerned: and for theſe reſpects *S. Auguſtine* in the place cited (b) by you,

(a) *Pag.* 95.
Edit. 1.

(b) *Pag.* 102.

had good reafon to fay : That *it is hard to know what makes an Heretique*. But it is ftrange that you fhould hold it to be fo hard a matter, to giue a generall definition of *Herefy* or *Heretique*, fince in this very *Section* you difpatch it quickly, faying : *He is iuftly* (c) *esteemed an Heretique, who yields not to Scripture fufficiently propounded*. Or (as you fay elfewhere,) *It is fundamentall* (d) *to a Chriftians Fayth, and neceffary for his faluation, that he belieue all reuealed Truths of God, wherof he may be conuinced that they are from God*. Nay, if you will fpeake with coherence to your owne grounds; it is eafy for you to define in all particular cafes what is damnable *Herefy* : for you (I fay) who meafure all *Herefy* by oppofition to Scripture; and further affirme, that Scripture is cleere in all *fundamentall* points. For by this meanes it will be eafy for you to difcerne what error oppofeth thofe *fundamental* Truths, which are *cleerly* contained in Scripture.

4.   In your difcourfe concerning the Controuerfy between Pope *Stephen*, and *S. Cyprian*, you fhew a great deale of paffion againft the *Roman* Church, which you impugne out of an Epiftle of *Firmilianus*, who at that time was a party againft the Pope, and who in particuler did afterward recant togeather with the other Bifhops who once ioyned with *S. Cyprian*, as we haue already fhewed out of *S. Hierome*, & may be alfo feen in an Epiftle of *Dionyfius Alexandrinus apud Eufeb.hift.l.6.c.7.* wherin *Firmilianus* in

par-

particular is named (& therfore you are inexcufable, who fay they perfifted in their opinion;) wheras the proceeding of *S. Stephen* was
neceſſary to preuent a pernicious error of *rebaptizing* of ſuch as had been baptized by Heretiques, which afterward was condemned by the
whole Church. And as for *S. Cyprians* mild proceeding, which you ſo much commend out of
your ill will to S. *Stephen*, becauſe he was *Pope*;
S. *Auguſtine* faith: *The things which* (e) *Cyprian in*
anger hath ſpread againſt Stephen, I will not ſuffer to
paſſe vnder my pen. Wherfore you could not haue
picked out an example more in fauour of Popes
then this. And you muſt giue vs leaue not to
credit what you ſay, *That both Stephen and Cy-*
prian erred in ſome ſenſe. For *Stephen* only affirmed, that Baptiſme was not inualide preciſely
becauſe it is giuen by Heretiques, as *S. Cyprian*
affirmed it to be; but yet if the Heretiques erred either in the *Matter* or *Forme* of Baptiſme,
Stephen neuer affirmed ſuch Baptiſme to be va-
lid, which had been more then he granted, euen
to the Baptiſme of Catholiqnes.

5. Your Argument to proue, that (f) concerning our greater ſafety, we diſpute againſt
you as the *Donatiſts* did againſt Catholiques, I
haue anſwered (g) in the *Firſt Part.* You would
make men belieue that we are like the *Donatiſts*,
who *waſhed Church wall, and veſtments of Catho-*
liques, broke their Chalices, ſcraped their Altars &c.
But I pray you conſider, whether *Chalices, Veſt-*

ments,

(e) *De Bapt.*
cont. Donat.
lib. 5. cap. 25.

(f) *Pag. 222.*

(g) *Cap. 7.*
num. 7.

ments, *Palls*, or *Corporals*, and *Altars* do expreſſe
the Proteſtant Church of England, Scotland,
Geneua, Holland &c. or the Church of *Rome* ?

6.   You ſpend diuers pages in propounding
Arguments for the opinion of *M. Hooker*, and
M. Morton : That *wherſoeuer a company of men*(h)
doe iointly profeſſe the ſubſtance of Chriſtian Religi-
on , which is fayth in Ieſus-Chriſt the Sonne of God
and Sauiour of the world , with ſubmiſſion to his do-
ctrine in mynd and will; there is a Church wherein
Saluation may be had , notwithſtanding any corrup-
tion in Iudgment or practiſe : yea although it be of
that nature that it ſeeme to fight with the very foun-
dation , and ſo haynous as that in reſpect thereof the
people ſtayned with this corruption , are worthy to be
abhorred of all men , and vnworthy to be called the
Church of God . But becauſe theſe and ſuch mon-
ſtruous Aſſertions proceed from other errours
which I haue already both cleerly , and at large
confuted; to wit, the Fallibility of the Church,
the Diſtinction of points fundamental and not
fundamentall &c. I referre you to thoſe places:
and heere onely obſerue into what precipices
they fall , who deny the vniuerſall Infallibility
of the Church . And it is ſtrange that you your
ſelfe did not ſee the manifeſt contradictions inuolued in this wicked doctrine . For how can it
be *a Church wherein Saluation may be had , and yet*
be vnworthy to be called the Church of God ? How
can that man haue *fayth in Ieſus Chriſt , with ſub-*
miſſion to his doctrine in mind and will, who is ſuppoſed

pofed to ioyne with his beliefe in Iefus Chrift, other errors fufficiently propounded to be repugnant againft Gods word, or Reuelation ? Can fubmiffion in mind or will, or obferuation of his Commandments ftand with actuall voluntary error againft his word? Is it not a prime Commandment to belieue Gods word? Do not your felfe affirme, that it is *Infidelity* to deny whatfoeuer is reuealed in Scripture? How then can a Church be faid to haue meanes for faluation and life, wherin is wanting *Fayth* the firft ground of faluation ? The Fathers fometimes called the Donatifts, Brethren, by reafon of their true *Baptifme*, not for their poffibility to be faued, according as *S. Auguftine* faid to them: *The Sacraments of Chrift* (i) *do not make thee an Heretique, but thy wicked difagreement.* And *Optatus* fayth: *You cannot* (k) *but be our brethren, whom the fame Mother the Church hath begotten in the fame bowels of Sacraments, whom God our Father hath in the fame manner receiued as adopted Children*; namely, on his behalfe, and for as much as concernes the vertue of *Baptifme*. The Conclufion of your difcourfe may well befeeme the doctrine for which you bring it : *A learned man* (l) *anciently was made a Bifhop of the Catholique Church, although he did profeffedly doubt of the laft Refurrection of our bodies* You might haue added, that he would not belieue that the world fhould euer haue an end; and further abfolutely refufed to be baptized : And that he would not, as the Hiftory

(i) *Epift.*48.

(k) *Lib.*4.

(l) *pag.*122.

ſtory recoūteth, liue a ſingle life as other Prieſts, but that he would liue with a wife . For *Syne-ſius*, who is the man you meane, publiquely pro-teſted all theſe things ; and you are wiſe inough to take only what might ſeeme to ſerue your turne , as this , concerning the ſingle liues of Prieſts did not, becauſe it ſheweth that in thoſe anciēt times, Prieſts could not liue with wiues. And now I aske, whether in good earneſt you belieue, that one may be made a Biſhop , who will not belieue the Reſurrection , nor wilbe baptized, or whether he may be baptized a-gainſt his will? The Anſwere therfore may be ſeen in *Baronius*, who (m) demonſtrates out of the Epiſtles of *Syneſius* himſelfe, that he did theſe things, not to be made a Biſhop, wiſhing (as he affirmeth) rather to dye , then to endure ſo great a burthen; wherin ſaith *Baroniu*: he ſeemes only to haue done in words , that which *S. Am-broſe* pretended in deeds, which was to be eſtee-med incontinent, and vnmercifull, ſo to hinder his being made Biſhop. But theſe extraordinary proceedings may be admired, but ought not to be imitated. To ſay , that the ten Tribes, not-withſtanding their Idolatries , remained ſtill a true Church; cannot but make any Chriſtian ſoule tremble , to conſider to what damnable abſurdities, and impieties they fall who leaue the *Roman* Church . You falſify *Magallanus* (n) as if he with *M. Hooker* affirmed , that, *If an Infidell* (o) *should purſue to death an Heretique,*

only

only for Christian professions fake, the honour of Martyrdome could not be denied to him : which is contrary to the words and meaning of *Magallanus*. For he expresly teacheth, that they do not participate of the *grace* of the Church, but are *dead parts,* and consequently not capable of faluation: Only he fayth, that they may be called mébers of the Church, becaufe the Church can iudge and punifh them. It is impoffible that any Catholique Author fhould teach, that an Heretique, remayning an Heretique, (that is, actually and voluntarily, denying a reuealed Truth fufficiently propounded for fuch)can be a Martyr. But fuch as you are may affirme what you pleafe. The words of *Salutanus* (p) which you cite, and fay, that they are *very remarkable,* do only fignify by way of doubt, whether *fome* of the Heretiques of whom hefpoke, and who in fimplicity followed their Teachers (as he exprefly fayth) may not be excufed by ignorance. And fince you affirme, that hefpeakes of *Arians*, I would know, whether you do not thinke *Arianifme* to be a damnable *Herefy*, vnles accidentally ignorance excufe fome particular perfons .

(p) De Gra. tern. lib. 3.

7.   You fay, that (q) the Errors of the *Donatifts* concerning the inualidity of the Baptifme giuen by Heretiques , and of the *Nouatians,* that the Church ought not to abfolue fome grieuous finners , *were not in themfelues hereticall &c. Neither was it in the Churches intention* (or in

(q) Pag. 131.

F f f   *her*

her power) *to make them such by her declaration* . If these errours neither in themselues , nor by the declaration of the Church be hereticall , I pray you, how are they hereticall? May a mã in these tymes hold them without note of Heresy ? So you must fay , vnles you grant the definitions of Gods Church to be infallible . For *S. Augustine* professeth , that this point concerning re-baptization cannot be determined out of Scripture alone, as hath been fayd before. Or if you fay, this Errour may be confuted out of Scripture , then you must grant that it is in *it felfe hereticall* , which you deny . But no wonder if by denying the infallibility of the Church , you be brought to such ftraytes . I goe on now to the next .

CHAP.

C H A P. V.

N this *Section* , you handle three points . *First*, that the Church is infallible onely in *fundamentall* points. *Secondly*, that the Generall Councels; and , *Thirdly* , that the Pope may erre in points fundamē-tall. Concerning the firſt , I haue ſpoken in the *firſt Part* ; the ſecond and third, are particu-lar diſputes, from which you ought to haue ab-ſtained, if you had meant to haue touched in-deed the point of our Controuerſy. But ſince you will needs fill you Booke with ſuch parti-culars , I muſt alſo goe out of the way , to an-ſwere your obiections .

2.   If I tooke pleaſure, as you doe, to fill my Margent with quotations of Authours, I could eaſily ſhew how you miſtake and wrong our Schoole-men ; as if they held that ſomething which in it ſelf is not infinit, but really diſtinct from the diuine Authority , were the chiefe Motiue of fayth , *the firſt and furtheſt principle into which it reſolues :* wheras their difference is only in explicating vnder what preciſe and for-

mall confideration, God is the formall obiect
of fayth : fome affigning the *Diuinity* it felfe ; o-
thers, the authority of God *commanding* ; others ,
which is the common opinion , teaching , that
it is refolued into the diuine , or Prime *Verity* :
and laftly euen thofe whome it feemes you call
vnwife, and vnwarry Writers agaynst Luther, doe
not teach that the Authority of the Church is
the *chiefest, first , and furthest principle into which*
fayth *refolues* ; but at the moft, that her Propofition is neceffary to an Act of diuine fayth ; eyther becaufe they conceyue that matter of faith
ought to concerne the common good of Religion , and fo require a *publique* Authority or
Propounder ; or els becaufe they hold that her
Propofition in fome fort enters into the formall
obiect of fayth in refpect of *vs* ; Neither are the
Authors of this opinion only Writers againft
Luther , as you fay , but diuers other Schoole-
Deuines .

   3.   Wheras you fay, that there is no queftion
but that Fayth is *fupernaturall*, in regard of the
Efficient Caufe, and of the *Obiect* , both which
ought to be *fupernaturall* ; it feemes you are willing to diffemble the doctrine of your great Reformer *Zwinglius*, who (a) out of his exceffiue
Charity, placed in heauen, *Hercules, Thefeus, So-*
crates, Ariftides &c. (who had no fupernaturall
Fayth, nor beliefe of God) as alfo the Children
of the Heathens dying without (b) Baptifme.
Were not fuch Charitable men, very fit to reforme

(a) Tom. 2.
expofit. fidei
Chriftiane
fol. 159.
(b) Tom. 2.
fol. 540.

forme the Church?

4. You fall againe vpon the sufficiency of
Scripture, which point I haue already aniwe-
red,& shewed in what sense all points of fayth
may be contained in Scripture; to wit, in as
much as the Scripture doth recommend to vs
the Church, and diuine vnwritten Traditions.
Neither can you alleage any one Catholique
Author,ancient or moderne, who speaking of
the sufficiency of Scripture, excludes Tradition, by which euen Scripture it selfe is deliuered to vs. And as for *S. Augustine*, and *S. Basill*
whom you alleage for the sufficiency of Scripture, they be so cleerly for Tradition,that they
haue been taxed by some Protestants for that
cause; as likewise for the same reason some
chiefe Protestants haue blamed *Clemens Alexan-*
drinus, *Origen*, *Epiphanius*, *Ambrose*, *Hierome*,
Maximus,*Theophilus*,*Damascene*,*Chrysostome*,*Ter-*
tullian,*Cyprian*,*Leo*, *Eusebius*, and others,as may
be seene in (c)*Brereley*. But though Scripture
alone did particularly containe all points necessary to saluarion;doth it follow, thinke you,
from thence,that the Church is not infallible?
May not both Scripture, and Church be infallible in what they deliuer? Doth not your selfe
grant, that the Church is infallible for points
fundamentall; and for the same points the Scripture is also sufficient, and cleere? Which euidently sheweth,that you cannot deny, but that
the *Infallibility* of the *Church*, may well stand

(c)Tract. 1.
Sect. 8.
Subd. 22;

Fff 3   WITH

with the fufficiency of *Scripture*, & confequently to oppofe either the Scripture or Church, is
fufficient to make one an Heretique: and this is
fufficient for our purpofe. Yea, fince you cannot deny, but that it is Herefy, to oppofe the
Scripture, and that you alfo grant that the Scripture affirmes the Church to be infallible in
fundamentall points, it followes, that euen according to you, euery one who oppofeth the
Church in fuch points is an Heretique, euen becaufe he oppofeth the Church; although the
further reafon heerof be, becaufe he oppofeth
the Scripture, which recommends the Church.
So that all which you haue faid about the fufficiency of Scripture alone, is in diuers refpects
nothing to the purpofe.

(d) Pag. 136

5. You affirme, that *(d) Eckius, Pighius, Hofius, Turrianus, Costerus, do euery where in their
writings fpeake wickedly, and contumelioufly of the
holy Scriptures.* And becaufe this is a common
flander of Proteftants againft Catholique Writers; I do heere challenge you to produce but
one, I fay, but *one* only place, either out of any
one of thefe whome you name, or any other Catholique Doctor, who fpeakes *wickedly* or *contumelioufly* againft holy Scriptures. But be fure you
do not confound fpeaking againft Scripture it
felfe, with fpeaking againft the abufe therof, or
againft the letter of Scripture wrefted to fome
hereticall fenfe; againft which our Authors
fpeake, and cannot fpeake too much. And *S. Hierome*

rome with other Fathers do the fame.

6.   You proceed, and fay: *The Teſtimony* (e)
of the preſent Church workes very powerfully & pro- (c) *Pag.139.*
bably, firſt vpon Infidels to winne them to a Reuerend
opinion of Fayth and Scriptures &c. *Secondly, vpon*
Nouices, weaklings, and doubters in the fayth, to in-
ſtruct & confirme them, till they may acquaint them-
ſelues with, and vnderſtand the Scriptures, which the
Church deliuers as the word of God. Thirdly, vpon all
within the Church, to prepare, induce, and perſwade
the Mind as an outward meanes to imbrace the fayth,
to read, and belieue the Scriptures. But the fayth of a
Chriſtian findes not in all this, any ſure ground wher-
on finally to reſt, or ſettle it ſelfe : Becauſe, diuine
Fayth requires a Teſtimony *abſolutely diuine,* and
yet, *our Aduerſaries yield that the Teſtimony of the*
preſent Church is not abſolutely diuine, (to which
purpoſe you cite in your Margent ſome of our
Authors) and therfore it cannot rely vpon the
Church.

7.   This your diſcourſe is neither pertinent,
nor true. For the Queſtion is not, as I haue often
told you, whether or no, our fayth be reſolued
into the Authority of the Church: but whether
we may not truly infer, that whoſoeuer reſiſteth the Church in thoſe points which ſhe doth
infallibly propoſe as reuealed by God (which
infallibility you yield to her for all fundamentall points) be not an Heretique, becauſe at
leſt by reſiſting the Church, he conſequently
comes to oppoſe the *Teſtimony* or *Reuelation* of
God,

God, which is the formall obiect of Fayth. Befides, if the Teftimony of the Church worke
but *probably* vpon Infidels, and Nouices, who
by you are taught to belieue that fhe may erre
(vnles you will circumuent them, by diffembling her fallibility) they will haue wit inough
to tell themfelues, that fince fhe may erre, and
fpeakes but *probably*, fhe cannot worke fo *powerfully* vpon them, but that they may ftill doubt
whether fhe do not actually erre, and deceiue
them. And how can the Church worke vpon
all *within* her, to prepare, *induce, and perfwade the
mind to imbrace the fayth, to read and belieue Scriptures?* Are they *within* the Church before they
haue *imbraced the Fayth?* Or muft they want
fayth till they read, and belieue the Scriptures?
Or rather (fince accoiding to your Principles
all fayth depends on Scripture) muft they not
belieue the Scripture, before they imbrace the
fayth, and confequently before they be in the
Church? How then doth the Church *prepare,
induce,* and *perfwade* them that are *within her,* to
imbrace the fayth, and to *read, and belieue the Scriptures?* If our fayth muft reft and fettle only v-
pon the Written Word of God, how doth *S.Ire-
neus* (f) affirme, that many Nations haue been
conuerted to Chrift without Scriptures? Were
they conuerted only to an humane fayth?

    8.   And wheras you fay, that the Authority
of the Church is not *abfolutely diuine,* and therfore cannot be the laft, and formall Obiect of
fayth,

(f) *Lib . 3.
cap. 4.*

fayth, it is but an Equiuocation, and you infer
that which we do not deny. *Coninck* whom you
cite in your Margent, and tranflated by halues,
anfweres your Obiection in the very wordes
which you alleage. *Although (* fayth he *) the
Church* (g) *be directed by the infallible afsistance of
the holy Ghoſt, and in that fenfe her Teſtimony do in
fome fort rely vpon the diuine Authority, and receiue
from it ſtrength (* all which words you do not
tranſlate *) yet it is not truly, or properly the Teſtimony or word, and reuelation of God, but properly it is a
humane Teſtimony.* You fee then, that the Teſtimony of the Church in fome fenfe is *Diuine,*
that is, infallibly directed by the holy Ghoſt;
which is inough for our purpofe, although it be
not *Diuine* in another fenfe, that is, her words
are not the immediate voyce of God, as Scriptures are, becaufe fhe doth not propofe any
new Reuelations, made immediately to her, but
only infallibly declares what Reuelations haue
beene made to Prophets, Apoſtles, &c. Your
felfe affirme, that the Church is infallible in
Fundamentall points, and confequently her Teſtimony is not meerly *humane* and fallible, and
yet it is not abfolutely diuine; and fo you muſt
anfwere your owne Argument: and you muſt
grant that the Church being infallible in fome
points, may be to vs a ground fufficient for our
infallible affent, or beliefe for fuch Articles.
And if you will tell vs that fayth muſt be refolued into fome Authority which is abfolutely

(g) *Difp.* 9.
dub. 5. *concl.*
2.

Di-

Diuine, as *Diuine* fignifies that which is diftinct from all things *created*, you will find your felfe gone too far. For Scripture it felfe, being a thing created, and not a God, is not Deuine in that fenfe. And the Apoftles, who receiued immediate Reuelations from God, when afterwards they did preach, and *declare* them to others; thofe *Declarations*, (which fuppofed the Reuelations already made) were not in the opinion of many Deuines, the teftimony or word of God, but of men infallibly affifted by God: And yet I hope you will not hence inferre, that it had not been *Herefy* to oppofe the *Declarations* of the Apoftles, although they did not preach new Reuelations, but only declare, and propound fuch as had been already made to them.

9. Your wordes (which are indeed but words) That *Scripture* (h) *is of diuine Authority, the Belieuer fees by that glorious beam of diuine light which fhines in Scripture*, I confuted heeretofore. And what greater côfutation can there be then by your own words, *the Belieuer fees.* For if he *fee*, how doth he *belieue*? Or if he *belieues*, how doth he fee? Efpecially fince you fay he *beliues*, and *fees*, vpon the fame *formall obiect*, or *motiue*. Yet that Scripture is knowne by it felfe, you proue out of *Bellarmine*, who fayth: That *the Scriptures* (i) *which are contayned in the Propheticall and Apoftolicall Writings be moft certayne and diuine, Scripture it felfe witneffeth.* But thefe words will proue to be againft your felfe. For *Bellarmine* in

that

(h) *Pag.* 141.

(i) *De verb. Dei lib.* 1. *cap.* 2.

that place difputing agaynft the *Swenckfeldian*
Heretiques, who denyed all Scriptures, fayth :
That, *he doth not alledge* (k) *Teſtimonies of Scrip-* (k) *Ibid.*
ture as if he thought that his Aduerſaries made any
great account of them, but leſt the Scriptures, the
Authority whereof his Aduerſaries did ſometymes a-
buſe agaynſt vs who reuerence them, may be thought
to fauour their doctrine . Is this to affirme that
Scripture is certainely, and euidently knowne
by Scripture? Or rather contrarily to fay, that
it muft firft be belieued, before it be powerfull
to perfuade? And therefore immediatly after
the wordes by you cited which are, *The Scri-*
pture ſelfe witneſſeth; he adds thefe (which you
as you are wont, leaue out *) whoſe predictions of*
things to come if they were true, as the euent after-
ward did manifeſt, why ſhould not the Teſtimonies
of things preſent be true? Where you fee, that he
proues not the Scripture *by that beame of light*
which euidenly ſhines in Scripture, but by *predicti-*
ons, which we grant to be a good inducement,
or, as Diuines fpeake, an *Argument* of *credibili-*
ty, and yet no *infallible* ground of *fayth* to belieue that Scriptures are diuine; and much leffe
a *beame of light* cleerly conuincing vs, that Scripture is Scripture. For one may be infpired to
prophefy, or fpeake truth in fome point, and for
others be left to humane difcourfe, or error, as it
hapned in *Balam*, and the friends of *Iob* . And
therfore *Bellarmine* in that very place, brings
other extrinfecall Argumentes, as Miracles,

exemplar, and viſible ſtrange puniſhments of
ſuch as preſumed to abuſe holy Scripture &c.
Which euidently ſhewes, that he intended to
bring Arguments of Credibility, and not infallible grounds of fayth, wherby we belieue that
Scripture is Scripture, which we muſt take
from the *infallible Teſtimony* of the Church by
meanes of *Tradition*, wherof *Bellarmine* ſayth:
(m) *De verb.* *This ſo neceſſary a point, to wit, that* (m) *there is ſome*
Dei non ſcri- *diuine Scripture, cannot be had from Scripture it*
pto lib.4.c.4. *ſelfe.* Wherby it is manifeſt that you plainely
corrupt *Bellarmines* meaning, when you go a-
bout to proue out of him, that Scripture can be
proued by Scripture alone, the contrary wherof
he affirmes, and proues at large againſt the Heretiques of theſe times. The place which you
cite of *Origen*, only proues that thoſe who already belieue the Canonicall Bookes of Scripture
may proue out of them, that Scripture is *diuine-*
(n) *Epiſt. 2.* *ly inſpired,* as *S. Peter* (n) ſayth. Neither doth the
verſ. 21. Authority of *Saluianus* proue any thing els.
  10. Your ſaying, that we yield to the
(o) *Pag.144.* Church, an *abſolute* (o) *vnlimited Authority to*
145. *propound what ſhe pleaſeth, and an vnlimited power*
to ſupply the defects of Scripture; I let paſſe as meere
ſlaunders. As alſo, that *the Authority of the Church*
(p) *Pag.144.* *is abſolute, not* (p) *depending on Scripture, but on*
which the Scripture it ſelfe depends. And you can-
not be ignorant of that, which hath been ſo often inculcated by Catholique Writers, that the
Scriptures in *themſelues* do not depend on the
Church,

Church, but only in refpect *of vs*, who learne
from her what Bookes be Canonical Scripture,
which is to fay, not the Scriptures, but our
weake vnderftanding, and knowledge of Scripture relies on the Church, which our Sauiour
Chrift commandes vs to heare. And your felfe
grant, that the Church(*g*) is *the ordinary outward*
meanes to prefent, and propound diuine verities to
our Fayth. You will not deny that your knowledge of the *Trinity, Incarnation* &c. depends on
Scripture, will you thence infer that the *Bleffed*
Trinity, Incarnation &c. in *themfelues* depend on
Scripture? as if God had not been God, vnleffe
Scripture had beene written. Befides, to fuch as
belieue Scripture we may proue the Church
herfelfe by Scripture, and fhe in all her definitions doth confult, examine, and fubmit herfelfe to Scripture, againft which fhe neuer did,
nor euer can define any thing; & in this fenfe
alfo fhe depends on Scripture. But to make
good your flaunder, you (*r*) cite *Bellarmine*, after your wonted fafhion. *If we take away* (*s*) *the*
Authority of the prefent Church of Rome, (*this of*
Rome is your addition) *and of the Trent-Coun-*
cell, the decrees of all other Ancient Councels, and the
whole Chriftian fayth may be questioned as doubtfull,
for the ftrength of all doctrines, and of all Councels
depends vpon the Authority of the prefent Church.
Would not one thinke by thefe words that the
ftrength of all doctrines depéds on the Church?
wheras *Bellarmine* only fayth, that we *could* not

(q) *Pag.* 142.
143.

(r) *Pag.* 144.
(s) *De effect.*
Sacram. lib,
2. *cap.* 25.
§. *Tertium*
Teftimonium

Ggg 3   infalli-

infallibly *know, that there were such Generall Coun-*
cels, and that they were lawfull Councels, and that
they defined this or that; but because the present
Church which cannot erre doth so belieue, and teach
vs. Which words demonſtrate, that *Bellarmine*
doth not ſpeake of fayth, or doctrines in *them-*
selues, but in reſpect *of vs.* And do not you your
ſelfe teach that it is the Church, which *directs*
vs to Scripture, and that ſhe likewiſe is the *ordi-*
nary outward meanes to preſent, and propound di-
uine Verities, without which Propoſition no obiect
can be conueyed to our (t) *fayth?* And what is this,
but to acknowledge, that in the ordinary way,
without the guidance, direction, and Propoſition of the Church we haue no fayth at all.

11. You likewiſe cite theſe words out of (u)
Bellarmine: The Scriptures, Traditions, and all do-
ctrines whatſoeuer depend on the Teſtimony of the
Church (he meanes ſay you, that of Rome) *with-*
out which all are wholy vncertayne. But *Bellarmines*
words are theſe: *Since the Scriptures, Traditions,*
and all doctrines whatſoeuer depend vpon the Teſti-
mony of the Church, all things willbe vncertayne,
vnles we be moſt aſſured which is the true Church.
You ſee *Bellarmine* ſpeakes not of the *particular*
Church of *Rome,* as you in your Parétheſis would
make him ſeeme to ſpeake. And as for the *Vni-*
uerſall true Church, what principle of Atheiſ-
me is it, (as you very exorbitantly (w) affirme) to ſay, that if we did not know which were
the true Church, we could haue no certainty
of

(t) *Pag. 142.*
143

(u) *De Ec-*
cleſ. mil. lib.
3. cap. 10 §.
Ad hæc ne-
ceſſe eſt.

(w) *pag. 145*

of Scriptures, Traditions, or any thing els ? Do
you thinke that it were safe to take the Scriptures vpon the credit of a falfe Church? As wel
might you take them vpon the credit of Turkes,
or Infidels. And therefore, not the Affertion
of *Bellarmine*, but the contrary to it, is a plaine
principle of Atheifme. Doe not you proue the
neceffity of a perpetuall vifible true Church,
becaufe otherwife men fhould want that ordinary meanes which God hath appointed for
our inftruction, Direction, & Saluation? Now,
if we might haue *Scriptures*, and true *Fayth* from
a falfe Church, your more zealous Brethren,
who deny a perpetuall vifible *true* Church,
might eafily anfwere all your Arguments, and
tell you, that a true Church is not neceffery for
fayth, and Saluation. And befides, is it not in
effect all one to fay (for as much as concernes
our inftruction) Chrift hath no vifible Church;
& to fay, that we cánot know which is the true
vifible Church of Chrift ? All the infallibility
which we afcribe to the Church, is acknowledged to proceed from the affiftance of God; how
can he be faid not to belieue a God, who belieues
the Church, becaufe fhe is affifted by God ? Re-
méber that euen now I told you, that according
to your owne affirmation, the Church is the
ordinary meanes wherby Diuine Truth is conueyed to the vnderftáding : and yet you thinke
your felfe free from Atheifme. The Apoftles of
tvemfelues, were but mortal, frayle, & fubiect to
errour,

errour, and yet I hope, you will not thinke it a
Principle of Atheifme to fay, that all our fayth
depends on them.

12. You taxe vs for teaching, that *much of
the Matter, or Obiect of fayth is not contayned in
Scripture any way*. But I haue already more then
once fayd, that we belieue nothing but what
is contained in Scripture in fome fort, eyther
in it felfe, or from fome Principle from which
it may be certaynely deduced, or in thofe places of Scripture which recōmend the *Church*, &
vnwritten *Traditions* to vs; as if one fhould in
his laft Teftament expreffe diuers particulars,
and fhould in the fame Teftament referre the
reft to fome third perfon, whome he had fully
inftructed concerning his further will, & meaning; whatfoeuer things were performed according to the direction of that third perfon,
might truly befayd to be contayned in the Teftament; although they might alfo be fayd not
to be cōtained therin, becaufe they are not mē-
tioned in particular. And according to this explication, *Canus*, and *Stapleton* whome you cite,
and other Catholikes are to be vnderftood,
when they teach, that we belieue diuers things
not comprehended in Scripture.

(y) *Pag. 146.*   13.   But you aske, *with what ingenuity* (y) *or
confcience doe they pretend Scripture in ech Controuerfy agaynSt vs, fince by their owne Confefsion many of their Affertions are meere vnwritten Traditions, leaning only on the Authority of their Church?*

I

I anſwere, that ſome points of faith are expreſly contained in Scripture, yet not ſo enforcingly as they might not be colourably eluded, if we tooke away the declaration of the Church. Some others, are not contained in Scripture, any other way then in the generall principles of the Churches authority, and diuine Traditions; as, for example, that ſuch Bookes in particular are Canonicall writings . Some others are comprehended in Scripture, only probably. Others are contained ſo cleerly, that they may ſeeme ſufficiently euident to a man not peruerſe; and according to theſe diuerſities we do more or leſſe alledge Scripture. If one were diſpoſed to vſe ſuch Arguments as you bring, I might aske on the other ſide, to what purpoſe do you alledge Councels, Fathers, & Reaſons, if out of Scripture alone you can conuince all errors againſt your doctrine? May not diuerſe arguments be rightly alledged to proue the ſelfe ſame Concluſion ?

14.   Once againe, you returne to the ſufficiency of only Scripture (that is, you returne to ſpeake nothing which concernes the Queſtion in hand) which you proue out of *Bellarmine, though heerin* (ſay you) *as not ſeldome* (z) *contra-* (z) *Pag.147 dicting both himſelfe, and his fellowes.* How conſonant the writings of *Bellarmine* are, both to themſelues, and to the common doctrine of other Catholique Authors, this may ſerue for a ſufficient proofe, that all his Aduerſaries could

H h h   neuer

neuer fhew yet in all his works any one contradiction, but fuch as themfelues had firft forged,
and then obiected. And although in this generall caufe I do not willingly meddle with perfonall things: yet that you may learne heerafter
to fpeake with more circumfpection, but chiefly for the merit of a perfon, fo eminent in learning and dignity, and yet more eminent in fan-
ctity, I will not forbeare to affure the world and
you, that when fome yeares fince, a perfon of
high authority in the world, had made himfelfe
beleue that he had difcouered many contradictions in *Bellarmine*, D. *Dunne* in a conference
that he had with a perfon of Honour & Worth,
from whom I receiued it, though I hold it not
fit heer to giue his name, declared that there was
no ground for this, but that all his works were
fo confonant and coherent to one another, as if
he had been able to write them all in one houres
fpace. And if you, D. *Potter*, be of another opinion, you fhall do well to produce fome inftáce
to the contrary, which may fhew a reall contradiction betweene fome paffage, and fome other
of his works, wherin it is odds that you will be
anfwered, and he be defended. Let vs fee alfo
for the prefent what you bring to make good
your affeueration. *The Cardinall* (fay you) *grants*
(a) that a Propofition is not *de fide*, vnles it be
concluded in this Syllogifme: *Whatfoeuer God* (b)
reuealed in the Scripture is true: but this or that, God
hath reuealed in Scripture: ergo, it is true. If matters

of

(a) *Bellarm.*
de verb Dei
interpret.
cap. 10. ad
arg. 15.
(b. *pag.* 145.

of fayth must be reueaied in Scripture, as this reason
suppoſes, then the Propoſall of the Church cannot
make any vnwrittenVerity to become matter of fayth:
yet to ſalue the ſoueraigne power of his Church, he
makes all the ſtrength, and truth in this Syllogiſme to
depend on the Teſtimony of the Church, and by con-
ſequence the truth of the Concluſion, which euer re-
ſembles the weaker premiſſe.So as if this be true, there
is no truth in the Scriptures, or in our Religion, with-
out the atteſtation of the Church. But now how
many corruptions, ſleights, and vntruths are
couched in theſe lines? Let vs examine them a
little. *Bellarmine* hauing taught, and proued at
large,that the *interpretation* of *holy Scripture* belongs not to priuate perſons, but to the Church
of God, which,*in reſpect of vs,*is to iudge of Scripture, and of all other Controuerſies in Religion: and hauing made this Obiection againſt
himſelfe; *If our fayth depend* (c) *vpon the Iudg-*
ment of the Church,then it depends vpon the word of
men, and therfore doth rely vpon a moſt weake foun-
dation; he giues this anſwere : *The word of the*
Church,that is, of the Councell or Pope, when he tea-
cheth as out of his Chaire, is not meerly the word of
man ;that is, a word ſubiect to error, but in ſome ſort
the word of God; that is, vttered by the aſsiſtance, and
direction of the holy Ghoſt: nay I ſay, that the Here-
tiques are thoſe who indeed leane on a rotten ſtaffe:
And then he comes to the words which you cited : *For we muſt know that a Propoſition of Fayth is*
concluded in this Syllogiſme : Whatſoeuer God hath

(c)*Vbi ſupra*

Hhh 2　　　　　　　　*reuea-*

reuealed in Scripture is true : God hath reuealed this in Scripture : ergo it is true . Of the premiſſes in this Syllogiſme , the firſt is moſt certaine among all ; the ſecond is moſt firme , or certaine among Catholiques , for it relies on the Teſtimony of the Church , Councell , or Pope (heere you breake off , but *Bellarmine* ads) *of which we haue in holy Scripture manifeſt promiſes that they cannot erre. Act.15.It hath ſeemed to the Holy Ghoſt, & to vs : And Luke 22.I haue prayed for thee , that thy fayth may not faile. But amongſt Heretiques it doth rely only vpon coniectures , or the Iudgement of ones own ſpirit , which for the moſt part ſeemeth good, and is ill ; and ſince the Concluſion followes the weaker part , it neceſſarily followes , that the whole fayth of Heretiques , is but coniecturall , and vncertayne .* Thus farre *Bellarmine .* And now wherein I pray you conſiſts his contradicting both himſelfe , and his fellowes ? Perhaps you meane , becauſe heere he teacheth that euery Propoſition of fayth muſt be reuealed in Scripture ; and therefore contradicts his other doctrine , that beſids Scripture there are vnwritten Traditions. But the vanity of this obiection will by and by appeare among your other corruptions , which now I ſet down. *First* , you ſee *Bellarmine* ſpeakes not of fayth in generall, but only of matters of fayth contayned in Scripture , his whole queſtion being about the *Interpretation* thereof , that is. Whether we are to rely on the priuate ſpirit , or humane induſtry of conferring places &c. or els vpon the Church .

And

And therefore ; *Secondly*, he fayth not , as you
cite him in a different letter , by way of an vniuerſal negation, that a *Propoſition is not de fide*, or
not belonging to fayth , *vnles it be concluded in
this Syllogiſme : Whatſoeuer God hath reuealed in the
Scripture is true* : but *this, or that God hath reuealed
in Scripture &c.* (from whence it would follow
that nothing at all could be belieued which is
not contained in Scripture) but he onely fayth
that *a Propoſition of fayth is cōcluded in this Syllogiſme* ; which includes no vniuerſall negation, but
is meant onely of thoſe Propoſitions of fayth
which depend on the interpretation of Scripture , which was the ſubiect of his diſcourſe .
And therefore I wonder why you ſhould ſay in
generall ; *this reaſon ſuppoſes that matters of fayth
muſt be reuealed in Scripture* . For , to teach that
ſome matters of faith are in Scripture, doth not
ſuppoſe that all matters of fayth muſt be contayned in Scripture , and yet all the contradiction that heere you find in *Bellarmine* muſt be
this : Such Propoſitions of fayth as are contayned in Scripture , are concluded in this Syllogiſme : *Whatſoeuer God hath reuealed in the Scripture &c. Ergo* all Propoſitions of fayth muſt be
concluded in this Syllogiſme ; *Ergo* there are no
vnwritten Traditions. A goodly contradiction!
Thirdly, where did *Bellarmine* euer teach that the
Propoſall of the Church can make *any vnwritten Verity to become matter of fayth*, as you ſpeake?
The Church doth not make Verities to be mat-

ter of fayth, but only declares them to be such.
Fourthly, you leaue out the words which cleerly
explicate in what sense the Testimony of the
Church may be sayd to be *humane*, or diuine;
by which your Argument to proue that the declaration of the Church cannot be a sufficient
ground of fayth, had been answered, and your
fallacy discouered. *Fifthly, Bellarmine* neuer affirmed, as you say he did, that the strength and
truth of the *Minor* in the sayd *Syllogisme* depends
on the Testimony of the Church, but only that
it is *most certaine among Catholiques* by the Testimony of the Church, becaufe, as I haue often
faid, the Church cannot make any one Article
to be *true*, but only by her declaration can
make it *certaine to all Catholiques*, as *Bellarmine*
faid. *Sixtly*, you leaue out *Bellarmines* words,
wherby he proues the infallibility of Church
and Pope out of Scripture; and accordingly in
the *Seauenth* place, that which he expresly sayth
of the vncertaine coniecturall ground of Heretiques, which can produce only a coniecturall
and vncertaine Fayth, becaufe the Conclufion
followes the *weaker* part, you make him apply to
the Testimony of the Church as if it were vncertaine, which contrarily in the words by you
omitted he proues to be most certaine & infallible; and therfore the *Conclufion* which relies
vpon a Propofition deliuered by her, is not fubiect to error. *Eighthly*, you returne to the flaunder, that if *Bellarmines* doctrine be true, *there is no*
truth

*truth in the Scriptures, or in our Religion, without
the attestation of the Church:* as if *Bellarmine* had
taught, that the *truth* of Scripture, and of all
Chriſtian Religion depends on the atteſtation
of the Church, which could not in you proceed
from ignorance, but from a purpoſe to deceiue
your Reader. For *Bellarmine* in that very place
which you cite, declares himſelfe ſo fully and
clearly that you cannot be excuſed from wilfull
ſlaunder. I will put downe the place at large,
that heerafter you, and your Brethren may either ceaſe to make the ſame Obiection, or els
endeauour to confute the Cardinalls anſwere.
Bellarmine then, makes this obiection againſt
himſelfe: *If the Pope iudge of Scriptures, it followes
that the Pope or Councell is aboue the Scripture: and
if the meaning of Scripture without the Pope or Councell be not authenticall, it followes that the word of
God takes his force and ſtrength from the word of
men:* And then he giues this Anſwere: *I anſwere,
that this Argument of which Heretiques make greateſt account, conſiſts in a meere Equiuocation. For it
may be vnderſtood two manner of wayes that the
Church doth iudge of Scriptures: the one, That ſhe
ſhould iudge whether that which the Scripture teaches
be true, or falſe: The other, That putting for a moſt
certaine ground, that the words of Scripture are moſt
true, ſhe ſhould iudge what is the true interpretation
of them. Now, if the Church did iudge according to
the former way, ſhe ſhould indeed be aboue the Scripture, but this we do not ſay, though we be calumnia-
ted*

*ted by the Heretiques as if we did , who euery where
cry out , that we put the Scripture vnder the Popes
Feet. But that the Church or Pope doth iudge of Scriptures in the latter sense, which we affirme , is not to
say, that the Church is aboue Scripture , but aboue the
Iudgment of priuate persons For the Church doth not
iudge of the Truth of Scripture, but of the vnderstanding of thee , and mee , and others. Neither doth the
Word of God receiue strength therby , but only my vnderstanding receiues it For the Scripture is not more
true or certaine , because it is so expounded by the
Church ; but my Opinion is truer , when it is confirmed by the Church.* What say you now Doth *Bellarmine* teach , that the *Truth* , or *certainety* of
Scripture or of the *Minor* in the foresaid Syllogisme, depéds on the Church? But in the meane
time how many corruptions haue you committed in this one Citation?

15.　You cite *g*) *Waldensis*, to proue that the
(g) *pag. 149.*
(h) *Walaen.*
lib. 2. *Doct.*
*fid. art.*2.
cap. 19. §. 1.
(h) infallibility of the Church is planted only
in the Church vniuersall, or the Catholique Body of Christ on earth, comprehending all his
members. But though we cannot allow of *Waldensis* his doctrine in some points, wherin he
contradicts the consent of other Catholiques;
yet he doth not teach what you affirme, but only that the infallibility of the Church consists in
the succession of Doctors in the Church, which
is against your assertion (*Pag.* 150.) that *the
whole Militant Church (that is, all the members of
it) cannot possibly erre &c.* And therfore the doctrine

&rine of *Waldensis* is sufficient for our maine
Queſtion againſt you, that whoſoeuer erreth in
any one point deliuered by Doctours and Paſtours ſucceeding one another in the viſible
Church, is an Heretique, and without repentance cannot be ſaued, whether the point be of
it ſelfe fundamentall, or not fundamentall. For
Waldenſis maketh no ſuch diſtinction, as you do:
Nay, which is directly againſt your preſent Aſſertion heere, and your doctrine els where, this
Author (*doctrinal.fidei tom.1. Art.2. cap.47.*) hauing prefixed this Title before that Chapter;
That the Pope hath infringible power to determine
verities of fayth, and to ouercome and cancell all he-
reticall falſities; doth in the whole Chapter it
ſelfe proſecute and proue the ſaid Title out of
the Fathers. And to the next Chapter 48. hauing alſo giuen this Title : *Of the Prerogatiue of*
the perpetuall immunity, and purity of the Romane
Church from all contagion of Hereſy ; he proues it
in like manner through the whole Chapter.
You muſt therfore be well aduiſed how you
cite Authors out of one place, without conſi-
dering, or enquiring what they ſay in another.

16. Together with *Waldenſis*, you cite *Sylue-*
ſter, ſaying: *The Church which is* (i) *affirmed not to*   (i) *Summa*
be capable of error, is not the Pope, but the Congrega-   *verb. Eccle-*
tion of the faythfull. But this is a plaine falſifica-   *ſia cap. 1.§.*
tion. For in that very place he teacheth; That   4.
the Pope vſing the Councell of Cardinals, or his
members, cannot erre, but may erre as he is a

particular perfon. And then adds : *In this manner is to be vnderstood the Gloffe, Cauf. 24.q. 1. can. à
recta. Which fayth the Church which cannot erre is not
the Pope, but the Congregation of the faytl full.* So as
you fee that thefe are not the words of *Syluefter,*
as you affirme, but of another, which yet he in-
terprets plainely againft you. And that you
may be wholy inexcufable, he doth heer referre
himfelfe to another place , namely, *Verb. Conci-
lium, §. 3.* where he exprefly proues, that a
Councell cánot erre, no more then the Church,
becaufe if the Councell could erre, the whole
Church might erre. For the Church doth not
meet togeather, but only the Councell , or the
Pope. Adding further, that the doctrine of the
Church vpon which S. *Thomas* fayth we are to
rely as vpon an infallible Rule, is no other then
that of the Councell. And as for the Pope , he
fayth, that we muft not ftand to the Popes declaration, becaufe he hath better reafons then
can be alleaged to the contrary ; but becaufe he
is *Head* of the Church, whofe office is to determine doubts in fayth. And a little after he exprefly fayth *:* That the Pope cannot erre when
recourfe is made to him in doubtfull matters as
to the *Head* of the Church , becaufe (fayth he)
*this errour would redound to the errour of the whole
Church.* And likewife in this very place of *Sylue-
ster* which you cite, he alfo referres himfelfe to
Verb. fides.§. 2. where at large he proues the Popes infallibility, faying: *That it belongeth to fayth,*

that

that we rely vpon the Popes determination in things belonging to fayth or manners , because the Church cannot erre in such things , and consequently he , as head of the Church, that is, as he is Pope cannot erre, although he determined without aduice of the Cardinals. With what confcience then , do you cite this Author againft his words , meaning, and defigne and afcribe to him words which he citeth out of another, and, as I faid, explicates againft you? And with the like fidelity, after Syluefter, you do ftrangely alledge the Gloffe *Cauf.* **24** *c m. à recta* with an, *Et,* as if the words which you cited out of *Syluefter* (*The Church which cannot erre is not the Pope &c.*) had been different from that Gloffe, wheras they are nothing but that *Gloffe,* and not the words of *Syluefter.*

17 . They (you meane Catholique Do-&ours) grant, that the *infallibility of the Church reacheth not* (k) *to all questions and points in Religion that may arife, but only to fuch Articles as may belong to the subftance of fayth , fuch as are matters effentiall and fundamentall , fimply neceffary for the Church to know and belieue .To omit others* D Stapleton *is full* (l) *and punctuall to this purpofe . He distinguisheth Controuerfies of Religiõ into two forts. Some ,* fayth he, *are about thofe doctrines of fayth which neceffarily pertayne to the publique fayth of the Church ; others about fuch matters as doe not neceffarily belong to the fayth , but may be varioufly held, & difputed without hurt or preiudice of fayth.* Heer is fuch a Caos of words, and corruptions,

(k)*pag.149.*

(l) *Princip. Doctr. lib. 8. contr.* 4.*cap.* 15 .

as I fcarce know where to beginne to vnfold them. *Stapleton* in the place by you alledged hath this Affertion. *The infallibility of teaching in matters of fayth, granted to the Church, hath place only in defining infallibly, and propofing faithfully thofe doctrines of fayth, which eyther are called in queſtion, or otherwife belong neceſſarily to the publique fayth of the Church.* And afterward he affirmeth, that *thofe things belong neceſſarily to fayth, and publique doctrine of the Church which all men are bound explicitely to belieue, or els are publikely practifed by the Church, or els which the Paſtours are bound to belieue explicitely, and the people impliciteby in the fayth of their Paſtours.* By which words it is cleere that *Stapleton* fayth not, that the infallibility of the Church reacheth only to fuch Articles as are *matters eſſentiall, and fundamentall, and fimply neceſſary for the Church, to know and belieue,* as you affirme; but to all points which are called in queſtion, or which are publiquely practifed by the Church, whether they be fundamentall, or not fundamentall: and therfore you do miſalledge him when you fay, that, *he diſtinguiſheth Controuerfies of Religion into two forts: Some are about thofe doctrines of fayth, which neceſſarily pertaine to the publique fayth of the Church &c.* For *Stapleton* explicates himfelfe, as you haue heard, that whatfoeuer is called in queſtion, or practifed by the Church, is the Obiect of her infallibility, which is the thing we intend to proue againſt Proteſtants; that to oppofe, or que-

queftion any one doctrine, or practife of the
Church is to refift an *infallible* Authority, and
confequently to be an *Heretique*. And that *Stapleton* neuer dreamed of your imaginary reftrai-
ning the infallibility of the Church to points
fundamentall, is cleere by another place which
you (m) cite as out of *S.Thomas* and him, in this
manner: *Some are primitiue Articles, of the fub-* (m) *Pag.* 40
ftance of Religion, effentiall in the obiect of fayth. O-
thers are fecundary, probable, accidentall, or obfcure
points. For *Stapleton* in that place fayth, that *cer-*
taine doctrines (n) *are either primary Principles of*
fayth, or els, though not primary, yet defined by the (n) *Staplet.*
Church, and fo, as if they were primary. Others are *Rel. controu.*
Conclufions deduced from thofe principles, but yet not 1.*q.* 3.*art.* 6.
defined. Of the firft kind are the Articles of fayth, and
whatfoeuer is defined in Councels againft Heretiques
& c. *Of the fecond, are queftions, which either belong*
to the hidden works of God, or to certaine moft obf-
cure places of Scripture, which are befide the fayth,
and of which we may be ignorant without loffe
of fayth, yet they may be modeftly, and fruitful-
ly difputed of. And afterward he teaches, that
whatfoeuer the Church doth vniuerfally hold, ei-
ther in doctrine or manners, belongs to the founda-
tion of fayth: and proues it out of *S. Auguftine*
(o) who cals the Cuftome of the Church, *Eccle-* (o) *Serm.* 14.
fiæ morem fundatifsin ū & fidem fundatifsimam, con- *de verbis Do-*
fuetudinem Ecclefiæ fundatifsimā, authoritatem fta- *mini. ep.* 28.
bilifsimā fundatif imæ ecclefiæ. Could any thing be 89. 96.
more cleere to fhew, that according to *Stapleton,*

the infallibility of the Church reacheth further
then to thofe points which you call *fundamentall*, and that it belongs to the very *foundation* of
Fayth, that we belieue whatfoeuer the Church
holds? And that it is not lawfull for any to difpute againſt fuch determinatiõs of the Church?
Which doth ouerthrow your diſtinction of
points *fundamentall* & not *fundamentall*; thogh
you alledge the authority of *S. Thomas* and *Sta-*
pleton in fauour thereof. For *S. Thomas* (o) in
the very place by you cited, after he had fayd,
that there are fome obiects of fayth which we
are bound *explicitely* to belieue : addeth ; that
we are bound to belieue all other points, when
they are fufficiently propounded to vs , as belonging to fayth . You might gayne more reputation to your felfe , and allow your aduerfary more eafe , if you would once refolue to
cite your Authours with more fincerity .

(o)2.2.q.2.
art.5.

18. To proue , that the infallibility of the
Church extends only to fundamentall points,
you alfo alledge *Maldonatus*, who fayth: That *he*
will not repugne (p) *if one will affirme , that thofe*
words Io. 14. *verf.* 16. *He fhall teach you all things ;*
be referred to thofe other words ; Whatfoeuer I haue
fpoken to you : as if our Sauiour did fay, that the holy
Ghoſt was to teach thē nothing, but that which he him-
felfe had taught them. But do you in good earneſt
belieue, that our Sauiour taught the Apoſtles
fundamentall points alone , which all Chriſtians are bound explicitely to belieue ? Or will
you

(p)Jn Joan.
14. 26.

you fay, the Apoftles were infallibly affifted only when they deliuered fundamentall points of fayth? So you muft fay, if Chrift did teach them only points fundamentall, and the holy Ghoft taught them onely thofe thinges which Chrift had taught them, vnles you will fay, they were infallible without the afhiftáce of the holy Ghoft. You fee he had good reafon to fay, that (q) by denying the vniuerfal infallibility of the Church, & *limiting* the promifes of Chrift made to her, you opened a gap for men to fay that the Apoftles in their Preaching and Writing were not vniuerfally infallible. And heer I aske, whether it be not a *fundamentall* errour againft fayth, and *Saluation*, to deny the truth of any one point fufficiently propounded as reuealed by God? and fince without queftion it is fo, you muft eyther grant, that the Church can erre fundamentally and damnably agaynft fayth, which yet your felf deny; or els you muft yield that her infallibility reaches to all points fuffi-ciently propounded as diuine Truths, whether they be in themfelues *fundamentall,* or not *fundamentall*, which is as much as we defire.

(q) *Firft Part. cap. 3. num. 13.*

19. Agaynft the infallibility of the Church you bring a long argument, (*pag.* 157. 158.) the force whereof is this: Nothing according to vs can be belieued by diuine fayth which hath not beene defined by the Church: But the Church hath not defined that fhe is infallible in all her decrees: Therfore we cannot belieue

by

by diuine fayth that she is infallible in all her decrees.

20. Before I answere your Argument , I must reflect that you do not sincerely alledge these words out of *Bellarmine*; *Vntil* (r)*a doctrine be declared or defined by the Church, so long it might be eyther doubted of, or denyed without danger.* For *Bellarmine* makes no such generall Rule, but only speaking of the opinió of Pope *Iohn the two and twentith*; That the Saints doe not see God before the Resurrection (which is your owne errour) he excuseth him from Heresy , because at that tyme the Church had not defined the matter. Where you see *Bellarmine* speakes only of a particular point , which that Pope not conceauing to be contayned in Scripture, and the thing hauing not been expressely defined by the Church nor euidently knowne to haue beene the vniuersall sense thereof; it was not at that tyme a matter of fayth . And he himselfe before his death retracted his errour . But to come to your Argument, I wish you would be carfull not to obiect against vs , what your selfe must answer. For doe not you teach, that the Church *workes vpon all* (s)*within her, to prepare , induce , and per-suade the mind to imbrace the fayth , to reade and be-lieue the Scriptures?* And that the *ordinary meanes* (t)*appointed by God to present , and propound diui-ne Verities , is the Church?* And therefore we cannot in the ordinary course belieue Scriptures , or any other diuine Verity, but by the *Pro-posall*

(r) *Lib. 4. de Roman. Pont. cap. 14 §. Respondeo inprimis.*

(s)*Pag. 139.*

(t)*Pag. 142. 143.*

posall of the Church. But this doctrine (that the
Church is the firſt Inducer to imbrace the faith,
and the ordinary Meanes without which we
cannot belieue) is not *propoſed* by the Church,
and therefore it is not a thing which we can
belieue . You likewiſe grant that the Church is
infallible in all fundamentall points . And I
aske in what decree, definition , or declaration
hath the Church *propoſed* to vs , that her ſelfe
cannot erre in *fundamentall* points, eſpecially
with your addition , that ſhe may erre in points
not *fundamentall ?* Now, to your Argument I
anſwere : *Firſt ;* That it is not neceſſary, that the
Church ſhould by any particular decree teſtify
her owne infallibility , becauſe it being euident
that ſhe is the ſelfe ſame Church which was
founded by our Sauiour Chriſt , and continued from the Apoſtles to this Age, by a neuer
interrupted ſucceſſion of Paſtours , and faythfull people ; it followes that ſhe is the Church
of Chriſt: which being once granted , it is further inferred , that all are obliged to haue recourſe to her , and to reſt in her iudgement for
all other particular points which côcerne faith,
or Religion ; which we could not be obligd to
doe , if we were perſuaded , that ſhe were ſubiect to errour. Which yet is more euident, if we
add, that there can be no Rule giuen in what
points, we ſhould belieue her, and in what not :
and therefore we are obliged to belieue her in
all. Moreouer , ſince the true Church muſt be

Iudge of Controuersies in fayth , as we haue
proued , it cleerly followes that she must be infallible in all points. Which vniuersall infallibility being suppoſed out of the *generall* ground of
Gods prouidence , which is not defectiue in
things neceſſary, we may afterward belieue the
ſame infallibility, euen by the Church herſelfe,
when she teſtifies that *particular* point of her
owne infallibility: As the Scripture cannot giue
Teſtimony to it ſelfe, till firſt it be belieued to be
Gods word, yet this being once preſuppoſed , it
may afterward giue Teſtimony to it ſelfe, as S.

(u) 2. *Tim.*
3. 16.

Paul affirmeth, that, *All Scripture is diuinely* (u)
inſpired &c. *Secondly* I anſwere, that the Church
hath many wayes declared her owne infallibility, which she profeſſeth euen in the Apoſtles
Creed , *I belieue the holy Catholique Church.* For she
could not be *holy*, if she were ſubiect to error in
matters of fayth , which is the firſt foundation
of all ſanctity; she could not be *Catholique* , or *V-
niuerſal* for all *Ages*, if at any time she could erre,
and be Author that the whole world ſhould erre
in points reuealed by God; she could not be *One*,
or *Apoſtolicall* , (as she profeſſeth in another
Creed) if she were *diuided* in points of fayth, or
could ſwarue from the *Doctrine* of the *Apoſtles*;
she could not be alwayes exiſtent and *viſible*, becauſe euery error in fayth deſtroies all Fayth, &
the Church. So that while the Church , and e-
uery faythfull perſon, belieues & profeſſes the
Sanctity, Vniuerſality, Vnity, and *Perpetuall Viſibi-*
lity

lity of the Church; ſhe, and they belieue & proclaime her infallibility in all matters of fayth : which ſhe doth alſo auouch by accurſing all ſuch as belieue not her definitions ; and while in all occaſions of emergent Controuerſies, ſhe gathers Councels to determine them, without examining whether they concerne points fundamentall , or not fundamentall ; while in all ſuch holy Aſſemblies , ſhe ſayth with the firſt Councell ; *It hath(w)ſeemed to the holy Ghoſt and vs,* while ſhe propoſeth diuers points to be belieued, which are not contained in Scripture; as that thoſe who are baptized by Heretiques, cannot without ſacriledge be rebaptized; that Baptiſme of Infants is lawfull ; that Eaſter is to be kept at a certaine time againſt the Heretiques called *Quartadecimani*; that the Bleſſed Virgin, the moſt Immaculate Mother of God, was eternally a moſt pure Virgin; that ſuch particular *Matter* and *Forme* is neceſſary for the validity of Sacraments; that ſuch particular Bookes, Chapters, and lines are the word of God , with diuers ſuch other points ; of all which we may ſay, that which *S. Auguſtine* ſaid about *Rebaptization* of Heretiques : *The obſcurity of this Queſtion* (x) *before the ſchiſme of Donatus and ſo mooue men of great note , and Fathers and Biſhops endued with great Charity , to diſpute and doubt without breach of peace : that for a long time in ſeuerall regions there were diuers and doubtfull diſcords , and that which was truly belieued was vndoubtedly vnſettled*

(w) *Act. 15.*

(x) Lib. 1. ſont. Donat. cap. 7.

blished by a full Councell of the whole world. And
yet the point declared in that Councell was
neither fundamentall, in your fenfe, nor contained in Scripture. And to the fame effect are
the words of *S. Ambrofe*, who fpeaking of the
Heretiques, condemned in the Councell of
Nice, fayth that, *They were not condemned by hu-*
mane (y) *induftry, but by the authority of thofe Fa-*
thers: as likewife the laft Generall Councell of
Trent defines; That *it belongs to the Church* (z) *to*
iudge of the true fenfe, and interpretation of Scri-
pture, which muft needs fuppofe her infallibility. And laftly, the thirft that euery one, who
defires to faue his foule, feeles in his foule to
find out the true Church; and the quiet which
euery one conceiues he fhall enioy, if once he
find her, fhewes that the very fenfe, and feeling
of all Chriftians is, that the Church is infallible. For otherwife what great comfort could
any wife man conceiue to be incorporated in a
Church, which is conceiued to be fubiect to error in matters of fayth?

(y) *Lib.1.de*
fid. ad Gra-
tian. cap. 9.
(z) *1.Sef. 4.*

21.   For want of better arguments you alfo
alledge (a) fome Authors within the *Roman*
Church of great learning (as you fay) who haue
declared their opinion, that any particular
Churchs, (and by confequence the *Roman*) any
Councels though Generall, may erre. But
though that which you affirme were true, it
would fall fhort of prouing that the Catholique
Church is not infallible in all points. For, befides

(a) *pag.161.*

sides particular Churches, or Generall Councels, there is the common Consent of all Catholiques, knowne by perpetuall sacred Tradition; and there is likewise the continued Succession of Bishops and Pastors, in which if one
should place an vniuersall infallibility, it were
sufficient to ouerthrow your assertion of the
fallibility of the Church. And euen your selfe
teach, that the Church is infallible in all fundamentals, and yet you affirme that any particular, or Generall Councell may erre, euen to
Heresy, or *Fundamentall*, and *Damnable* errours :
And therfore you must grant, that according
to your Principles, it is one thing to say, Generall Councels may erre, and another, that the
Catholique Church may erre. But yet for the
thing it selfe, it is a matter of fayth, that true
Generall Councels, confirmed by the Pope,
cannot erre. And if any hold the contrary, he
cannot be excused, except by ignorance, or in-
aduertence. And as for the *Romane* Authors
which you cite, *Occham* is no competent witnes; both because that worke of his dialogues
which you cite is condemned, and because he
himselfe was a knowne enemy, and rebellious
against the sea Apostolique. Besides the words
which you cite out of him against the Authority of Councels are not his opinion, but alledged for arguments sake, for so he professeth expresly in the very preface of that worke, and often repeats it, that he doth not intend to deliuer

　　　　　　　　　any

any opinion of his owne. Thirdly, wheras he alledgeth reasons for, and against Councels, he alledgeth but fiue against them, and seauen for them. Lastly before he comes to dispute against Councels he doth in two seuerall (b) places, & in the very beginning of those Chapters of which the one is by you cited, deliuer his opinion in the person of his Disciple to be directly for the infallible authority of Councels. So as heer is a double corruption, the one, the citing words for his opinion which are not so : the other, the concealing those which are his, and directly to the contrary . *Clemangis* his workes are forbidden . That worke of *Cusanus* which you (c) cite , he afterward retracted . *Panormitanus* in the place (d) cited by you, may seeme to speake of Councells , disagreeing from the Pope : and though he say, that if the Councell erred , it did not follow that the whole Church should erre, because the faith might remaine in others; yet that doth not conuince that he held a Generall Councell together with the Pope might erre : For *Canus* hath the very same Obiection and Answere, and yet, as we shall see anon, he holds it to be a matter of faith, that General Councels confirmed by the Pope cannot erre . Neuertheles if *Panormitanus* did hold that Generall Councells with the Pope might erre , he can only be excused , because he did not affirme it with pertinacity . *Petrus de Aliaco* hath indeed (e) the words which you cite:
but

(b) *Dialog. lib. 5. 1. part. cap. 25. & c. 28.*

(c) *Concord. Cathol.*
(d *Jn cap. Significasti. extra. de Electione .*

(e) *Quæst. in Uesper. art. 3.*

but they are not fpoken by him as his opinion, but as the opinion of fome others : & fo he hath alfo the cleane contrary propofition, *viz*. that a generall Councell cannot erre, nor euen the *Romane* Church; which you might as well haue alledged for his opinion as the other : but the truth is, that neither are alledged by him as his owne doctrine, but as the opinion of others, as I faid, which he exprefIly fayth that he doth forbeare to difcuffe for the prefent, contenting himfelfe onely with thefe three Conclufions which expreffe his owne opinion. Firft, that alwayes there is fome Church which is ruled by the law of Chrift (which according to his former explication is as much as to fay, that there is alwayes fome Church which cannot erre.) The fecond, that it is not conuinced out of Scripture, that any particular Church is in fuch manner conformed to the rule of Chrifts law. The third is, that it is conuinced out of Scripture, that alwayes there is fome vniuerfall Church which neuer fwarues from the rule of Chrift. Neither will it aduantage you, that he teacheth that any particular Church may erre; For as I haue often told you, the *Roman* Church in the fenfe which I haue heertofore declared, is all one with the *Vniuerfall* Church, and fo his doctrine that the *Vniuerfall* Church cannot erre directly proues, that the *Romane* cannot erre. And when he teacheth, that the Vniuerfall Church cannot erre, he doth not diftinguifh

betwixt

betwixt points fundamentall, and not fundamentall, as you do. You cite out of *Canus* thefe
words : *I confeffe* (f) *that euery Cenerall Councell
doth reprefent the whole Church. But when you vrge,
that the Church cannot erre; it is true in that fenfe in
which faithfull people vnderstand it; which is, that the
whole Church together, that is, all faythfull people do
not erre: But this doth not hinder, but that the greater part of the Church may erre.* I fhould fcarcely
haue belieued it to be poffible for any man aliue
who pretends to haue credit, & common fame
to peruert the fenfe of this Author, as you do,
vnles I did fee with mine owne eyes both what
you write, and indeed what *Canus* affirmes. For
in the Chapter next precedent(g) to that which
you cite, he hauing affirmed, that a Generall
Councell confirmed by the Pope makes a thing
certayne, and belonging to fayth (in refpect of
vs) addeth, that this *Conclufion is fo certayne that
the cotrary is hereticall*, which he proues by diuers
good conuincing reafons, and among the reft,
that *if fuch a Councell could erre, there were no way
certaine to decide Controuerfies of fayth.* And in the
place which you cite afterward, he impugnes
their opinion who affirme that a Generall Cou-
cell is infallible before it be confirmed by the
Pope, which they endeauoured to proue becaufe the Coutel reprefents the whole Church,
and therfore can erre no more then the vniuerfall Church it felfe. To which Argument he
anfweres in the words which I fet downe, and
which

(f) *Canus
loc. lib. 5. c.
5. §. At con-
tra.*

(g) *Cap. 4.
§. Tertia Co-
clufio.*

which you alledge to proue that *Canus* held a Geनerall Councell might erre, namely : *(But when you vrge that the Church cānot erre , it is true in that fenfe in which faythfull people vnderstand it , which is , that the whole Church together , that is , all faythfull people do not erre :*) and therefore it is euident that you bring them directly agaynst his words and meaning , & bring the *Obiection* for his anfwere. And befides what we haue already related out of him, within fiue lines after the words cited by you , he fayth , *The Councell would be infallible if it were confirmed by the Pope* . I leaue it to your owne confideration , what iudgement euen you would frame of any other befide your felfe , if he fhould cite Authours in this manner.

22. You haue no reafon to be fo much offended, that we equall *diuine vnwritten Traditions*, with the written word of God. For we haue fo reuerend an opinion of Gods word , as that wherfoeuer we find it , our fayth belieues it to be moft infallible: nor can we belieue that pen, inke, and paper can add any certainty to the Truth thereof. Without caufe alfo you accufe the *Romane* Church of fupine negligence , becaufe fhe hath not as yet giuen a Catalogue of vnwritten Traditions, as well as of all the Bookes of Scripture. For you might alfo condemne the Ancient Church, which did not for diuers ages deliuer any Catalogue of Canonicall Bookes , which yet afterward, fhe did as occa-

L l l   fion

fion required. And as the Councell of *Trent*
by reafon of your herefies, whereby you denyed diuers Canonicall Bookes of Scripture, fet
downe a perfect Canon of Scripture : fo, as iuft
& neceffary occafio may require, the holy Ghoft
by which fhe is directed, will not fayle to affift
her in making a Catalogue of vnwritten Traditions. I cannot find but that your moderne
Brethren will gladly admit of fome Apoftolicall Traditions agaynft the Puritans; and why
then doe you not make a Catalogue of them, as
you haue done of the Bookes of Scripture ?
Your famous Archbifhop of *Canterbury* fayth :
For fo much as the Originall (i) *& beginning of thefe*

(i) M . Wit- *names, Metropolitan, Archbifhop &c. fuch is their An-*
gift in his *tiquity, cannot be found, fo farre as I haue read, it is to*
his defence *be fuppofed, they haue their Originall from the A-*
&c. pag.351 *poftles themfelues: for as I remember S. Auguftine*
hath this Rule in his 118. *Epiftle.* And in proofe
of this Rule of *S. Auguftine* he adds: *It is of cre-*
dit (k) *with the Writers of our tyme, namely with M.*
(k) Vbi fu- *Zwinglius, M. Caluin, M. Gualter; and furely I*
pra pag.352. *thinke no learned man doth diffent from them.* Are
not I pray you thefe, and the like *Traditions*,
vpon which your *Hierarchy* depends, of fome
confequence, and worth your labour to put
them in a Catalogue? Or doe you not hold the
Traditions of the *Apoftles* to be infallible true?
(l)pag. 163.   23. It is but a Calumny to affirme, that (l)
we receiue the definitions of the Church, with
no leffe deuotion then the holy Scriptures. For
you

you cite(m)that very place of *Bellarmine*, where he (n) setteth downe at large fiue singular Pre-rogatiues of the holy Scriptures aboue the defi-nitions of the Church, in which respect your fault is lesse excusable. It is your owne doctrine that the Church is infallible in all fundamen-tals, and yet you will not euen in respect of such points, equall her Authority with that of holy Scripture.

24. At length you come to teach that Ge-nerall Councels may erre euen damnably, and yet you also teach, that *their authority is imme-diately* (o) *deriued from Christ:* and that *their de-crees* (p) *binde all persons to externall Obedience.* But will you haue men in matters of fayth *ex-ternally* belieue themselues, & dissemble against their conscience? And thinke that they do so by authority from Christ? The truth is, that you might as well say, the Church is inuisible, as to say, that her infallibility consists not in Generall Councels, but in this, that euery mem-ber of the Church cannot erre damnably: For, towards the effect of instructing men in doubts concerning fayth, all comes to one effect. And with what colour of truth, doe you say (*pag.* 164.165.) that you *giue Generall Councells much more respect, then do most of our Aduersaries*, since Catholiques belieue thē to be infallible, which you deny?

25. But you would gladly proue, that Councels are fallible, because they are *discour-*

(m)pag.169.
(n, De Conc.
l.2. cap.12.

(o)Pag.162
(p) Ibid.

(r) *Pag. 167.* *fiue in their deliberations, and* (r) *vfe the weights &*
moments of reafon, for the drawing out of Conclu-
fions from their Principles, wherin it is confeffed they
may miftake.

26. It is true, we grant that the Church
coynes no new Reuelations, but only declares
fuch to vs, as haue been already deliuered in the
written, or vnwritten word of God; to finde
which out fhe vfeth meanes, by fearching out
true Records of Antiquity, by difcuffing the
writings of Fathers, by confulting the holy
Scriptures, Traditions &c. becaufe it is the will
of God that fhe vfe fuch meanes. But the thing
vpon which fhe finally relyes in her Definitions, *ex parte Obiecti*, is the Reuelation, or atteftation of God, which is the *Formall* and laft *Mo-*
tiue of fayth; and *ex parte Subiecti*, in behalfe of
herfelfe, fhe relies vpon the infallible affiftance
of the holy Ghoft, directing her not to propound any falfhood infteed of a reuealed truth.
Thus we read in the firft Councell *Act. 15. Cum*
magna difquifitio fieret: After great fearch, & examination of the Cafe, by citing Scriptures, relating Miracles, and the bleffing of God, declared by the good fucceffe, and conuerfion of fo
many Gentiles; the final determination did not
rely vpon thefe induftries, but, *Vifum eft Spiritui*
fancto, & nobis. It hath feem,d to the Holy Ghoft, and
vs: Which words expreffe both the *formall Mo-*
tiue, and chiefe *efficient* Caufe of fayth, as alfo
the *free,* and *voluntary concurring* of the Apoftles,

ſtles, aſſiſted by the Holy Ghoſt. And yet I hope
you will not out of theſe diligences, & *diſcourſes*
of the Apoſtles inferre, that this Councell was
fallible: Or that there was no more certainty in
the Concluſion, then in the Arguments themſelues, of which ſome, abſtracting from the aſſiſtance of the holy Ghoſt, and the Authority of
the Apoſtles, were but, as the Deuines ſpeake,
Arguments of Credibility, and diſpoſitions to
fayth, as Miracles &c. Or will you perhaps with
your firſt Patriarch *Luther*, reprehend euen this
Councell of the Apoſtles, and ſay with him :
That Iames, whoſe (s) *opinion the whole Councell*
followed, changed the verdict of Peter, whoſe iudg-
ment, that the Gentiles ſhould not be conſtrained to
obſerue the Iewiſh Ceremonies, was moſt true, & cō-
ſequently the opinion of Iames and the Councell could
not be true? You grant (as I muſt often put you
in mind) that the Church is infallible in fundamentall points, muſt ſhe therfore vſe no induſtry, to attaine to the knowledge of ſuch
points? And Proteſtants, who hold Scripture to
be the only Rule of fayth, vſe meanes of conferring Text, conſulting the Originals, Prayer,
&c. for attayning the true meaning of Scripture; and yet you will not grant, that your
fayth is fallible : becauſe you will ſay, it doth
not rely vpon thoſe ſaid fallible meanes, but finally (as you apprehend) it reſts in the word
of God. And if any Catholique Author equall
the definitions of the Church with the holy

Scri-

(s) *In Aſſert.*
art. 29.

Scripture, his meaning is, that both the one, and the other, are so infallible, that they cannot deliuer any vntruth. For in other respects we grāt many singular Prerogatiues to the holy Scripture, more then to the definitions of Councels, as may partly be seen in (t) *Bellarmine*.

27. Your obiection that the great *Councell* (u) of *Chalcedon* corrected *the Second of Ephesus*, and that *S. Augustine* sayth, *Prouinciall Councels* (w) *may be corrected by Plenary, and Plenary Councels, the former, by the latter*, hath beene answered a hundred times; and I doubt not but that you haue read *Bellarmine* who (x) shewes that the second Councell of *Ephesus* proceeded vnlawfully, wherin *S. Flauianus* Bishop of *Constantinople* was murthered by the faction of *Dioscorus*, and the Popes Legates were driuen away, and finally the *Eutichian* Heresy was confirmed: for which causes that Councell was annulled by Pope *Leo*. You haue pickt out a pretty example to proue that lawfull Councels, confirmed by the Pope may erre. To the words of *S. Augustine, Bellarmine* answers, that (y) either they are vnderstood of vnlawfull Councels, such as was the second of *Ephesus*; or els, they are to be vnderstood of Questions concerning matter of fact, as whether *Cæcilianus* had deliuered vp the Bible; or finally, that latter Councels may be said to correct the former, because some decrees which concerne manners may by change of circumstāces proue inconuenient, although

in

(t) *De Conc. lib.2.cap.12.*
(n) *Pag.170.*

(w) *De Bapt. cont. Donat. lib.2.cap.3.*

(x) *De Conc. lib.1.cap.6.*

(y) *De Concil. lib.2.c. 7.§.Respondeo Primò.*

in the beginning, they were very holy and fit.
Which interpretation is gathered out of *S. Au-*
guſtine himſelfe, who ſayth: That Councels may
be corrected, when *Experience* doth manifeſt
ſomething which before did not appeare. Now,
experience hath no place in vniuerſall doctrines,
but in particular facts, or lawes, which reſpect
particular circumſtāces of time, and place &c.
Your ſecond Citation in your Margent out of
S. Auguſtine, (a) whoſe words you did not recite, *Bellarmine* anſweres in the place which I
haue cited now. And heertofore I haue declared at large in what ſenſe, and vpon what occaſion, and reaſon, *S. Auguſtine* againſt the *Do-*
natiſts made recourſe to Scripture alone.

    26. You begin to impugne the Popes in-
fallibility, by ſaying, that *Charity-Miſtaken*
meanes by *his infallible Church, only the Pope.*
Which ſaying of yours doth well declare how
fallible your affirmations are. And that if the
Pope define that to be white, which the eye
iudges to be blacke, it muſt be ſo admitted by
vs, you pretend to proue, out of I know not
what papers of the Ieſuites found in *Padua,* in
witnes wherof you alleage *Paulus Soarpius,* a ſeditious, ſcandalous, and condemned Author: &
we muſt by no meanes belieue you without better proofe. You cite alſo out of *Bellarmine,* theſe
words: *If he* (the Pope) *ſhould(b) erre, and com-*
mand the practiſe of vice, or forbid the exerciſe of
vertue, the Church were bound in conſcience to be-
                           lieue

(a) *Lib.* 3. çōt. *Maxim.*

(b) *De Rom. Pont. lib.* 4. *c.* 5. §. *Quod antem,*

lieue vices to be good , and vertues to be bad. Who
would not thinke by thefe words of *Bellarmine,*
as you corrupt him, that indeed we might belieue Vice to be good, and Vertue il ? The direct
contrary wherof he affirmes; and from thence
infers that the Pope, whom the Church is obliged to obey as her Head , and Supreme Paftor,
cannot erre in decrees of manners prefcribed
by him , to the whole Church . Thefe be his
words. *If the Pope did erre in commanding vices, or*
forbidding Vertue, the Church were bound to belieue
that Vice is good and Vertue ill, vnles she would finne
againft her confcience. For in doubtfull things , the
Church is bound to fubiect herfelfe to the Iudgment of
the Pope, and to do what he commands , and not to
do what he forbids: and left she should finne agaynft
her confcience , she is bound to belieue, that what he
commands is good & that what he forbids is ill. For
the auoyding of which inconuenience. he concludes, that the Pope cannot erre in *Decrees con-*
cerning manners, by forbidding Vertue , or commanding Vice . If one fhould proue that Scripture cannot erre in things concerning manners , becaufe otherwife Chriftians , who are
bound to belieue whatfoeuer the Scripture
fayth, fhould be obliged to belieue Vertue to be
ill, and Vice to be good ; would you infer that
indeed we are to belieue, Vertue to be ill , and
Vice to be good? Or rather that indeed Scripture could not propofe or command any fuch
thing? This is that which *Bellarmine* fayth. But

your

your felfe is he, according to whofe principles
we might be obliged to imbrace vice &c. For
fince you affirme, that the *authority* (d) *of Gene-* (d) *Pag.*16
rall Councels is immediately deriued from Chrift, and
that, their *Decrees bind all perfons to externall Obe-*
dience; and feing you hold that they may erre
pernicioufly both in fayth, and manners; What
remaines but that we muft be obliged, euen by
authority immediately deriued from Chrift himfelfe,
to erre with the Councell, and at left externally
imbrace Vice.

29. You come afterward to difcourfe thus:
Thefe men (e) *deale not plainely with vs, when they* (e) *Pag.*
pretend often in their difputations againft vs, Scri-
ptures, Fathers, Councells and the Church; fince in
the iffue their finall and infallible argument for their
fayth, is only the Popes Authority. It were indeed a
happy thing, and a moft effectuall way to end
all Controuerfies if people would fubmit themfelues to fome vifible liuing Iudge, by whom
they might be inftructed, & by whom it might
be declared who alledge Scriptures, and Fathers
right or wrong. Which fince you, and your Brethren refufe to do, no wonder, if we be con-
ftrained to alledge Scriptures, and Fathers, as
you likewife do, though you fay, that Scripture
is infaillible, and that all Controuerfies muft be
decided by it alone. Befides, though the Pope be
infallible, yet he is not fo alone, as if he did exclude all other infallible meanes: for Scriptures,
Generall Councells, and the Confent of the

whole

whole Catholique Church are alfo infallible.
And therfore (as I was faying) it is no wonder
that we alledge other Arguments befides the
decrees of Popes alone. For fince in our difputes with you, we abound with all kind of arguments, why fhould we not make vfe therof?
And if you will know the reafon why Councells be gathered to the great good of the
Church, notwithftanding the Popes infallibility, you may read *Bellarmine*, who giues (f) the
reafon therof. I hope you will grant that *S. Peter*
was infallible, and yet he thought good to gather a Councel, *Act.* 15. for greater fatisfaction
of the faythfull, and to take away all occafions
of temptation in the weaker Chriftians. What
eftimation Antiquity made of the Popes Authority I haue fhewed heertofore. And if fome
who haue written *Pleas*, or *Prefcriptions* againft
Heretiques, do not *without more adoe, appeale* (g)
all Heretiques to the Popes Tribunall, you haue no
caufe to wonder; fince commonly the firft error
of all Heretiques, is to oppofe the Pope, and the
Church of Rome, and therfore they muft be
conuinced by other Arguments. *Tertullian*
in his *Prefcriptions* againft Heretiques doth particularly aduife, and direct that Heretiques are
not to be admitted to difpute out of Scripture,
and that it is but in vaine to feeke to conuince
them by that meanes: and yet you hold that the
Scripture is not only infallible, but the fole Rule
alfo of fayth: How then do you infer againft

(f) *De Rom.*
Pontif. lib.
4. cap. 7 §.
Refpondeo
3d.

(g) *Pag.* 173.

V s

vs, that if the Pope be infallible, *Tertullian*
fhould haue appealed all Heretiques to his
Tribunall; fince he doth not appeale them to
Scripture, which yet he belieued to be infallible. And neuertheles the two Authors whom
you cite, *Tertullian*, and *Vincentius Lyrinenfis*
fpeake, as much in aduantage of the Pope and
Church of Rome, as can be imagined. *If (* fayth
Tertullian) thou liue (h) *neere Italy, thou haft the* (h) *Pref-
Citty of Rome, from thence Authority is neere at cript. cap.*
hand, euen to vs (Africans.) *A happy Church, into 36.*
which the Apoftles haue powred their whole doctrine
together with their bloud. And *Vincentius Lyrinen-*
fis cals the (i) Pope, and Church of *Rome,* the
Head, and other Bifhops as *S. Cyprian* from the (i) *In fuo*
South, S. Ambrofe from the *North* &c. and others *Com.*
from other places, the *fides* of the world. And I
cited thefe words out of him before, who fpea-
king of Rebaptization, faith: *Then* (k) *the bleffed* (k) *Jn Com.*
Stephen refifted, together with, but before his Collea- *part. 1.*
gues, iudging it as I conceiue, a thing worthy of him,
that he should furmount them as much in Fayth, as
he did in the authority of his place. Of the oppofition of fome particular men to the Pope we
haue fpoken already, and in your faying that his
Authority hath beene oppofed by Generall
Councels we will not belieue you, til you bring
better proofe. That the diuifions of the Eafterne
from the Latine Church proceeded from the
ambition, & pretenfions of the Bifhop of *Rome,*
you proue by the Authority of *Nilus,* a Schif-

mati-

matique, an Heretique , and a profeſſed enemy
of the Church of *Rome*, and of Proteſtants alſo,
vnles they haue a mind to belieue that the holy
Ghoſt proceeds not from the Sonne. And how
can *Nilus* affirme as he doth, that the Pope refuſeth to haue the groundes of that diſſenſion fay-
rely heard and diſcuſſed in a generall Councell?
For vnder *Vrbanus* the ſecond a Councell was
held at *Barium* in *Apulia*, where the Græcian Biſhops being preſent, were conuicted of errour,
in denying God the holy Ghoſt to proceed from
God the Sonne, *S. Anſelme* (l) our Primate of
Canterbury being the chiefe diſputant in the
behalfe of the Latins. Whereupon the Græcian
Emperour that then ruled *Alexius Comnenus* became Catholicke, and cauſed the Græcian Biſhops to hold Communion with the Roman
Church ſo long as he liued, as *Baronius* ſheweth.
And greater cauſe I haue to wonder, that you
would now reuiue this Cauill of *Nilus*. For
to ſay nothing of the Councell of *Lyons* in
France vnder *Gregory* the tenth, where the Pa-
triarke of *Conſtantinople* was preſent , and o-
ther Hierarchs of *Greece* to the number of 40. beſides innumerable Biſhops and Prelates of the
Latins, being more then a thouſand in all, ſome
Kings being therein perſon , and all by their
Embaſſadors, namely *Michael Paleologus* , and
Andronicus his Sonne Emperours of the Eaſt,
in whoſe name their Embaſſadours recanted &
abiured all errors againſt the Roman Church,
namely

(l) *Anſelm.*
lib. de pro-
ceſ. Spirit.
ſanct.

Baronius
tom. 12. An.
1118.

Baron. ad
an. 1274.

namely that about the Holy Ghoſt: to preter-
mit (I ſay)this inſtance, who doth not know,
that in the generall Councell at *Florence*, the
matter was debated vnder *Eugenius* the fourth,
where the Græcians with their Emperour ,
and their Patriarch, and the Legates of three
other Patriarches, and the *Armenians*, and the
Deputyes of the *Ethiopians* were preſent , and a
perfeƈt concord was then made: from which
the Greekes departing afterward, were ſubdued
and made ſlaues to the Turke. And that they
might ſee the cauſe of their deſtruƈtion to be
pertinacity in their Errour about the Holy
Ghoſt, vpon the very feaſt of Pentecoſt (as *Bel-*
larmine proueth) the Citty of Conſtantinople *Lib.* 2. *de*
was taken, their Emperour killed , and their *Chriſto.cap.*
Empyre extinguiſhed. And it is well knowne 30.
that the true cauſe of their diſſenſion , whereupon a ſeparation at laſt enſued, was the Controuerſy between *Ignatius* lawfull Patriarch of
Conſtantinople , whom the Pope ſtill kept in his
Communion, and *Photius* an ambitious Intru-
der into the Patriarchate , by ſtrength of the
Imperiall Power. Which Schiſme hath enlarged
it ſelfe, by addition of the hereſy, about the pro-
ceſsion of the holy Ghoſt. For want of better
matter, you bring heere that old Obieƈtion a-
bout the Councels of *Conſtance* and *Baſil*, defining that the Councell is aboue the Pope. The
Anſwere whereof you may read in *Bellarmine,* *(m) De Cõ.*
that (m) the Popes who were depoſed, were in *lib.* 2. *c.* 19.

time

time of Schifme, when it was not knowne who
was the true Pope; in which cafe the Church
hath power to prouide herfelfe of an vndoubted Paftour : To fay nothing that two of thofe
Popes voluntarily renounced their pretence.
As for the decree of the Councell of *Conftance,*
that all ought to obey a Generall Councell ; he
anfweres, that either it is meant for time of
Schifme, or if it be vniuerfall, that the Councell
could not make any fuch definition of fayth,
becaufe it was neuer confirmed by the Pope,
for as much as concernes that point. And the
Councell of *Bafill* was in that particular exprefly repealed by diuers Popes; and the whole
Church receiued *Eugenius* as true Pope, who
yet was depofed by that Councell. To difproue
the Popes infallibility, you cite *Victoria* faying :

(m) *Relect.*
4.de Poteft.
Papæ &
Conc. prop.
12. ad fin.

Giue me (n) *Clements, Linus, Siluefters, and I will
leaue all to their pleafure. But to fpeake no worfe of
latter Popes, they are much inferiour to thofe ancient
Ones.* But you alleage this Author according to
your wonted manner, that is, very vnfaithfully. For he in that place fpeakes only of Difpen-
fations in Lawes, the facility and frequency
wherof *Victoria* diflikes in thefe latter times;
Which being wholy matter of *Fact,* doth nothing preiudice the Popes Infallibility for
points of *Fayth.*

(o) *Pag. 176.*

30.　To proue that there is nothing but vncertainty in prouing the Popes infallibility, you
alledge fome places out of *Bellarmine,* but with
fo

fo great confufion and fraude , that they ferue
only to proue the certainty of your ill dealing .
Bellarmine diftinguifhes two Queftions: The
one, whether *S. Peter* had any Succeffor in being
head of the Church , and this he fayth is moft
certayne , and *De iure diuino* , or by diuine inftitution. The other ; whether it be *de iure diuino* ,
or of diuine inftitution , that *S. Peters* Succeffour
muft be the particular Bifhop of *Rome,* and this
he fayth is not fo certayne (though it be true)
becaufe if *S. Peter* had placed his Sea in fome o-
ther Citty, or els had chofen no particular Citty at all ; yet his Succeffour had been , *iure diuino,* Head of the Church ; howbeyt in that cafe,
he had not beene the particular Bifhop of *Rome* .
Neuertheles , becaufe *S. Peter* did in fact , choofe
Rome , it is vpon that fuppofall a matter of
fayth , that the Bifhop of *Rome,* & *S. Peters* Succeffour is all one . As for example by the Law
of God all lawfull Superiours are to be obeyed,
and therefore though it be not of diuine infti-
tutió , that this or that man fhould be fuperiour ;
yet fuppofing that in fact he be Superiour , the
general diuine Law pitches, & faftens vpó him ,
& obligeth vs to obey him in particular . This
being prefuppofed , let vs now heare what you
alledge out of (q) *Bellarmine. S. Peter fate many
yeares Bifhop of Rome, & there he died* You chãge
the very Queftió. *Bellarmines* words in the Title
of the Chapter are : *Petrum Roma vfque ad mor-
tem Epifcopum fuiffe. That S. Peter was Bishop of*
Rome

(q) *De Rom.
Pont. lib. 2.
cap* 4. §. *Re-
ftant.*

Rome till his death. And he explaines his meaning to be, That *S. Peter was Bishop of Rome, and that he kept that Bishoprick till his death* : which is a different thing from what you say; That *S. Peter* sate *many yeares Bishop of Rome, and there he died.* For he might haue been many yeares Bishop of Rome, and also died at *Rome,* and yet not died Bishop of Rome ; as one may be Bishop of London for some yeares, and dy at London, & yet not dye Bishop of London. No w *Bellarmine* sayth, that *S. Peter* died Bishop of *Rome,* which indeed was the maine point; and proues, that the Bishop of Rome is *S. Peters* successour; wheras to dye at *Rome* is accidentall to his being Bishop of *Rome,* and in fact diuers Bishops of *Rome* died in *France,* and els where. But let vs goe on. You say that the first reason by which *Bellarmine* proues that *S. Peter* died Bishop of *Rome,* is so weake , that himselfe sayth only *suadere videtur, it seemes to perswade.* This *Bellarmine* sayth only of one reason, besides which he bringeth diuers other demonstrations : neither is it necessary for the certainty of any truth, that euery reason for it , be euident. And it is the doctrine of Philosophers, that the best methode is, to begin with probable Arguments, and then to ascend to demonstrations. Moreouer in this very subiect *Vdalricus Velenus* , a Lutheran, wrote a Booke to proue that *S. Peter* was neuer at *Rome,* and to that purpose he brings eighteen reasons , which he calls *Persuasions* , & yet he holds them

for

for euident *Demonstrations*. If then *Bellarmine,* out of his great modesty say, that his first reason seemes to *persuade*, must you thence inferre, that it doth not *demonstrate* ? And indeed it is a very good , and solid argument. After this you go forward , and cite *Bellarmine* saying : *There God comanded him to fixe his Chaire , & to leaue his full Power to his heyres and Succeßours, the Popes.* And then you adde: But what certainty of this ? *Indeed (* saith *Bellarmine)it is no where (* r *) expreſſed in Scripture, that the Pope(* you should add *of Rome,* as *Bellarmine* hath it *) succeeds Peter , & therefore happily it is not of diuine right that he succeeds him ;* Yet, *it is not improbable, that (* s *) God commanded him to fasten his Seate at Rome , and it may be deuoutly so belieued .* And it may be truly belieued, that you corrupt *Bellarmine. First ,* when you speake of Popes, you leaue out, *of Rome,* in which word consisteth the maine point. For *Bellarmine* teaches, that it is most certaine, and *de iure diuino , that S. Peter* should haue Popes to succeed him, but he holdeth it not so certaine, whether it be of *diuine institution* , that his Succesſour should be Pope of *Rome ;* that is , haue his Seate fixed at *Rome,* although *de facto* it be there. *Bellarmines* wordes are : *It is not all one, that a thing be a point of fayth , and that it be of diuine institution. For it was not a diuine Law that S. Paul should haue a cloake, yet it is a point of fayth that S. Paul had a Cloake. Though then it be not expreſly contained in Scripture , that the Bishop of Rome should*

(r) *De Rom. Pont. lib. 2. cap.12.§.Obseruandum est tertio.*

(s) *Ibid. § Et quoniam.*

sue-

succeed S. Peter (thus far you goe, and leaue out the words immediately following, which explicate the whole matter :) *Yet it is euidently deduced out of Scripture that some must succeed S. Peter: but that he who succeeds him is the Bishop of Rome, we know by the Apostolicall Tradition of S. Peter; which Tradition, Generall Councels, Decrees of Popes, and Consent of Fathers, haue declared, as heerafter shall be demonstrated.* And according to this cleere explication he said a little before: *Because S. Marcellus Pope in his Epistle ad Antiochenos, writes that S. Peter came to Rome by the Commandment of our Lord ; and S. Ambrose* (t) *and S. Athanasius* (u) *affirme, that S. Peter suffered Martyrdome at Rome by the commandment of Christ ; it is not improbable, that our Lord did also expresly command that S. Peter should so settle his Seate at Rome, that the Bishop of Rome should absolutely succeed him. But howsoeuer this be, at left this manner of Succession proceeds not from the first institution of the Popedome, which is deliuered in Scripture.* Do you not see what *Bellarmine* deliuers for certaine, & what for lesse certaine? It is certaine that *S. Peter* must haue Successours; it is certaine that in fact his Successour is the Bishop of *Rome*: but it is not so certaine, that by diuine institution, his Successour is the Bishop of Rome, but that might proceed from the act of *S. Peter*, who actually liued and died Bishop of Rome, though he might haue chosen some other particular Diocesse. These things *Bellarmine* deliuers very cleerly;

(t) *In Orat. cont. Auxentium.*

(u) *In Apolog. pro fuga sua.*

cleerly; but you do fo inuolue his words, as one
would belieue, that he held it for vncertaine,
whether actually the Pope of *Rome* be *S. Peters*
Succefsour, or whether it be certaine, and of diuine inſtitution, that *S. Peter* left any Succef-
four at all: both which are plainely againſt his
meaning, and exprefse words.

31. Your other obiections are fo old and
triuiall, that they deferue no Anfwere : I fayd
already, that in time of Schiſme the Church
hath power to declare, or elect a true and vndoubted Pope; and in the meane tyme God in
his Prouidence can gouerne his Church without new definitions of Popes, of which there
is not alwayes fo precife neceſſity, as that the
Church may not fubſiſt without the for a time ;
as for three hundred yeares from the Apoſtles
tymes, ſhe was without any one Generall
Councell; and as the Iewes for two thoufand
yeares were without Scripture. If any ſhould
enter fymonically, & be accepted by the Churh
as Pope, God will eyther not permit him to define any matter of fayth, or els will aſſiſt him
not to erre pernicioufly, not for his owne fake
but in refpect of the Church which cannot be
ledde into errour, as ſhe might, if that reputed
Pope could define a falfhood, becaufe the members are obliged to conforme themfelues to one
whome they efteeme their Head. And you your
felfe muſt fay the fame. For fince all the fpirituall Power, and Iurifdiction of your firſt Prela-

tes, was deriued from *Rome*, you muſt affirme, that a Pope accepted for ſuch by the Church, is ſufficiently enabled for all neceſſary acts and functions, notwithſtanding that ſecret impediment : For otherwiſe you might endanger the Authority of your owne Prelates. And the ſame you muſt in proportion ſay, of all publique Magiſtrates. The ſame anſwere ſerues to your other Obiectiō, that we are not ſure whether he that is elected Pope be baptized. For it belongs to Gods prouidence, not to permit any whome the Church hath elected for her head, to erre perniciouſly, though indeed your ſuppoſitions are neuer to be admitted; but we are to belieue that whoſoeuer in a tyme free from Schiſme, is accepted by the Church for true Pope, is ſuch indeed. And I wonder you doe not reflect, that theſe obiections are alſo againſt your owne Biſhops. Or if you ſay, that your ſpirituall Iuriſdiction comes from the Temporall Prince, the ſame difficulty wil remaine cōcerning him. For I ſuppoſe you will not ſay that one who is not baptized, and conſequently not a Chriſtian, can meerly by vertue of his Temporall Power giue ſpirituall Iuriſdiction. And though you ſay that it is not want of *intention* in the Miniſter which can make voyde the Sacrament of Baptiſme; yet you will not deny, but that there may be other *eſſentiall* defects, hindring the validity therof: as for example, if by error the water be ſo mingled, that it be not

elemen-

elementall water ; or if the forme of the words
in Baptifme be not pronounced entierely &c.
For in your forme of Publique Baptifme it is
faid: *That water, and, in the name of the Father, of
the Sonne, and of the Holy Ghoſt, are effentiall parts
of Baptifme*: and this you haue gained by your
obiections. And finally if your doctrine be true
that *intention* in the Minifter is not necefsary,
the Pope cannot (according to your doctrine)
want Baptifme for want of due intention in
the Minifter. You proceed.

32. *No Papiſt* (x) *in Europe (excepting only* (x) *pag.* 180.
*thofe few, that ſtand by, and heare his Holynes when
he giues out his Oracles) can be infallibly fure what it
is which he hath defined.* A goodly Obiection ! As
if there were no meanes to know what one
fayth, vnles he heare him fpeake. For ought I
know you neither haue feene the Pope, nor
Rome, will you therfore thinke, you are not
fure that there is a Pope, and *Rome*? Haue you all
this while fpoken againſt a thing in the aire,
while you impugned the Pope? Can no body
know what the Apoſtles fpake, or wrote, except them who were prefent at their preaching,
or writing? Or can no body be fure that the Bible is truly printed vnles he himfelfe correct the
Print ? I grant that you who deny the ertain-
ty of Traditions, haue caufe to belieue nothing
befide what you fee, or heare. But we acknowledge Traditions, and fo muſt you, vnles you
will queſtion both the preaching, and writing

of

of the Apoftles. And befide hearing or feeing,
there are other meaning, as Hiftory, Letters,
true Relations of many , and the like . And
thus we haue anfwered all your obiections a-
gainft the fallibility of the Church , Councels,
and Pope , without defcending to particular
Controuerfies , which are difputed off among
Catholiques without breach of fayth,or Vnity.
But heere I muft put you in mind , that you
haue left out many things in the fixt Chapter of
Charity Miftaken againft your promife, notwithstanding that to anfwere it alone,you haue
imployed your third, fourth, and fifth *Section.*
You haue omitted (*pag.44.*) what it is that maketh men to be of the fame Religiō : & (*pag.46.*)
diuers differences betwixt you , & vs ; as about
the Canon of Scripture; fiue Sacraments; neceffity of Baptifme, and reall prefence; vnwritten
Traditions; Primacy of *S.Peter* ; Iudge of Controuerfies; Prayer *to* Saints,and *for* the foules in
Purgatory: and fo, that we are on both fides refolued to perfift in thefe differéces &c. Why did
you not fay one word to all thefe particulars?
Why did you not anfwere to his example of the
Quartadecimani, who were ranked for Heretiques, although their error was not *Fundamen-*
tall in your acception? as alfo to his example of
rebaptizing Heretiques, for which the *Dona-*
tifts were accounted Heretiques, although the
errour be not of it felfe fundamentall ? The
fame I fay of his Example, drawne from the
Noua-

Nouatian Heretiques : And of his reaſon, that if
diſobedience to the Church were not the rule
wherby hereſies, & ſchiſmes muſt be knowne,
it were impoſſible to conclude what were an
Hereſy, or *Schiſme:* As alſo to his Aſſertion proued out of *S.Thomas,* that error againſt any one
reuealed truth deſtroyeth all fayth &c. But neceſſity hath no law, you were forced to diſſemble what you knew not how to anſwere.

CHAP. VI.

THIS *Section* is chiefly emploied in relating ſome debates betweene Catholiques ; and is
ſoone anſwered , by diſtinguiſhing betweene a *potentiall*
and *actuall* Vnity ; that is, we
deny not, but that Controuerſies may ariſe a-
mongſt Catholique Doctours, as well for matters concerning practiſe, as ſpeculation : But
ſtill we haue a *Iudge* to whoſe known determinations, we hold our ſelues obliged to ſubmit
our vnderſtanding, and will : whereas your debates muſt of neceſſity be endles, becauſe you
acknowledge no ſubiectiō to any viſible liuing
Iudge,

Iudge, whome you hold to be infallible in his determinations. All the inſtances which you alledge agaynſt vs, proue this , and no more. For ſome of them concerne points not expreſ‑ ly defined by the Church : Others touch vpon matters of faſt, and as it were ſuites of Law in the Catholique Clergy of England , wherein you ought rather to be edifyed , then to obieſt thē as any way preiudicial to the *Vnity* of faith, becauſe Pope *Clement* the 8. in his tyme, and our holy Father *Vrban the* VIII. could , and did , by their decrees end thoſe Controuerſies, & forbid writing Bookes on all ſides.

2 . I wonder you will , like ſome of the country Miniſters, tell vs that we haue *enlarged the Creed of Chriſtians one moyty.* And to proue it, you cite the Bull of *Pius Quintus* , which is properly no *Creed*, but a Profeſſion of our faith. And if this be to enlarge the *Creed*, your Church in her 39. *Articles*, hath enlarged the twelue Articles of the Apoſtles *Creed*, more then one moyty thrice told. For the Church makes no new Articles of fayth, as you muſt likewiſe ſay in defence of your Church‑Articles. Was the Creed of *Nice* , or of *S. Athanaſius &c.* new Creeds, becauſe they explicate old truths by a new word of *Homouſion* , or *Conſubſtantiall?* It is pretty that you bring *Pappus* and *Flaccus*, flat Heretiques, to proue our many Contradi‑ ſtions . Your comparing the Decrees of the Sacred Councell of *Trent*, which you ſay , that
both

both the Dominicans and Iefuites pretend to
fauour their contrary opinions, to the *Deuill in*
the old oracles, is by your leaue wicked; & which
you might vpon the fame pretenfe as blafphe-
moufly apply to the holy Scriptures, which all
Heretiques, though neuer fo contrary in themfelues, do alledge as fauouring them : Which is
a fufficient Argument to fhew againft Proteftants, that no writing, though neuer fo perfect,
can be a fufficient *Iudge* to decide Controuerfies. And you were ill aduifed, to make this obiection againft the Councell of *Trent*, fince in
his Maiefties Declaration before the 39. *Arti-*
cles, printed 1631. it is faid : *We take comfort in*
this, that euen in thofe curious points in which the
prefent differences lye, men of all forts, take the Arti-
cles of the Church of England to be for them. And it
is worthy the obferuation, that the difference
betwixt the *Dominicans* and *Iefuits*, (who as
you fay do both pretend to haue the Councell
of *Trent* on their fides) is concerning a Queftion, which you conceiue to be the fame with
that which is difputed among Proteftants, and
in which Proteftants *of all forts take the Articles of*
the Church of England to be for them. Your demand, why the Pope determines not that Controuerfy betwixt the *Dominicans* and *Iefuits*,
might as well be made againft the whole Ancient Church, which did not determine all
Controuerfies at once, nor on a fudden, but after long, and mature deliberation, fooner, or
latter,

latter, as occaſion did require In the meane
time, the Pope hath commanded, that neither
part cenſure the other; and his Command is
moſt religiouſly obſerued by them, with a readines to ſubmit their Iudgment, when the holy
Ghoſt ſhall inſpire him to decree it, one way or
other. And who aſſured you, that the point
wherin theſe learned men differ, is a reuealed
truth, or capable of definition, or is not rather
(b) *Pag.*112. (as you ſpeake) *by plaine* (b) *Scripture indeter-*
minable, or by any other Rule of fayth.

3. It is worthy to be obſerued, that after you
had told vs that the diſſentions of the Church
of *Rome* are of greater importance, then any a-
mong the Reformed; you can name only two,
which may haue any colour of difficulty, the
reſt being meere Scholaſticall diſputations in
obſcure points for the better explanations of
the Myſteries of our Fayth againſt Infidels, and
Heretiques. The one concernes the Popes Authority: And in particular his Superiority a-
boue Councells; to which we haue anſwered
more then once: & all Catholiques agree that
he is the Vicar of Chriſt, the Succeſſour of *S. Pe-*
ter, & the Viſible Head of the Church, to whom
all particular perſons, and Churches are ſubiect. The other, is touching a Contrariety bet-
(c) *Adam.* ween *Sixtus* 5. and *Clement* the 8. about the E-
Tanner.tom. dition of the Bible: which obiection, *Adamus*
3. diſp. 1. q. *Tannerus* anſweres (c) ſo fully, that I haue
4. dub. 6. n. thought good to ſet downe his words, wherin
364. he

he affirmes, That *this Queſtion hauing been diſpu-*
ted in the Vniuerſity of Ingolſtad, for being ſatisfied
concerning the truth, he wrote to F. Ferdinandus Al-
berus, (who afterward was Vicar Generall of
the Society of I E S V S,)and he by letters dated 28. Aug. 1610. anſwered in theſe words,
which I haue thoght beſt to ſet down in Latin,
as they lye(the ſumme of them being this, that
the Decree of Sixtus was neuer ſufficiently pro-
mulgated;)that ſuch as haue not the Booke it
ſelfe, may read them heere. *Circa Biblia Sixtina,*
poſt diligentem inquiſitionem & diſcuſsionem, hanc
denique reſponſionem dederunt ij, qui huic rei incum-
bebant, qua omnis tollitur difficultas, & cui omnes
meritò acquieſcent. Reſponſio ſic habet. Certum eſt,
Bullam de ijs Biblijs non fuiſſe promulgatam; cuius
rei certiſsimum indicium eſt, in Regiſtro huiuſmodi
promulgationem non reperiri : & Illuſtriſsimus Car-
dinalis Bellarminus teſtatur, ſe cùm ex Gallia Romam
redijſſet, à pluribus Cardinalibus audiuiſſe, Bullam illã
non fuiſſe promulgatam, & id quidem illi ſe certiſsi-
mè ſcire affirmabant. And the ſame *F. Alberus* addeth: *Sciat præterea R.V. hæc eadem ex S. D. N.*
(Pope *Paul* the 5.) *habita fuiſſe, vt tutò his adhære-*
re liceat, & oporteat. And in his letters dated the
4. *of September* in the ſame yeare 1610. for confirmation of the ſame matter, he adioyneth
theſe words: *Item P. Azor, eo ipſo tempore, quo*
cæperunt (typis) *publicari illa Biblia, cùm inſtarent*
aliqui, Papam poſſe errare, quia videbatur iam erraſſe
de facto in Biblijs; Reſpondit publicè P. Azor, Bullam

illam

illam non fuiſſe publicatam , quamuis in impreſsione
legeretur ſubſcriptio Curſorum; nam hoc factum fuiſſe
per anticipationem Typographi, ita iubente Potifice, ne
impreſsio tardaretur. Huius rei teſtis eſt P. Andræas
Eudæmon · Ioannes , qui tunc aderat diſputationi .
Thus he. And befids all this , *Po. Sixtus* himſelfe
marking that *diuers things had crept in which nee-*
ded a ſecod Reuiew, had declared that the whole worke
should be re-examined , though he could not do it by
reaſon he was preuented by death , as is affirmed in
the Preface before the Bible ſet forth by Pope
Clement the 8.

    4. If any Catholique Writers teach abſo-
lutely, that it is ſufficient to belieue with an implicite faith alone, you know and acknowledge
(*pag.* 198. and 71. and 241.) they are reiected
by the reſt. And yet that doctrine is neither ſo
abſurd , nor dangerous as the opinion of *M.*
Hooker, and *D. Morton* as you relate, with much
ſhew of fauouring them ; Who yet not only
grant, that one may be ignorant of ſome *funda-*
mentall Articles, but alſo may deny them, without ceaſing to be a member of the Church: No,
nor ſo *hurtfull* , as your owne doctrine , who
muſt (if your diſtinction of points be to any
purpoſe)teach that an Error againſt a reuealed
truth in points not *fundamentall ,* is not damnable. Yea after you haue ſet downe the Creed, *as*
(d) Pag. 241. *a perfect ſummary* (d) *of thoſe fundamentall truths,*
wherin conſiſts the Vnity of fayth , and all men are
bound actually to know neceſsitate præcepti; you add,
                                       but

but happily not so, necessitate medij, vel finis ; so that
vpon the matter (speaking of things to be belieued *necessitate medij*, it will not be easy for you to
free your selfe , euen from that for which you
impugne the Authors who do at least say , that
we must belieue all Articles implicitely , in the
explicite beliefe of the Article of the *Catholique Church*: and yet that Article you do not belieue as you ought, while you deny her vniuerfall Infallibility in propounding diuine Truths.

5. I will end with a notorious falsification
which I find almost in the end of this your *Section*. For, in your first Edition (*pag.* 65. *Marg.*)
you cite *Tanner* saying (*in Colloquio Ratisbon.
Sess.* 9.) *If the Prelates of the Church did erre in defining any doubt, Christian people by vertue of such a
gouernement , might , yea ought to erre.* And
these words you bring to proue, *that whatsoeuer the Pope , assisted with some few of his
Cardinalls and Prelats , shall define, that must be
receiued though it be falfe and erroneous* ; wherein you difcouer eyther intollerable ignorance,
or fupine negligence , or willfull malice . For
Tannerus in that place proues the infallibility of
the Church , that is , of the Prelates of the
Church , becaufe the people are obliged to belieue their Paftours; and fince it is abfurd to fay,
that they can be obliged to belieue that which
is erroneous , it followes that the Prelates of
Gods Church cannot define any errour: yea, in
expreffe termes he fayth; (f) *I fay not , that the* (f) *Fol.* 106.
Pope

Pope is to be obeyed, when he erres ; but fay only, that if the Superiour might erre, & yet were endued with publique authority, the people might be led to errour. And in this very fame manner, you falfify *Bellarmine* in your fecond Edition (*pag.* 172) fpeaking to the fame purpofe, as I fhewed in this fecond (g) Part. Laftly, I muft put you in mind that you leaue out the difcourfe of *Charity Miftaken* (*pag.* 64.) wherein he anfwers the vulgar obiection, that we haue differences among vs of *Thomifts, Scotifts, Benedictins* &c. and yet (*pag.* 84.) you bring this very fame obiection as frefhly as if it had neuer beene anfwered.

(g) *Cap.* 5. *num.* 48.

CHAP.

CHAP. VII.

HE maine points treated in your *seauenth Section* are : the diftinction of points *funda-mentall* , and that the *Creed* is a perfect Summary of all fundamentall points of fayth. In anfwere whereof I employed the *third,*and *fourth* Chapter of the *Firſt Part.*

2. You fay , that the *Rule of fayth,* (a) *being cleerly , but diffufedly fet downe in the Scriptures , hath beene afterward fummed vp in the Apoſtles Creed :* and in the Margent you cite *S. Thomas ,* as if he did affirme that the Rule of fayth is *cleerly* contayned in Scripture : Whereas he rather fayth the contrary in thefe words : *The Verities of fayth* (b *) are contayned in Scripture diffufedly, & in fome things obfcurely &c. fo that to draw the Verity of fayth out of Scripture , there is required long ſtudy and exercife .* Is this to fay the Scripture is cleere, euen for *fundamentall* points?

3. I fee not how you can proue that the Creed containes all fundamentalls , out of thofe Letters called *Formata, formed* ; the manner whereof is fet downe by (c *) Baronius .* Among other things

(a) Pag. 216.

(b) 2.2. q.t. art. 9. ad 1.

(c) Ann. 325. num. 44. & 407. num. 3. apud Spond.

things one was, to write the firſt letter in Gre-
ke of the Father , the Sonne , and the holy
Ghoſt; & of *S.Peter* : the one, faith *Baronius*, being to profeſſe their fayth againſt the *Arrian*
Heretiques of thoſe times; the other , to ſhew
their Communion with the *Catholique Church* ;
becauſe he was eſteemed truly *Catholique* , who
was ioyned in Communion with the Succeſ-
four of *S.Peter*. And this *Baronius* proues out of
Optatus. Wherby it appeares that the intention
of thoſe *formed* Letters was not to expreſſe all
fundamentall points of fayth , but particularly
aymed at the *Arrians* : & beſides the Articles of
our *Creed*,they contained the Primacy of *S. Peter*,teaching vs that it is neceſſary for euery true
Catholique to be vnited with the Sea of *Peter.*
You cite the circular letters of *Sophronius* , *Taraſius* , *Pelagius* Patriarch of Rome , and *Photius*
of Conſtantinople,& for thoſe of *Pelagius* you
cite *Baronius* (Ann. 556. n.33.) But the letters
of *Pelagius* which *Baronius* ſets downe at large,
do not ſo much as mention the Apoſtles Creed :
and beſides the foure ſix *Generall Councels* , he
profeſſes to receiue *the Canons which the Sea Apoſtolique* (that is,the *Romane* Sea) hath receiued ,
the Epiſtles of the Popes, *Celeſtine* , *Sixtus, Leo,
Hilarius, Simplicius, Felix, Gelaſius* (the firſt) *A-
naſtaſius, Hormiſda , Iohn , Felix , Boniface, Iohn,
Agapetus* ; and then adds: *This is my Fayth.* I
wonder by what Logick you will inferre out
of theſe Letters,that the Creed alone, explaned
by

by the firſt Councells, containes all Articles of
fayth, ſince *Pelagius* profeſſes to receiue diuers
other things not contained in the Creed. *Sophronius* alſo (*Sext. Synod. Act.* 11.) in his letters
recites, and condemnes by name a very great
number of particular Hereſies, and Hetetiques
which are not mentioned in any of the *Creeds,*
and adds a full condemnation of all Heretiques. Neither are you more fortunate or faythfull in *Taraſius*, who in his *Confeſsion* of fayth
doth exprefly teach Inuocation of our blefsed
Lady, Angels, Apoſtles, Prophets, Martyrs,
Confeſſors &c. as alſo worſhip of *Images*, of
which he was a moſt zealous defender againſt
the *Iconomachi*, and was the chiefe in the *ſea-
uenth Synod,* who condemned thoſe Heretiques.
And ſince he was a mã famous both for ſanctity and miracles, we may note by the way, what
perſons they were who in ancient times oppoſed Proteſtants in thoſe *Iconomachi. Photius* likewiſe is by you misalledged. For he in his Letter
to Pope *Nicholas* ſet downe by *Baronius* (*ad Ann.*
859.) wherein he maketh a profeſſion of his
fayth, ſayth: *I receiue the ſeauen holy Generall
Counſels.* And hauing mentioned the ſix Councels, and what Heretiques were condemned by
them, he adds : *I alſo receyue that holy, and great
Councell, which was the ſecond held at Nice, which
caſt out, and ouercame, as filth, the Iconomachi, that
is, the oppugners of Images, who therfore were Chri-
ſtomachi, that is, oppugners of Chriſt, as alſo the im-*
pugners

pugners of Saints. Tell me now, I pray you, by
what art can you extract out of *Photius* his Letter, an argument to proue, that the Apoftles
Creed *as it was explaned in the Creeds of Nice, Con-*
stantinople, Ephefus, Chalcedon, and Athanafius,
comprehends a perfect Catalogue of fundamentall
truths, and implyes a full reiection of fundamentall
herefies (as you affirme *pag.* 217.) fince he exprefly profefses to receiue alfo the feauen Generall Councels, and that in particular, which condemned the *Impugners of Images,* that is, fuch as
your felfe, and other Proteftants are? Will you
grant that the Creed *implies a reiection* of the errour of the *Iconomachi,* or oppofers of Images, as
of a *Fundamentall* Herefie? Who will not wonder at your ill fortune in mis-alledging Authors? Yet I grant that fraude can neuer be imployed better, then to the difaduantage of him,
who vfeth it.

(d) *pag.* 220.   4. You fay, *(d)* to litle purpofe, that; *the*
(e) *Replique* *learned Cardinall Peron thinks* (e) *it probable, that*
?4p. 1. *the Article of the Catholique Church, and the Com-*
munion of Saints is all one, the latter being only an
Explication of the other. But what is this for your
purpofe, which was to proue that Articles not
expreffed in the Creed, cannot be reduced to
the Catholique Church ; *Becaufe no learned Ro-*
manift will fay that the new doctrines of the Romane
Church are contained in the Communion of
Saints? For Cardinall *Peron* only means, what
he fayth in exprefse words; That the Catholique

que Church confifts not in the fimple nūber of
the faithfull, euery one confidered a part; but in
the ioynt Communion alfo of the whole body
of the faythfull : From whence it doth not follow, that the Church is not fhe, who ought to
deliuer, and propound diuine Verities to vs as
fhe is the Mother and Teacher of all Chriftians.
Doth not *Charity* and Communion in the fpirit
of *Loue* include *Fayth*; and confequently fome
infallible Propounder of the Articles therof?
The Explication of *Azor*, concerning the Article of the Catholique Church which you
bring, maketh nothing in the world to your
purpofe. I haue told you already, that while we
belieue the *Vnity*, *Vniuerfality*, *Perpetuity*, *San-*
ctity of the Church, we ioyntly belieue her *In-*
fallibility, and freedome from all error in fayth.
But it is a meere flaunder to talke, as if we held
that fhe had *foueraigne and infallible power to pref-*
cribe, or define what fhe pleafes. You fay, that the
Creed is a fufficient Rule of fayth, *to which no-*
thing effentiall can be added, or may be detracted : As
if the addition of *Materiall* obiects, added any
thing to the *Effence* of faith, which is taken, not
from the materiall *Obiect*, or the things which
we belieue, but from the *Formall Obiect*, and
Motiue, which is the *Teftimony* of Almighty
God .

    5.   Though it were granted, that the Creed
being rightly vnderftood, contaynes all fundamentals, yet doth it not follow that Prote-

ſtants agree in them, both becauſe they may diſagree in the meaning of ſome of thoſe Articles ;
as alſo, becauſe diſagrement in any one point
of *Fayth* , though not fundamentall , cannot
ſtand with the *Vnity* , and ſubſtance of fayth,
euen in ſuch points as both of them belieue. As
for the Authour of the *Examen pacifique* , I haue
told you already, that he is no Catholique.

6. You ſet down your owne opinion about
the neceſſity of good workes, which you know
is contrary to many of your prime Brethren ;
yet, this I will not vrge for the preſent, bnt only ſay, that you forget that *Charity Miſtaken,* a-
mong other inſtances , alledges this to proue
that all points of fayth are not contained in the
Creed; to which you giue no anſwere at all, but
only tell vs what your owne opinion is. And
that it may appeare how you comply with your
promiſe, not to *omit without Anſwere any one thing
of moment*; heare what *Charity Miſtaken* ſayth to
this purpoſe, in theſe words. S. *Peter ſayth, that*
S. *Paul in his Epiſtles had written certaine things,
which were hard to be vnderſtood, and which the vnlearned, and vnſtable, did peruert to their owne deſtruction. S. Auſten declares vpon this place , that the
places miſvnderſtood concerned the doctrine of Iuſtification, which ſome miſconceiued to be by fayth alone.
And of purpoſe to countermine that error, he ſayth,
that S. Iames wrote his Epiſtle , and proued therin
that good works were abſolutely neceſſary to the act of
Iuſtification. Heereupon we may obſerue two things;*
the

the one, that an error in this point alone, is by the iudgment of S. Peter, to worke their deſtruction, who imbrace it: and the other, that the Apoſtles Creed which ſpeakes no one word therof, is no good rule, to let vs know all the fundamentall points of fayth. Did not all this diſcourſe deſerue ſome anſwere from one, who profeſſes *to omit nothing?*

7. But now you come to a new buſines, and ſay: *If the* (f) *Romane Church be not guilty of Manicheiſme; why is ſingle life called Chaſtity, and commended as an eminent degree of ſanctimony?* As if (forſooth) Marriage muſt be ill, becauſe a ſingle lyfe is better. Why doe you not lay the ſame aſperſion vpon our Sauiour Chriſt, who propoſed Chaſtity as one of the Euangelicall Councells; vpon *S. Paul,* who ſayth that (h) he who doth not marry, *melius facit, doth better;* & vpon the Ancient Fathers, who ſo highly extoll a ſingle life? You cannot be ignorant but that among diuers degrees of *Chaſtity,* Catholique Deuines do alſo place *Coniugall Chaſtity,* which they hold to be good, and meritorious, though yet inferiour to the other.

8. You goe on, and aske, why Marriage is ſayd to be incompatible with (i) *holines,* or with (k) *Gods fauour;* nay counted a (l) *pollution worſe then* (m) *whoredome?* With better reaſon we may ſay, why doe you peruert and corrupt Authours agaynſt your owne conſcience? *Innocentius,* whome you cite ſayth only: *It is not lawfull that they ſhould be admitted to ſacred functions* (that is,

(f) Pag. 239.

(h) *1. Cor.* 7.

(i) *Innocent. Papa diſt.* 82. *can. Proposuiſti.*
(k) *Idem.*
(l) *Bell. de Clericis cap.* 19. §. *Iam verò*
(m) *Coſter. Enchirid. c. de Cælib.*

holy

holy Orders) *who liue with their wiues, becaufe it is written:* Be holy, becaufe I am holy, *fayth our Lord.* Is this to fay abfolutely, that Marriage is incompatible with holines, becaufe it is incompatible with that holines which by the Churches Ordination is required in Priefts ? S. *Paul* fayth, that an *vnmaried woman* (n) *and a Virgin thinkes of things belonging to God, that she may be holy in body and foule.* Will you hence inferre, that the *Apoſtle* affirmes, Marriage to be incompatible with holines, becaufe it is incompatible with that peculiar holines, which Virginity is apt to breed? Thofe words, *Be holy, becaufe I am holy,* are taken out of *Leuit. chap.* 11. *verf.* 44. where the Iewes are forbidden to touch certaine beafts: and yet I hope you will not accufe God of *Manicheifme,* as if the eating of fuch beafts were incompatible with holines ? The other words alledged by *Innocentius, Thofe who are in flesh cannot pleafe God,* are vnderftood, as I faid, of that particular holines and pleafing of God, which is required in thofe that take holy Orders. To proue that *Bellarmine* accounts Marriage a *pollution,* you alleage out of him thefe words: (o) *Not only the Marriage of Prieſts, which is facriledge & not marriage; but euē the Marriage of holy perfons is not exercifed without a certaine pollution & turpitude.* But why doe you take pleafure in alledging Authours againft their owne meaning ? *Bellarmine* to proue how cōgruous & conueniēt it is, that Priefts fhould lead a fingle lyfe, after many

Autho-

(margin notes)
(n) I. Cor. 7.

(o) *De Clericis cap.* 19. §. *Iam verò.*

Authorities of Scriptures, Councels, & Fathers proues it also by reason it selfe, in regard that Marriage is a great impediment to Ecclesiasti-call functions; and beginning with the action of sacrificing, he sayth: Matrimony, as *Saint Hierome* saith *lib.* 1. *in Iouinian.* hinders the office of *sacrificing,* because there is required most great purity and sanctity therein, as *S. Chrysostome* in his *sixt Booke of Priesthood* doth declare; and it cannot *be denyed, but that in the act of Marriage there is mingled a certaine impurity and pollution, not which is sinne, but which arose from sinne. For though Caluin exclayme against Pope Siricius,* who is so ancient that he sate *an.* 385. *because he called the Marriage of Priests, Pollution; yet that not only the Marriage of Priests, which is not marriage but sacri-ledge; but also the Martrimony of holy persons is not exercised without a certayne pollution and turpitude, appeares by the rebellion of nature, and the shamefast-nes of men in that act, who alwayes seeke to be hidden, as S. Augustine hath obserued, lib.* 14. *de Ciuitate Dei. cap.* 17. Thus *Bellarmine :* and indeed *S. Au-gustine* in the next *Chap.* expresly speakes *de pudo-re Concubitus non solum vulgari, sed etiam coniuga-li.* And now what but malice can reprehend any one tittle in this doctrine of *Bellarmine?* or rather in the doctrine of the Fathers by him cited, which containes against you, Sacrifice, & single life of Priests ? Moreouer you falsify both *Inno-cetius* and *Bellarmine,* who speake not of *Marria-ge in it selfe,* of which you make them speake in

your

your Text, but of the act thereof ; and therfore *Innocentius* fayth : *Qui exercent cum vxore carnale confortium*; And *Bellarmine* fayth: *Non exercetur fine pollutione quadam &c.* Which is not euen fo much as to fay, the act it felfe is pollution, but only, *Non exercetur fine pollutione &c.*and this alfo not abfolutely,but with a limitation, *non fine pollutione quadam &c.* For Matrimony of it felfe, may ftand with moft perfect Chaftity,yea with Virginity, as appeareth in the moft *Immaculate Mother of God.* And at this day, a married man may be made Prieft, if his wife confent, and o-ther Conditions prefcribed in the holy Canons be obferued. And wheras you fay , *It feemes by S. Augustine, they* (the Manichees) *did not forbid meates, or marriage as abfolutely impure, or to all: only their choyce Elect ones muft obstaine ; the other vulgar, their Auditors, were lefte at their liberty :* This obiection taken out of *Peter Martyr,* is anfwered by *Bellarmine* in the Chapter next to that which you cited, that *S. Auguftine lib. 30. contra Fauftum cap. 6. writes, that the Manichees did abfolutly forbid Marriage ,becaufe though they did permit it to their Auditors, yet it was only for that they could not do otherwife. You cannot* (faith *S.Auguftine*)*fay that you do not forbid (* Mariage *) becaufe without breach of friendfhip you tolerate many of your Auditors,being either not willing,or not a-ble to obey you in this.* Thus *S.Auguftine. But we do not only permit , or tolerate the Marriage of Chri-ftians , but do alfo commend them. And befides the*

Ma-

Manichees did so permit Marriage to their Auditours for satisfying their lust, that they iointly warned them to auoid procreation of Children, which is manifestly to detest Marriage. But Catholiques do therfore chiefly commend Marriage, becaufe it is knowne to haue been instituted by God for the procreation of Childrē. Thus *Bellarmine.* And now I hope you fee how free he is from *Manicheifme,* & that the places which in your Margent you alledge out of *S. Aug.* to proue that fome of the Manichees might marry, are brought by you very cōtrary to his expres wor-des, in the place which now we haue heard *Bellarmine* cite out of him. The doctrine of *Cofterus* (a) that, *though a Priest be guilty of a grieuous facriledge if he cōmit fornicatiō; yet he fins more grieuoufly, if he contract Matrimony,* is very true, becaufe Matrimony in a Prieft is no Matrimony at all by reafon of his folēne vow of Chaftity, & the Churches prohibition, as *Bellarmine (*o) proues at large out of Councels & Fathers: and fo I fay to you, with *S. Iohn Chryfoftome, Though you call (*p) *fuch a Contract Marriage, yet I eftecmee it worfe then Adultery.* What fay you to *S. Chryfoftome,* who fayth, that Marriage after a folemne vow of Chaftity, is not only worfe then fornication, as *Cofterus* faid, but euen then Adultery? as S. *Ambrofe* alfo cals (q) the Marriage of a vowed Virgin, *Adultery.* Now fuppofing this doctrine of Catholiques, that the Matrimony of Priefts is no Matrimony; it followes that by attem-pting to contract Matrimony, befides the finnes

(a) *Enchiria: cap. de Ce: lib.*

(o) *De Ma: trim. Sacr. l. 1 c 21.*

(p) *In Epift. 6. ad Theo: dorum.*

(q) *In lib. ad Virginem lapfam, c. 5.*

Qqq of

of fornication and Sacriledge, he cōmits a grieuous diſobedience to the Church, a ſacrilegious
irreuerence againſt the Sacrament of Matrimony, which he celebrates inualidly; and may be
preſumed alſo to add a profeſſion of *Hereſy*, as if
the Church could not forbid, or make voyd the
Marriage of Clergy men; as in fact, *Luther*, &
ſuch Apoſtata's, ſinned not only againſt Continency, againſt their vow, againſt the Sacrament
of Marriage, againſt the precept of the Church;
but alſo againſt *Faith* : & laſtly both they and al
Prieſts that marry, doe to the vttermoſt of their
power, adde a greater immobility in ſinne,
then if they did cōmit fornication, without at-
tempting to marry. But I beſeech you doth he,
who teaches that a double ſinne is committed
by abuſing Marriage, teach thereby that Marriage is ill, & vnlawfull; or rather doth he not
ſhew that in it ſelfe it is holy and muſt not be a-
buſed ? If one ſhould not onely commit inceſt
within the forbidden degrees, but alſo attempt
to marry, ſhould not he cōmit a greater ſinne
by the abuſe of Marriage ioyned with inceſt,
then by inceſt alone? Or is it not a greater ſinne
both to commit Adultery, and attempt Marriage with the Adultreſſe, while his lawfull
wife liues, then onely to commit Adultery ?
The one by the lawes of the Kingdome is puniſhed with death, but not the other. So as it
is cleere that the doctrine of *Coſterus* cannot be
blamed, but by ſuch as oppoſe the Church, and
all

all Antiquity , about Marriage after a folemne
vow of Chaſtity. But if *Coſterus* deſerue blame,
what fay you to your Patriarch *Luther* , who
teaches, that (r) if the Councell ſhould grant
Churchmen liberty to marry , he would thinke
that man more in Gods grace, who during his
life kept three harlots, then he who marryed
according to the decree of the Councell : and
that he would command vnder payne of damnation , that no man ſhould marry by the per-
miſſion of ſuch a Councel, but either liue chaſt,
or if that were impoſſible, then not to deſpaire,
though he kept a harlot . O holy Reformer of
the Romane Church ! What can pleaſe theſe
men ? If the Church permit them not to marry , they will Apoſtatate vnder pretence of re-
forming her corruptions ; If they be permitted to marry , they will rather chooſe to be in-
famouſly wicked , then to marry . In your
firſt *Edition* , you fay , that Marriage is (by
vs)*counted a Crime*; and you proue it out of *Pe-*
lagius diſt. 61. *can. Catinenſis* , where it is faid :
Aduiſe, that one may be choſen, who neyther hath
a wife , nor children , nor any Crime repugnant to
the Canons . But with what conſcience can you
deceyue your vnlearned Reader , ſince the Latin , euen as you alledge it, hath the quite contrary to your Engliſh, as is euident by the words
which i haue now fet downe , in which, Marriage is diſtinguiſhed from a *Crime ?* But what
if after all this your obiecting *Manicheiſme* to

(r) *Tom.* 2.
Ger.fol. 214.

vs , eyther your felfe, or at leaft many chiefe
Proteftants be found more lyable to that Herefy , if they will fpeake with coherence to their
other grounds ? For as the *Manichees* in your
opinion did not forbid Marriage to all , but only to their *Elect* : fo doe Proteftants fay , that
thofe who haue the gift of Chaftity not onely
may , but ought to abftaine from Marriage, becaufe they teach that there are no workes of Supererogation , but that men are bound to performe whatfoeuer God doth infpire them to; &
confequently fuch *Elect* Perfons fhould finne a-
gaynft the law of God if they married , which
is more then Catholiques affirme, who doe not
teach that the prohibition of Priefts to marry ,
proceeds immediatly from the law of God.

9. You goe from Marriage to Meate , and
(s)*Pag.*239.fay : *And for Meates*; (s)*why is abftinence from
flesh accounted a perfect Christian fast , yea holy and
meritorious? And why is he that eates flesh in Lent,
punished with a more grieuous pennance , then he that
commonly blafphemes the name of God , or defiles his
Neighbours bed , or abufes himfelfe by drunkennes ,
or others by rayling , flaundering , &c .* But thefe
Arguments might better befeeme fome illite-
rate rayling Lecturer , then a man of your place.; efpecially in a Treatife tending to Pacifica-
tion. For how doe you thinke we can be faued,
if we were indeed guilty of Manicheifme , and
fuch abfurd impieties, as thofe whereof you
talke . Abftinence from flesh , is meritorious ,

not

not becaufe flefh of its owne nature is euill, as neither was the forbidden apple; but becaufe obedience to lawfull Superiours is good : and if fafting to fubdue the flefh, and ouercome temptations were not holy, why did not the Anciēt Fathers cōmend feafting, as highly as fafting ? For I will not thinke you to be fo great a ftranger to the Fathers, that you can be ignorant how frequently they extoll fafting. And I defire to know, whether you do not thinke, that his Maiefties Lawes, and in particular his Proclamations about keeping Lent, do not bind in confcience ? And if you anfwere me at all, I befeech you forget not this demand; and whether the obferuation of them be not holy, and forafmuch as belongs to that particular obiect, a perfect Chriftian faft, and meritorious in that fenfe, and degree, according to which you grant that other works are meritorious, or deferuing a reward ? For the other part of your obiection, that he that eates flefh in Lent is punifhed with a more grieuous pennance then he that blafphemes &c. you fhew how modeft a man you are, and with all, that you are little (t) *In Au-*feene either in the *Canon*, or *Ciuil* Law. For *thentica, vt* the Ciuill Law commaunds, that (t) Blaf *non luxu-*phemers fhould be punifhed with death, be- *rientur ho-*caufe, fayth the Law, *Hunger and earthquakes,* *mines. No-* *and plagues, come by reafon of fuch crimes.* In the (u) *Cap.* (u) *Canon La*w, Blafphemers, befide *other punifh-* *Statuimus* *ments, are to ftand as Penitents at the Church* *de maledicis* *doore*

Q q q 3

doore for the fpace of fome Sundayes, and for
fome fridayes to faft in bread & watei &c . and
by other decrees of Popes the fame finne is grieuoufly punifhed, as in particular the Councell
of *Lateran* vnder *Leo* the 10. commands, That
none be abfolued from Blafphemy without a
grieuous penance : and to the fame purpofe *Iu-
lius I I I.* and *Pius V.* haue made veiy feuere
decrees. Neuertheles it is alfo true, that greater
punifhment may *in foro externo,* be appointed
for fome finnes which are leffe then other, as
S.Thomas doth (w) truly affirme. Do not your

(w) 1.2.q. felues more vfually punifh fuch, as without li-
105.ar.2. ad cence eate flefh in Lent, then them who take the
9.2nd, 2.2. Name of God in vaine, or abufe themfelues by
q.39. art. 2. drunkennes, or wrong their Neighbours by dead 1. traction? And befides, to eate flefh in Lent may
be an act of Herefy, which how grieuous a finne
it is, hath been explicated heertofore.

10.   By occafion of mentioning the *Manichees,* you charge your Margent, as your fafhion
is, with a deep peece of erudition, that the name
(forfooth) of their founder *Manes,* is conforme
to the Greeke word, which fignifies *Madnes.* But
if we delighted is take hold of fuch goodly occafions of Vanity, we could fay, that he was a
Perfian, and his name was firft *Cubricus,* which
he changed into *Manes,* which in the *Babylonian*

(x) Epiph. Tongue fignifies (x) a Veffell. But let vs leaue
haeref.66. thefe toyes to Grammar Scholiers.

11.   It feemes you are willing of fet purpofe
                                                    to

to miſtake the point in queſtion, which was; whether the *Creed* containe all fundamentall points of fayth or no? about which *Charity Mi-ſtaken,* hauing inſtanced in ſome points of fayth not contained in the Creed, as the Scriptures, and Sacraments; he adds theſe words: *Beſides that, there are (* **y** *) ſome great differences betweene them (* meaning Proteſtants *) and vs about the vn-derſtanding of the Article of the deſcent of Chriſt our Lord into hell, and that other of the Holy Catholi-que Church, and that alſo of the Communion of Saints, which we belieue, and they deny to inuolue both Prayers for the dead, and Prayers to Saints, as that we ſhould not be much better, either for our knowing, or confeſsing that the Creed containes all fundamentall points of Fayth, vnles withall there were ſome certaine way how to vnderſtand them a-right, and eſpecially vnles vnder the Article which concernes the holy Catholique Church, they would vnderſtand it to be endued with ſo perfect infallibi-lity, and great Authority, as that it might teach vs all the reſt.* This ſolid diſcourſe you mangle as you pleaſe, ſtill forgetting the promiſe you made in your Preface to the Reader not to omit *any one thing of moment.* For you anſwere not a word to his particular inſtances of Prayer for the dead; or to Saints; nor to his generall exce-ption, that we ſhould not be much better for knowing that the Creed containes all funda-mentall points of fayth, vnles withall there were ſome way of vnderſtanding them aright.

(y) *Pag. 86,* 87.

If

If you anfwere, that Prayers for the dead, or to Saints, are not *Fundamentall* points, whether they be denied, or affirmed; then you muft grant that you forfooke the Church of *Rome* for things indifferent, and *not fundamentall* one way or other. For thefe two points, and fuch as thefe, were the pretended errours, wherewith you feeke to cloake your *Schifme*. To the other you anfwere ; *The Church of England* (z) *queftioneth not the fenfe of thofe Articles; She takes them in the old Catholique fenfe: and the words are fo plaine, they beare their meaning before them.* Why do you anfwere to thefe two points of the Catholique Church, and our Sauiours defcent into Hell, rather then to the other which *Charity - Miftaken* doth mention? And in thefe two of which you take notice, why doe you vfe fo much tergiuerfation? Why doe you not plainely, and honeftly acquaint vs with the meaning of them. If you fay, that by the Catholique Church is vnderftood a Church alwaies vifible, & not capable of errour in *fundamentall* points, many of your chiefe Brethren will contradict that which you iudge to be plaine : and your Church of England fpeakes fo generally, *Art.* 19. *of the Church,* that, as it is affirmed in the Preface, *men of all forts may take* that Article *to be for them.* And as for the other Article of our Sauiours defcent, if it befo *plaine as it beares the fenfe before it,* how comes *Caluin* to vnderftand it one way, *Brentius* another, *Beza* another, and other

(z) P*ag.240.*

ther Proteftants in another, differently from Catholiques, with whome neuertheles fome o-ther Proteftants agree, who teach a *Lymbus Patrum*, as *Lafcitius, Oecolampadius, Zwinglius, Peter Martyr, Bullinger*, and *(a) Bilfon*, and we may adde *D. Pott er* as one different from all the reft, who fayth, the fenfe is *plaine*, and yet he keeps it to himfelfe.

(a) Vide Brereley tract.3.Sect. 7. vnder M. num.26.

12. But, *the Roman Doctours (b) cannot agree among themfelues about this Article.* Is there any Catholique that denies *Lymbus Patrum*, or that Chrift defcended *to Hell* as it fignifies *Lymbus?* Yes; becaufe, fay you, *(c) Stapleton* affirmes *the Scripture is filent that Chrift defcended into Hell, & that there is a Catholique,& an Apoftolique Church. Bellarmine (d) on the cotrary is refolute, that the Article of the defcent is euery where in Scripture : and Thomas grants (e) as much for the whole Creed.* What is all this to the purpofe? It is one thing to difagree in the doctrine of Chifts defcent, & another, whether that doctrine which they belieue be proued out of Scripture, or deliuered by the Church out of Vnwritten Traditions. Among Proteftats who hold Scripture only to be the Rule of faith, it is all one not to be contained in Scripture & not to be a point of faith; but not fo with Catholiques, who befides Scripture, belieue infallible vnwritten Traditions. And wheras you fay; *Bellarmine* is refolute, that the Article of the defcet is euery where in Scripture, and in Latin *Scripturæ paffim hoc docent:*

(b)Pag.240.

(c) Contr. 3. q. 5. art. 1.

(d) 4 . De Chrifto. cap. 6. & 12. (c)2.2.q. 1. art. 9.ad 1.

Bel-

Bellarmines wordes are ; All men agree that
Chriſt deſcended into Hell *aliquo modo,* in ſome
máner or ſenſe , becauſe Scripture euery where
teaches ſo much. Why did you leaue out *aliquo
modo ,* which words might well haue ſhewed
that there was no contrariety betweene *Bellarmine* & *Stapleton* . *S. Thomas* doth not purpoſely
diſpute , whether all Articles of the Creed be
contayned in Scripture , but onely vpon an o-
ther occaſion teaches , that the Creed is not an
Addition to Scripture, *out of which it is taken ,* &
that the truths belieued by fayth are contained
in Scripture *diuers wayes ,* and in *ſome obſcurely;*
which doth in no wiſe exclude the Authority
of the Church to declare the meaning of the
Creed . For if ſome be contayned in Scripture
but *obſcurely ,* who ſhall declare them to vs, but
the Church ?

(f)*pag.*240.   13.   As, for *the ſenſe of that* (f) *Article, ſome
hold that Chriſt deſcended really into Hell . Others ,
virtually , and by effect* : This *virtuall* deſcent is
taught by one only , namely *Durand ,* and therfore your *Others* is but an exaggeration ; and e-
uen he doth not deny *Lymbus Patrum ,* or that
the Fathers were there, nor that Chriſt deſcended thither in ſome ſort , but only differeth frõ
others, whether he deſcended *ſecundum ſubſtan-
tiam* : which doctrine , or rather doubt of his
(for he leaueth the thing doubtfull) is reiected
by all other Deuines , as erroneous.

(g)*pag.*240.   14.   *By Hell ſome* (g) vnderſtand the loweſt
pit,

pit, or the place *of the damned, as Bellarmin at first* ;
others, the Lymbus Patrum , as Bellarmine at last.
Would not one conceiue by your words, that in
the opinion of *Bellarmine,* Chrift defcended only into the place of the damned ? And yet your
confcience cannot but tell you , that *Bellarmine*
neuer doubted , but that Chrift defcended into
Lymbus Patrum, and only propofed it as doubtfull whether or no he defcended into the Hell of
the damned, and refolued *probabile eſt: It is pro-*
bable that the foule of Chriſt defcended to all the in-
fernall places , or Hells . But afterward in his *Re-*
cognitions he retracted his opinions for as much
as concerned the place of the damned; whereby
it is cleere, that he neuer doubted of our Sauiours defcent to *Lymbus*; and that you affirming
the contrary , doe without doubt , defire to deceiue your Reader .

15.   You fay, that *it is the moſt important* (h)
and moſt fundamentall of all Articles in the Church (h)*pag.*242.
to belieue , that Iefus Chriſt the Sonne of God , & the
Son of Mary, is the only Sauiour of the world: wherin you giue a deadly blow to *D. Morton,* who teaches that the *Arians* denying our Sauiour to be
God, do notwithftanding make a true Church :
and if the opinion of *M. Hooker* for which you
bring diuers Arguments , be true , you cannot
exclude the *Arians,* or *Trinitarians* from being
members of a true Church .

16.   To cleere the côfufednes of your Church
in her 39. *Articles,* you lay the fault vpon vs.

But by your leaue, if you read , either Catholique Deuines, or the Councell of *Trent*, you will
find , that they fpeake moſt cleerly and diſtinctly. But *Charity Miſtaken* doth truly fay , that
*you are very carefull not to be too cleerly vnderſtood;
and therefore in many Controuerſies whereof that
Booke (* of the 39. Articles *)ſpeakes , it comes not
at all to the maine queſtion between them and vs &c.*
Which affirmation of his, is moſt true, both in
the points by him ſpecified, & in diuers others ;
as for example : The *third* of our Sauiours deſcent into Hell. The 26. of the Nature and effect
of Sacraments. The 27. will haue the Baptiſme
of Children to be retained, but doth not ſpecify whether or no it be neceſſary. The 28. about
the Lords Supper, is ſo generall, and of ſo large
a ſize, that it may reach to *Zuinglians, Caluiniſts,*
& *Lutherans,* who yet in this Article are known
to be as farre aſunder from ech other , as Eaſt
from Weſt. I omit other Articles, and only vrge
that which *Charity Miſtaken* preſſeth , and you
wholy diſſemble, that : *Thoſe Articles do not ſo
much as ſay, that the Articles of doctrine which they
deliuer are fundamentall, either all, or halfe , or any
one therof, or that they are neceſſarily to be belieued by
them, or the contrary damnable if it be belieued by vs.*
Is this to keep your promiſe, not *to omit without
anſwere any thing of moment in all his diſcourſe?*
Certainly this which *Charity Miſtaken* doth vrge
heere, is according to your principles, the very
quinteſſence of all other points. I will not ſtand

to

to examine how truly you affirme, that our Wil is *essentially free from all necessity.* Such motions of our Will as preuent the deliberation of reason, are they not necessary? The Will in good Philosophy cannot suffer *coaction*, but it may be *necessitated,* without changing the essence therof.

17. To the demaund of *Charity Mistaken;* (*Why do they not particularly enumerate all the Bookes which they acknowledge to be of the New Testament, as they had done them of the Old; but only because they must so haue named those Bookes of S. Iames, and others for Canonicall, which the Lutherans haue cast out of their Canon?*) You answere that the *Lutherans* do now admit the Epistle of *S.Iames,* and the rest, as Canonicall: which you proue by *D. Gerhard* a Luthera. But if this be so, you do not answere his Question, what the reason is, why your Church doth not *particularly enumerate all the Bookes which they acknowledge to be of the New Testament, as she had done them of the old?* Besides, what Authority had *D.Gerhard* to speak for all the Lutherans, of which there be diuers sorts, condemning one another? If once you deny the infallibility of the Church, what infallible ground hath *D. Gerhard* this day to admit of those Bookes, which yesterday other *Lutherans* reiected? In the Bibles of *Luther* to this day, the *Epistle* to the *Hebrewes,* the *Epistle* of *S. Iames,* and *S. Iude,* and the *Apocalyps* of *S. Iohn,* are excluded from the Canon.

18. Now that none of thofe Bookes which we hold for Canonicall, be Apochryphall, as you teach, *Bellarmine* (m) proues at large, and anfwers all your obiections. And if any heertofore doubted of fome of them, the Authority of the Vifible Catholique Church of Chrift ought to preponderate all doubts of particular perfons. And it is ftrange that you cite *S. Augustine* againft the *Machabees*, who in that very place which you cite, fayth : *The Scripture* (n) *of the Machabees is receiued by the Church not vnprofitably, if it be read and heard foberly :* which latter words are vnderftood only againft defperate inferences of the *Donatifts*, who vpon the example of *Razias* in the Hiftory of the *Machabees* did kill and precipitate themfelues; as is cleere by his other enfuing words in the fame place. *We ought not then to approue by our confent, all things which we reade in the Scriptures to haue been done by men, euen adorned with praifes by the teftimony of God himfelfe, but to mingle our confideration with difcretion, bringing difcretion with vs, not grounded vpon our owne Authority, but vpon the Authority of the holy and diuine Scriptures, which permit not vs to praife or imitate all the actions euen of thofe, of whom the Scripture giues good, and glorious Teftimony, if they haue done any thing, that hath not been well done, or that agreeth not with the confent of the prefent time.* In which words we fee *S. Augustine* calls the Bookes of the *Machabees,* Scriptures, euen as afterward he cals Canoni-

call

(m) *De verbo Dei l.* 1. *per multa capita*

(n) *Cont. ep. Gaudent . lib.* 2. *f.* 23.

call Bookes in generall, Diuine, and holy Scriptures; and that the Sobriety of Circumspection, which he aduiseth to be obserued, in reading them, is not, how far they be true or false, but whether the example of *Razias* recounted by them, is to be imitated more or lesse. What you alledge out of *S. Gregory* (o) is easily answered. For he doth not call the *Machabees, not Canonicall,* as if he would exclude them from the number of true, and diuine Scriptures, but because they were not in the Canon of the Iewes, or in that which he had at hand when he wrote his first draught of his *Commentaries* vpon *Iob.* For he was at that time the Popes Nuncius, or Legate at *Constantinople,* and the Greeke *Rapsody* of *African Canons* had vntruly put out of the Canon the two *Bookes* of the *Machabees,* though they were receiued in *Africa* as Canonicall, by the decree of the *African* Councell. And therfore you were ill aduised, vnder colour of commending Pope *Gregory,* (but indeed the more to impugne vs by his authority) to write *Greg: M.* or *Magnus,* the *Great,* wheras he was not Pope, but only *Deacon,* when he first wrote those Commentaries vpon *Iob.*

(o) *Moral. lib. 19.c. 17.*

19. You cite *S. Hierome præfat. in lib. Salom.* *The Church reades the Bookes of Iudith, Tobias, and the Machabees, but she doth not receiue them among Canonicall writings.* But *S. Hieromes* words are these : *As the Church reades Tobias, Iudith, and the Machabees, but receiues them not among the Canonicall*

nicall Bookes ; fo may she read Wifedome , and Eccle-
fiafticus, for the edification of the people , but not for
the confirmation of Ecclefiaſticall doctrines. Thus *S.*
Hierome . And you had reafon to cite his words
by halues : For he afterward retracted what he
faid of the Bookes of *Iudith ,* and *Tobias (* with
which the Machabees are yet ioyned in the
words cited by you *)* faying in his Preface vpon
the Hiftory of *Iudith : The Booke of Iudith is read*
by the Hebrewes among the Hagiographs , whofe an-
thority is eſteemed leſſe fufficient to decide Contro-
uerfies : but for as much as the Councell of Nice hath
reckoned it among the holy Scriptures, I haue obeyed
your requeſt. Where you fee that *S. Hierome* affirmes, that the moſt ancient, and graue Councell
of *Nice ,* receiued the Booke of *Iudith* in that
fenfe, in which the Iewes did not receiue it; &
confequently as a Booke efteemed fufficient to
decide Controuerfies, which the Iewes denied.
And in another place the fame Father fayth:
Ruth, Heſter, and Iudith haue beene (q *) fo glorious,*
as they haue giuen their names into the facred Vo-
(q) *Ep.*140. *lumes.* Where you fee that *S. Hierome* placeth *Iu-*
dith with *Ruth* and *Heſter ,* the former wherof
you admit for Canonicall , and part of the latter. In his Preface vpon the Booke of *Tobias ,* he
(r) *Ep.*100. fayth : The Hebrewes *(* r *)* cut off the Booke of
Tobias from *the Catalogue of the diuine Scriptures.*
And againe : *The iealoufy of the Iewes, doth accufe*
vs, that againſt their Canon we tranflate the Booke of
Tobias into Latin : but I iudge it better to difpleafe
the

the iudgment of the Pharisees, and to obey the Com-
mandment of the Bishops. And elſewhere he placeth (t) the *Machabees* among Canonicall (t) *In Iſa.*
Bookes, ſaying: *The Scripture reports that Ale-* *c. 23.*
xander king of the Macedonians came out of the land
of Cethim. And wonder not if *S. Hierome* ſpake
not alwayes in the ſame manner of the Canon
of the *Old Teſtament*, ſince vpon experience,
examination, and knowledge of the ſenſe of the
Church he might alter his Opinion; as once he
ſaid of the Epiſtle to the Hebrewes, that it (u) (u) *Ad Pau-*
was put out of the number by the greateſt part of men: *linum.*
and yet elſewhere he receiues it (w) as the Epi- (w) *Ep. ad*
ſtle of *S. Paul.* And if you will haue a generall *Darda num.*
explication of *S. Hierome* concerning his reie-
cting of Bookes, not admitted by the Hebrewes,
heare it in his owne words : *Wheras I haue repor-*
ted (x) what the Hebrewes vſed to obiect againſt the (x *Aduſ*
Hiſtory of Suſanna, and the Hymne of the three Chil *Ruſſ. Apo-*
dren, and the Story of the Dragon Bell, which are in *log. 2.*
the Hebrew; I haue not declared what I thought, but
what the Iewes were wont to ſay againſt vs. And he
cals *Ruſſinus a fooliſh Sycophant* for charging him
with the opinion of the *Hebrewes* about theſe
parts of *Daniel.* And *S. Hierome* explayning himſelfe in this manner, is acknowledged by (y) (y) *Anſwe:*
Couell, and (z) *Bankcroft*. How then will you *to Burges.*
excuſe your Church, which in her *ſixt Article* *pag. 87.*
ſayth in generall of all the Bookes which you (z) *Confe-*
eſteeme Apochryphall, among which are the *rence before*
Hiſtory of *Suſanna*, the Hymne of *the three Chil-* *his Maieſty.*
　　　　　　Sſſ　　　　　　　　　　　*dren.*

dren, and that of the *Dragon* : (*The other Bookes*
(*as Hierome sayth*) *the Church doth reade for exam-*
ple of life, and instruction of manners: but yet it doth
not apply them to establish any doctrine?) How can
she (I say) be excused, since *S. Hierome*, euen
according to the Confession of your owne
Brethren, doth explaine himselfe, that he vttered only what the Iewes *were wont to say against*
vs; and cals *Ruffinus* a *foolish Sycophant* for saying
the contrary ? So as, insteed of *S. Hierome*,
and the *Church* of God, you put on the person of *Ruffinus* against S. *Hierome*, and of the
Synagogue against the *Church of Christ our Lord*; &
so your whole *Canon* of the old Testament relies
vpon the Authority of the Iewes. And finally,
D . Potter while he grants that Catholiques and
Protestants disagree about the very Canon of
Scripture, forgets to answere what *Charity- Mi-*
staken (pag. 43. *&* 46 .) doth thence inferre, to
wit, that they cannot be accounted of one and
the same Religion, Fayth, and Church.

20 .   The Chymericall Church of your
(b) *Pag. 234.* (b) Maister, *D . Vsher*, consisting of men agreeing only in *fundamentall* points, is indeed a
Chymera, or *non Ens* . For it is impossible that
there can be a visible Church, which professing
fundamentall points, doth not in other points
eyther agree with vs, or you, or els disagrees
from vs both. For eyther they must hold, for
example, the Reall Presence, Transubstantia-
ti, Prayer for the dead, and to Saints, Worship
of

of Images, Supremacy of the Pope, Sufficiency
of one kind for the Layty &c. and then they a-
gree with vs: Or els they deny all thefe points,
and fo agree with you againft vs. And this is
that pernicious fallacy, wherby you deceiue
your felfe, and others; as if there were a vifible
Catholique Church, or company of men, holding all *fundamentall* points, and being neither
Romane Catholiques, nor *Luthcrans*, nor *Caluinifts*
&c. nor any other Church in particular; which
is a meere impoffible fiction. For Fayth is not
Fayth vnles it extend to all points fufficiently
propounded as diuine Truths, the leaft wherof
if any one deny, he giues his Fayth a deadly
wound, and his feeming Beliefe of other Articles auailes him nothing. To which purpofe this
faying of S. *Augustine* is remarkable: *If a man* (c) *De Bap-*
grieuoufly wounded (c) *in fome necefary part of his* *tifm. cont.*
body, be brought to a Phifitian, and the Phifitian fay, *Donatift.l.1.*
if he be not dreffed he will dye, I thinke they who *c.8.*
brought him, will not be fo fenfles, as to anfwere the
Phifitian, after they haue confidered and viewed his
other parts which are found; What, fhall not fo many
found parts haue power to preferue him aliue? And
fhall one wounded part haue power to bring him to
his death? In vaine then do you flatter your felues with a feeming found beliefe of the Articles of the *Creed*, if in the meane time you receiue a *deadly* wound, by oppofing any one
truth reuealed by God, and propounded by the
true Catholique Church. For as all the liuing

mem-

members of a mans body, are so vnited in one
life, that a deadly blow receiued immediately
but in one, doth necessarily redound to the destruction of all: so all the obiects of fayth, being
vnited in the same *Formall Motiue* of Gods testimony sufficiently propounded to vs, the deniall
or wounding of any one truth, which is vested
with that *formall Motiue*, and life of fayth, doth
ineuitably redound to the death, and destruction of all the rest. When by this occasion you
cite our late soueraigne Lord king *Iames* affirming, that (d) the things which are *simply neces-*
sary to be belieued, are *but few in number*; and yet
that *all* things are *simply necessary*, which the
word of God *commands* vs to *belieue*; it had beene
your duty to explaine the contrariety which
appeares betwixt those two sayings. For since
the word of God commands vs to belieue euery Proposition contained in holy Scripture,
which are many thousands, how are the things
necessary to be belieued, but *few in number?*

21.   But now I must put you in mind of not
performing your promise, not to omit *any one*
thing of moment. For besides other, you omit to
set downe what *Charity Mistaken* writes (e) a-
bout the true sense of the distinction of points
fundamentall and *not fundamentall*, which if you
had set downe as he deliuers it, it had cleerly
appeared, how through your whole Booke you
had still auoyded the true State, and point of
the Question. To which purpose you conceale

in

(d) *Epist.*
Casauboni
ad Card.
Per. ad Ob-
seruat. 3.

(e) *Pag. 73.*

in particular, what he alleageth out of *D. Dunne,* late Deane of *S. Paules,* who hauing put great ftrength in the diftinction of *Fundamentall* and *not Fundamentall* points , he wipes out with a wet finger the whole fubftance of his difcourfe by faying, That (f) difference in points which are not important is not to preiudice a mans faluation, vnles by not belieuing them he commits a difobedience withall (as certainely euery one doth, who denies any leaft point fufficiently propoūded to him, as reuealed by God , whofoeuer that Propounder be:) For (fayth he) *Obedience indeed* (g) *is of the Effence of Religion.*

(f) *Pag.* 96.

(g) *Pag.* 97.

Sff 3   *The*

The Conclusion.

AND thus hauing in this *Second Part* anſwered the particulars in *D. Potters* Booke, and hauing proued in the *Firſt Part*, that this truth, *Amongſt men of different Religions, one onely ſide can be ſaued*, is ſo euidently true, as no Chriſtian that vnderſtands the termes, can call it in queſtion; in ſo much as if any will goe about to perſuade the contrary, we muſt ſay with *S. Auguſtine*; *He doth erre* (a) *ſo much the more abſurdly, and againſt the true Word of God more peruerſly, by how much he ſeemeth to himſelfe to iudge more charitably*: It cannot but appeare, how much it importeth euery ſoule, to ſeeke out that one ſauing Truth, which can be found only in the *true Viſible Catholique* Church of Chriſt. Wherfore our greateſt care muſt be to find out that one *true* Church; which we ſhall be ſure not to miſſe, if our endeauour be not wanting to his grace, who *deſires that* (b) *all men ſhould be ſaued, and come to the knowledge of the TRVTH.* For, the words of the ſacred Councell of *Trent* are moſt true: *God commands not* (c) *impoſſible things, but by commanding warnes thee both to do what thou art able, & to aske what thou art*

not

(a) *De Ciuit.Dei.l.21. cap. 17.*

(b) 1. *Tim.* 2.4.

(c) *Seſſ.6. cap.11.*

not able, and helpes thee, that thou maiſt be able. Let not men therfore flatter, and deceiue themſelues, that *Ignorance* will excuſe them. For if they want any one thing abſolutely neceſſary to ſaluation, *Ignorance* cannot excuſe. And there are ſo many, and ſo eaſy, and yet withall ſo powerfull meanes to finde the true Church, that it is a moſt dangerous, and pernicious error, to rely vpon the excuſe of inuincible Ignorance. And I wiſh them to conſider, that he can leaſt hope for reliefe by Ignorance, who once confides therin : becauſe his very alledging of Ignorance, ſheweth that God hath put ſome thoughts into his mind of ſeeking the ſafeſt way; which if he, relying on Gods grace, do carefully and conſtantly endeauour to examine, diſcuſſe, and perfect, he ſhall not faile to *find* what he *ſeekes,* and to *obtaine* what he *askes.* Neither will the ſearch proue ſo hard and intricate, as men imagine. For, as God hath confined ſaluation within the Communion of his Viſible Church ; ſo hath he endued her with ſo conſpicuous Markes of *Vnity,* and agreement in doctrine; *Vniuerſality* for Time, and Place ; a neuer interrupted *Succeſsion* of Paſtors ; a perpetuall *Viſibility* from the Apoſtles, to vs &c. far beyond any probable pretence that can be made by any other Congregations; that whoſoeuer doth ſeriouſly and vnpartially weigh theſe Notes, may eaſily diſcerne to what Church they belong. But all this diligence muſt be vſed with perfect indiffe-

differency, and conftant refolution to proceed
in this affaire, which is the moft important of
all other, as at the hower of their death, and the
day of their finall accompt they would wifh to
haue done: For nothing can counterpoyfe an
Eternity of *Felicity,* or *Mifery.* Their Prayer will
be much holpen with Almes deeds, offered to
this intention of obtaining *Light* of Almighty
God, according to that faying of the Prophet
Efay: *Breake thy bread (d) to the hungry, and needy,*
and harbourles ; when thou fhalt fee the naked couer
him, & defpife not thy flefh. Then fhall thy L I G H T
breake forth as the Morning, and thy Health fhall
foone arife, and thy Iuftice fhall goe before thy face,
and the Glory of our Lord fhall imbrace thee. Then
fhalt thou call, & our Lord will heare: Thou fhalt cry,
and he will fay; Lo, heere I am. And fo he will not
fayle to fhew thee *Where he is:* Namely, in his
owne Catholique vifible Church. Fafting likewife giues ftrength and wings to our Prayer:
for *Prayer is good* (e) *with fafting.* But nothing is
more neceffary then that they roote out of their
foules, preiudice of Opinion, Feare, Hope, A-
uarice, Intereft, humane Refpects, and fuch eyther corruptions of nature, or temptatios of our
Enemy; to which men will the more eafily be
led to yield, by the defire which they haue naturally to leade a life in liberty, and not to aduenture the loffe of fuch conueniences & de-
lights, as they are wont to like fo well ; as alfo
not to incurre thofe difaduantages and afflicti-
ons

(d) *Cap.* 58.
v.7.8.

(e) *Tob.* 12.
8.

ons to which a contrary courfe might make thē
fubiect. Some of thefe thinges, are excellently
pointed at by *S. Augustine*, when he writes a-
gainft the *Donatist* Heretiques of his tyme,
which euery man ought ferioufly to confider
how farre they may perhaps concerne himfelfe.

How many (fayth he) *being* (f) *conuinced by eui-*   (f) *Epist. 48.*
*dence of truth, did defire to be Catholiques, but did
deferre it from day to day, for feare of offending their
friends or kinsfolkes? How many were tyed, not by
truth, wherein they neuer much confided, but by the
heauy chayne of obdurate custome? How many did
belieue the faction of Donatus to be the true Church,
becaufe too much afuredues made them drowzy,
difdainefull, and flouthfull? To how many did the
reports of ill Tongues fhut vp the way to enter,
who fayd, that we put, I know not what, vpon the
Altar? How many thinking that it was no matter on what fide one were a Christian, did therfore
remaine among the Donatists, becaufe there they
were borne?*

And afterward: *We were frighted to enter, by reafon of falfe reports, which we fhould
not haue knowne to be falfe vnles we had entred,* into the Catholique Church (as daily we heare
from the mouth of Proteftants conuerted to
Catholique Religion.) *Others fay. We did indeed belieue, that it imported nothing, in what
Company, we did hold the fayth of Christ. But
thankes be to our Lord, who hath gathered vs from*

T t t   *diuifion*

diuision, and hath shewed to vs, that it agreeth to
one God, that he be worshipped in Vnity.

F I N I S.

Faults

Faults escaped in the Print.

GOod Reader, whereas through the abſence of the Author of this Worke, and by reaſon of an vncorrected written Coppy ſent vnto the preſſe, many errours & miſtakings haue happened in the printing, eſpecially hauing byn côſtrained, through the difficulties of theſe times, to vſe the help of ſtrangers, and ſuch as are ignorant in our tongue ; It is in all humble manner deſired, that (theſe ſaid Circûſtances duly conſidered) thou wouldeſt in no wiſe heerin condemne the ſaid Authour as acceſſary heerto, but fauourably affoarding thy Cenſure heerof, and in reading ouer the Booke, to correct them with thy pen, they being heere exactly gathered by himſelfe, and ſet downe as followeth.

EPiſtle Dedicatory. Pag. 7. lin. 3. Catholiques *Corrige* Catholique

In the Preface.

PAg. 2. lin. 26. indifferent *Corrige* in different
Pag. 7. lin. 26. transfered *Corrige* transferred

In the firſt Part.

PAg. 38. lin. 26. one, the other *Corrige* one, and the other
Pag. 44. lin. 6. *contentions* Corrige *contentious*
Pag. 45. lin. 29. as there is *Corrige* as in Job is
Pag. 51. lin. 15. affirme knowledge *Corrige* affirme that our firſt knowledge
Pag. 54. lin. 3. it *Corrige* is
Ibid. lin. 24. then *Corrige* them

Pag. 56. lin. 25. languages. *Corrige* languages?
Pag. 57. lin. 25. *Hoſpinians* Corrige *Hoſpinianus*
Pag. 59. lin. 1. *Caerlile* corrige *Carlile*
Pag. 61. lin. 11. No! *Corrige* No.
Pag. 67. lin. 7. feditions *corrige* feditious
Pag. 78. lin. 6. not *corrige* no
Pag. 79. lin. 1. feuerall *corrige* feuerally
Pag. 89. lin. 16. they holy *corrige* the holy
Pag. 95. lin. 30. *deleatur* be
Pag. 99. lin. 4. fayth *corrige* he fayth
Pag. 102. lin. 8. *Hold* corrige *hold*
Pag. 103. lin. 1. Circumcifion *D. Potter* corrige Circum-
cifion. *D . Potter*
Pag. 105. lin. 3. errours : But (x) *corrige* errours (x):But
&c. for the letter (x) is not referred to *Philaletes*, but to
the *Moderate examination* &c.
Pag. 111. lin. 2. at *corrige* it
Pag. 113. lin. 9. Text *corrige* Texts
Ibid. lin. 17. or *corrige* nor
Pag. 115. lin. 16. nor. *corrige* not .
Pag. 119. in the Title Chap. 111. *corrige* Chap. 1111.
Pag. 124. lin. 2. *beliene* corrige *belieue*
Pag. 126. lin. 25. *their* corrige *there* (for in Latin it is
(*ibi*) not (*illorum.*)
Pag. 135. lin. 17. of few *corrige* or few
Pag. 136. lin. 22. danably *corrige* damnably
Ibid. lin. 26. *damnably* corrige damnably. I meane, it ought
not to be in a different or curciffe letter , becaufe it is not
D. Potters word , though it follow out of his doctrine.
Pag. 140. lin. 5. before, to auoyd *corrige* before. To auoid
Pag. 141. lin. 4. *fuppofes*; it doth *corrige fuppofes*. It doth
Pag. 146. lin. 25. *name ; confeſſe* corrige *name, J confeſſe*
Pag. 147. lin. 19. *which* corrige *with*
Pag. 149 lin. 10. *deleatur* we
Pag. 155. lin. 11. we was *corrige* he was
Pag. 161. lin. 10. & 26. *Napier* corrige *Napper*
Ibid. lin. 19. *goodly* corrige *godly*
Ibid. lin. 29. *wilernes* corrige *wildernes*
Ibid. lin. 31. *Hailbronerus* corrige *Hailbronnerus*
Pag. 162. lin. 15. for that *corrige* that for
Ibid. lin. 17. conld *corrige* could

Pag. 163. lin. 29. *haue alfo* corrige *haue not alfo*

Pag. 165. lin. 22. men depart . *corrige* men to depart.

Pag. 174. lin. 5 *Chriſtopher Potter*, corrige D. *Chriſtop. Potter*,

Pag. 183. lin. 20. at laſt *corrige* at leaſt

Pag. 184. lin. 29. your grounds *corrige* your owne grounds

Ibid. lin. 30. *inough* corrige *enough*

The like alſo pag. 185. lin. 2. 6. 7. 8. *inough* corrige *enough*

Pag. 185. lin. 9. *deleatur* not

Pag. 187. lin. 6. breach in *corrige* breach, in

Pag. 190. lin. 1. & 2. And D. *Potter corr.* And yet D. *Potter*

Pag. 193. lin. 7. Reformation : *corrige* Reformation .

Pag. 197. lin. 18. fenceleneſſe *corrige* fencelefneſſe

Pag. 200. lin. 25. *manuer* corrige *manner*

Pag. 204. lin. 6. after *impoſſible*, adde , and *damnable* .

Pag. 209. lin. 26. correct the parentheſis this : (What? do you meane that they are his owne conceyts , and yet grounded vpon euidence of Scripture ?)

Pag. 212. lin. 16. *the gouernment* corrige *her gouernment*

Pag. 215. lin. 18. *Auguſtines* corrige *Auguſtine*

Pag. 218. lin. 14. *deleatur that*

Pag. 221. lin. 16. Gods Church , *corrige* Gods Word ,

Pag. 225. lin. 24. A godly *corrige* A goodly

Pag. 230. lin. 5. for *corrige* from

Pag. 233. lin. 18. *ſee by a* corrige *ſee now by a*

Pag. 235. lin. 2. ſummoned *corrige* ſummoned

Pag. 238. lin. 22. theſe *corrige* thoſe

Ibid. lin. 24. *certainly* corrige *certainty*

Pag. 239. lin. 9. from Authority . *corrige* from diuine Authority .

Ibid. lin. 20. any hereſy *corrige* an hereſy

Pag. 245. lin. 18. *moſt impudent* corrige *moſt impudent*

Pag. 248. lin. 1. euen *corrige* euer

Ibid. lin. 28. began *corrige* begun

Pag. 251. lin. 25 *Our of* corrige *Out of*

Pag. 252. lin. 27. writ *corrige* write

Pag. 257. lin. 8. Church , becauſe *corrige* Church : yet becauſe

Pag. 259. lin. 23. Greeke Turke *corrige* Great Turke

Pag. 263. lin. 17. the parentheſis ſhould end after the word baptiſme)

Ibid. lin. 19. repeated) ſo *corrige* repeated : and ſo

Pag. 264. lin. 8. certificate *corrige* certificate.
Pag. 271. lin. 23. *Argumenta* corrige *Argumente*.
Pag. 272. lin. 11. :hould corrige *should*
Pag. 274. lin. 26. drawes *corrige* drownes.
Ibid. lin. 31. disbelieued *corrige* disbelieue
Pag. 276. lin. 4. (or as *corrige* or (as
Pag. 279. lin. 7. or *corrige* nor
Pag. 293. lin. 12. reitering *corrige* reiterating
In the title of pag. 294. by errour, is put 264.
Pag. 298. lin. 25. fundamentall *corrige* fundamentalls
Pag. 299. lin. 10. truth *corrige* truthes

In the Second Part.

PAg. 2. in the tittle *Part.* 1. Corrige *Part.* 2.
Pag. 9. lin. 6. do, with truth you *corrige* do with truth, you
Pag. 12. lin. 22. *the many* corrige *there are many*·
Pag. 14. lin. 3. *Chap.* corrige *Pag.*
Pag. 19. lin. 27. *Priest* corrige *Priests*
Pag. 23. lin. 1. & 2. second directly *corrige* second is directly
Pag. 28. lin. 19. deleatur *will*
Ibid. lin. 20. *doth* corrige *doe*
Pag. 33. lin. 26. spirit, as he was who *corrige* spirit as he was, who
Pag. 37. lin. 8. your *Text* your *corrige* your *Text* you
Pag. 45. lin. 24. geuerall *corrige* generall
Pag. 50. lin. 5. *man bound* corrige *man is bound*
Pag. 61. lin. 5. in *fact* corrige of *fact*
Pag. 78. lin. 28. seeme *corrige* seene
Pag. 86. lin. 29. ingenious *corrige* ingenuous
Pag. 88. lin. 14. Meanes *corrige* Newnesse
Pag. 94. lin. 19. mattes *corrige* matters
Pag. 97. lin. 18. it is giuen *deleatur* it is
Ibid lin. 29. *Church wall* corrige *Church walls*
Pag. 103. lin. 5. the Generall *deleatur* the
Ibid. lin. 13. you Booke *corrige* your Booke
Pag. 14. lin. 7. *vnwarry* corrige *vnwary*

Pag.

Ibid. lin. 17. after *vs* ; *corrige* after *vs* . And blot out all
the words following. Neither are the Authors &c. vnto
the next, and 3. Paragraph, as put in by errour.
Pag. 105. lin. 26. Doth not *corrige* Do not
Ibid. lin. 28. and for *corrige* and that for
Pag. 109. lin. 3 . translated *corrige* tranflate
Ibid. lin. 30. if you *corrige* if ftill you
Pag. 111 lin. 14. *felfe* corrige *it felfe*
Pag. 127. lin. 20. deleatur *may*
Pag. 131. lin. 8. he had *corrige* I had
Pag. 143. lin. 16. belieue *corrige* belie
Pag. 145. lin. 13. & 14. thefe words only [*James changed*
the verdict of Peter] fhould be put in a different letter , as
the direct affirmation of *Luther*.
Pag. 162. lin. 2. meaning *corrige* meanes
Ibid. lin. 5. fallibility *corrige* infallibility
Pag. 168. lin. 19. D. *Morton* corrige *M. Morton*
Pag. 169. lin. 3. *medij*, corrige *medij*)
Pag. 171. lin. 4. *fundamentall,* and that *corrige fundamen-*
tall, and *not fundamentall* , and that
Pag. 177. lin. 16. Councells *corrige* Counfells
Pag. 186. lin. 28. *Manes* corrige *Manes*
Pag. 191 lin. 23. D. Morton corrige *M. Morton*
Pag. 197. lin. 20. *are in* corrige *are not in*
Ibid. lin. 25. *S. Hierome* corrige *S. Hieromes*

In the Margent. 1. *Part.*

Pag. 12. *Reioynders* corrige *Reioynder.*
Pag. 61. *fect. 6. 26.* corrige *fect. 6. pag. 26.*
Pag. 157. *lib. cont. Parmen.* corrige *lib. 1. cont. Parmen.*

In the Margent . 2. Part.

Pag. 13. *Petricon.* corrige *Petricor.*
Pag. 92. (c) *pag. 93.* corrige (c) *pag. 92.*

FINIS.